The

WORLD

of

TRANSLATION

the world of TRANSLATION

With a new introduction by Gregory Rabassa

PEN American Center, New York

Third Printing: February 1987

The World of Translation *was originally made possible through contributions from Harcourt Brace Jovanovich, Victor Weybright, and a grant from the National Endowment for the Arts.*

Acknowledgement is gratefully made to the estate of William Butler Yeats for the right to reprint "Mary Hynes," and to Robert Duncan and New Directions Publishing Corporation for the right to reprint "After a Passage in Baudelaire," from Roots and Branches *by Robert Duncan (© 1964 by Robert Duncan).*

Printed by Wickersham Printing Company
Cover design: Mervyn E. Clay

Contents

CONTENTS

Preface to the Third Printing

The art or craft of translation has so long been subject to a welter of criticism, mostly negative, that it is difficult to find some way to disabuse readers of ever so many inaccurate notions as to what it is all about. There seems to be a demand on the part of critics and readers for the version in another tongue to be the absolute equivalent of what it had been in the original language. This is patently impossible, no two snowflakes are ever alike, nor does 2 ever equal 2 outside of a mathematical formula because the second 2 is, among other things, younger than its predecessor. Sticking with mathematical notions, what translation aims at is not the *equals* sign but, rather, the more useful one of *approaches*. So our criterion must state that the best translation is the closest approach.

The essays in this collection deal with myriad approaches to what a translator must be thinking of as he or she works and what the criteria to be used in judgment of the product are. Some are very specific and treat small yet important details in putting ideas and circumstances from one language into another; others transcend these limitations and consider the matter of what translation is or should be per se. The value of the essays, beyond their intrinsic worth, lies in the fact that they add to the current and growing concern with translation. Too long has this craft played second fiddle (maybe second 'cello is better, since no two languages can possibly play on the same strings or with the same tone to other creative uses of the word, spoken or otherwise. This new interest in what things might sound like elsewhere has even got authors to thinking about "What will I be like in Urdu?", showing that although writing takes place in different languages (and cultures), literature is essentially one.

No translation ever seems to endure as long as the original (with certain exceptions, such as the King James Version, and yet there are new translations of the Bible every day), which constrains us to focus on the problems of the craft and whether, indeed, by examining what we do in it we might someday come up with a system or method or formula for making translations that are not just adequate for our here and now, but proper ones that will last a bit longer and let us partake for a longer stretch of time of the moment and place that produced the original. Studies of the problem or problems entailed have been much more forthcoming in the past few decades than ever before. George Steiner's *After Babel* has opened ever so many doors and given us new paths to follow in our consideration of this art of choice, all the way from the equivalency of words, the *mot juste*, to an attempt at making a parallel of the histories and cultures that have produced it, both singularly and collectively.

PEN American Center has been in the forefront of this effort to bring translation into a focus worthy of its status as an art separate from mere mechanical reproduction (if that were possible). Its Translation Committee has labored hard and long and brought forth statements and documents that lay down not only norms to be followed by translators as they work, but also what they deserve in return from those who benefit from their work. Now, as is the case with writers in other genres, the translator has recourse to organizations such as the PEN Committee, the American Literary Translators Association, and the American Translators Association to turn to for an exchange of ideas and helpful hints. This collection of essays represents one of the earlier gatherings of translators in this country and the fact it is now in a new edition bespeaks the authenticity of what I have said above. It is an invitation to consider what goes into the making of a translation and, one might hope, for writers to join in this newly recognized confraternity and try their hands at it.

Gregory Rabassa
October 1986

Introduction

Lewis Galantière

Conference papers rarely make good reading. Written to be read aloud, they fall somewhere between the speech, which is hortatory and calculated to persuade, and the essay, which is discursive and was rudely defined by Dr Johnson as "an irregular indigested piece." Except, perhaps, papers presented at meetings on the exact sciences, once in print they are rarely heard of again.

This collection of papers on translation has some chance of meeting a better fate. One difference between it and other books on the subject known to me is the emotion stirred in the reader by so many of its contributors. Few publishers can have any notion that these second-class citizens of the Republic of Letters are animated by the professional conscience and respect for their craft here displayed. Even the occasional speaker who seems to be thinking about his subject for the first time (how many novelists are prepared to write a treatise on the novel?) is possessed by these feelings. Particularly moving are the pieces written by those who have chosen to insert their ideas about the art of translation into accounts of their personal experience.

The variety of literatures dealt with is another of the merits of this volume. There is nothing here on Greek or Latin, but besides the European staples—French, German, Italian, Spanish—we learn in varying measure something of the essence of neglected litera-

tures: Bengali, Chinese, Danish, Irish (Gaelic), Japanese, Korean,
Polish, Sanskrit and Swedish; and about the oral literatures of the
Black African and the American Indian, and the difficulties of trans-
lating out of English into French, German, Italian and Polish.

On the problems of translation—literary translation only, for there
are other kinds—this book is rich in matter. On the principles
alleged to govern this art there is less to be expected, if only because
translation is, obviously, not even an inexact science. What are sometimes called rules consist in a handful of venerable clichés reiterated
since the time of Cicero, Horace and the irascible St. Jerome, not one
which has not been violated by one or other of the very greatest
translators. What is certain is that there exists no corpus of rules
on which consensus has ever prevailed. Instead, we have what I shall
call *obiter dicta*—though many are not the less valid for that.

It is part of the enjoyment to be taken from these papers that
dicta, some superficial and some profound, pullulate and clash. One
speaker maintains that a good translator should not translate a book
he does not like. Before we can ask how he is to earn a living, another says: the translator's qualifications are decisive and his feelings are
not. The truly professional translator will be able to render any
author's text "loyally." "The poorer the language, the more difficult
it is to translate," we read. I applaud, on the assumption that by
"language" is meant quality of writing. A translator says with a sigh,
"The truest translation would obviously come from the author himself." To which another retorts that if one is bilingual it is much
easier to rewrite what one has written in the second language than to
translate it. Golden words, though they may baffle you.

Whether most translators are aware of it or not, their alleged
rules tend to fall within the scope of the categories established by
Dryden three centuries ago. Here they are: *metaphrase* (word for
word, line for line), *paraphrase* (the sense strictly preserved, the
words not), *imitation* (free re-creation inspired by only "hints" in
the original). As to the first, Dryden called it "but a foolish task";
Browning is probably the most celebrated poet to have proved him
right. Ivan Morris, examining a literal version made by "probably
the most distinguished expert on classical Japanese," calls it "the
nadir of translation." Paraphrase, Miss Muchnic points out, is the
method used by most translators and the one accounting for "the
highest incidence of casualties." What Dryden thought of "imitation"
many respected critics and translators of poetry would dispute today.
"To state it fairly," he wrote, "imitation of an author is the most
advantageous way for a translator to show himself, but the greatest
wrong which can be done to the memory of the dead." Neither the

Iranians nor Mr. Edmund Wilson are offended by Edward FitzGerald's *Rubaiyat of Omar Khayyam*. Ezra Pound's "imitations" (he did not call them that), which were for years received with scorn, founded a "school" to which some of the most gifted of American and British poets belong, and it would appear from what is said here by Léon Damas and by Mr. Quasha (for whom Pound is a "hero") that only imitation could properly render Black African and American Indian chants into our languages.

In recent years a new method of translation (though long established in authorship) has emerged: *collaboration.* One of the finest living authors, Isaac Bashevis Singer, who writes in Yiddish but publishes in English, tells us here with sparkling humor and hard sense, what he has learned about translation from collaboration with his translators. It seems to have been in the translation of contemporary Russian poetry that collaboration began between poets who knew little or no Russian and sensitive Russianists (if that is the term), though not themselves poets, to produce Russian poetry in our tongue. To this practice, Mr. Daniels puts forward a succession of vigorous objections, initially founded on the premise that the Russianists furnish our poets no more than a crib. Soon, however, he concedes that "conscientious coaching" also goes on, that it has "quite improbably given us some good poems," and he ends by generously avowing that this may be "the only way of getting at poetry in inaccessible languages." The practice has spread from Russian to other languages. It is not clear that W. H. Auden's translations from the German, and latterly the Icelandic, belong in this category, for his are among the rare collaborators whose names appear as co-translators.

There is no harm in enunciating dicta as firm beliefs. I myself have long insisted that if the literary translator is not a writer he is nothing. And as the literary translator who seeks to earn a living by his craft is expected to work in every variety of general literature, from novels and biographies to books on current problems and events, it follows that he should, ideally, possess his own language beyond the possession of it by every other category of writer. How to amass this treasure, I do not know, though he can strive for it by following the advice once given to the American Translators Association by Richard Howard. I paraphrase: "Read everything in your own language that you can: great books, varieties of books." Which means that the translator shall love words, love language; and that he ought to possess that intellectual curiosity upon which he can build a broad general culture. For without that culture he will not begin to seize the *whole* of his author's text.

"Begin to, " I say, for to seize the whole—"the context" as Elsa
Gress calls it in her paper—obviously requires some degree of mastery
of the foreign language, and equally obviously (one would think)
a capacity for participating in the mentality, the genius, of the people out of whose language he is translating. Empathy, that quality is
often called.

All this is elementary and will be news to no veteran translator.
These remarks are not addressed to our poets and poet-scholars who
during the past thirty years have brought into existence, almost unnoticed, a new age of translation which, in inventiveness of form,
audacity of experimentation and brilliance of achievement, is comparable to any since that of the Tudor and Stuart translators. (I inter-
rupt myself to point to an equally remarkable phenomenon, the
crowding of American youth into public and university halls to
listen to poets, come from half way round the globe, as they read
their own poems aloud in their own tongues with their translators
present to read their versions of the same poems.) Nor do I write
for the score of prose translators of surpassing excellence who have
emerged in our time. I like to think that this volume will be read by
many aspirants to a career in translation; indeed, that it may fall
into the hands of earnest students of foreign languages whose attention has not hitherto been directed to translation, either as a career
or as an avocation. There is a crying need for the professional preparation of young people to take up this line of writing from which so
much spiritual and intellectual satisfaction can be derived. Goethe
wrote to Carlyle: "Say what you will about the inadequacy of translation, it remains one of the most important and worthiest occupa-
tions in the realm of world affairs." This may have seemed an exaggerated claim in 1827, in a Europe of virtually isolated peoples.
Today, in our close-knit world, it is unassailable—though paradoxi-
cally, neither to language teachers nor to publishers does it seem
self-evident. The need has been met, and translators are well
regarded and well rewarded, only outside the field of literature. The
oral translators (conference interpreters) are in practice a guild,
recognized as professionals. And so are the non-literary writer-trans-
lators who serve the scientific institutes and laboratories, electronic,
bio-chemical and other basic industries, the government bureaux, the
patent lawyers, none of which can do without impeccable translation.
Only in literature do we find young people who "want to write"
stumbling unprepared into translation as into book-reviewing, as a
pis aller, with an obscure feeling of guilt at having "nothing of their
own to say."

Guilt? Matthew Arnold wrote of a prose translation of Faust that it was "so good, it makes one regret that Mr. (Abraham) Hayward should have abandoned the line of translation for a kind of literature which is, to say the least, somewhat slight." Poor Mr. Hayward. Signora Pivano writes in her moving and quietly dramatic account of a career as translator in the Mussolini era, "My own very strong opinion . . . is that a translation can be a creation." Her great compatriot, Croce, wrote that "A good translation is a work of art." Nearly all the classic translators, from Lord Berners and Amyot down to Arthur Waley, are immortalized only by their translations.

Where are the professionally prepared literary translators to come from? Mr. MacShane's heartening report on his translation seminar at Columbia University confirms that translation can be taught; though not quite—coached, rather, as a singing master coaches those who have already been taught to sing in the performance of operatic roles. His students have graduated from language study, already know something of their "source" literatures. It is distressing to find how few professors of modern languages feel any responsibility for the breeding of a generation of translators. Worse, foreign language teaching as a department of *litterae humaniores* seems to be threatened. In August 1970, The New York Times sent a reporter around the country to inquire into the causes of the decline in student registration for foreign language courses. Here is how the executive director of the American Council of Foreign Language Teachers accounted for it: "We've gotten carried away with the way we have been teaching languages for the last one hundred and fifty years . . . . [Students] want a speaking knowledge about other countries' urban problems, family life and dating customs." Language teaching is for tourists, evidently. The director of the Language School at Middlebury College is equally set on learning 'em to talk: "Teachers of foreign languages, as opposed to foreign literatures, are rarely rewarded by the schools." And the university administrators, meanwhile, are beginning to look upon foreign languages as they look upon Latin. "The academic controversy," the Times' roving reporter writes, "generally centers on whether a minimum number of college credits should be required for graduation." The world of learning, like the newspaper, is to live from day to day. Ten years ago crash courses in Swahili were improvised because we had a Peace Corps. Today, the foreign-language requirement is to be deemed "irrelevant" under the pressure of "stiff competition from such new subjects as minority studies." The fact that the translator will continue to be the supreme cross-fertilizer of cultures and civilizations, even if on tape and not on paper, even if on television and not in books, is irrelevant. In this age when most of the seminal and instantly influential ideas that circulate round the globe reach men through the medium of translation, no language teacher may permit himself to dream of combining with his colleagues of other disciplines to construct a curriculum leading to the degree of B.A. (Trans.) or B.Sc. (Trans.).

And the publisher? Fifty years ago a publisher bought a foreign book that seemed to promise a profit, commissioned a translator to whom he paid a pittance, and sent the translator's copy to the press without scrutiny. Later, experience led him to set up a desk where that copy was read for literacy and intelligibility. In recent years, our best publishers have employed sub-editors with some knowledge of foreign languages. There has been further progress: a few editors now work as patiently with translators of important works as they do with novelists, say. But the trade as a whole regards the translator—Mr. Purdy tells in these pages—as a "nuisance" and an "expense." Miss B. J. Chute addresses the publishers on their traditional attitude to translators in a manner so witty and cogent and good-tempered that one cannot imagine what they could find to retort. And the head of a distinguished family firm, John Macrae, after giving his colleagues their comeuppance, goes on to demonstrate, by a fascinating and perhaps unprecedented example, that what the trade lacks is imagination and daring; that not only books on "timely" subjects can be "created" in the publisher's office, but that the stimulation of translation can create literary works for the American publisher's list—and at a profit.

Money is what the publishers talk about, and it is fascinating, in a repellent way, to see how they cling to the belief that every material concession made to the translator can come only out of their pockets. I ask their leave to make a shocking suggestion. Let the Association of American Publishers take a look at the way the Dramatists Guild handles a parallel problem and consider how it might be adapted to the conditions of their trade. Translators of plays are called in the theatre "adaptors." Even where plot and setting are left untouched, a feeling for theatre, an ability to visualize a scene is essential. And the only words used, dialogue, must be adapted; that is, it must be instantaneously intelligible through the ear. No time to reflect on what the actor said; the actor has gone on talking—the same or another actor. Thanks to the powerful influence of the Dramatists Guild, it has been customary for decades that the adaptor shall be paid a minimum of one-third of the author's royalties. Nothing is more fair. Whether a book or a play, the venture is a gamble for all three: producer (publisher), author, and adaptor (translator). Everybody agrees that it is the quality of the text read or heard by us, in our tongue, that makes a foreign work a best-seller or a stage hit; even more so a book, where the talents of director, cast, scenic designer do not intervene.

Is it not scandalous that whereas the author's business agent goes on drawing commissions, sometimes for years, the author should be deemed to owe nothing to the translator who re-created his text in a way to assure him the rewards he derives? I urge again that Mr. Macrae's story be read. Of course he does not describe a routine operation. I wrote above of terms "adapted to the conditions of the trade." Today, the excellent translator commands terms far better than the merely competent translator. The competent translator should command terms better than what we may call the apprentice translator. (We have all been apprentice translators in our time.) And most of all, the publisher should weed out the incompetent translator and combine with others to find means to assure his ancient and respectable trade that literary translation shall cease to be in any significant part a species of "moonlighting" and become a profession.

The PROCEEDINGS

of the

Conference on Literary Translation

Opening Remarks

Charles Bracelen Flood

As the President of the American Center of P.E.N., it is my pleasant
privilege to welcome you here, and to declare that this Conference
on Translation is now in session.

Those of us in the American Center greet you not only as distinguished colleagues in the world of letters, but as friends. There is
a long tradition of warm hospitality in P.E.N. We know that this
week is going to be professionally rewarding for all of us, but we also
want it to be a very pleasant occasion for all of our guests, and particularly for those who have come from other countries to be with us.

I am a novelist, and it seems particularly appropriate to me that
you, as translators, are being greeted by a novelist rather than by
a translator. My novels have been translated into several languages,
and I am well aware that I am in the presence of those who have
increased my audience—and my income. I am grateful that my books
can be read in such languages as Swedish and Dutch and Italian, and
I am grateful to those who have made this possible. I pay tribute
to translators not only as a writer, but as a reader. When I lived for
some years in the Far East, I studied those literatures in translation,
sometimes as part of formal study and as research for lectures I was
giving, but also in an effort to make a personal adjustment to the
very different cultures in which I was living. For me the translations by such men as Donald Keene and Ivan Morris were an

important part of learning to live in the very different atmosphere of
Japan, and the fact that these men are members of our Translation
Committee in the American P.E.N. gives me more satisfaction than
you can easily imagine.

Apart from these personal reasons for feeling that it is appropriate
that you should be greeted first by a novelist, I think that this is
symbolic of what we hope to achieve in these meetings. We are not
here to discuss translation in the abstract, but to place translation
in its living form between the writer at one end of the room, the
publisher at the other end of the room, and the reading public just
beyond. Throughout this week, everything that is said here will be
said in the presence not only of distinguished translators, but in the
presence of poets, playwrights, critics, publishers—everyone involved
in the process of communication by words. We have here the opportunity to test each person's ideas against the past experience of each
other person, and to do this in an atmosphere which is not academic,
but quite realistically professional.

It is really this concept of professionalism which has led us over
the years to this conference and this morning. International P.E.N.
will be fifty years old next year, and throughout its history translators have played a leading part in this organization which exists to
bind ever more closely the international literary community. We are
well aware of the part played by the Polish P.E.N. in holding extremely successful conferences on translation in Warsaw in 1958 and 1965,
and we think it is particularly fortunate that we have two of our
Polish colleagues with us, so that we may share their depth of
experience in this type of interchange of ideas and plans. International P.E.N., through the London Center, has produced works in
cooperation with UNESCO, and many other P.E.N. Centers have
their own individual projects in relation to the field of translation.

Regarding the American Center, our own involvement with translation became greatly accelerated in 1959, when the novelist, B.J.
Chute, on assuming the presidency, established our Translation
Committee, with Theodore Purdy as its first chairman. This led to
the establishment of the American Center's annual award for translation, a prize of one thousand dollars which was made possible
through the generosity of the late Harry Scherman. This is the prize
which will be awarded, in his memory, at our dinner on Thursday
evening.*

When I became President of the American Center, a year ago, I had
a most useful series of discussions with Miss Chute, who has maintained her interest in translations and the problems of translators. In
discussing the various priorities which we should assign to different

* Awarded to Sidney Alexander for his translation of *The History of Italy* by
  Francesco Guicciardini (Macmillan, 1969).

projects, we agreed that the time had come for American P.E.N. to step forward and to claim a far larger role in the field of translation in the United States. The National Center for Translation at the University of Texas was in the process of dissolution, and we felt that an entirely different approach should be tried by us. With little money but with a core of prominent professional translators, we felt that our Translation Committee was ideally suited to further the cause of translators in this country, and throughout the world. I approached Robert Payne, a man of great intellect and energy who has more than one hundred titles to his credit as author, editor, and translator, and asked him to accept the Chairmanship of our Translation Committee. He accepted, and from that moment there has been a burst of energy in our work in this area which has never been equalled. One of the greatest pleasures that I have had in my presidency has been working with Robert Payne, and in working towards this day. He organized a most distinguished and imaginative committee, and we began discussing various projects, which have included the Manifesto on Translation and the guidelines for a model contract for translators which will be discussed during the course of this week.

In our meetings as a committee, again and again we came to the idea of a conference of translators. This was clearly the hardest project to organize and to finance, but gradually we became hypnotized by the overwhelming desirability of this idea, and all of us chose to look not at the obstacles, but at the goal beyond. In reaching this goal we had great help from men who are not primarily engaged in the field of translation. A generous gift from the publisher Victor Weybright enabled us to begin planning this meeting, and a similar gift from the economist and financial writer Eliot Janeway enabled us to expand our original plans. Our Executive Secretary, Kirsten Michalski, then approached the National Council on the Arts in Washington, showing them our plans and the money we had already received, and the Council voted us a large sum which enabled us to increase our invitations to translators from other countries. Then we had to settle down to the hard work of organizing the details of this conference, and in this connection I must again mention the extraordinary efforts put forth by our Executive Secretary, Kirsten Michalski, without whom this Conference would not be taking place, and our Corresponding Secretary, Barbara Rice Jones, who has helped her in making efforts far beyond the normal scope of her job.

So, at last, the idea became a reality. We have already achieved
much this past year in working to publicize the inadequacies of the
conditions under which translators must work. We have served
notice upon publishers that the lot of the translator must be improved.
We have had publicity concerning our efforts, and now it is up to all
of us to make concrete proposals that will make this a real turning
point in the history of translation as a field in this country and elsewhere. Copies of the proceedings of this Conference, in thousands
of copies, will be sent to publishers, to universities, to writers' organizations, throughout the world. It is my hope that we will be able
to enhance the image of the field, and to improve the working
conditions, in such a way that many young people throughout the
world will look upon the career of translator as being possible and
attractive for them. If we can improve the conditions for translators, and hence improve the quality of translations themselves, we
will have done a great service for every literature in our world.

Dedication

Robert Payne

I would like to dedicate this conference to the memory of three men
who helped the Translation Committee in its work and who died
in reeent years. One was James Putnam who was a man of enormous
energy, tranquility and gentleness; another was Joseph Barnes, who
had a wonderful knowledge of Russian and was also a man of great
energy and sweetness and tranquility; and finally, only a few days
ago, there died another man who helped us a great deal—Franz
Schoenberner. It is not surprising to me that he also, like all the
others, had that gentleness and sweetness and energy. So the Conference is dedicated to their memory, and this will be inscribed
in the records.

Bill of Rights

Since translation of works of literature
by the very nature of the task is the creation of a new work,
the translator must be regarded as sovereign.
The translator's chief obligation is to create
the work in a new language with the appropriate
music and the utmost response to the silences of the original.
The unit in translation is the entire work:
and the imagination of the translator is concerned
above all with this unity.
The privileges of the translator therefore include
the right to be regarded as the maker of a new work, and
he should be recompensed accordingly.
His name shall be given a proper prominence, and
he shall possess continuing rights over his work during its life.
The honor of translation demands that translators
of literary works shall in future be regarded
as artists rather than as skilled craftsmen.

The Publisher's Dilemma

Theodore M. Purdy

It is cause for surprise, but also for real gratification, that the Committee on Translation of the P.E.N. American Center should have decided to open this conference on the translator and his problems with a discussion of the subject as viewed by a publisher.

For, while the author-translator relationship is obviously most important, it is far too often forgotten that the product of this relationship, a new version of a literary work in another than the original language, cannot really come to life without the help of that *tertium quid,* the foreign publisher (foreign, that is, to the author, and usually to the translator) who is to bring out the work.

I regret to have to admit that the publisher often plays the part of the villain in the eternal triangle which is played out around the cradle of a recently published book. This is because the interests of author and translator are basically the same. Both wish to attain publication of a valid version in the new language which will convey the inspiration, the intellectual qualities, and the style of the book to new readers, and will increase the reputation of the author as a writer of international stature. And (let's face it) both wish to make some money.

The publisher also hopes to make some money, of course, but for practical purposes today (save in the case of a few non-profit university presses and foundations) all book publishing is a speculation,

9

a gamble. The public may not realize it, but up to 100% of most books "sold" to booksellers are returnable after one year, yet the publisher has to pay at once the printer, the salesmen, the editors, and his overhead—a mysterious expression that includes everything from those absolutely essential three-hour business luncheons down to the electric-light bulbs.

Without boring you with complicated figures and statistics, it costs a publisher in the United States about $5000 to produce 5000 copies of an ordinary unillustrated hardcover book of around 200 pages, destined to be sold to the public at $5.95 in the present market. He has to give the bookseller the average current discounts (from 40% to 50%) off the retail price. If he sells in advance of publication half the printing (a high figure) he will take in roughly from eight to nine thousand dollars. Out of this apparent surplus of three or four thousand dollars, he then must pay for advertising and promotion, and pay the author's royalty, which in this case might come, at 10% of the retail price, to between $1500 and $2000.

Sooner or later, the publisher also has to face the problem of the copies returned unsold by the bookseller. I believe the present average for the industry ranges from 15% to 17%, though it can be higher. This means that the publisher (and the author proportionately on his royalty account) may be debited for an additional $1300 or so. A final accounting may show a more favorable balance after a season or two, but it is clear that both author and publisher receive very slender profit margins, considering all the work and capital, whether intellectual or commercial, that each in his own way has put into producing the book.

Now, where does the translator come in? For the author, he is a necessity if he wishes to penetrate international markets. For the publisher, frankly, he is too often a nuisance, an added expense. This is sad but true.

I think that we will all admit that many serious and self-respecting publishers here and abroad do wish to enhance the variety and appeal of their lists by including translations of significant contemporary works and of literary classics originally written in foreign languages. I do not need to point out to this group the supreme importance of the translated book as a means of communication. You are going to discuss all week better ways of achieving this form of communication. And, from the publishers' standpoint, bringing out translations can gain, for an imprint, international recognition. I need only mention the careers in this country of Alfred A. Knopf, of Kurt and Helen Wolff, now of Harcourt Brace Jovanovich, as examples of this, and there are similar examples in London.

Gallimard in Paris, Mondadori, Feltrinelli, and others in Italy, have built up high standards for their translations of foreign books and have made money out of it. Publishing translations undoubtedly lends a certain prestige to any list.

But, unfortunately, many publishers here still tend to think of translators as a necessary evil. Some even seem inclined to try to conceal from the public the fact that a book has been translated. Too often the translator's name does not appear on the title page or jacket of the book, nor in the advertising, or it appears only in the smallest type. And book reviewers are no better. In spite of the efforts made by the P.E.N. Translation Committee and others, they do not always mention the translator in their reviews.

I have been to many sales conferences where editors and management have presented translated books apologetically, and have even urged the salesmen not to mention that a novel is "from the French" unless asked. How often have I heard the phrase: "It's translated but you'd never know it, it reads so easily, just like an American novel."

What can be done, then, to overcome the handicaps, financial and otherwise, under which translated books often appear in the American market?

Let us suppose that your publisher is a man of good will, sincerely interested in publishing foreign literature, well translated. He may have a knowledge of certain languages or he may have scouts or agents in Europe and elsewhere whom he can trust. He may go on yearly pilgrimages to Frankfurt-am-Main, where, in the heady atmosphere of the bar at the Frankfurter Hof or the Intercontinental, he will find he has acquired American rights in quite a few books he hasn't and generally cannot read. Or the book may come to him from an agent of standing, or it may be submitted by the foreign publisher and taken after being read by an expert here.

Anyway, he decides to put it on his list. At this point the spectre of the translator appears, and the publisher thinks: "My God, it's 100,000 words long—that means at least $2000 extra for the translation fee. With those illustrations we'll have to charge at least $9.95 for it." Visions of angry board meetings dance in his head.

What can he do? He can ask the original foreign publisher or agent, who controls the rights, to grant him a lower royalty scale, starting at 7½% or so. This will not actually pay for the translation, but it may, so to speak, assuage the pain of it a little. Yet it must be remembered that in the long run this saving comes out of the author, and it is not going to make for happy cooperation between the author, the translator, and the publisher of the translation.

Another expedient in the case of a translation into English—and it is often a dangerous one, for reasons I will give—is to arrange to share the translation cost with a London publisher. In days of yore, when Americans depended on England for much of their intellectual fare, it was almost taken for granted that the translation of an important foreign novel or other work would be made in England and sold later to the American publisher. This is no longer true, but, because the fees paid to translators in England have for a long time been lower than those paid here, many titles, particularly fiction, have been rendered into English by English translators rather than American translators. I say "rendered" because much of the work, even when signed by good names in the field, has been of hack quality, no doubt because the translator received only a low flat fee of two or three guineas per thousand words, and no share in royalties or other proceeds, (Rates in England have tended to rise considerably recently, it should be noted, which is another reason why more American translators are being used.)

Today I am glad to say that this seems to be changing, particularly in cases where U.S. publishers acquire English language rights throughout the world, or take U.S. rights before a book is sold in London. The English are now more willing to accept translations made in the United States than they were, though it must be admitted that there are still great differences in our literary accents.

What is important, of course, is to remember that a good translation is absolutely necessary if a book is to be well reviewed and sold in this country nowadays, and this is, of course, true in London and Canada as well as here. Cost should not be the primary factor—it is an investment for the future. Get a good man, a qualified professional, who will if possible consult the author if problems arise, treat the translator as an equal figure in the triangular love affair of which the book is the heart, and give him an incentive to do his best work by allowing him to share in all the proceeds of what is, after all, a mutual gamble.

In closing, let me bring up one other possible source of funds to pay the costs of translation: money from public sources, from foundations, corporations, or other institutions. In the case of scientific, educational, and scholarly works, such funds may be readily available. The university presses and specialized publishing houses often enjoy subsidies expressly for such purposes. In the case of literature—of belles lettres, fiction, history, poetry and the classics—although money may be available in the form of grants or scholarships, it is much harder for a translator to get help, whether to learn his craft or to pursue it when immediate advances from commercial sources are not sufficient to allow him to do good work.

Might it not be a very worthwhile project for the American Center of P.E.N., with the advice and consent of our distinguished guests, to start a fund which would help to finance writers in their neglected works of literary value? This fund should probably cover translations from foreign languages into English and also encourage the translation of important books of American origin into foreign languages. Here, of course, there is a government program but it is a rather inadequate one. Publishers, authors, foundations, large companies, and educational institutions would be asked to contribute.

The amounts involved are relatively small. The fund could be held and administered by P.E.N. as a commercially disinterested party. Other centers in other countries might be invited to participate, or they might start their own funds.

In conclusion, at practically all conferences or meetings of translators, the old saw of *Traduttore = Traditore* must inevitably be brought up. Let me be the one to do so now, and as an admitted traitor from the publishing fraternity, to offer you in slight amends this idea of a P.E.N. Fund for Translators.

On Translating

from Renaissance Italian

Sidney Alexander

Some years ago I asked Marc Slonim, a distinguished scholar, a fellow member of P.E.N., and accomplished polyglot, for his judgment on the various translations of *Dr. Zhivago* then in circulation. "Well," said Marc, "the English version is accurate enough but the music is gone. The American [English and American, you understand, being two separate languages] takes far too many liberties. The French have made it all too neat, like a play by Racine; the German is impenetrably thick; the Italian—well, let's not talk about the Italian (I have already counted 1,850 errors) and. . ." (and here he smiled a wee sad knowing smile) "and the Russian—well, the Russian—is ... untranslatable."

I'm afraid we have to begin with this. To the degree that a work of literary art approaches the condition of poetry—that is, the inseparability of form and content—it cannot be translated. Robert Frost defined poetry as "that which gets lost from verse and prose in translation." Except in freakish and rarely lucky circumstances how can one transplant, from one national plot to another, meanings which are inherent in the very curl of the words? Poems are wildflowers which, plucked, die in your hand.

And those prose works wherein the meaning resides as much in the rhetoric as in the "facts," those works where *"le style est l'homme,"*

15

offer the same problems as a poem. In such works the double-axed
Italian equation *traduttore-traditore* applies with terrible pertinence.

Languages are not merely verbal and sonic systems of symbolism—
they also are various ways of looking at the world. They help shape
and express national character. An Italian is reluctant to use the
imperative. It's poor breeding; it's too direct. And so in Florence
(where I have lived for fourteen years) nobody says to a shopkeeper,
"Give me . . .*Mi dia.*" Even that formal imperative is too brusque.
Instead one employs the indicative: *"Mi da . . ."* "Give me . . ."
with a kind of interrogative lilt to remove any trace of demand, or
an evasive imperfect, *"Volevo un pacchetto di sigarette . . ."* *"I was
wanting* a pack of cigarettes." Or *"Vorrei . . ."* "I would like . . ."
Italians use conditionals and subjunctives much more frequently
than we do in English. Naturally. They *think* more conditionally.
They distrust blacks and whites. Life is more complicated than
simple affirmations and negations. And all this is reflected in Italian
syntax, everyday syntax.

And if to this built-in difference between languages we add the
intensely personal vision of a literary artist—it doesn't matter
whether he writes prose or poetry, history or novels—obviously the
verbal structure that results is unique, by definition untranslatable.

And yet we must translate. Else we are locked in our separate
boxes. We must communicate across cultures; we must devise a simu-
lacrum that seems—at one and the same time—to reproduce the
original work and yet exist as a work of art in itself.

For three years—more—I was involved in the translation of Francesco Guicciardini's *Storia d'Italia* (published for the first time in
1561), a work colossal in scope, in significance, the greatest European
history between Thucydides and Gibbon, a *selva oscura* full of
demons for the unwary translator. I don't claim to have conquered
all those demons, but I enjoyed the struggle, and I did make my way
through the wood.

As I plunged into that verbal thicket of Guicciardini I became
aware of one demon who plagued me more than all the others. He is
what I would call the demon of time-translation: the challenge of re-
creating, transmitting, not merely from one language to another (with
all those inevitable traps) but from one *century* to another, in this
particular case, from the sixteenth to the twentieth.

Now, there is a theory and practice of translation which begins
with the proposition that the only viable literature is contemporary.
Listen to these snatches of dialogue:

MENAECHMUS II

Look, kiddo, what's with it, with you and me, that can make
You curse out a man you don't even know? Would you like
A nice hole in the head for turning loose your lip?

PENICULUS

God damn it to God Damn.

And in another play by the same author:

LYSIMACHUS

Good. Keep plugging and in twenty years you'll get a Ph.D.

DEMIPHO

What would I want with a Ph.D.?

And again:

MENAECHMUS

Well, I'll be God damned! What's on the schedule now?. . .
What do you guys want? What's all the racket about?. . .

MESSENIO

. . .I'll start distributing
a crack in the puss here, a sock in the jaw there. . .
By the heavyweight Hercules, you thugs are gonna lug
him away. . . .

And so on and so on.

Would you know that all this purports to be speeches from the
comedies of Plautus (254-184 B.C.): *The Menaechmi* and *The
Merchant*?

We are all too familiar with this "modernizing" practice in the type
of historical novel in which such incongruities as "Shove over, King!"
erupt out of the eighteenth century to strike our unbelieving ears. Or
consider this example from a novel dealing with ancient Athens, whose
craftsmanship is flawed by the inability of the English to forget at
times that they are English. Thus this author's Attic warriors become
British landed gentry riding to hounds, teeth to the wind: "The torch
burned red above the gate tower; we leaped to our feet dismayed. The

army was half a mile away; most of them naked by this time, oiling and
scraping down or mending their armor before the action. Our eyes
all turned to Alcibiades. 'These colonials,' he said. 'People who turn
up to a party while one is still dressing. Someone has gone white-
livered, I suppose, and the rest daren't wait.' "

But even this might be forgiven. Isn't the marvel of Greece its
eternal contemporaneity?

Or let us take a recent case in which a popular novelist has a great
sixteenth-century sculptor (one in whom I have a special—one might
say, a vested—interest) address himself to the marble with the cheer-
leading adjurations of a football coach. "Go! Go! Go!" he says to
himself before he strikes mallet to chisel.

Well, now, if we demand that the language of the historical novel
be congruous with its period, why do we not apply the same canon
to translation of texts (whether fiction or nonfiction) from, let us
say, the sixteenth to the twentieth century?

A strong, perhaps the strongest, tendency in translation today is
what the Italians would call an *aggiornamento,* a bringing up-to-date,
a modernization, a renovation. And this is so in a double sense:
spatially and temporally, horizontally and vertically. We attempt,
that is, to domesticate works from a foreign hearth, to give them all
citizenship, so to speak, in our own native tongue; and we want them
all to sound as if they were written in the twentieth century. The
highest praise that can be given to a work translated into English is
that it sounds as if the original were written in English, *now, today.*
The classics of centuries, of the most farflung quarters of the earth,
must all appear to be products of twentieth-century America or
England.

For many many years now, I have been immersed in the Italian
Renaissance: in one case, writing a series of historical novels built
around the figure of Michelangelo, in the other, translating Guicciardini's classic history. In both situations I found that I was facing
a similar linguistic problem: the necessity of *inventing* a language that
would achieve the magical feat of making past present and yet keeping
it past. T.S. Eliot, complaining about Professor Gilbert Murray's
translation of Euripides, recognized this dual obligation which language, dealing with the past, must perform. "Professor Murray has
simply interposed between Euripides and ourselves a barrier more impenetrable than the Greek language. . . . And it is inconceivable that
anyone with a genuine feeling for the sound of Greek verse should
deliberately elect the William Morris couplet, the Swinburne lyric, as
a just equivalent . . . We need an eye which can see the past in its
place with its definite differences from the present, and yet so lively

that it shall be as present to us as the present. This is the creative
eye. . .''

Of course, all literature—whether it deals with Aristotle the
Stagirite or Aristotle the Onassis—must be contemporary in its
impact on the reader, or it is dead. When I was embarked on the
second volume of my Michelangelo trilogy some headline-bound
friends asked with some irritation: "Why don't you write contemporary novels?" "I *am*," I was fond of replying: "I *am*. I'm writing
contemporary novels set in the sixteenth century." History is *about*
the past but the art of narrative is the past made present. The historian stands on the bank and watches the stream of time, charts its
current, analyzes the direction of its flow. The historical novelist
plunges us directly into the stream; his main business is not explanation but evocation. One tells you what happened. The other makes
it happen to you now. Hence all true works of narrative art—whether
the subject be the Athens of Pericles or the Florence of Lorenzo il
Magnifico—are written in the present tense although the theme and
syntax may seem to deny it.

There are really two ways of modernizing antiquity: one is to
bring the past into the present; the other is to bring the present into
the past. The first method simply *uses* the past: exploits it, extracts
raw material from it. Perhaps the most inexhaustible of these mines
in European literature are the Homeric myths—all the Greek and
Latin dramatists excavated there, and later, over the centuries, we
find everybody in Europe quarrying in the same pits. In our own
time we have seen Jean Cocteau's transformation of Greek tragedy
to surrealist wit; Joyce's colossal Bloomsday; Robert Graves'amalgam
of astonishing erudition and Grenadier psychology; and Eugene
O'Neill's capacity to find Oedipus in a bar. But, although in these
cases this exploitative use of the past is perfectly legitimate, re-
dressing old boys in modern clothes is not valid in literary translation.
Like the historical novel, it must achieve humanization and a distant
perspective diminished in long depths of time, as if we were looking
at real actors through the wrong end of a telescope. If the language
is all present, we have destroyed that special piquant Morocco-bound
flavor that comes from rummaging through ancient manuscripts,
immersion in another world. If the language is all past, our modern
consciousness batters in vain against the fortress of an impenetrable
jargon. We are all too familiar with translatese, that mysterious
tongue invented in the nineteenth century to separate us from the
Greek and Latin classics. Who hasn't broken his teeth against
Professor Jebb's Sophocles:

Lycean King, fain were I that thy shafts also, from thy bent bow's
string of woven gold, should go abroad in their might, our champions
in the face of the foe; yea, and the flashing fires of Artemis wherewith
she glances through the Lycian hills.

Or E. P. Coleridge's Euripides:

ANDROMACHE

Thinkest thou God's hand is shortened and that thou wilt not
be punished?

MENELAUS

When e'er that comes I am ready to bear it but thy life will I have.

ANDROMACHE

Wilt likewise slay this tender chick, whom thou hast snatched
from 'neath my wing?

This is not English of any known period and I dare say (although
my Greek is limited to five words of Demotic) that this isn't Greek
either. It is no language known to man.

Professor Dudley Fitts in his excellent introduction to *Greek Plays
in Modern Translation* wittily gives us the nineteenth-century recipe
for rendering classic Greek texts. "For serious prose imitate the
Bible and Sir Thomas Browne; for poetry mix Swinburne with
Shelley in lyric passages, assorted Elizabethans in the dramatic."

Must we, therefore, in translating from an old text choose between
this no-language and "Get-with-it-Jack" language? Between unimaginative literalism or pastiche, or unimaginative modernism? Which is
worse, archaicism or twentieth-century colloquialism (archaicism in
reverse) both keeping us equally at a remove from the life of the past
which we are trying to revivify? Must we shrug our shoulders and
accept the *traduttore-traditore* alternative, casually opting for that
kind of betrayal most harmonious with our nature? Is the gobblede-
gook of the old translatese more or less preferable to some modern
renderings that make Propertius sound like Ol' Ezra himself, and
Ovid like an exile from Haight-Ashbury?

Now, setting aside translatese and hot-house archaicism, the other
theory—that translating old texts means bringing them up-do-date,
making them contemporary—is by no means limited to the twentieth
century. In fact, the very Plautus I quoted before did precisely that
with old Greek comedy.

Recently in Sicily, I experienced another version of *aggiornamento*. I was with a group of art students, attempting to lecture at the temple of Concordia, and thrown into ever more furious frustration by the portable radios and phonographs bellowing *calcio* games and Italian rock music in the temple. The culmination of this incursion of modernity into my lecture came when an ice cream vendor began to nail—with a nail, a very twentieth-century nail, mind you—his price list onto one of the fifth-century B.C. Doric columns. When that evening I lamented loudly about all this to a classics scholar, he replied, philosophically: "But that's how it most likely was in the fifth century!" My friend is probably right but I persist in feeling that popularization, even vulgar popularization, is not identical with incongruity, that vulgarization within the same culture, the same epoch, does not necessarily destroy the fragile time structure, while incongruity sends it toppling to the ground. *Gelati* and Greek temples don't mix. But the bellowing of a fifth-century B.C. vendor hawking sacrificial pigeons in front of a temple is perfectly all right.

What I'm trying to say is that the past must be made alive but its flavor must not be destroyed in the process. And that is magic indeed. To revivify the dead and yet keep their life at a remove from our lives. Perhaps it can't be done at all but we should try. Otherwise we lose our past.

Now, as I have said before, the notion that old texts must be made contemporary is by no means limited to the twentieth century. In his book on Elizabethan translation, F. O. Mathiessen cites numerous examples of this *aggiornamento* tendency of the Elizabethans— to whom translation was an act of patriotism, conquering foreign classics as one was conquering the new world. Hoby's *Courtier,* North's *Plutarch,* Florio's *Montaigne*—all in their various ways Elizabethanized their Italian, Greek, or French originals; not just translating but transforming the style of the original into the robust rich-imaged action-lashed diction and syntax of that freebooting boisterous society. For example, where Castiglione writes, *"Per levar dal animo,"* Hoby gives us, "To roote that out of your mind"; where the Italian says *"sciocchi"* or "foolish," Hoby writes, "Untowardly assheades." It's all marvelously vigorous and it brings a new classic into English literature. But is it Castiglione? Hoby is robust where Castiglione is polished. The difference is, as Mathiessen points out, "the difference between English and Italian society in the first half of the sixteenth century." Languages are not merely different verbal systems: they are also different ways of looking at the world. Does the acquisition of immediacy, in Elizabethan translation, compensate for the loss of that sense of distance and difference? Should we not be more aware

that we must serve as *agents of communication* between one culture
and another by transmitting those differences, not destroying them?

Hoby and Castiglione, after all, were almost contemporaries, both
of the sixteenth century. But when the translator is building bridges
not merely from one language to another, but also from one century
to another, he has no right, it seems to me, to obliterate all sense of
that gap of centuries. I would maintain that a translation of a classic
—whether from antiquity or from the Renaissance—is not "true" if
the reader ceases to be aware of its antiquity. When I read:

> While thus the hero's pious cares attend,
> The cure and safety of his wounded friend,
> Trojans and Greeks with clashing shields engage
> And mutual deaths are dealt with mutual rage,

I don't hear Homer, I hear Alexander Pope. Gifford's Juvenal:

> Whene'er Ogulnia to the Circus goes,
> To emulate the rich, she hires her clothes. . .

transports me to the eighteenth century, not to the second. And when
a present day Italianist tells us that his prime object in rendering a few
preliminary chapters of Guicciardini's *Storia* "has been to provide an
accurate and legible English text rather than to reproduce the style
and periods of the original. . ." I reply: "Then you are translating
only partial meanings, meanings which are paraphrasable, separable;
in the interests of a spurious clarity, you destroy nuance; most seriously, by uprooting the work linguistically from its epoch, you offer
the reader a corpse dressed in the latest fashion, instead of the illusion
of a living past."

For it is an illusion, mind you. All revivification, whether in translation or historical novels, is *trompe l'oreille*. But in translating old
classics, we certainly cannot conjure up that necessary artful illusion
if we limit our choice to archaism, or the no-language of translatese
(out of time entirely), or the archaism-in-reverse of modern colloquialism, or an "accurate and legible"—that is, neutral and bloodless
—English.

Perhaps a few words about the stylistic problems I faced in translating Guicciardini's *Storia d'Italia* may be pertinent. None of Guicciardini's writings were issued during his lifetime. Only in 1561 were the
first sixteen books out of twenty of the *Storia* published in Florence.
And three years later the first four appeared separately in Venice. But
within the very sixteenth century that saw its first publication, the

History of Italy was swiftly translated into French, Latin, Spanish, Flemish, as well as the first English translation (in the Elizabethan sense) by Geoffrey Fenton. In the cinquecento alone, there were more than one hundred Italian editions, both integral and partial. Poor Messer Francesco Guicciardini is another of those not infrequent cases of posthumous literary success.

The English version by Sir Geoffrey Fenton, an Elizabethan literatus, first published in London in 1579, is most curious. Fenton knew no Italian and his "translation" (considered his major work and greatly successful in his time) was derived not from Guicciardini's original text but from the one foreign language Fenton knew, French. Fenton based his work on the 1568 French version of Chomedey; what we have, therefore, is a translation of a translation! Fenton's dependence on the French version is proved by the fact that he maintained in his English text the spellings of proper names used by Chomedey instead of adopting, which would have been more logical, the Italian spellings. Thus we have Petillane for Pitigliano, Triuulce for Trivulzio, Francisquin Cibo for Franceschetto Cibo, Ceruetre for Cerveteri, and so on.

Furthermore, I have discovered that Fenton indulges throughout his text (which is remarkably faithful, considering that it is second-hand) in numerous excisions, paraphrases, omissions, ellipses, and revisions, frequently in the interest of courtly bows to the English ruling house.

Political and religious considerations play their part (Fenton was a Protestant and agent of the Crown) and so when he comes to translate Guicciardini on Pope Alexander VI, he tends to sound like the God of the King James Bible fulminating against backsliders and fornicators, whereas Guicciardini, in these passages, is characterized by a whiplash of condemnation that is, however, cold, controlled; the whip is tongued with ironic barbs that cut and draw blood. For example, note this cobra-tail of a Guicciardinian sentence referring to Cesare Borgia, the Pope's son, with its mock rhetorical echo effects:

> ... *Et tra questi qualcuno, accioche a esseguire i pravi consigli, non mancassino pravi instrumenti, non meno detestabile in parte alcuna del padre.*

becomes in Fenton:

> ... and amongst others, one no less detestable than the father to whose cursed counsels he became a wicked instrument.

I am lucky to possess the 1618 edition of Fenton's version. It's a delicious book. It plunges me right back to William Shakespeare, to Hakluyt's *Voyages,* to Drake, to Marlowe, and to the King James Bible—all that marvelous sinewy English of the Elizabethan. Here is how Fenton begins his History:

> Hauing in hand to write the affaires and fortunes of Italy, I judged
> it conuenient to draw into discourse, those particularities that most
> nearest resemble our time and memorie, yea euen since the selfe
> Princes of that country calling in the armies of Fraunce, gaue the first
> beginning to so great innouations; a matter, for the variety, greatnesse,
> & nature of such things, verie notable, and well worthie of memorie:
> and for the heauie accidents, hateful, bloudy, and horrible: for that
> Italy for manie yeares was trauelled with all those sorts of calamities,
> with the which mortal men are wont to be afflicted, as well by the
> iust wrath and hand of God, as through the impiety and wickedness
> of other nations.

Beautiful! And surely we are in the late sixteenth century, only thirty-eight years after Guicciardini's death. But sixteenth-century England, not sixteenth-century Italy. This text would solve only half our dilemma, which is reproduction of language and epoch. In any case, to render it available to the modern reader, Fenton's knotted Elizabethan English would require a translation, in which case we would have a translation of a translation of a translation!

The only other integral English version of the *History of Italy* is that by Austin Parke Goddard, published in ten volumes in London over the years 1753 to 1756. Goddard was expert in Italian, had studied and lived in Italy for many years at the invitation of Cosimo III, the Grand Duke of Tuscany, who was a friend of his family. Furthermore, aside from his expertise in the language, Goddard's intentions were to adhere scrupulously to Guicciardini's phraseology rather than redo it "in a very elegant style."

But unfortunately the road to paraphrase is paved with good intentions. Goddard extracts wholesome lessons from Guicciardini and then puts them into courtly periwigged English. What he has accomplished is, for the most part, a good, sometimes sparkling paraphrase of the *Storia d'Italia,* clothing it in the opulent Gibbonsonian style of eighteenth-century historical rhetoric. Much more serious are Goddard's frequent variations of meaning, reinterpretations, polite omissions, invented gallantries—a general transformation of Guicciardini's feeling-tone from solemn Latinate obliquity and acerbity to a very English mixture of manners and morals.

More serious is the fact that both Fenton and Goddard omit practically all of the famous forbidden passages, the sections in Book III concerning the incestuous loves of the House of Borgia; Book IV on the effect of the new discoveries of Columbus, and on the Portuguese interpretations of Sacred Scriptures; Book X on Cardinal Pompeo Colonna inciting the people of Rome to rebel against the Papacy, as well as numerous Guicciardinian anti-clerical ironies such as his remark that the Holy Ghost must have inspired the cardinals in the election of Adrian VI, and so on.

Hence we have the unusual situation that, since Guicciardini's classic was first published more than four hundred years ago, the only two integral versions in English of his work are both disqualified as true translations, one because it was not based on the original Italian text, the other because it is a paraphrase.

I come back to my original premise. There is a theory and practice of translation, in our day especially, which in an effort to avoid translatese leaps to the other extreme, and gives us Romans of antiquity who talk pure Hemingwayese.

But I should say that a true translation, while rendering available to the modern reader the speech of another time and culture, will also preserve the savor of that speech, the flavor of that time. A pinch of antiquity must be added. A good translation of a sixteenth-century text should be redolent of its period. It should take us back there; we should not only understand it, we should be permeated by it in a kind of historical osmosis, research through the pores. To render Guicciardini in clear modern English available to the modern reader may be admirable pedagogy, but it is not the art of translation.

I have called Guicciardini a Proustian historian—that is, he creates a vision and a logic manifested in a certain kind of language. The stylistic challenge I set myself, therefore, was more than searching for English equivalents that would avoid archaicism, on the one hand, and clear modern English (again, archaicism in reverse), on the other, I have tried instead to re-create an English that would be faithful to the literal meaning of the text, and yet convey Guicciardinian involutions, his Ciceronian periods, his Proustian *longueurs*—an English that would convey in the twentieth century the flavor of a personalized Latinate Italian style of the sixteenth century.

Enmeshed in this web, I found that I was searching the processes of Guicciardini's thought. Sometimes I had to cut the interminable sentences, balanced like some incredible trapeze act, clause upon (and within) clause, often a page high. Sometimes I had to clarify Guicciardini's casual way with antecedents and pronouns, substitute proper names for his strings of ambiguous he's and him's. (Those scholars who claim that Guicciardini never writes other than crystal-clear merely betray their ignorance of the text.) Great monuments are not marred by scratches, and Guicciardini's marvelous rhetoric is not without its faults of over-elaboration, density, impenetrable thickets.

The true translator must only clear up as much of this Sargasso Sea as is absolutely necessary to make for passage. But to clarify what was ambiguous in the original is not translation but explication. The job of the translator is not to make clear that which was not clear, but to render in another tongue (and sometimes another century) the same degree and kind of ambiguity wherever it occurs.

Guicciardini's chief literary fault is his prolixity, the inevitable outcome of his obsessive search for detail, his quest for truth by amassing all particulars. This gave rise to the legend of the Laconian (condemned because he had used three words where two would do) who was offered his freedom if he read entirely through Guicciardini's interminable account of the siege of Pisa, but who pleaded—after attempting a few pages—that he be sent instead to row in the galleys.

Scholars debate whether Francesco Guicciardini is more *res* than *verba,* but I should say that if there is a discrepancy between his hard skeletal thinking and the rhetorical artifices in which it is shrouded, this literature is very important. To transform it into simple modern English is to destroy those obliquities which are the very mark of the man: his intellectual clarity, his astuteness, his diplomatic visor glinting at all times.

For the Embattled Reader

Frances Keene

There are times when the importance of translation is primarily that of a bridge between the Embattled, or at least surrounded, Reader and his threatened freedom. At such times, the act of translation becomes a moral and political act: he who engages in the translation of forbidden books, books which edify toward a no-longer-permissible goal, or which incite to action directly leading to that goal, is as much a freedom fighter as the clandestine printer who sets his type for him or the distributor who risks his life in streets and byways to circulate the message—or the reader of the message himself.

Such times are not confined to war, as nearly all of us present today know at first hand. Suppression of books, of the voice of the 'outsider,' is a favorite activity of the well-organized repressive society. What would the minds of an already restive populace do if exposed to a steady stream of literature that permitted an open vista of better times or a wide-angled view of a future more desirable than the present?

Censorship is always for the reader's "good"—it spares him invidious comparisons, reconciles him to the darkness of reality by freeing for circulation those (often escapist) publications that seem unobjectionable for public consumption in a time of crisis. And crisis can become, in the police state, an everyday affair for is not the state perpetually threatened, and must it not perpetually be defended in word, thought, and—only lastly—deed? How easy, the solution to suppress, or at least strictly limit, the circulation of so-called seditious material, thus supposedly removing the risk-fraught temptation to look over the wall!

But such censorship is less easy with works in translation for here the censors, the common garden variety, are often at a loss. Whitman circulated freely in Fascist Italy long after Corrado Alvaro's *L'Uomo e' forte* (Man is Strong) had been—after many misunderstandings—impounded. Vittorini's translations of Hemingway flourished in paperbound 'for train reading,' and could be bought at the kiosks in the stations or the booksellers outside. Steinbeck's *Grapes of Wrath* and Dos Passos' *Manhattan Transfer* beckoned while native works on the plight of the starving migrant worker, say, or the struggle to survive as a marginal man in the great cities, or the moral confusion of the conned draftee in a war of whose goals the draftee himself was ignorant were, of course, suppressed or denied official sanction—hence never saw the light of print. The censor was alert to home-grown dangers first and, logically enough, he took a stiff line with works which *he could clearly see* might rock the boat.

But how clearly can the censor, even the multi-lingual censor, see when presented with a classic of another language written a century prior to the situation in which he finds himself? Unless he is willing to see beyond the lines as the Embattled Reader does, how is the censor to know that *Moby Dick,* that vast cathedral whose every gothic arch is carved of purest whalebone, is a deeply disturbing incitement to the examination of conscience—hence "seditious" by nature? And so Cesare Pavese's translation circulated freely under Fascism for who, it was thought officially, would bother with that vast book and from another language, at that? An old story, a kind of fable. Censors, beware of fables for their truths go marching on.

But it is not only literary works that can cause trouble. Georges Sorel's works on syndicalism—spoon-fed to Mussolini in his neophyte days by Angelica Balabanoff and important for the formation of Fascism's own early form of syndicalism—were taken from the open shelves and placed in rooms to whose access special permits were required. This in Bologna, the seat of one of the greatest pioneering universities in the western world. The reader asked and, if he could prove an historian's rather than a labor leader's need to consult the works, a key was given unto him which he passed to a satrap who proceeded to unlock the coveted works. The reader took notes; he did not write his findings until the dust of Bologna had been wiped from his feet. If he was a foreigner it was easier to gain access . . . if *he* was a *she* it was easier still.

Still later in the regime, Spinoza was locked up. As a Jew, he might have perverted the minds of students, in some insidious way reaching forward across the centuries to beguile them to questions, to think, to find an inner peace that was not state-related or induced. In Spinoza's *Theological Political Treatise,* he clearly explains in the Preface that his work will concern itself with man's problems in seeking to guarantee the greatest possible freedom for his own ideas. Given his period, Spinoza saw repression in terms of organized religion rather than of the state but he warned his readers against orthodoxies of all kinds:

"If deeds only could be made the grounds of criminal charges,
and words were allowed to pass free, seditions would be divested
of every semblance of justification . . . "

The Fascist authorities thought otherwise and, except for scholars, the works of Spinoza were hard to come by after 1938.

And of course Martin Luther disappeared first from the bookstalls, where his aphoristic *Table Talk* at least had been in relatively frequent demand, then from the open shelves in the libraries. Too involved he was in this case, not with his Articles but with the peasants and their revolt—despite his ultimate stand—to fit comfortably in the authoritarian, stratified society then in the making in Italy. Totalitarianism and, later, racist philosophy could scarcely countenance a writer who, regardless of religious questions, could write:

"I have often wondered what led the heathen to say so many
beautiful things of death which is so fearful and hateful. But when
I consider the world, I wonder no more; for there were so many
stupid scoundrels in authority in the world who did them evil, that
they had nothing to threaten them with but death," *(Table Talk,*
New York, 1893, p. 100)

Or again, at the time of the campaign for the Purification of the Race, to read: "There is no doubt that in remote times a great number of Jews fled to Italy and Germany. The eloquent heathen Cicero [mentions] their numbers in Italy . . . It was a mighty nation," can scarcely have fitted in with official propaganda. (Ibid., p. 87)

On the other hand, there was a brief period in the middle thirties when books by Miguel de Unamuno and Salvador de Madariaga were more freely obtainable in Italian translations in Italy than in Spain. This was, one was led to believe, because Italy's own brief thaw was on, to dazzle the eye of the native or foreign scholar with a brief illusion, a ray of hope that more liberal times were ahead.

Few were fooled, therefore repression returned full force along with
anti-semitic laws, the laws for the purification of the Race!

What are the particular attractions of a foreign literature in times
of stiff repression? There is a wide range. Often the publisher feels
that his purpose has been served if, in the book he chooses to have
translated, the conscious evocation of nostalgia can "shake up" his
readers' emotions. Translations of Mann's and Gide's novels into
Russian must have worked this way. The same books could serve
as manuals of polite customs *(les bonnes moeurs)* in cruder times,
hence in part the popularity of *Gone with the Wind* with its unconscious echo of *"quel ramo del Lago di Como . . ."* Manzoni's dear
long-winded call to arms which fired the Italians to freedom at the
time of the Risorgimento (hard as it is today to imagine its having
"fired" anyone). More activating than nostalgia and manuals of
moeurs are translations that stimulate the mind to critical comparisons: a world in which the unflattering, seminal books of Faulkner,
the treacherously simple poems of *The Spoon River Anthology* with
their comment on the human condition could circulate freely must
surely be, if not a better, then a freer world than the one in which
the books were available in translation—and Mme. Fernanda Pivano,
among us today, has translated all of *Spoon River* and some of
Faulkner into Italian in the parlous times of which I am speaking.
(The publishers Laterza and Einaudi were in the forefront of those
houses that kept a stream and then a trickle of translations flowing
into the parched literary landscape. It is not surprising that Feltrinelli was the first to publish *Dr. Zhivago,* when you think back and
recall that Gorky's *The Lower Depths* was partly composed in
Italy whither the author had fled in pre-Fascist times to escape another form of tyranny at home.)

Two technical difficulties confront the translator under totalitarianism, whether of right or left. Both are primarily semantic in
nature. How to translate terms which have but a single meaning in
such a way as not to alarm the authorities and so delay or prevent
publication? Victor Alba has told me of his problem in translating
citizen which must consistently be rendered *subject* in contemporary
Spain. But the Michael Harringtons of the world, in writing on
poverty or urban blight, know nothing of "subject," hence the
translation is perforce false to the original. However, if *citizen* is used,
the production of the book is slowed down. My own problem
was in rendering *liberty* and *freedom* into suitable Italian, this in
the Quaderni di Giustizia e Libertà, clandestine publications, it is
true, whose editors would therefore be willing to risk accurate renderings: but you all realize that, of the commoner western languages,

only English has the two terms, Spanish, French and Italian having some form of *libertas,* and German having *Freiheit.* In English we often use liberty to signify absence of organized restraint or pressure, and freedom as freed from some sort of the foregoing or free of the threat of the same. Nuances, if you will, but at times significant.

The second difficulty is moral as well as semantic: in an effort to make a point more emphatic, the political translator is sometimes tempted to give a slightly more positive case to a word or phrase than the original can be strictly interpreted as having. In, "I am somewhat inclined to agree. . ." from let us say, a Lewis Mumford in a housing discussion with Italy's famed architectural planner and historian (and long-time anti-Fascist leader) Bruno Zevi, how easy it would be to omit the *somewhat.* After all, the sense is not traduced: the point is simply made stronger. The emotions that enter in political translation must be scrupulously curbed, else in trying to do justice to one's own cause, one tends "somewhat" to betray the original.

Today, translation continues this same role in Greece, in Brazil, to a very real extent in Spain where selective intellectual repression has been refined to an art—time can elevate 'most anything! Colleagues, alert to the intimate pain that suppression of native works can bring to the mind in afflicted countries, have borne witness to the correspondingly high level of translated work available in totalitarian lands. There is scarcely need, in the presence of our honored colleagues from behind the curtain, to dwell on what certain native writers must undergo. Yuli Daniel, in his great story *Atonement,* has said it for us all. Quoting a poem of one of his protagonists, Daniel writes:

> Mankind, in haste, will seek out a false prophet,
> Mankind will find itself a leader,
> And it will run blindly to and fro
> And its leader will frown sagely
> And once again brother will rise against brother,
> Reason against reason, evil against evil . . .
> Inventing our doctrines, loitering under the heavens
> What fools we were, who could not see
> That the pivot of life lies in the balance
> Of good and evil, darkness and light.

As we return to our work of translation, to our job of giving birth to a new work based on fidelity and, hopefully, with taste and deep commitment, on the original, let us remember that for the Embattled Reader the darkness has often been dissipated, if only a little, by the light translations have cast on his appalling gloom. Let us keep our own standards high and courageously perform these mixed marriages of the mind which, at their best, have borne truly vigorous fruit.

The Publisher as Obstacle

John Macrae III

Two years ago I was told by the Czechoslovakian state publisher that it was common for a moderately well-known American novel to sell out an edition of 40,000 copies in Prague alone. If the work of a contemporary foreign writer sells 40,000 copies in one year in the entire United States the event is publishing news. I do not present this as an unqualified statistic. There are many cultural and economic factors to consider. It is enough to say, however, that Americans are less hungry for the printed word, at least in book form and in translations, than are readers from other countries. Though American readers do not naturally seek out foreign literature, publishers, by insisting upon quality translations, can make such literature accessible to a far wider readership than exists today.

Traditionally, the quality of translation is not the first concern of the American publisher. This has been true of the United States' most distinguished publishers, including the two or three outstanding literary publishers who during the last half century have recognized and introduced many of the most important French, German and Spanish language writers to American audiences. Publishers generally assume that the readership for uncelebrated, though talented, foreign writers is finite, possibly identifiable as a group of only four or five thousand souls. Because the target audience is said to be small, it has not been considered prudent for publishers to expend large enough sums to attract first-rate translators. Thus the works of good and occasionally important foreign writers are frequently rendered into the English language by translators who have little concern for literary quality and whose single attractive feature to the publisher is their willingness to accept low pay. Certainly there are exceptions to this sad publishing tradition, yet exceptions are generally reserved for a few masterworks—classics from Greece and Rome, and a few Russian, German and French works. In most cases these are standard works whose school and college markets are well established. Rarely does the publisher's concern for contemporary literature in translation permit him to invest the resources—both money and editorial talent—necessary for such works to win large and lasting American audiences.

Another obstacle to quality translations, and therefore a problem for publishers, is the newsworthy or topical book. Many such books today seem to relate personal encounters, often between the individual and his state. The success, artistically and commercially, of such works does not turn on literary quality. Instead success is largely dependent upon timely publication. Speedy translations rarely satisfy anyone, yet one must acknowledge the necessity for bringing out original political or scientific developments while the news is fresh. Less excusable, however, is what seems to happen to many important foreign-language writers who, because of their essential morality, are considered political writers. Solzhenitsyn's fate, for example, at the hands of American and British publishers has been unfortunate. Most recently two of his major works were poorly translated under the direction of American publishers. It is not enough to lay the blame on competition and the need to publish books as news, "the race to publish first." Any novel of importance stands a better chance of finding a lasting audience when the translation reveals fully the writer's narrative gifts. Readers need not be linguists to appraise readability, and for most of us it is the book in translation that determines the original work's value as literature. It seems that in the case of Solzhenitsyn, Pasternak before him, and with too many other writers, the quality of the writer's mind and his writing style have been jeopardized unnecessarily by the publisher's haste.

When the publisher considers "promising writers" who are not internationally known, he is faced with an apparently unresolvable dilemma: on the one hand, an ill-equipped translator is one who is selected only because he is inexpensive or is incapable of or unwilling to take the time to translate the work effectively. On the other hand, the publisher who is willing to take the necessary financial risk to insure a quality translation for a little-known work must recognize that the work's sale rarely repays his investment. To solve this dilemma, publishers frequently turn to foundations for translation grants. Another answer is for publishers to publish fewer books in translation, to concentrate on the few outstanding writers. Wouldn't we all be better off—writer, translator, publisher and the reading public—if fewer literary works in translation were offered each year? If each publisher were to decide that only quality translations—and let me add that a fair measure of quality in this regard is its high cost —are to grace his list, then the selective process would become more rigorous. One expects that only important works would slip through the tighter editorial net. Critics—and eventually the reading public— would begin to respond to what we have to assume would be higher publishing standards. Few reviewers now take the trouble to chip through the imposing matrix of uninspired books in translation to locate the occasional gem. If standards are raised, who other than poor, i.e. "cheap," translators will suffer? Even publishers are beginning to realize that low initial cost frequently breeds expensive failure, a fact well-known to many translators. A friend and translator Alistair Reid, remarks that the only thing lost in translation is *money.* Mr. Reid's remark concerns his loss and ours, too. If publishers wish to protect their literary investments they must support translators and involve them routinely, along with authors, in the work's financial success.

Recently, several of us have met to draft a P.E.N. translation manifesto. Its crucial tenet, simply stated, is that a foreign literary work for American readers is only as good as its translation. It is not my concern here to appraise the translator's art. As a publisher my concern is to help create the environment that will allow the best foreign writing to appear in appropriate translation. To test the quality of a book in translation one has only to judge its effect on the reader. Is the magic intact? Have unfamiliar ideas, customs and life experiences been rendered in a comfortable American idiom? The translator, as Gregory Rabassa points out, is not the creator. He is the messenger, the bilingual communicator between cultures, whose concern is to reveal the creative artist, the author. The translator must never intrude. His works succeed only when the reader is unaware of his existence. The translator has then prepared the way for the reader to enter directly the mind of the author. The few who are capable of this fine art deserve our full support, for it is they who offer our readers access to much of the world's literature.

In the case of specialized works, scholarly monographs, and even contemporary poetry, it does not seem that effective translations are possible without subventions, either from the academic community or from foundations. In the case of poetry the subvention must be large enough to allow the publisher to produce a bilingual edition.

The recent experience or example that is close to us, myself personally as publisher and editor, is our program to publish Jorge Luis Borges. Though celebrated, Borges has not had a popular success in this country. Our plan was to publish all his works in new translations involving close collaboration between the author and an American translator. I found that Borges had a "collaborator-translator" in mind, and we agreed to publish seven titles in English, offering Borges' translator, Norman Thomas di Giovanni, larger than usual advances to help defray the costs of his moving to Buenos Aires to be with the author. Di Giovanni and Borges work together daily, discussing subtle cultural differences between America and Argentina as they affect the work. The first book, *The Book of Imaginary Beings,* was published by Dutton last fall. Though it is one of Borges' minor books, we have sold 10,000 copies and arranged for a sub-stantial—$22,500—paperback sale. The translator and author share all earnings equally. Thus, even though we had not looked upon Borges as an investment—we simply wanted to publish Borges well and to break even financially—his first book produced a handsome return. The next book, which will come out in the fall, is his major collection of stories; we paid an advance of $10,000, again 50% to Giovanni and 50% to Borges through the publisher of record in Latin America.

Someone may wish to know how we can tell if the translation is appropriate: the foreign work must be rendered into English in such a way as to make it attractive and accessible to the American reader, that is the first concern. Further, the publisher must be certain that it is faithful and accurate and that the translator has not left out anything of importance or added anything of his own making. We do check that. One must be sure that the translation reads smoothly and that the idiom is familiar to the American reader and, most importantly, that the author's intent is preserved. Here is an example: when Alistair Reid was translating a Colombian writer, he came upon a section in the Spanish-language edition which said that a man and woman were dancing in a house of pros-titution—they were doing the tango, and "light came between them." What the author meant by this was not just that light shone between them but that they were dancing the tango far apart; and, when you dance the tango in a whorehouse, light does not usually

separate the dancers. So this was really an important point of information which the translator would have missed unless he had access to
the author, as Reid did. Obviously a literal translation is not enough.
It is helpful for the translator to sit down and work with the author,
to be sure that he understands the author's intent and translates the
culture not just the words.

I made a comment earlier about the need for "reconstruction" in
the case of Senor Borges. I would like to elaborate on this a little.

The "reconstruction" is done in collaboration with the author.
Because Borges is almost blind, Norman di Giovanni reads parts of
the book to Borges in English and Spanish, then they discuss them
and add to the original or subtract from it, making a new work in
English. The author changes things as he goes along, sparked by the
relationship with the translator. In this case, the translator and
author, working closely together, have collaborated every step on the
way to the completed English text.

In many cases, however, such collaboration is impossible and the
author is in no position to judge whether the translator is using the
most appropriate idiom. Should the author be incapable of offering
good advice in this regard, I think the publisher would support the
translator if, in his opinion, the final work—the completed manuscript in English—is improved because the translator has taken the
trouble to capture the writer's meaning and style, not just the literal
equivalent of his words. As publishers involve themselves routinely
in translation problems they will remove the biggest obstacle to the
success of foreign literature in America.

The Interaction of Literary and Technical Translators

Dale S. Cunningham

The literature of translation as a subject abounds with beautifully written descriptions of the translator's cultural mission. No one can deny the importance of the translator to civilization—countless essays and books recount the positive effects of translation. Yet, at the same time, one can envisage the possibility of an equally large literature on what has been *lost* to civilization for the lack of an even greater, more adequate translation effort.

To be sure, it is relatively easy in science and technology to point out specific instances of how thousands or even millions of dollars and innumerable hours have been wasted in the duplication of re-search. But even in these fields, one can rapidly reach the domain of pure speculation. For example, it is a fact that half of the world's medical literature is *not* in English. The American National Institutes of Health serve the entire English-speaking world with a very adequate, heavily subsidized bibliographic program that is so modern, it is computerized. Yet, in spite of the fact that half the medical knowledge is not in English, the physician who queries the computer is invited to exclude these non-English items from the results of the literature search. In other words, we admit that the English-speaking countries of the world have not been able to cope with the question of translation as effectively as we have with that of bibliography and information retrieval. As a result, we can merely imagine what bad effects the lack of translation may eventually have on our health.

Indeed, the very survival of civilization as we know it may some day come to depend upon translation. It has been related that a short phrase in the Japanese reply to an Allied ultimatum towards the close of the Second World War could have several meanings. The translator selected one which sealed the door to further communication and dialogue. As a result, the first atomic bombs were dropped. Yet, few Americans seem to be troubled by the fact that no college in the country offers a degree in translation.

Perhaps similar speculations in the area of the humanities will not produce nightmarish results, but they are nevertheless disheartening. There is simply no way even to begin measuring the pleasure or inspiration which has been lost for the lack of a translation. However, it is not my purpose to add yet another encomium on the role of the translator or to dwell on speculative areas of what happens when there is an absence of translations or the production of bad translations. Rather, I should like to discuss a more controversial subject: What is a translator?

I wish we had a dissertation-level study of the vast number of definitions from the literature of translation as a subject. In the absence of such a study, however, I can only guess about the findings. I think that one trend would be a tendency to define translators more by the type of material translated than by the basic unity of translation as an activity. This is unfortunate, for it perpetrates a split between categories of translators which has a harmful effect on the entire profession.

When this suggested study of translator definitions is carried out, a second finding would probably emphasize the opposing viewpoints of theorists who hold that the translator is above all a language specialist and those who praise subject-matter expertise as the ultimate criterion. I belong to the former group, for I feel that emphasis on subject matter again is a force which divides what should be a unified profession. Instead of being primarily translators concerned with carrying out a difficult intellectual activity professionally, we become poets, physicists, playwrights, writers, or even housewives who also translate. When translation has been made secondary to whatever else one may be, it is easy to go an additional step and regard translation as something which requires no more thought or preparation than clerking or shining shoes. If the activity of translation is belittled in this way by some translators, then it should cause no wonder that translation is rarely taught and that the public leaves the translator's door displeased to find that translation cannot be performed somewhat faster and cheaper than typing.

Utopian definitions of translations are obviously uselss to us. Extreme statements about required abilities in the target language, the source language, or subject matter can only lead to the portrayal of a fabulous creature. As long as "human" can be used synonymously with "imperfect," we can hardly attribute a trinity of perfections to the translator when we wish to speak to or about the real translator who lives in the real world.

I should like to suggest a more realistic definition of the translator which would make it easier to regard translation as a profession, and to facilitate full-time translation for greater numbers of people. Publishers, public health officials, and others who need translations could stop kicking their problems under the table and take steps to get the translations that are presently not being done. Finally, a more realistic definition of the translator would help show the feasibility of teaching translation and pave the way for even more professional translators in the future.

In taking sides on the controversy of language mastery versus subject-matter expertise, I have considered elementary logic, theory, and practice. By *logic,* I mean that translation is a language art and service in the broadest sense. The subject-matter expertise basic to translation is language expertise. By *theory,* I mean that the science underlying translation is linguistics. By *practice,* I refer to my own personal experience. Throughout my apprenticeship and now as a full-time translator, I have consistently dealt with language, namely the embodiment of ideas and the expression of thoughts and subject matter rather than the actual areas of expertise per se. Questions of subject matter have arisen, of course, but this happened as frequently when I was translating poetry and books on art as when the material before me was mathematics, medicine, or engineering.

I believe my stress on language and linguistics can be justified by more than purely subjective feelings. Editing is not a new subject to translation, and I have written more extensively on translation and editing myself.[1] Philology—when defined as historical linguistics—cannot provide an answer and has done little for translation as a science or a profession. However, while nineteenth-century linguistics may have contributed little to translation outside of the field of lexicography, modern structural or descriptive linguistics as it has developed from the work of de Saussure, the Prague School, Bloomfield, and others has begun to be a major force.

[1] See p. 51 for all footnotes.

Of the several books presently available which directly apply linguistic principles to translation,[2] that by the brilliant linguist Eugene A. Nida is particularly significant, even in the choice of a title: *Towards a Science of Translation.*[3] The knowledge symbolized by the vast bibliography of books and papers on machine translation[4] has not yet been evaluated and interpreted for what may be the most significant benefit to be derived from these efforts: a new awareness and understanding of natural language which should eventually be accompanied by the application of this new knowledge in further developing translation theory and in improving human translation. Linguistic research now seems aimed at providing machine-aided computer aids for humans.[5]

Help for human translators and progress in translation theory can also derive from the use of modern linguistic techniques in studying human acquisition of language. There are more than practical advantages in knowing how to learn still another language, or about it, for the purposes required (e.g., reading, speaking, translating); research on thought processes themselves may lead to greater theoretical understanding of the act of translation. For example, work by Noam Chomsky suggests[6] at a simplistic level of interpretation, that the thought processes involved in acquiring a language as a child are perhaps the most complicated that any human being experiences in life. Possibly this may explain why only a small percentage of all people ever learn to handle even their native language with superior skill. In any case, it suggests that translation is not the easiest profession to which one can aspire and that the source and target language abilities of a translator far overshadow the importance of subject-matter knowledge in the trinity of skills. Acquisition of specialised knowledge is a process which begins relatively late in life—and only subsequent to the acquisition of learning at least one language! Furthermore, a certain portion of this effort represents the learning of vocabulary, jargon, or perhaps what could best be designated the language (or sublanguage) of the specialized field.

Thus, the translator would then be defined—ideally, but not unrealistically—as a person who masters both target language and source language. Subject matter, if it need be mentioned at all, would be discussed only in terms of the *language* of any particular subject area. As a result, when a translation that approaches perfection is desired or required, it will readily be understood that editing of various types is the medium through which a perfect or nearly perfect translator can be constructed—as a composite if such a person is not available as a single individual. And the rarity of perfect translators in our world is a well-known phenomenon.

Many problems presently encountered by translators (and their clients) can readily be solved by a language approach to translation that views translation and editing as different, separate problems.

In brief, the types of editing which must be considered with respect to translation are as follows: 1) editorial comparison of the target and source languages for completeness and sense (distortion of fine points); 2) editing for subject-matter vocabulary: technical terminology and technical usage; 3) target language editing for elagance (correctness) and style (consistency).

There is probably nothing new in this for an audience of translators, but it may be interesting for you to consider my presentation in a graphic form (see Table 1 on page 50).

It should be noted that this view is not restricted to a special type of translation. Human as it may be to want to do the whole job oneself, this seems to be expected or even required today only in the translation of poetry or other literature. Of course, there is a great deal of satisfaction involved in doing a job from start to finish, and perhaps even in being truly Renaissance in spirit and proceeding to set the type and roll the presses, too. However, I often wonder if the original author, the translator, the publishers of both, the reading public, and even art would not be better served by the literary equivalent of collaborations which have worked so well in scientific and technical fields. All writing being a literary act, the postulation of a "scientific-technical" translator as opposed to the "literary" translator appears as patently false to me as the introduction of "subject-matter expertise" into the definition of the translator.

Let me refer you to a paper by I. J. Citroen, "The Myth of the Two Professions—Literary and Non-Literary Translation."[7] In this paper, you can find numerous examples of excellent writing from scientific papers and of literary works which contain passages with highly specialized vocabulary from science, technology, or other fields.

I know that many of us at this meeting have had the good fortune to know Dr. Alexander Gode personally. In speaking to the technical translator, he has said "Woe to the person who forgets that technical literature is literature." Time does not permit citation of many lyrical passages from technical and scientific literature without a trace of technical vocabulary. However, the corollary to Dr. Gode's admonition should be clear; the literary translator will frequently find that he must also be a scientific or technical translator as well.

No one can possibly know all the sub-specializations of a subject, not to speak of larger, related fields. For example, the American Medical Association Style Manual lists well over one hundred "Classifications of Materials," most of which could be regarded as medical (sub)sub-specializations.[8] Thus, any competent translator must know how to elicit information from "native speakers" of the sublanguage in specialized fields. By "native speaker," I mean a subject-matter expert who may be monolingual. "Expert" evokes the image of a scholar, advanced degrees, doctors or lawyers, but experts in subject-matter vocabulary can also be hairdressers, dancers, supermarket clerks, mechanics, or a wide variety of other non-academic individuals. The original document determines who the expert will be. In the case of Gunter Grass' translator, Ralph Manheim, it was a stone-cutter. However, the monolingual (possibly even illiterate) expert has to be helped by the translator, and this can demand special skills or training in linguistics.

By viewing translation wholly as a language activity, and by refusing to see translation as a number of professions or a subservient craft secondary to another profession, I believe I have demonstrated the essential unity of translation. To be sure, I recognize the fact that not all translation work requires the same abilities and intellectual preparation. I was recently told that a great deal of "translation" in banks consists in knowing the difference between "pay" and "collect" in several languages and being able to use the correct rubber stamp. Of course, a person trained to do nothing but this would hardly be a translator, but otherwise the differences are chiefly of degree. It should also be clear by now that I believe the greatest interaction between literary and scientific-technical translators should be continuous and occur in one and the same person. At the same time, I recognize that some people will always be happiest banging rubber stamps for an eight-hour day, while others can only be satisfied by struggling with a poem—possibly as recreation after a day's translation work filled with birth certificates, business letters, legal documents, patents, and various scientific or technical papers. For this reason, I should like to describe the work of the American Translators Association and present some suggestions for extended interaction between all individuals involved in translation.

This association was established in 1959 and incorporated in 1962. It is affiliated with the Fédération Internationale des Traducteurs (FIT) which is supported by the national translator organizations which constitute its membership and by grants from UNESCO towards publication of the journal Babel.

In 1964 I adapted an earlier statement of purpose which I believe was largely the work of the first President of ATA, Dr. Alexander Gode. It can stand today without a change: "ATA serves as a forum and clearing house to advance the standards of translation and to promote the intellectual and material interests of translators and interpreters in the United States. Translation has always been a difficult art and an exacting craft, but only in recent times has it become a full-time occupation. In seeking to safeguard the interests of this new profession as well to represent those who work in the field on a part-time or a vocational basis, ATA strives toward the goal of making the translator fully professional. Although the new status of translation has come about in the wake of scientific and technological developments, the Association appreciates the importance—to the profession as a whole—of the tradition of translation as a scholarly and literary pursuit and welcomes to membership those who are interested in the field as well as translators and interpreters active in any branch of knowledge."

Historically, ATA has passed through four fairly distinct phases and is presently entering a fifth. In the early days, the number of members was small, and the percentage of literary translators was quite high. I am sure that many of you here today are well acquainted with Frances Frenaye, Frances Keene, Herma Briffault, Gertrude Schwebell, Harriet de Onis, Clara and Richard Winston, Lewis Galantière, Theodore Purdy, and Heinz Norden—just to mention a few who have been members of ATA or have otherwise participated in its work.

Dr. Gode was our Renaissance man and genius-in-residence during those early days. A brilliant translator of all types of literature, the creator of Interlingua, an auxiliary language widely used in medical-journal abstracts, and a profound thinker who could express himself forcefully and eloquently in at least three languages that I know of, Dr. Gode wrote much of what ATA published and inspired most of the rest. He also typed it all, cut the stencils, ran the mimeograph machine, and either supervised or motivated just about everything else connected with running the affairs of the association.

The second period of ATA's history was fortunately brief, for it was marked by internal dissension, more characterized by personalities than issues. What was concrete involved whether ATA should be some sort of super agency and union or whether it should continue its attempt to become a truly professional society. The officers were reelected by the membership, ATA grew in numbers, and more members became active in assisting Dr. Gode.

The third phase was one of relatively great activity in terms of national conventions and publications. It was nevertheless characterized by volunteer work donated by a handful of individuals— Dr. Kurt Gingold, Henry Fischbach, and Dr. Eliot Beach should be mentioned in particular.

As an organization approaches a membership of five hundred, how-ever, an almost completely volunteer effort that extends to the stuff-ing of envelopes becomes unworkable. Illnesses and the pressures of work forced one person after another into inactivity; publications became relatively infrequent, conventions less ambitious. ATA did not accomplish much during this fourth period of its brief life.

The then President, Boris Anzlowar, and the Board of Directors made various attemps to correct the deficiencies. However, it is only within the past quarter, under the leadership of the current President, Daniel P. Moynihan, that a truly professional association manager has been hired. ATA has thus entered a fifth stage in its history, which we hope signifies its coming of age as a professional associa-tion.

At present, ATA can guarantee that its members will receive three publications with a certain regularity. In the past, the most regular has been *Babel,* the official organ of Fédération Internationale des Traducteurs which is published with the assistance of UNESCO. Its languages of publication are officially English and French, but occasional articles are published in other languages. The journal not only reaches all members of ATA, but many members of all other member societies of FIT; thus, if you have something of importance to say on the subject of translation, I suggest that *Babel* be a journal you consider seriously. I can assure you that papers by American translator-authors will be welcomed.

The ATA journal is called simply *American Translator.* Material with any urgency or without lasting value is distributed to members in a newsletter which has usually been entitled *ATA Notes.* In the past, the ATA has also published the *Professional Services Dictionary, Dictionaries Ahoy!* by Lewis Bertrand, and *Translator's Tool Chest.*

Finally, ATA cooperated in the publication and distribution of the *Translation Inquirer.* [9] This periodical was another of Dr. Gode's brainchildren and represents a sort of living dictionary. The first section contained words and frequently their contexts with equiv-alents in the language or languages desired. A second section had only unsolved queries, and the third section presented replies to queries in previous issues and additional comments on previous replies. Currently, this is not being published, but it may be revived in some form.

I have no preconceptions about how ATA and P.E.N. would interact most effectively, for there are many possibilities ranging from loose affiliation though close liaison to a far greater incidence of overlapping membership. However, I do feel that a group which in some way could reach nearly all American translators could be far more effective that either ATA or P.E.N. is at present. Thus, I will leave the "how" to the future, and present a few of the concrete things that could be accomplished by concerted action.

Revival of the *Translation Inquirer* does not seem to be a wise move in view of the past, but modifying the basic idea and using modern technology to realize something practical might be a very worthwhile project. A great deal of work is presently being done on developing computerized dictionaries.

For many years, I have been troubled by the lack of a bibliography on translation as a subject. Without a reference work, the education of translators must remain a haphazard thing indeed, whether the process is one of self-training or is carried out in formal courses. The omission is an expensive one. As far as education is concerned, it means that the student must waste vast amounts of time either unearthing whether work has been done in the area of interest to him or else repeating the effort of thought and discovery which others have already performed. The results are inevitably inferior. The person with an average sort of mind will be less well trained and more poorly informed than is necessary. The brilliant person merely wastes talent in duplicating the efforts of others instead of building on them.

The lack of a basic reference work therefore affects, at least in the long run, the professional standards of translators and their work. This lack may have led to omissions in the *Manifesto on Translation* which heralded the present conference.[10] Let us not waste our human resources by holding meeting after meeting of translators in order to duplicate past efforts. Instead, we should aim to add new knowledge to what is already known and new practical solutions to problems that translators encounter in their work.

Once again, I am aware of the immensity of the problem and of the fact that neither P.E.N. nor ATA is financially strong enough to undertake such a project on its own. When a bibliography was first suggested nearly fifteen years ago,[11] it might have been possible for a few individuals to carry out the work. In view of the explosion in information in our field as well as others, it would now appear more sensible to spread the work more widely and again to use computers in the indexing effort.

In concluding, I should like to mention under the heading of professionalization some other areas in which the interaction of P.E.N. and ATA might be mutually beneficial. It is obvious that a modern sort of dictionary and a comprehensive bibliography would have an effect on translation as a profession. The concerted efforts

of a large confederation of translators could also be helpful in fur-
thering the education of translators, and perhaps even in educating
the public. This goes beyond the formulation of model contracts,
other guidelines, and bills of rights and duties. There should be
greater efforts in assuring that the translator receives credit for
his work so that he can be appropriately praised or blamed. I also
feel that there should be more effective ways of criticizing translations. Sometimes a radical approach is needed. Robert Addis has
demonstrated this approach, which I feel is worth quoting.[12]
A critic quoted from Racine:

> *Que le jour recommence, et que le jour finisse*
> *Sans que jamais Titus puisse voir Berenice,*
> *Sans que, de tout le jour, je puisse voir Titus!*

and then an unacceptable published version:

> The sun shall rise and set and rise again
> While Titus seeks his Berenice in vain,
> And Berenice, in vain, her Titus seeks!

This is followed by a long dissertation on literature being essentially
untranslatable. Mr. Addis suggests that the criticism could have been
as concise as the following version:

> And the days shall wax, and the days shall wane,
> And Titus shall seek his love in vain;
> And I shall not see him again.

   Mr. Addis is a translator who demonstrates how effective the interaction of scientific and literary translation can be when it occurs in
an individual translator. However, when this interaction does not
occur as frequently as it should, the mingling of persons specialized
in a single direction could furnish valuable experiences for everyone
involved at larger scale meetings. Certainly, many practicing technical translators have much to learn about writing, and it is not inconceivable that they could teach literary translators some useful techniques in solving terminology problems.
   On a very practical level and given the present situation, I should
like to suggest that more people could be full-time competent professionals in the field of translation if they were to divide that time
between the two supposedly different fields. In this connection,
I want to quote from Mr. Addis once again. He suggests that

. . . those who love translation enough to wish to make it their life's
work, hence must need to make a living at it—most of them, notwith-
standing their own oftentimes considerable literary interests and talents
—taught themselves to translate *science and technology*, for only there
(in our society) is where the translation money is.

Has English-speaking society ever been willing to *pay* for a good
"literary" translation? The instances must surely be rare. It is cheaper,
of course, to lament reverently that Racine, Goethe, Pushkin and the
rest are "untranslatable." (An expensive economy, methinks.)

The Russians look at these things differently. They know that good
translations can be *bought*—by proper training and compensation of
translators. And they buy them, and they get them. The Russian translations of Goethe, Shakespeare and others are powerful, beautiful—
and they are *read!* In Russia it is also known that our English translations of their great works of literature are, for the most part, hideous.

So, when the translation money moves to "literature," rest assured
that our good translators will move with it. And good translations
will abound. Shakespeare said it all: "What is aught but as 'tis valued?"
Is not the low estate of "literary" translation in the English-speaking
world, and very especially in the United States, exactly equal to the
low value that we have placed on it?

This is, of course, one very obvious way to test this thesis—if anyone
is *really* interested.

Mr. Addis' assertions could and should be discussed at length, but
there is no time for that today. I cite him to emphasize once again
the main point I should like to make: the interaction of all translators will benefit them and their profession—not only materially,
but intellectually and ideally as well.

Table 1: The Ideal Translator as an Individual or a Composite

	A	B	C	D	E	F
Target Language	+++ (t)	+++ (t)	+/++	+++	0	+++
Knowledge of TL			*			*
Native Speaker of TL	*	*		*		
Source Language	+++ (t)	++	+++ (t)	0	+++	0
Knowledge of SL		*				
Native Speaker of SL	*		*		*	
Subject-Matter						
Vocabulary	+++	+/++	+++	+++	+++	0
TL Knowledge of SM		*	*			
TL Expert in SM	*			*		
SL Knowledge of SM		*	*			
SL Expert in SM	*				*	
Editorial (Writing) Skill	+++ (e)	++ (e)	++ (e)	0/+	0/+	+++ (e)
Target Language	*	*		*		*
Source Language	*		*		*	

TL: Target Language, SL: Source Language, SM: Subject Matter; *: Level at which the evaluated skill occurs; 0, +, ++, +++: Evaluation of the skill; (t), (e): Translator and editorial training respectively, or their equivalents.

A: The ideal translator who rarely exists except as a utopian dream.

B: A well prepared translator in a given field.

C: A similarly well prepared translator who could translate in the reverse direction or function as B's editor.

D: A subject-matter expert who can advise on terminology in the target language.

E: The counterpart of D for questions on usage and subject-matter vocabulary in the source language.

F: A writing expert who can polish the language of the translation.

NOTES

1. Kuz'mina, E. B., ed. *Redaktor i perevod*. Moscow, Izdatel'stvo "Kniga," 1965; Cunningham, D.S., "Translation and Editing," submitted to *Delos* for publication.

2. Federov, A. V., *Vvedenie v teoryu perevoda,* Moscow, Izdat. Lit., 1958; Revzin, I. I., and Rozentsveig, V. Yu., *Osnovy obshchego i mashinnogo perevoda,* Moscow, 1964; Catford, J. C., *A Linguistic Theory of Translation,* Oxford University Press, 1965; and Kade, O., *Zufall und Gesetzmaessigkeit in der Uebersetzung,* Leipzig, VEB Verlag, 1968.

3. Nida, E.A., Leiden, E. J. Brill, 1964. See also his *Learning a Foreign Language* , New York, Friendship Press, 1967 (Rev. Ed.), and *Bible Translating,* London, United Bible Societies, 1961 (Rev. Ed.).

4. See Delavenay, E., (K. Delavenay, tr.), *An Introduction to Machine Translation,* New York, Praeger, 1960; Delavenay, E. and K., *Bibliography of Mechanical Translation,* Mouton & Co., 1960; *Current Research and Development in Scientific Documentation,* No. 12. Washington, D.C., National Science Foundation, 1965; *The Finite String,* Center for Applied Linguistics; and *T. A. Information,* Paris, Edition Klincksieck.

5. Automatic Language Processing Advisory Commitee (ALPAC), *Language and Machines,* National Academy of Sciences, N.R.C. publ. 1416, 1966.

6. Chomsky, N., *Syntactic Structures,* 1964, *Current Issues in Linguistic Theory,* 1966; and *Topics in the Theory of Generative Grammar,* 1966; *Aspects of the Theory of Syntax,* 1965, MIT Press; *Cartesian Linguistics: A Chapter in the History of Rationalist Thought,* 1966, Harper & Row; and with G. A. Miller, "Introduction to formal analysis of natural languages," in Luce, R. D., ed., *Handbook of Mathematical Psychology,* 1963, Wiley, II: 269-321.

7. *Babel,* XII (4): 181-188 (1966)

8. *Style Book and Editorial Manual,* AMA, 2nd ed., 1963, pp. 82-84

9. Science Service-Interlingua Division, New York, published 1959-1969.

10 For comment, see the editorial exchange in *Van Taal tot Taal,* 14(2): 20-21 (March, 1970)

11. Jumpelt, R. W., "Internationale Bibliographie der Uebersetzungstheorie," *Van Taal tot Taal,* 1(3): 2-5 (April 1957).

12. *American Translator,* 2(4): 13-14 (December 1968).

The Art of Translating

Elsa Gress

Being an amphitriune—writer, critic, and translator in one— I shall take off in all directions, but hopefully arrive *somewhere*, using as my basic theme the following quote, from Ernst Cassirer's *An Essay on Man:*

> *Language must be looked upon as an* energeia *rather than as an* ergon.
> *It is not a readymade thing, but a continuous process. It is the ever-repeated labor of the human mind to utilize articulated sounds to express thought.*

Myths and religions have always refused to consider the multitude and variety of languages as an inevitable necessity or a consequence of the given order of things. They ascribe human faults or guilt to the "confusion of languages," and there are striking parallels to the Biblical story of the Tower of Babel in other religions. Even after the Renaissance, many philosophers and writers retained the dream of a Golden Age, when one language, *lingua Adamica,* bound all humans together in a community of thought and feeling. Some dreamt also of a future, when one language would again connect all human beings or, at least, be the tool of one common science. Without *characteristica generalia* no *scientia generalis* was the belief of Leibniz, who thought it possible to construct a perfectly univocal

53

language, which would reduce all brainwork to mathematical calcula-
tion. This perfect language would lead men to the perfect science of
God. Giambattista Vico had a more realistic idea of language as
sprung from symbolic action in a kind of poetic state of innocence,
and developed with the development of society into a highly differentiated stage, with rationalistic-scientific use of language as a lately
added element. But he also believed, as did the ancient Greeks, in
the original "organic" connection between word and action—the term
Logos, indeed, implies both.

Leibniz' idea of the perfect language—just imagine him knowing
of computers—has been carried over in our age by the logical-positiv-
istic school of philosophy and other forms of logical and semantic
philosophies, but Wittgenstein, who originally favored this idea,
in his later philosophy discarded the possibility of constructing a
perfect language. We would never be able to abolish confusion and
ambiguity, was his final conclusion.

Poets have, of course, always been aware of that, consciously or
not; indeed, their works rest partly, if not mainly—as modern theor-
eticians since William Empson have insisted—on the exploitation of
the ambiguities of language (and of languages). It is another matter,
that all thinking—including poetic thinking—has tried, and will continue to try to clarify language for its own purposes, and this is the
way languages develop. The firm, metaphysical belief that language,
as it exists and is used, is something given and equipped with a kind
of hidden intelligence or spirit that surpasses the intelligence of its
users, is, however, widespread and deep-rooted. Hegel made it philosophically respectable, and many of his modern followers argue
from the same belief, which does not make it any more right. Of
course, any language, as a sum of the communication of generations,
can contain more *potential* knowledge and more ideas than even its
wisest individual users possess. But all this is only potential, and language is made intelligent only by intelligent use. In the process of
use, new elements are added, so that the words and idioms expand
and change with time, while new idioms are continuously added. On
the other hand, just as language can further the expansion of consciousness, it can also hamper this expansion, because, as Bertrand
Russell pointed out, it is "a cemetery of dead philosophical and
metaphysical metaphors." The consciousness of this fact, and even
more the unconscious *feeling* of it, is, I believe, the main reason
for many anti-verbal activities today in art and in life.

However, it remains the greatest responsibility of the writer and
of the translator not just to use language adequately for the project
at hand, but also to try to improve it as our chief means of commun-

ication and to sharpen parts of it into new weapons for thought and imagination. Today we have a greater confusion of language, and of languages, than ever before, and also a greater need of communication across the linguistic barriers. Since translation from one language into another, no matter how closely related, is not a mechanical process, this situation of communication is a highly complicated matter as well as a highly important one. Translation is an art, or more correctly expressed, ought to be one. Already in the early nineteenth century, W. von Humboldt was aware that the real difference between languages is not one of sounds and signs, but one of *Weltanschauungen,* or attitudes to life. Electronic "brains" are presumably already able to manage any mechanical transfer of fairly unambiguous messages from one tongue to another when nuances and over- and undertones are not of the essence. But translation of literature, where these things are always of the essence, takes *people,* preferably artistically gifted people.

In reality it is, of course, not always—or even very often—artists of language who do the translating, and most translations, consequently, are not art. Already in the seventeenth century John Denham complained:

> Such is our pride, our folly and our fate,
> That only those who cannot write, translate. . . .

And such is still the sad state of affairs all over the world. But that does not alter the fact that the translator should be an artist, and that a translation worth its salt is a work of art.

How much the personal gifts of language and what one might call the quality of faith involved, mean to the artistic quality of a translation is clearly seen when comparing modern, presumably superior versions of the Bible in various vernaculars to the original translations of it, the most recent example being the New English Bible compared to the King James Version. It is easier for modern readers to read and undoubtedly more clear and correct in details, but the loss of poetic quality corresponds to the loss of imagination and sense of language in the modern group of translators, and indicates that their respect of scholarship has replaced the faith and fire of the original translators. (Besides, who wants the corrections *now,* when the damage of the errors has been done?) The Bible, apart from this, is the most obvious example of the necessity of translation in the cultural life of a nation, since for centuries after the Reformation it was the most important, if not the only book available in the non-Catholic areas of Europe. But there are earlier

examples—e.g., Thomas Aquinas based his Aristotelian philosophy
on a Latin translation of Aristotle. Without translation, Western civilization from antiquity on would be unthinkable in its present form.
And today translations are both a bigger part of the cultural output
anywhere, and a greater necessity than ever.

Having established this fact, which few will doubt, let me turn to
the present practical situation of the person exclusively or intermittently engaged in translation, and the more specific questions he will
be asked, or will ask himself, if he is a person of conscience. While the
necessity and usefulness of translations cannot be sensibly disputed,
the question of the quantity of translations and their selection or
non-selection is open and relevant. In a world that is steadily shrinking, as far as surmounting distances is concerned, while the linguistic
barriers are as numerous and real as ever, we find in some cases—
particularly in the smaller European nations—a true flood of translations, while in other cases—the larger nations—there is, comparatively
speaking, only a trickle. Should there be fewer in the former cases
and more in the latter, and, more important, *what sort* of books,
plays, etc., should be translated?

Naturally, a great number of translations that are done and being
done is not from any reasonable point of view "necessary," and the
larger nations are spared more of these than the smaller ones. On the
other hand, a great many essential and highly qualified works of every
conceivable kind are not translated at all, or are translated very late
and often inadequately, which seems a greater problem. For it is
in everyone's interest that the right works reach the right people,
within and across the national frontiers. And this has little or nothing
to do with the popularity of the books in the first place—sadly
enough, since the popular books anywhere are the ones that stand
the best chance of being translated. The need of an international,
subsidized board, under the United Nations (if that would not be the
kiss of death) taking care of a steady supply of qualified translations
of qualified works in connection with an information service, independent of political and governmental control, is becoming steadily
more urgent. It could never be entirely fair, and would often err,
but it would ensure a non-commercial exchange of works and would
further the cultural relations and conditions immeasurably.

As it is, the selection of works for translation and distribution is
more than accidental; it is chaotic and dominated by culturally
irrelevant or directly anti-cultural considerations. And as for the
possibilities of the "right readers" anywhere to get to the right
books—and get the right message from them—one must be pessimistic. For, although a knowledge of other languages and particularly

of the *lingua franca* of the post-war world, English, is certainly more widespread than ever (particularly in the smaller nations such as the Scandinavian countries) this solves few problems and raises others. In the first place, much of this "knowledge" of English, or, rather, of a synthetic sort of American, mistaken for the "in" language of the young, is not actual knowledge which will enable the possessor to read and understand anything but the most uncomplicated texts. And even apart from this code non-language of the young, increasing numbers of presumably English-speaking citizens derive their linguistic prowess from various types of "nature method" courses based on the assumption that anybody can learn anything in easy lessons, in this case that the acquisition of a few hundred basic words and idioms gives access to the world of another language.

But it is, of course, not true that the commonest basic words are also the most important in the sense of being meaningful, nor is it true that anybody can learn a foreign language, unless this is equated with the ability to express the most ordinary everyday concepts with a very limited vocabulary. What is beyond this low level is dependent on the learner's individual learning powers, ear for language and sense of combination, and at a still higher level on his intuition, imagination, and creative powers. One does not become an Isak Dinesen or a Joseph Conrad by being able to sing *Eleanor Rigby* or pass the time of day in faultless English. If this applies to the best-known foreign language in the parts of Europe that are most enlightened linguistically, it can safely be assumed that the knowledge of other languages there and elsewhere is considerably more shaky. So the usual excuse of publishers who reject valuable works for translation with the remark that those who are interested can now read the book in the original, is invalid, apart from the fact that it is not always easy to obtain the originals, although paperback editions have greatly improved this situation. In reality, few readers will get as much out of the originals as they would from a good translation. To be able to read in the original a "whodunit" or a factual book about a field known to the reader is not the same thing as being able to read more complicated literature in a foreign tongue, and nothing indicates that this will ever change substantially.

When we come to the larger nations, there is not even this mostly superficial knowledge of foreign languages to count on. The knowledge of even the so-called major languages is deplorably scarce in the United States, as in England, and the knowledge of other languages than these is virtually nonexistent. So the large nations should logically be the most anxious to establish a responsible translation

policy like the one sketched above. They are missing a lot without
even knowing it.

The second big question of and to and by the translator does not
concern quantity and selection of texts, but quality. This question
of quality is "eternal," and has been asked from the days of Horace
as it will be asked in the future. It can be reduced to the ultimate
question of whether qualitative translation is really possible.

The answer is, in a way, simple. Even an elementary knowledge of
more than one language makes it plain that words in one language do
not simply correspond to words in another, they are not like mechanical symbols, their content is defined and circumscribed in different
ways, their very meaning varies from one context to another. With
a more thorough knowledge of several languages one realizes that
it is literally not feasible to translate complicated messages of any
kind, let alone literature, so that *all* nuances, tones, associations and
connotations are truly rendered in translation.

The impossibility of true and exact rendition of a text from one
language to another, however closely related, is most apparent when
one tries to translate a text of one's own. If one knows the other
language well enough to handle idioms with some ease, one will find
it much easier to rewrite the text in the other language than to
translate it. The fact that one knows not just the text, but intentions and associations connected with it so that the usual guesswork
and selection is out of the question, makes it reckless work to try
to render the text faithfully. Isak Dinesen, alias Karen Blixen, knew
as much and *wrote* her texts in English and Danish respectively rather
than translate them. She thought, incidentally, that translation is a
much misunderstood and underrated profession, which should be
highly paid, when highly qualified.

The fact that exact and full translation is impossible where literature is concerned does not, of course, indicate that good, and even
eminently good translation is not possible nor that it does not occur,
even though it is none too common. The fundamental thing, to my
mind, is to remember that *what is translated is a context meant to be
read as a context,* not an accumulation of words and idioms with
definite meanings and stamped-on values.

It is the old story of the spirit and the letter. Naturally, there are
translator's faults and mistakes which do mark a translation as in-
secure in its very essence. There are words meaning these particular
things and certainly not others; there are idioms used this particular
way and certainly not in other ways. But even boners in such details
only spoil the translation that is weak in concept anyway, while
they only mar but do not destroy the translation which convincingly
renders the tone and structure of the text and respects its coher-

ence. A few false notes do not spoil a good singing performance, nor will any number of correct notes save the performance which is without musicality.

Though this truth can be observed and subscribed to by any knowledgeable person, translations are quite regularly done by people who know only the letter (if they know that), while the spirit is a mystery to them. It does not make it any better that the same pedantic criteria which in the last instance are unrealistic—since they are criteria of correctness rather than of use—are regularly used in judging and criticizing translations. Various categories of faults are used: faults of sloppiness, fatigue, knowledge, etc., and "unforgivable" mistakes are pointed out with no regard for the whole. Still, every practicing translator knows that mistakes of one kind or another are all but inevitable in any larger work because of the "word-fatigue" that occurs about halfway, if for no other reason. Petty souls can always find faults of some sort, and any translation can, like any original work, be unraveled and found not fault-proof. It takes no qualification to do so, apart from a little knowledge and some ill will.

But it does take both literary and linguistic know-how to evaluate the essential qualities in a translation to see whether a tone has been rendered or not, and whether tricky problems have been solved or left unsolved. It takes, in other words, more to see if a translation as a whole is right than to establish whether it is correct in detail. This is why evaluations, in any true sense, of translations are rare, while quibbling with details is common. Which is a pity, since good translation certainly needs the encouragement of adequate evaluation. And I mean adequate, not just any recognition.

It should be clear from all this that the usual complaint—i.e. that a translated book is not the same as the original—is unreasonable. It cannot be. There will always be open questions where the translator resorts to his own interpretation, even to his own rewriting, and the result may approach the original in effect but will not be identical or congruous with it. The question is rather: is the translation good, in that it represents the original without violating the language in which it appears?

This points to the not unexpected, but still surprising fact that there are translations that do not just "cover" the original, but are *better*, just as there are translations which do represent the original, but are noticeably inferior reading. The degree of correctness, as already indicated, has little to do with this, although it certainly cannot be said that correct translations are necessarily inferior and incorrect ones good by the same token. One may say, however, that too much effort can mar a translation as effectively as too little effort. Many contemporary American books that use plenty of slang thus become completely distorted in Scandinavian translations which conscientiously try to render all slang expressions with corresponding Scandinavian ones. This is wrong, no matter how right the individual terms may be, simply because slang is another phenomenon altogether in America and has other social uses. A suggestive approach is preferable to a convulsive attempt to cover everything, here as in other cases.

The translation that is "too good" will usually be so by virtue of an added tone or refinement of style. How many foreign writers have been praised for virtues that were not in the original? And how many have been blamed for faults due to the translation? Airy qualities like irony, humor, sadness, whimsical mirth have a way of sneaking in or out in the process of translation.

Is the "too good" translation "right?" That the translation which takes away qualities from the original is wrong, no matter how correct, goes without saying. But the *added* qualities—are they in order? It would depend on the character of the recipient language. If, e.g., one tones down a pretentious text, or mixes a bit of irony in an insufferably solemn text when translating into Danish—which is a muted language, full of understatements and ironies—one would certainly obey the unspoken laws of the Danish language and probably serve the original well. Only where such over- and undertones jar against the basic notes of the original or completely distort the intentional images can it be called encroachment.

This brings up another "eternal" question: what should a translator know best—the foreign language or his own?

This was discussed endlessly in the period of Neo-Classicism, and the question still pops up in cases of doubt. The ideal is easy to see: the translator should know both languages to perfection. In reality there is, however, practically always a choice. And the writer-translator, who is himself creative, will usually hold that knowledge of one's own language is most important, while the academic type will insist that the knowledge of the nuances of the foreign tongue is the most important thing.

Once more it should be emphasized that it depends. It is possible to translate without much knowledge of the foreign tongue. The Danish poet, Sophus Claussen, whose knowledge of English was very slight, thus recreated Shelley's "Sensitive Plant" beautifully by writing down all possibilities of each word, according to the dictionary, pasting the notes all over his room and combining it all by the aid of hunches and his own considerable poetic powers. But the method is hardly commendable, even for a genius. To be creative in his own language is, however, doubtless of great value to a translator. It gives the necessary dash and daring. And the talk of how translating other writers can spoil your own writing is, I believe, unfounded. It belongs with the romantic idea of original genius and talent as fragile things which do not bear discipline, technical knowledge, or influences from outside. The fact is rather that a writer can profit greatly from studying other writers' worlds and styles—a task to which few writers are prone—and studying them closely while translating their texts. Of course a writer translating can, like any other translator, get sick and tired of the job, but that is another matter entirely.

Translation of poetry is a special case, calling for more creativity and imagination in the translator than even the most refined prose, and being even more of a squaring-the-circle proposition. But the same fundamental law goes for this as for other types of translation: the context is the thing. And it *can* be done, though it happens rarely.

Finally a less important, but often recurring question: how far should the translator try to identify with the writer? To the truly professional translator, this is a subordinate problem; he will be able to render a text loyally whether it happens to be by his favorite writer or not. Indeed he will probably render it more loyally if it is *not* by his favorite writer. Too great love for the writer or the subject does not result in good translation *by itself*—any more than a bit of antipathy to both or either need result in bad translation. An extreme case of identification is a Danish translator of *Dr. Zhivago,* who ended up thinking he *was* Dr. Zhivago. But, even apart from such extremes, a translator may well castrate a text out of sheer respect for it. And there are naturally also extreme cases where the translator's disgust with writer and subject makes him incapable of doing justice to both. But, generally, the translator's qualifications are decisive, and his feelings in the matter are not. This is something non-professional translators and laymen find hard to understand. I have often been upbraided for translating writers whom, as a critic, I have repudiated. But such are the hazards of the profession.

There are other hazards that can be annoying, while rewards are few, and payment, on the whole, miserably low in the profession. One hazard I may be particularly exposed to, as a combination of writer-critic-translator in one, is the extraordinary interest in and fanaticism about linguistic and idiomatic details that lead readers to write endless letters to editors, and even threatening letters to

writers and translators. It also leads writers and translators into
vicious polemics, often about seemingly unessential details. This
interest, which often overshadows the spectacular events of the day
in the minds of those involved, and this fanaticism about the correctness or incorrectness of some term is not due to pedantic nuttiness
in all those cases, and it does show that language—and the individual
conception of it—is of the greatest importance and loaded with the
explosives of emotion. This is explicable enough, since much mental
and a lot of emotional life is expressed in language, even though not
all mental or emotional life is language or all language mental or
emotional life. The linguist, E. Sapir, pointed out that language is
the most self-sufficient and most massively resistant social phenomenon—"It is easier to kill a language than to dissolve its individual
form." And biology now tells us that language, including dialects
and "jargons," is probably a means of hereditary selection, so that
the multitude of languages—and ways to use language—is ineradic-
able, though frontiers will continuously shift.

While all this explains the interest, it does not explain the moralistic indignation about linguistic matters that too often rests on
ignorance of the nature of languages and ambiguity of words. This
indignation at "wrong uses" sometimes looks like a derailed moral or
even religious feeling. Fanaticism goes, of course, with ignorance
disguised as rock-bottom faith and knowledge. Goethe said that he
who does not know foreign languages knows nothing of his own.
This covers a number of the cases but not all. The conviction that
one's idea of the language in question, acquired at an early age, must
be correct in all details, is *also* found combined with a theoretical
knowledge of the manifold nature of language and of the fact that
languages throw light on one another. It is, of course, human to
raise one's own ideas and feelings to the status of universal laws, but
here, as everywhere in the field of art and ideas, tolerance is called
for—not passive tolerance, but active interest and openness. Naturally, there is good and bad language, fine or less fine ear for language
to consider. But it is never a question of absolutes. The better language is built exactly, by artists who break rules to communicate
better but who respect rules where *they* further communication.
So, to rhetorical questions from people who ask you as a translator
whether you think you are the Good Lord, remaking language, and
to those who blame you, often at the same time, for being untraditional *and* for using clichés, the answer must be:

All language is "use of clichés" insofar as it consists of clichés and
would otherwise be incomprehensible. Clichés only become reprehensible when they render oversimplified or distorted ideas which
cause the dilution of language and—by that token—of thought and

emotion. No user of language can avoid clichés, unless he is content with laughing and screaming, but it is the simple duty of the writer *and* the translator to avoid distortion of ideas and confusion of concepts. He has the duty to be untraditional, when it furthers communication, but only then. There are no other criteria. And this answers indirectly the question of playing God: the writer—and translator—does indeed play God in this connection. Language is not given, let alone God-given, in its present form, or in any past or future form either; it is a process of breaking down and building up that never ends. Artificial languages are still-born, exactly because they are not processes but finished things. Those who write and translate are directly involved in this process, more actively and creatively so than others, and they build the language by using it as communication as effectively as they possibly can. And, conversely, they break it down by using it ineffectively.

Translation—is it art, mediation of art, an important weapon in the fatal fight against parochialism as a state of mind? Or is it something uncreative, unimportant, a paradise for pedants? The process can be both, and the individual result can be one or the other. It is not a matter of indifference *what* it is. It is not unimportant who does the translating and how, and in these days of accelerated developments and multitudes of new works and movements, it should be increasingly obvious how important it is that translation should be an art, and treated as such—which implies that translators themselves know when they are being artists and when not. Pleading "experience" is not enough.

The Necessity of Translation

B. J. Chute

First of all, I would like to thank you for granting me a passport to
your country of Translation. I am not a translator, only a profound
and grateful admirer of that impossible art.

My credentials for being here are brief. In 1959, when I became
president of the American Center of P.E.N., I knew exactly what
I wanted to do as my first official act. I wanted to form a Committee on Translation. This was a direct result of the Translators' Conference held in Warsaw in 1958 under the auspices of the Polish P.E.N.
and the International Federation of Translators, and of the report on
it which was given by Theodore Purdy at a P.E.N. dinner. Moreover,
it seemed to me, after hearing his report, that Mr. Purdy was ideally
suited to be the new committee's first chairman. He served nobly
in this capacity for three terms, being succeeded by other able and
dedicated chairmen who carried on the committee's work, and
arriving finally at our present chairman, Robert Payne, whose energy,
skill and determination brought this conference into being.

I am awed by translation, and I am fascinated by the shoptalk of
translators. In their ranks, certainly, there are some of the most
interesting and articulate members of the literary world—present
company most definitely included. But it is not your ability to
verbalize or to translate that I want to talk about today. It is not
even your beaux yeux. In fact, it is not your presence at all with
which I am concerned. It is, on the contrary, your invisibility.

65

You do not need me to tell you how invisible you are. You are indispensable, but you are unnoticed. You are a bridge between cultures and nations—quite literally, the Golden Gate—and any reader can walk across you, but few readers are even aware that you are there. Perhaps it is this very invisibility that makes it so difficult for the translator to make a living at his craft. If he is not there, so to speak, why does he need to eat?

Still, it was not the economic problems faced by translators that prompted me to found the P.E.N. Translation Committee. The literary world is full of people who have to earn their daily bread outside of it, in order to go on doing what they want to do. Most poets are not showered with gold; most novelists sell very few books. And surely no one takes up literary translation under the illusion that he is going to find a pot of gold at the end of the rainbow.

I hope, and am sure, that the many economic problems faced by the translator will be discussed at this conference, and discussed energetically. All of us here recognize their vital importance. But of course you are not meeting here this week, at this very special and unique conference, only to concentrate on the pot of gold. You are here to celebrate the rainbow.

And people like myself, who are not translators at all, are here to celebrate you.

Which brings me to the subject of this talk, which is "The Necessity of Translation." Because the truth of the matter is that you translators can take up other crafts or businesses. You might become many things, from auto mechanics to Chairmen of the Board, and still be able to follow your chosen vocation as a hobby, a private art a solitary joy. There are other ways of making a living, and most of them are more remunerative than translating, and if all of you left your posts tomorrow, I am certain that all of you could find other employment and daily bread.

In short, you can live without us.

But, Heaven help us, we cannot live without you.

And so, when I ostensibly address you today, I am really not talking to you at all. I am talking to all those faceless people out there who, quite literally, must have you. I am talking to the publishers and editors, to the critics, the writers and the readers. Many of you fit into these categories at one time or another, and all of you fit into the last category—that of the reader. But, from this point on, I must put you on notice that, if you are listening only with the ears of a translator, you are eavesdropping.

If I were asked to sum up in one word my reason for feeling that a Translation Committee was essential to the American Center of

P.E.N.—quite apart from the obvious fact that P.E.N. is an international organization and therefore exists through *translated* relationships—I think that the word I would choose is "climate." For translation to flourish in this or any other country as it should (as it must), an ideal climate would supply certain basic necessities: recognition of the fact that the translator is indispensable; appreciation of the difficulty of his role (that it is an art as well as a craft); proper financial return for his labors, and credit given where credit is due.

All these have been matters of concern to the P.E.N. Translation Committee over the past ten years, and progress has been made. The Translation Prize and the medals, the Manifesto, the Minimum Basic Contract which is being worked out, this conference of distinguished translators from many countries—all these are genuine signs of progress. They are strong beginnings, sturdy shoots of a seed that has been well tended. Ecologically, all those bright green leaves cannot fail to improve the atmosphere; and indeed they do. But there remain two sources of pollution—to continue the metaphor—which cannot be the concern of committees only. These are ignorance of the role of the translator, and indifference toward him.

In these matters, I am a confirmed optimist, and so I believe that ignorance can be cured by information, and indifference by concern. If you have a diamond and believe it to be a piece of glass, that is ignorance. Believing it to be glass, you will treat it without respect. And that is indifference. A really good work of translation is a diamond, not glass, or, to mix my jewels with utter carelessness, it is a pearl beyond price. The more the craft of translation is respected, and the more the necessity for good translation is recognized, the more good translations will be published.

The whole responsibility by no means lies with editors and publishers, but some of it certainly does, and I want to talk about them first and at some length, because this is an area in which my experience is specific and I can supply documentation.

Since 1960, I have pursued a small but vigorous personal project, which is represented in my files by a folder marked "Editors and Publishers, Harassment of." This file is concerned with matters of translation, and most of it consists of correspondence—sometimes brief and sometimes lengthy—which has taken place between a publisher or editor and myself on those numerous occasions when the name of the translator has been omitted from either the book jacket or the advertising—carrying the invisible profession to its logical conclusion.

I do not need to tell you that this file folder is a stout one. Some of the correspondence has been decidedly energetic; almost all of it has been productive. I have found this to be a battleground on which non-translators, like myself, can at least carry a spear on behalf of translators. When I write a letter of protest (and I am sure that there must be editors who wince whenever they see my name on an envelope), I have—in spite of the spear—no axe to grind. All that most of my letters say is 1) that I am a member of P.E.N. who has been connected with the Translation Committee, 2) that I am a novelist who is acutely aware of the debt that writers owe to translators, 3) that I am distressed to note their failure to give proper credit to the translator, 4) that, since there could be no American edition without the translator's services, I hope that the whole thing is merely an oversight on their part, and not a policy, and 5) that I remain sincerely theirs.

It should please you to know that only rarely does one of my letters go unanswered, and that in most cases the answer is not only admirably prompt but constructive. Let me quote from a few typical letters that I have received from publishers and editors of major houses. Here is one.

> You are absolutely correct, and we profoundly regret the oversight which will be corrected in any subsequent editions of the book. Thank you very much for calling this to our attention.

Here is another:

> You are so right in checking us on the omission of the translator's name. It was indeed an oversight, and we shall make every effort not to let it happen again. We shall try to do better, and thank you for writing.

Or this engaging expression of regret:

> Am I embarrassed! I was on vacation when the ad for the book went through, or the omission of a credit to the translator would not have happened. In fact, I now push credits for the translator to the point that not only does the name appear on the front of the jacket of such translations for which I am responsible, but a note about the translator follows the note about the author at the back of the book.

That letter closed "Remorsefully yours." And here is another letter in response to my cry of outrage when a full-page advertisement of a major novel appeared in The New York Times with the translator's name nowhere to be seen, not even in the tiniest print.

I agree with you 100% that translators deserve recognition—actually
more than they have usually received—for the difficult work they do.
The name of the translator should have appeared in the ad you saw in
the Times, and I shall see to it that his name is included in ads that
appear around publication date or thereafter.

This publisher was as good or better than his word. The name of the
translator appeared in very large black letters in every subsequent advertisement, and, in one double-column ad, four out of the six
reviews which were quoted contained a full sentence praising the
quality of the translation and mentioning the name of the translator
in each case, so that credit was given not once but four times. (Perhaps there will come a day in this publishing house when the authors
will find themselves demanding equal time with the translators.)

On this occasion, I wrote an especially appreciative thank-you
note, adding what I fear was a somewhat ungracious postscript to the
effect that I hoped it might be possible, in future editions of the book,
to show the translator's name on the jacket.

Back came the amiable response.

I agree with you that the translator's name should appear on the
jacket of the book, and I am arranging that this be done in another
printing.

Happy ending? Yes. But not an unusual one. My bulging folder
tells me that many publishers and editors share my opinion that the
translator must be given proper credit and recognition. It has been
rare indeed for me to get no response to a letter. In some cases, I do
get an argument. I remember one exchange of letters that went on
for more than two months, and one of the arguments used against
my position was that "Ads are geared to sell books, not to advertise
translators, and I am sure that Mr. X would not disagree with this
statement."

Mr. X, of course, was the translator, and possibly he would not disagree with the statement (though I beg leave to doubt it), but I most
emphatically did. I wrote the publisher a two-page letter saying that
on many occasions, he had indicated that he cared just as much
about the cause of good translation as I did—in fact, he had often
proved it—and that I thought he had, therefore, a more than ordinary obligation to the profession. He did not reply, as he might have,
that my head was muddled with paradoxes; he did not annihilate me
with pure logic or assail me with sharp epithets. He responded generously, and he closed his letter with these words: "We will take the

ideas you expressed into consideration in the future. As you say, we are not at odds in spirit."

I feel very strongly that this kind of letter-writing in defense of proper credit to the translator is something that anyone can do, and one is really freer to do it if one is not a translator. I have developed, over the years, a hawk's eye for the omission of a translator's name, and it might encourage you to know that sometimes other names get omitted too.

My folder holds one vintage item: an advertisement for a paper-back book which omits—not the name of the translator, since the book was written in English; not the name of the designer of the book jacket, and most certainly not the name of the publisher. It omits the name of the distinguished author himself! I am happy to report to you that, upon inquiry, the editor was able to assure me that this did not represent the Wave of the Future. He said—and I detected a note of real sorrow—that the designer of the advertisement had felt that the author's name would "clash with everything else." He also said, "It will *not* happen again." And I believe him.

I only mention this episode to tell you that you are not alone. And also to point out that the omission of important names is not necessarily a company policy. It may only be the policy of an over-zealous advertising agency which has produced a lovely ad into which everything fits nicely except one trivial item. What have we here? The name of the translator? Out with it! Who cares about the translator's credit line?

Well, I care, for one. And so do a lot of other people. And, I think, more people all the time. There is nothing to stop anyone from keeping a weather eye on advertisements and following up invisible credit lines with visible letters of protest. I pride myself on having developed a considerable nuisance value, and I intend to go right on developing it until the habit of giving credit to translators in ads and on book jackets becomes automatic in publishing houses. I emphasize that, almost without exception, I have received answers that were courteous and concerned, sometimes even penitent. Once in a while, a lapse will be repeated by the same publishing house, and then one need only quote the original reply back to the editor or publisher who wrote it.

Incidentally, I think you might be amused—and possibly appalled— by some of the explanations that have been offered to me as to why a translator's name was omitted. Here is one letter that I shall always treasure:

It was our feeling that, since the translations were in the process of

revision, and revision by outsiders who had not originally been responsible for the initial translation, it would have been somewhat
confusing—*both morally and intellectually* [the italics are mine] —
to have used the name of one translator without clarifying the role
of their revisers. I do hope you understand that our feeling is very
strongly in favor of translations and translators. We do not deny
the proper role of the translator in the publication of our books, but
in this particular case it would have been unfortunate to have used
the name of the translators at this stage.

To this audience, I need make no comment.

Again, an editor writes, memorably: "The reason no credit was
given to the translator is that we took the English translation. It
was done so badly that it had to be re-done here in the editorial
offices."

Again, no comment. The moral is all too obvious.

On the other hand, there are occasional explanations which are at
least not quite so lame. In one case, the editor to whom I wrote had
had no direct connection with the book, and, when he made inqui-
ries on my behalf, he returned with the report that it has been
"a policy decision. The book was such a highly personal testament
—a man baring himself to the reader—that there was fear lest the
interpolation of another person between the writer and the reader
might hurt everybody." My friendly editor then added, "I don't
myself see that this is a reasonable excuse, and I am grateful to you
for doing something about it."

Editors, too, are sometimes captives of the situation, you see, just
as translators are. I would like to make a recommendation to all
editorial boards that anything called "a policy decision" be taken
out of its mothballs at least once a month and examined very critically.

Another letter explains in rather melancholy detail the process of
rearrangement which an ad for a major novel went through, and the
letter ends: "The ultimate result was that there was no room to
squeeze the translator's name in at all without reducing the size of
the type for the title, which nobody wanted to do."

As an explanation, that certainly leaves a good deal to be desired.
In fact, I can find in my files only one defense that does seem to
have the ring of authenticity. It is brief, and it reads as follows:
"The translator is in a Catholic order, and he feels compelled to
remain anonymous." With this I cannot quarrel. If a translator
chooses to remain anonymous, I shall not begin a new file folder
labeled "Translators, Harassment of."

I have gone into all this in so much detail because I think it is consoling to observe the weakness of most of the reasons given for omitting the translator's name and that it is encouraging to see how effective the pressure of even one individual can be, if it is unrelenting. It is only fair for me to say that one of the effects my own efforts in this direction have had on me has been to increase my respect for the publishing profession. They have their problems too, and I think the P.E.N. Translation Committee owes a great deal of its success to the fact that publishers and editors are members of it and take a very active part.

Then, there are the book reviewers.

Yes, reviewers leave out the names of translators. Yes, they respond to letters protesting the omission. Yes, they have their problems too, and these range from the carelessness of printers, to arbitrary editorial cutting, to the real difficulty that a reviewer faces when he does not know the original language in which the book was written and therefore does not feel equipped to evaluate the translation. However, as I take occasion to point out from time to time, if a critic has praised the quality of prose throughout an entire review, might it not be reasonable to suppose that the translator must have done his work rather well?

This brings us back to the original author himself, he who is translated. A good book, badly translated, becomes a poor book. Speaking as a writer myself, I will say categorically that I would be perfectly happy to reduce my own share in foreign rights to a considerable degree *if I could be sure of a good translation.*

This, of course, is the crux of the matter. How does an author know that he is getting a good translation? What protection does he have against a bad one, especially if his rights are handled through a large agency, or if translations—as my correspondence so often confirms—are not translations at all, but merely re-translations or editorial projects of the home office.

This is all difficult, and complex. But, again, I think the authors would find themselves receiving automatic benefits if the work of the translators were more widely respected and recognized. Lewis Galantière once said: "The translator is not the servant of his author, he is the servant of his author's book." So perhaps what is needed is a broader area of understanding and sympathy, since the author is also the servant of his book, and both servants have the same aim in view.

Publishers, editors, translators, reviewers, writers—even advertising agencies—we are not enemies of each other in this country of translation. We serve the same cause.

And, when all is said and done, this is the heart of the matter. Without translation, our world would narrow mercilessly. Like air and sunlight and good growing earth in the natural world, translation is our necessity in the creative world.

Whatever benefits this cause of good translation, benefits everyone. Through literature, we share experience, we share comprehension, we share our very hearts and minds. But we speak so variously, in so many tongues, and there is too much possibility for misunderstanding and misinterpretation in a world where we *must* learn not to misunderstand or misinterpret one another.

And so we turn to the translators, and we must trust the translators. We must work to guarantee that good climate of which I have spoken by insisting that translators receive proper recognition and support, not only through contracts and credit lines, but through the energy and good offices of those most direct beneficiaries—the writers and the readers.

It is as a writer and a reader that I thank you for your contributions to the craft and art of translation. It is as a writer and a reader that I pledge you—for what it may be worth—my continuing support, encouragement and concern. I wish you a better climate of public awareness. I wish your work sunlight and fresh air and good earth in which it can thrive. And I hope you truly do realize how very much we, who reap your harvest, owe to you. And how gratefully we acknowledge our debt.

The World of Translation

Thomas Lask

We live, as we know, in a sight-oriented environment. The word is being eroded by the pictorial image. The photograph, the motion picture, the television screen have become the modern literacy. In an older time, a feat such as the moon-shot would have demanded men of the greatest verbal skill to describe what had happened. Today,the most non-literate youngster can experience the thrill of space exploration by doing nothing more than reading a picture caption, and, with the aids of charts and models over television, understand the phenomenon if not better, certainly more quickly, than the youngster who has to plow through a book written six months ago.

It is a trusim that for the college students today and their peers it is the motion picture that is the great esthetic. As late as the 1930's, young people wanted to write novels. Today they all want to make motion pictures and, judging from a few that I have seen, frequently do. Two generations ago, it was the motion-picture star who received all the attention and the acclaim. Today it is the director, the difference between the hero of the novel and the novelist. The old joke (if it ever was a joke) "Did you read the book?" "No, but I saw the movie" is more relevant than ever. Recently I had occasion to write about a new life of T. E. Lawrence. I wondered how meaningful his name was to someone born during or since the last war. The best I could get from those I asked was "I missed the movie." That Lawrence had written books or even that he had done something that made him a subject for a movie was subordinate to the fact that he was in it. I suppose simply being in a motion picture is its own reward.

Even when the word is used to convey thought in some measure in advertising, in posters, in industrial design, it is often obscured or fragmented or so employed that the words and letters become part of and even subordinate to the overall design. They are just another element that includes pigment, texture, arrangement. This is amusing in a way, because we know that, when printing was first developed, the men in charge desired mainly to reproduce the manuscripts and codexes they already possessed. It took a while for them to realize that the printed word required other desirable qualities: clarity, simplicity, ease of comprehension. Now once again the word is perhaps disappearing into the viewable whole.

Even in poetry, in the most compact, explosive, most severely controlled art in which the word figures, the spatial element is asserting itself and has become a function of meaning. Concrete poetry has been described as poetry that is perceived rather than read, and not perceived in the sense that Henry James used the term, "perception at the height of passion," but perceived as an object.

These remarks may sound like the counsel of despair. But I mention them to indicate what seems to me the changing dimensions of the problem, the cultural problem and the problem of translation. A new version of the Church Fathers is not enough.

Consider the study of Swahili. A half-century ago those who thought about the matter at all would have acknowledged that somewhere there were enclaves of scholars devoted to the study of Swahili, probably as productive as other scholars but not as visible. Though no one would have thought of disturbing the quiet tenor of their ways, very few would have seriously urged that the discipline be expanded, that plans be prepared for incorporating the study into the mainstream of contemporary education. It was, after all, caviar to the general . But what had been considered exotic fruit seems to have been turned into manna for the many. I am not arguing here for or against its inclusion in our curricula, and I certainly don't know enough about the language to know whether the claims made for it as a device to strengthen the black man's image of himself in America are valid.

But sometimes, as we know, it is not the language so much as the fact of the language that is significant. It may become the symbol, the embodiment of a political or social idea, and its value as a meta-

phor may be greater than its value as a field of study. Or as great.
I don't know how much headway Gaelic has made in bringing Old
Ireland into the forefront of everyday Irish consciousness, and I suspect that a very small contemporary literature has resulted from its
study. The shadowy heroes of Irish legend remain shadowy still. But
it is defensible to claim that the Gaelic revival was a forceful and
integral part of the Irish renaissance that led to the establishment of
the state. The battle over Gaelic, as we can tell from James Joyce's
story, "The Dead," transcended details of grammar, syntax, even—
I will hazard—comprehension. Patrick Pearse, one of the most fer-
tile practitioners of Gaelic, was among the first to be executed after
the Easter rebellion. Thus in the case of the study of Swahili, a
translator's task may be more meaningful and greater than the simple preparation of accurate texts.

I am sure that you have noticed the tremendous surge of interest
among young people in the Far East, in fact in all things oriental, in
Indian sacred writings, Chinese poetry, Kabuki theatre, Zen Bud-
dhism and the like. It is an interest that shows itself in dress, in the
use of personal ornaments, in changing life styles. Two poets, very
influential among the young, Allen Ginsberg and Gary Snyder, have
been leaders in firming up this interest, Snyder with his poems
about Japan, Ginsberg with lines on Angkor Wat and the verses in
"Planet News." One of Snyder's most popular poems is on the subject of ecology, but it has an oriental touch and is called "The
Smokey Bear Sutra." I know that it will be argued that much of
this interest is faddish and superficial and, in essence, not new.
After all, Pound in the Fenollosa days was working in the field, and
our own Robert Payne's "The White Pony" goes back almost a
quarter of a century.

Still I believe this interest to be part of a significant cultural
trend—a turning away from the history of the western world, away
from the achievements that flowed out of the Mesopotamian lands,
out of the Palestinian shore, out of Greece and Rome. Whatever the
reasons, whether they are simply tired of hearing once again of the
glory that was Greece and the grandeur that was Rome, whether the
falling away of the classics broke the bond that made possible a kinship with the classical world, whether it is a disgust with the end
product of our civilization, the current generation is turning away
from the Judaeo-Christian tradition, its art products and its arti-
facts. I remember how enraged B. H. Haggin, the music critic, was
when a younger colleague remarked that going to concerts today was
an act of necrophilia.

The two or three cited examples of change are relevant, I believe, to the purpose of this conference because the translator can be a mediating force in them. Take the large number of *haiku* being written by those who do not have the foggiest idea of what they are about and who reduce the form to syllable counting and a mention of the seasons. Thus, if one can count to four and then to seventeen, one has the making of a poem.

Yasunari Kawabata, a recent Nobel Prize laureate, provides a challenge of a different sort. I don't doubt his eminence. Yet I must say that I must take much of it on faith. In English the words in his fiction are clear, the narrative transparent. Yet I have the uncomfortable feeling that all sorts of things are going on in his work that are getting by me. There is something above and beyond the tea ceremony, a complex of feeling and attitude that evaporates in translation. This is not intended as a criticism of Edward Seidensticker, the translator. The fault may well lie with me, but it will serve as an example of the difficulty of getting one culture into the language of another.

Parenthetically, it is this intangible element in translation that makes it hard to believe in the potentiality of the computer as a translator. I cannot imagine how an electronic machine would get the idiomatic, flavorsome, mouth-filling Yiddish of Sholem Aleichem into English, or the rich, subtle variants of dialect of *Huckleberry Finn* into Icelandic. A computer might work for the telephone book or the Sears-Roebuck catalogue. I have a pretty picture of a Ukrainian collective farmer curling up on a cold winter night with a copy of the Manhattan Yellow Pages.

Some months back I attended a reading by a Czech poet, who was asked later about the poetic influences at work in his country. He remarked that the up and coming poets were very much interested in Whitman and free-verse forms. Now free verse is scarcely a very revolutionary vehicle and we wondered about it. But the poet pointed out that Czech poetry had been so dominated by Russian forms, metrics and rhyme schemes that the very use of free verse represented an act of defiance. I wondered how a translator could get across into English the form of the work as well as the sense of freedom that was part of it.

Getting the qualities of one culture into another brings us perhaps nearer the heart of the problem. It has been argued, though not by Sidney Alexander, that a good translation should be very much of its own time, a work satisfying to and in a sense representing the sensibility of the age into which it has been reworked, a regrounding of the original into contemporary terms. The King James version of the

Bible is certainly an Elizabethan document. And Reuben Brower has
shown that Pope's *Iliad* expresses the heroic tradition in classical
and English poetry in a way that moderns, who find the heroic posture
too rhetorical for their taste, may be incapable of. As Mr. Brower
wrote, Pope expressed "the noblesse and splendor of the eighteenth-
century aristocratic ideal." And Dryden, responsible for another
classic translation, *The Aeneid,* has been described by Robert Fitzgerald as putting "a sophisticated civilization" behind Vergil's Roman
hero. But literary success in its own time may not be quite the
answer either. I think most ordinary readers, and I count myself
among them, would acknowledge a debt to Constance Garnett for her
translations from the Russian. Through her labors, a whole library
was made available to those who could not read the originals. Today
scholars talk rather of her inadequacies than of her services.

Gilbert Murray's translations of Euripides were considered in his
own time as near as one could come to the Greek dramatist. But
even before T. S. Eliot destroyed that assurance, many readers must
have felt that those versions had been dipped too strongly into a pre-
Raphaelite vat.

Is then Pound's battle cry, "Make it new," the only answer?
Should his "Homage to Sextus Propertius" be the model for all
those entering the field? It is interesting to me that, though Pound's
version is more than half a century old, the debate as to its merits
continues still. One need only look at the recently published study by
J. P. Sullivan. That Pound's practice answered some need seems
today reasonably obvious. And he has been very persuasive.
I recall one critic saying that the trouble with the translations of the
Noh plays was that there wasn't enough Pound in them. But even
those who don't go the whole way with him are not likely to employ
Victorianisms, inversions, poeticisms and the like. He has made
every translator think through his own practice.

Nothing in this paper is intended as a denigration of Western
values. Someone remarked to T. S. Eliot that we know more than
the past, and he is said to have answered, "Yes, and the past is what
we know." Obviously to make that past meaningful and relevant
to our time remains a great challenge. I understand that in one of
the branches of the City University a course is being given in Simon
and Garfunkel and Bob Dylan, who may represent the poetic ideal.
I have no objection to that, but I wonder if a similar course is being
given in Sophocles, who is not as easily available on records. But if
I did mention the non-Western areas it is because the translator's
problem in regard to them is urgent and complex. It is just not
enough today to offer another reading of *Don Quixote* or Cicero's

De Senectute. During the last war, the Third Fleet passed by the
islands of Micronesia and reduced whatever towns were there to dust.
If we can bring those islands into the twentieth century by those
means, we have an obligation, I think, to search out their humanity,
their characteristics as people, and we can do it most efficiently—
at present anyway—through their literature, written and unwritten.
The single great need today is to establish the humanity of all men,
regardless of the accidentals of speech, skin pigment, customs or
geographical location. The translator in that task can establish himself as a third world, not in the sense of a neutralist aloof from both
sides, but as the one who, knowing both sides well, can make the
best qualities of each known to the other.

The Ear in Translation

Gregory Rabassa

I take my text from Johnny Cash: "I've walked the line." What the translator must do first off is to walk the line. And in keeping with the image, he must always be aware that in a very deep sense he is the prisoner of his author, convicted on any number of counts. But at the same time he must be a model prisoner, a trusty, willingly at the mercy of the text he is rendering and of all the turns it might take. If not, he had best return to the original urge of writing something of his own inspiration and bust out.

When asked to participate in this conference I thought hard about something to say that would not be too obvious and also something that I have thought to be an important part of my technique. I was not long in arriving at the theme of "ear." Now, we must be careful, for the term is broad in English. Spanish and Portuguese are more exact and distinguish between hearing and the fleshy appendage. This second meaning does indeed have relevance to our craft because we are often called upon to go into the silk-purse business. When we decline to do this and are faithful to our text, "walking the line," we find that the translator is too often the recipient of criticism which is better directed at the author. I have always maintained that if Homer nodded in the Greek he should nod in English. And there are those authors who seem to be sound asleep a good deal of the time.

Ear is important in translation because it really lies at the base of all good writing. Writing is not truly a substitute for thought, it is a substitute for sound. We couch our thoughts in a language which is spoken, else we would have to resort to the formulas of mathematical science, which are the true substitutes for thought, with a beauty of their own, and which offer little in the way of aural feeling except in rare cases such as that of the remarkable google. So that when a person writes, he is speaking, and when a person reads, he is listening. Writing has drifted away from this idea of direct expression because it has the advantage of being outside of the inexorable flow of time; it is a flow which can be halted, reversed, and amended. Nevertheless, what we appreciate in writing is much the same as what we look for in rhetoric (although that poor word has suffered of late: first it meant freshman English, now it means intentionally hollow statements)—sound, whether heard or imagined; sound which can either enhance or detract from the meaning.

The translator with a tin ear is as deadly as a tone-deaf musician. In a great many cases a translation that has been deemed wanting suffers from the fact that the translator does not have the sense of ear that the original author had. The most common praise for a translation is that it reads as if the book had been written originally in English. One gets the feeling that the opposite is normally expected in a translation, which is too often the case, so the translator should be continually aware of this and should listen to what he is writing. I think that this sort of criticism or praise is much more to the point than the type which goes nit-picking after inaccuracies. This last type is most often produced by academics of the sort that Sara Blackburn has dubbed Professor Horrendo. In his anality he fetches his dictionary and finds that on page twenty the translation reads "chair" where the true meaning of the original was "stool." This is usually done in defense of the integrity of the author, but often in the innocence of not knowing that the author, who knows English quite well, has checked and approved the translation. Professor Horrendo has long been our bane, and we should be thankful when a far-sighted editor gives a translation to a writer rather than to a scholar for review.

This raises the question of which is more important in translation, accuracy or the flow of the prose. The question should really never have to be put, for we would hope that both would be present. This is not the case, however, and what we have too often is either an "imitation" or a trot. If a work sings in the original and does not in the translation, then the version is little more than a linear glossary;

if it reads well but is grossly inaccurate, we are faced with a sub-creation which may well have its merits but which is not what it purports to be. This defines the line I have mentioned above, the one which the translator must walk. Deciding whether a translation is good or not is very similar to passing judgment on a sonnet.

How should the ear be used in translation, then, beyond the obvious indications? There are so many variants that we will have to choose only a few, showing in a sense that the ear might well be the most important factor in the whole process. The most obvious place would be in the rendering of dialogue, which is the direct use of spoken language in writing. This is doubtless more difficult in fiction than in drama because it lacks the possible saving grace of the intervention of the actor or the director. Here is where the translator must have some freedom of action and where he must call upon a great deal of aural experience. More important than the words themselves are the characters, their status and their circumstances. Interjections are moments where the translator must almost certainly stray from the original words. For some cultural reason people tend to couch their cursing in words and imagery that are sometimes unrelated from one language to the other, and at other times barely touch by some thin filament of coincidence that may go back to the *Ursprach*. The elemental feeling, however, is universal to the species. I remember a specific case during the translation of *Hopscotch*. Oliveira, the protagonist, was attempting to straighten some nails with a hammer during the wild bridge-building episode in the second part of the novel. Naturally enough, at one point he hit his thumb with the tool. The Spanish expletive that he directed at the nail made reference to the whore that bore it. No one would say that in English this side of Hemingway. Rather than going to a book I went to the thesaurus of my experience (feeling close enough to Oliveira in this case) and to what I had heard as well as what I had said. I wrote what I and many like me would have said in English under such circumstances, chiding the nail for incestuous proclivities directed towards its dam. But in such cases one must always keep the person speaking in mind. There are times when one must decidedly not use his own instincts but must rely on an acute and remembering ear. There are far too many "goshes" and "gollies" in the mouths of stevedores and other rough and grown men. Cases like that are examples of times when the ear has not served the translator because it had never heard or was evidently turned off when he should have been absorbing the true equivalent in English.

Sometimes a work will have a decidedly local or regional tone in the foreign tongue which should be preserved in English. This can be exceedingly difficult for the translator because of the great

variety of possibilities. The easy way out is to give up and use straight
English. (I remember one book I was doing which had a lot of regional vocabulary, particularly for objects. To save time and trouble, for
those particularly thorny words I could not find anywhere and since
my barber, who was from the region, was off on vacation, I had recourse to the French translation, which had already appeared. I was
amused to find that in a majority of cases those words that I was trying to track down were missing. Think what some Professor Horren-
deau could have done to that book). The use of straight English in
these cases would in the end be unfaithful to the intent and impact
of the original. The most difficult solution would be the invention of
some sort of artificial but true-ringing English to convey the impression. In the wrong hands this could be a terrible disaster. It is tempting because it seems so easy. We have all read Ernest Hemingway's
Spanglish in *For Whom the Bell Tolls*. The first impression is simply
that Hemingway is translating Spanish literally. A closer examination
shows that this is not so, that Hemingway succeeded in putting into
words the *impression* that Spanish makes on one who is not a native
speaker but who understands the language fairly well. He has done
with syntax and vocabulary what Arte Johnson does with pure sound
impression with his Scandinavian storyteller. This is the best solution
but it calls for a master ear. The middle way is to find some local or
regional equivalent in English which rings at least somewhat true, and
again the ear must be the guide.

   A similar problem is that of those so-called "untranslatable" words.
Portuguese abounds in them, with such entries as *jeito* and the over-
stressed *saudade*. These words are really only impossible when the
concept behind them is hard to find in the second language, and this
is really what the translator is up against most of the time. Such
words can be left in the original, thus giving the translation a deli-
ciously exotic flavor which it should not have; or a footnote can be
used. I have seen this last technique and it horrifies me, but then it
is usually the work of some deadly-tongued Professor Horrendo who
lives in spastic fright that he might be a little off in his accuracy. The
best solution, of course, is the hardest, searching for some English
equivalent or near-equivalent that sounds true. Otherwise the very
sound of the foreign word will give the book a tone that it should not
have. While I was working on *The Green House* and in correspondence with Mario Vargas Llosa, he counselled against any possible
taint of the exotic. The setting was exotic enough and he did not
want the characters to appear as odd sorts for being in the midst of
it. Foreign words often over-stimulate the ear to the detriment of
meaning, and then too they suffer so much, all the more when the

foggy awareness of hypercorrection brings out such abortions as
"lahnzheray" and "repartay."

These few items out of many possibilities give an indication of the
importance of the ear in translating. There is argument for the fact
that it may be even more important here than in original writing, for
in translation the one doing the writing must be both listener and
speaker, and he could go astray in either direction. He must have
a good ear for what his author is saying and he must have a good ear
for what he is saying himself. We are faced, then, still with the intangibles of translation; what makes one version better than another
after the accuracy of both has been established? It can only be a
felicitous choice of words and structure which not only conveys the
meaning in English but enhances it by preserving the tone of the
original. Tone has many meanings, but most often it is associated,
figuratively at least, with sound. A deeper meaning which could
have relevance to translation is given the word by an old Indian
woman in *The Eyes of the Interred* by Asturias. Everyone has
both tone and soul in his living body, but the soul is a coward and
flees with the coming of death. The tone lingers and can bring
influence to bear on circumstances even though the body has died.
This might be the mystery of translation, the preservation of the
Asturian *tone* as we leave the cowardly soul to the scholars.

In its very last analysis, translation is an instinctive business.
Dictionaries can take care of the rest and, indeed, as Billie Holiday
sang, "You've got machines to do your work for you" with the
advent of computerized translation. Someday there may well be
a machine programmed for ear, but until that "bedlam millenium"
comes the translator is still the link between the author and a foreign
public. It is up to the translator to make the author sing, rage,
curse, and laugh in the second language as he has done in his own,
and this can only be done if the translator *listens* closely to the
text and then listens even more closely to what he has written himself, else he will produce an aphonic welter of definitions and con-
dign punishment will come from the academics as they slouch about
and seek their opening.

The Place of Translation in Literature

Juliusz Zulawski

Most of us here, at this Conference, are explaining their point of view on the question of translating from the other language *into* English. I will try to make a few remarks derived from my experiences of translating *from* English into the language of my own. There are some very special differences which could be subjected to a separate description. But the main problems are much the same.

I set myself to translate English and American poetry rather late. Usually the young writers take care of themselves first, and then, growing old, they widen their curiosity. Perhaps it is all the better for them. So, from 1933, I occupied myself only with prose writing and poetry of my own for many years, before—in 1950—I started translating besides, to run away from our century for a while.

Henceforth, I wrote quite a lot of essays and some books on poets of English language, and translated more and more of their works, beginning with the poets of the first half of the nineteenth century, as Byron, Shelley, Keats, then turning backwards to Pope, to Dryden, and then to the poets of the sixteenth century, as Spenser, Sidney, Chapman, and others, then again to the poets of the second half of the nineteenth century, as Browning, Arnold, and above all Walt Whitman, then to the poets of our twentieth century, as Frost, Hart Crane, and many others up to Robert Lowell. All in all, during these twenty years, I dealt with more than fifty English and American poets dispersed in the course of five centuries. Really a great confusion it seems to be. What is the meaning in such perpetual alternations of interest? Are we to consider a translator to be some kind of an actor, who plays by turns one part after another in different dramas?

It may be. But still it leads somewhere. As one can never fully discover the quality of a poem of foreign language until one attempts to translate it, so it seems impossible to apprehend rightly and appreciate any single poet—and even any generation of poets—out of their historical background and literary tradition, especially in respect to their language, idioms, hints, and so on.

At the same time, a translator has to exploit all the knowledge of his *national* language and its literary tradition; he must master it even better and of course with much greater responsibility than any writer who makes poetry or prose of his own. Because—as it ought ever to be remembered—any translated piece of work not only supplies the informations of a foreign writer, but is also to enter the translator's national literature as a new part of it. That is the fundamental and principal aim, which has to unite our common civilization, as it is, and out of that aim our art of translation has no meaning. In fact, not Homer himself, but Alexander Pope became once and for centuries to come the creator of the *Iliad* in English literature for all the English-speaking readers (regardless of the quality of his translation).

So, to translate, it is to enrich one's own national treasury, and to make the separate poetical expressions, individual judgments on life, and different visions of the world, more universal. In my country it was always appreciated, and the art of translation has its long and rich tradition extending from our times back to the sixteenth century. All the chief masterpieces of humanity were always well-known there.

But again and again, an old question arises. Is there a real possibility to translate poetry at all? To give in another language the similarity of expression, of structure, of melody, to create the full resemblance between the two poetical pictures—original and translated"? Of course, you could not say you know the poetry of Petrarch well enough, if you do not read his sonnets in the original. But still, in a good translation you have a chance to find something more than a "trot," and even more than a key. You can find a true poetical "idea" of any of these sonnets. I mean, you can find in another language a counterpart of the approximated, if not the same, poetical *importance*.

So, one can not avoid now the main and most awkward question: What is a "good" translation? What are the most important features, qualities, elements in it? What are the right, permissible compromises, and to what extent might these be used without spoiling the essence of the thing? During several years of work, I have changed my view quite a lot of times, and my present definition is probably still far from being satisfactory. In the same way that you try to explain which of two poems is better, although you know for sure, you can tell a good translation from a bad one all at once.

I think that you accept it as "good" when it gives you in different language a true image of the thoughts, realities, and poetical intentions of an original, and at the same time reveals itself as an equally integral, genuine piece of work. To convey that true image of the thoughts, realities and poetical intentions—it is, for a translator, a question of his fidelity to an original. To create at the same time an equally integral, genuine piece of work—it is a question of fidelity to the language and literature of his own.

That is our task. Not an easy one, sometimes really depressing, sometimes treated as fun with all its joys and disappointments. And that is the way a translation enters the national literature, and often remains there for good. It has entered once, and it is still there in the conscience of the readers. And, practically, this state of things holds true for most of the famous pieces of work, although sometimes its translations are not adequate. What then? Is it possible and desirable just to work out some new, better, more representative translation? Things are not as simple as that. For instance: All of Shakespeare has been translated in my country in the course of the nineteenth century. The translators were good and able, but, of course, they were under the influences of the poetical convention of their romantic age rather than that of the seventeenth century. In these translations, Shakespearian plays were widely read and presented on stage and hundreds of so-translated sentences and expressions passed for good into colloquial language. Perhaps because of that, our reviewers too often—as everywhere, as somebody here has already complained—omit the translator's name as if Shakespeare or, say, Moliere, did not write in English, or in French, but in Polish.

It sounds funny, but it is one more proof in daily practice how obviously a piece of work of a foreign writer, when translated, becomes a part of the new adopted literature.

Hence so great a responsibility is ours—responsibility as much towards a foreign writer, as towards our own literature. But as to old translations, already adopted, known by heart, and firmly placed in the tradition of literature—what are we to do? To correct it, to get rid of not quite adequate expressions which people are used to, or to bring it to "up to date" to the dismay of the readers?

In my practice I almost never touch a poem, already translated— only when it is a part of a larger piece of work, or one of a set which I want to gather. However, I am not against new translation. It could be useful. Especially in the case of the poets not well known by the readers in another country yet, or really very badly translated —as far as one can judge. Also Homer, Dante and Shakespeare, and others already adopted should be translated again and again, but under some special conditions. In his new experiments, a translator must take on a very hard responsibility. He must realize that he is going to replace something that is already as much an integral part of his own literature as any other piece of work. He must be quite sure he is better and really closer to the original in the frames of his literature.

I am rather against any so-called "modernization" of the old pieces of work, what seems to be everywhere so "up to date" now, against translating "from century to century," against any artificial fastening our ideas, our points of view, our knowledge of physical world, and our mood of life, as they are, to absolutely different ways of thinking of the past.

On Translating from Gaelic

Brendan Kennelly

I want to speak about Woman in Irish poetry, and more specifically
I'll speak on The Theme of Woman in Translations from the Gaelic.
It may be as well, therefore, to begin with a poem by one of the
most famous of Gaelic poets, the blind Raftery. This blind man was
one of the last of the wandering poets; and his countryside was the
West of Ireland. He fell in love with a beautiful girl called Mary
Hynes who, you may remember, was celebrated by Yeats in one of
his poems.

> Some few remembered still when I was young
> A peasant girl commended by a song,
> Who'd lived somewhere upon that rocky place,
> And praised the colour of her face,
> And had the greater joy in praising her,
> Remembering that, if walked she there,
> Farmers jostled at the fair
> So great a glory did the song confer.
> And certain men, being maddened by those rhymes,
> Or else by toasting her a score of times,
> Rose from the table and declared it right
> To test their fancy by their sight;
> But they mistook the brightness of the moon

For the prosaic light of day—
Music had driven their wits astray—
And one was drowned in the great bog of Cloone.

Strange, but the man who made the song was blind. . . . Perhaps it
was Raftery's blindness that made him create an image of ideal
beauty in his mind. After all, do not the poet and the blind man
live in a world of images? Raftery's poem, in Irish, would give you
an idea of the musicality of Irish poetry. A delighted verbal music is
one of its dominant features; its lively rhythms; its constant rhyming
and chiming, both internally and at the end of lines; its rich vowel-
sounds; its directness; its simplicity. It is a poem of praise; it seeks
to establish the uniqueness of the girl's beauty—hence, as we shall
see, the invoked comparisons with the beautiful women of France
and England, Spain and Greece. And finally you will notice how
close it is to the ballad, the poem of the people. Raftery was *of* the
people; he spoke out of them and *to* them. The ballad rhythm is as
near as one can get to the pulse of the blood of the people. There
is in it the swell of the city streets, the ease of the open road.

Here is Frank O'Connor's translation of Raftery's poem, "Mary
Hynes."

> Going to Mass by the heavenly mercy,
>   The day was rainy, the wind was wild;
> I met a lady beside Kiltartan
>   And fell in love with the lovely child;
> My conversation was smooth and easy,
>   And graciously she answered me
> 'Raftery dear, 'tis yourself that's welcome,
>   So step beside me to Ballylee.'
>
> This invitation there was no denying,
>   I laughed with joy and my poor heart beat;
> We had but to walk across a meadow,
>   And in her dwelling I took my seat.
> There was laid a table with jug and glasses,
>   And that sweet maiden sat down by me—
> 'Raftery drink and don't spare the liquor;
>   There's a lengthy cellar in Ballylee.'
>
> If I should travel France and England,
>   And Spain and Greece and return once more
> To study Ireland to the northern ocean,

> I would find no morsel the like of her.
> If I was married to that youthful beauty
>   I'd follow her through the open sea,
> And wander coasts and winding roads
>   With the shining pearl of Ballylee.
>
> 'Tis fine and bright on the mountainside,
>   Looking down on Ballylee,
> You can walk the woods, picking nuts and berries,
>   And hear the birds sing merrily;
> But where's the good if you got no tidings
>   Of the flowering branch that resides below—
> O summer sky, there's no denying
>   It is for you that I ramble so.
>
> My star of beauty, my sun of autumn,
>   My golden hair, O my share of life!
> Will you come with me this coming Sunday?
>   And tell the priest you will be my wife?
> I'd not grudge you music, nor a feast at evening,
>   Nor punch nor wine, if you'd have it be,
> And King of Glory, dry up the roadway
>   Till I find my posy at Ballylee!

In talking about Woman in translations from the Irish, I shall comment on what seem to me the most difficult challenges for a translator, and suggest ways in which I think it may be possible to cope with these challenges.

Firstly, then, the theme. There is an old Irish poem which nearly every Irish poet writing in English has tried to translate. It is called "The Old Woman of Beare." Frank O'Connor, one of Ireland's greatest translators, writes that "The Old Woman of Beare (County Cork) is one of the standard permanent figures of early Irish literature, a goddess who, having survived for long ages, finds herself a man in a Christian community." In his translation, O'Connor presents the workings of the old woman's mind, looking back on her youth.

> I, the old woman of Beare,
> Once a shining shift would wear,
> Now and since my beauty's fall
> I have scarce a shift at all.

Plump no more, I sigh for these
Bones bare beyond belief;
Ebbtide is all my grief,
I am ebbing like the seas. . . .

Oh, my hands as may be seen
Are so scraggy and so thin
That a boy might start in dread
Feeling them about his head. . . .

I have always admired O'Connor's poem and yet I have always
been unhappy about what seems to me one of the most important
elements in translation—I mean the poem's rhythm. Failure in
rhythm is like a contagious disease—it affects all the parts of the
poem. To me, the capturing of a rhythm in translation means the
exact portrayal of the subtle vicissitudes, the ebb and flow of emotion and thought, as found in the original. The finding of a right
rhythm in translation is like the transplanting of a human heart. And
so, for this poem, "The Old Woman of Beare," I wanted a rhythm
which would not merely approximate to, but which would literally
be the tide of her thoughts, ebbing and flowing, rising and falling. So
I broke up the stanzas. It seemed to me that this woman hated old
age for its indignity, its discourtesy, its dull decrepitude. This hatred
brings with it a love: love of her youth and of the memory of those
men who had made love to her. So far as I understand the poem,
there is both acceptance and anger in this woman, and I wanted the
rhythm to express this tension. I think I had in my mind images of
women such as Molly Bloom and Crazy Jane. The Old Woman of
Beare is a dramatic archetype. Here is my translation.

The sea crawls from the shore
Leaving there
The despicable weed,
A corpse's hair.
In me,
The desolate withdrawing sea.

The Old Woman of Beare am I
Who once was beautiful.
Now all I know is how to die.
I'll do it well.

Look at my skin
Stretched tight on the bone.
Where kings have pressed their lips,
The pain, the pain.

I don't hate the men
Who swore the truth was in their lies.
One thing alone I hate--
Women's eyes.

The young sun
Gives its youth to everyone,
Touching everything with gold.
In me, the cold.

The cold. Yet still a seed
Burns there.
Women love only money now.
But when
I loved, I loved
Young men.

Young men whose horses galloped
On many an open plain
Beating lightning from the ground.
I loved such men.

And still the sea
Rears and plunges into me,
Shoving, rolling through my head
Images of the drifting dead.

A soldier cries
Pitifully about his plight;
A king fades
Into the shivering night.

Does not every season prove
That the acorn hits the ground?
Have I not known enough of love
To know it's lost as soon as found?

I drank my fill of wine with kings,
Their eyes fixed on my hair.
Now among the stinking hags
I chew the cud of prayer.

Time was the sea
Brought kings as slaves to me.
Now I near the face of God
And the crab crawls through my blood.

I loved the wine
That thrilled me to my fingertips;
Now the mean wind
Stitches salt into my lips.

The coward sea
Slouches away from me.
Fear brings back the tide
That made me stretch at the side
Of him who'd take me briefly for his bride.

The sea grows smaller, smaller now.
Farther, farther it goes
Leaving me here where the foam dries
On the deserted land,
Dry as my shrunken thighs,
As the tongue that presses my lips,
As the veins that break through my hands.

You may say that whoever wrote that poem tended to go on a little, but it is this very insistence on her grief which provides one of the poem's most dramatic features. Again, Joyce's Molly Bloom and Yeats's Crazy Jane come to mind. Like the Old Woman of Beare, the thoughts of these two women have a brooding stamina, a tenacity which compels Joyce to give Molly Bloom the longest soliloquy in literature, and makes Yeats treat Crazy Jane as a vehicle for numerous aphoristic statements about life, love, time, sex, death, and eternity.

Now, this is not to say that poems in Irish about women are all very long. Here is a very short one about a girl who is equally attracted to men but who is, as yet, untroubled by the problems of old age. The poem is called "Etáin."

Who will sleep with Etáin tonight?
   That's still unknown.
One thing is certain though—
   Etáin won't sleep alone.

That is my first view of woman, then. It is a view which still persists in Irish writing: *woman as dramatic archetype.*

The second view of woman is one that is deeply characteristic of Irish poetry—*woman as the symbol of one's country.* There was a time when Irish poets were forbidden to speak directly of Ireland. They got around this problem by referring to the country as a beautiful woman who came to the poet in a vision. In this vision, the woman told the poet that she was preparing the way for the return of the saviour hero-king. This was not just a poetic convention, it was a device of human survival. There are many famous translations of this kind of poem; the most famous is probably James Clarence Mangan's "My Dark Rosaleen." From these two verses, you can see the desperate insistence on identity.

I could scale the blue air,
   I could plough the high hills,
Oh, I could kneel all night in prayer,
   To heal your many ills!
And one . . . beamy smile from you
   Would float like light between
My toils and me, my own, my true,
   My Dark Rosaleen!
   My fond Rosaleen!
Would give me life and soul anew,
A second life, a soul anew,
   My Dark Rosaleen!

O! the Erne shall run red
   With redundance of blood,
The earth shall rock beneath our tread,
   And flames wrap hill and wood,
And gun-peal, and slogan cry,
   Wake many a glen serene,
Ere you shall fade, ere you shall die,
   My Dark Rosaleen!
   My own Rosaleen!
The Judgment Hour must first be nigh,

> Ere you can fade, ere you can die,
> My Dark Rosaleen!

Now, looking at this poetry in Irish, we ask: what kind of poetry is it, and what problem does it present to the translator? I think if we recognize the first question, we can resolve the second. This poetry is obsessed with *vision,* and with *movement,* and because this visionary movement has behind it the purpose of racial survival, any translation must discover an athletic rhythm, a buoyant idiom, and a conclusive direction. This poetry is, as it were, "rigged" from the beginning, so that the promise of redemption can be made by the woman in the vision. In the poem I have chosen to translate, Egan O'Rahilly's "Dawn Dream," this is obvious if we look at the poet's simple but effective device. I have translated the first line as

> "One morning before Titan had opened his eyes"

and this is also the last line of the poem. The double-guarantee of the sleeping god Titan enables the poet to go out and meet the goddess Eevul with her news of delivery for Ireland. Between these two lines is that movement into optimistic vision which must be portrayed in rhythm, diction, and image. One must capture that feeling of exaltation which, according to John Synge, typifies the highest poetry. The peculiar exaltation of this poem comes from its fusion of two worlds: the dream-world of the queens with its air of supernatural confidence and eloquent promise, and the unspoken desperation of the poet's world, with its craving for the beautiful and its hunger for freedom. Here is my translation of "Dawn Dream."

> One morning before Titan had opened his eyes
> I rose from my bed and made my way up the mountainside
> And who would believe when I speak of the women I saw
> Who had lived one time towards the North in beauty and pride.
>
> There where they stepped I saw the plentiful land
> As morning mist surrendered boulder and slope,
> Grass was greener than ever, boughs crouched under fruit,
> The golden light of honey spilled over the stones.
>
> Each woman held a candle, the light pierced my eyes,
> I followed them where the Shannon twisted and twisted again,

All the way through Thomond, going it seemed out of time
Till I asked Queen Eevul what brought her into this world of men.

Eevul was quick to reply, out of the sun came her voice,
"The candles we carry through every season must burn.
This land that is crying must learn again to rejoice.
And we, the proud women, prepare for the hero's return."

Bewildered I woke from my sleep, her words in my head,
Her words shivered with truth in this world of lies,
And what in God's name comes next, I asked myself,
One morning before Titan had opened his eyes.

I hope I have captured something of the tone of desperate hope
and a little of that visionary movement which account for the living
quality of the original.

I would like now to speak of woman in some Irish love poems. An
effective way to do this perhaps is to read a poem by Patrick Pearse,
one of the leaders of the 1916 Rebellion. It is a poem about a woman
who is dead and whose memory haunts his sleep. I feel, however, that
Pearse may have had Ireland in mind as well—the poem is called
"A Cinn Aluinn" ("O Shapely Head"). Here it is in Irish first, and
then in translation. I have tried to find equivalents in English translation for the vowel music and the internal rhymes.

ᴀ Ċɪɴɴ Áʟᴜɪɴɴ

Ᵹ ċɪɴɴ áʟᴜɪɴɴ ɴᴀ mɴá ᴅo ᵹʀáᴅᴀʀ,
1 ʟáʀ ɴᴀ ɴoɪᴅċe cᴜɪᵯɴɪᵹɪm oʀᴛ!
Ᵹċᴛ ꝼɪʟʟeᴀɴɴ ʟéᴀʀᵹᴜʀ ʟe ᵹɪʟe ᵹʀéɪɴe,—
ᵯo ʟéᴀɴ ᴀɴ ċɴᴜᵯ ċᴀoʟ ᴅoᴅ' ċɴᴀoɪ ᴀɴoċᴛ.

Ᵹ ᵹʟóɪʀ ɪoɴᵯᴜɪɴ ᴅoᴅ' íʀeᴀʟ ᴀoɪᴅɪɴɴ,
Ᵹɴ ꝼíoʀ ᵹo ᵹcᴜᴀʟᴀʀ ᴛʀém' ꝼᴜᴀɴᴀɪᴅ ᴛú?
ɴó ᴀɴ ꝼíoʀ ᴀɴ ᴛ-eoʟᴀʀ ᴀᴛá ᴅom' ᴅeo-ᵹoɪɴ?
ᵯo ᴅʀóɴ, ʀᴀ ᴛᴜᴀmᴅᴀ ɴíʟ ꝼᴜᴀɪm ɴá ᵹᴜċ!

> My eyes once more adore at night
> My girl's shapely head
> But see in cruel morning light
> Worms bite into the dead.

Have I really known in deepest sleep
The joy her sweet voice gave?
Or was it truth that cut to the quick?
My heart is sick by the sullen grave.

It is conceivable, I think, that Pearse has *both* woman and country
in mind. Usually, however, Irish love-poems do not carry this kind
of ambiguous possibility; they are straightforward and direct. In
some of the best poems, for example, the opening line is blunt and
dramatic. I am reminded of John Donne's capacity for startling
beginnings. Some of Donne's opening lines are like a slap in the face.

For God's sake hold your tongue and let me love

and

Busy old fool, unruly sun . . .

In the translation of "Reconciliation," I tried to capture this
directness. The poet, I take it, is impatient with the woman's hesi-
tation. Her attitude of doubt irritates him, but there is no doubt
about his attitude.

Do not torment me, woman,
    Let our two minds be as one,
Be my mate in my own land
    Where we may live till life is done.

Put your mouth against my mouth
    You whose skin is fresh as foam,
Take me in your white embrace
    And let us love till kingdom come.

Slender graceful girl, admit
    Me soon into your bed,
Discord, pain will disappear
    When we stretch there side by side.

For your sweet sake, I will ignore
    Every girl who takes my eye,
If it's possible, I implore
    You do the same for me.

> As I have given from my heart
> > Passion for which alone I live,
> Let me now receive from you
> > The love you have to give.

In that poem, the poet is trying to clarify things; to get the matter settled once and for all. It is the woman who is holding things up. She is, potentially, a spoiler of something fine because of her refusal to cooperate.

Another poem which brings this out very strongly is "The Indifferent Mistress." The poem's impact derives from a series of contrasts which emphasize the poet's helplessness and his tendency towards masochism.

> She is my love
> Though she makes my life a hell,
> Dearer, though she makes me sick,
> Than one who would make me well.

> She is my dear
> Who has reduced me to a slave,
> She'd never let one sigh for me
> Or lay a stone on my grave.

> She is my treasure
> Whose eye is stern with pride
> She'd never put an arm under my head
> Or lie at my side.

> She is my secret
> Who won't speak a word to me,
> Who won't listen to anything under the sun
> Or turn an eye on me.

> My plight is sad.
> To a lonely death I move.
> She who spurns me, only she
> Can be my love.

It is a short step from that kind of self-punishment to hatred of the other. A good deal of Irish love-poetry is concerned with hate. Is hatred a poisoned love? It would appear to be so from this poem which is called "Hate Goes Just as far as Love."

Woman full of hate for me
　　　Do you not recall the night
When we together, side by side,
　　　　　Knew love's delight?

If you remembered, woman, how,
　　　While the sun lost its heat,
You and I grew hot—
　　　　　But why repeat?

Do you recall my lips on yours,
　　　The soft words you said,
And how you laid your curving arm
　　　　　Under my head?

Or do you remember, O sweet shape,
　　　How you whispered passionately
That God Almighty had never made
　　　　　A man like me?

But I gave all my heart to you,
　　　Gave all, yet could not give enough;
Now, I've your hate. O skin like flowers,
　　　　　This hate goes just as far as love.

If a man believes he loves a woman
　　　And that she loves him too,
Let him know one thing for certain—
　　　　　It is not true.

It is quite extraordinary that there is so much hate in the love-
poetry of Ireland. Indeed, completely independent of the tradition
of love-poetry, there is a tradition of hate-poetry, full of disgust,
revulsion, bitterness, and invective. This may be due in part to
Irish history, from that nightmare (as he called it) from which Joyce
sought to escape. But whatever the explanation, hate and love live
closely together in Irish poetry. There is even a poem, "Love and
Hate," in which the poet declares that he loves only one thing—hate.
It has been admirably translated by Frank O'Connor.

Hate only will I love,
　　　Love I will set aside,
The misery of love
　　　Too many a heart has tried.

My scorn upon the thing
    That such vain grief began
And many a good man made
    Into a sick man.

Even when it goes too far
    Hate's the better part,
One can bid Hate pack,
    Who can bid love depart?

Hate is healthy fare
    That leaves the body sound,
Nor herb nor medicine cures
    Love's bitter wound.

Once I saw a girl
    Choose a man in play;
Love he never knew
    To his dying day.

I whate'er befall
    Know a better fate—
This is all my song,
    I will love only hate.

But it would be dreadful if we came to the conclusion that when Irishmen try to write love-poems, the best they can do is explode into hatred. Much Irish love-poetry is like Chinese poetry in its delicacy. I have tried to translate a poem called "She" which seems to me to have this sort of delicacy. The images are simple, the rhythm easy, and yet the effect is, or should be, mysterious.

She
White flower of the blackberry
Sweet flower of the raspberry
Pure herb of beauty
    Blesses the sight of my eyes.

She
Heart-pulse and blood-secret
Sweet flower of the apple
Hot sun in cold weather
    Between Christmas and Easter.

Or here is another called "The Blackthorn Pin." It is an exhortation to a girl to exchange a blackthorn pin for a golden brooch. I am
not going to comment on whatever may be the symbolism of the
request.

> Sweet red-lipped girl, for many years
>   You have been loved by men.
> Your cloak should wear a golden brooch
>   And not a blackthorn pin.
>
> O graceful girl, just to all,
>   Whom none could ever win
> Why should your yellow cloak show but
>   A blackthorn pin?
>
> Well, wear it then! It is your secret
>   And will not be told:
> Give the blackthorn pin another hour;
>   Then raise the gold.

My final view of Woman is that of *critic of society*. The Old
Woman of Beare is, in one sense, a critic of the men who "swore the
truth was in their lies," though she doesn't hate them. But the poem
in which woman is predominant in this rôle is Bryan Merriman's
"The Midnight Court." In this poem, which has an epic structure,
the women of Ireland denounce all the timid Irish bachelors, and the
dreadful waste of fine manhood among the celibate clergy. The
women, in their midnight court, accuse the men and find them guilty
indeed. They even find the poet, Merriman, guilty; and he escapes
punishment only when, in fact, he wakes up to find that the court
has been a dream, and that all the women were merely complaining,
accusing phantoms of his imagination. But, dream or not, we still
have the voices of those women telling us what it meant to be frus-
trated in eighteenth-century Ireland. When Frank O'Connor's
translation appeared in the 1940's, it was banned—an ironical
proof that twentieth-century Ireland could be as sinisterly repressive as Merriman's eighteenth-century world. Here, in O'Connor's
translation of Merriman's vigorous couplets, is one of those young
women.

> Look at that waist! My legs are long,
> Limber as willows and light and strong.

There's bottom and belly that claim attention,
And the best concealed that I needn't mention.
I'm the sort a natural man desires,
Not a freak or a death-on-wires,
A sloven that comes to life in flashes,
A creature of moods with her heels in the ashes,
Or a sluggard stewing in her own grease,
But a good-looking girl that's bound to please.
If I was as slow as some I know
To stand up for my rights and my dress a show,
Some brainless, illbred, country mope
You could understand if I lost hope;
But ask the first you meet by chance:
Hurling match or race or dance,
Pattern or party, market or fair,
Whatever it was, was I not there?
And didn't I make a good impression
Turning up in the height of fashion?
My hair was washed and combed and powdered,
My coif like snow and stiffly laundered;
I'd a little white hood with ribbons and ruff
On a spotted dress of the finest stuff,
And facings to show off the line
Of a cardinal cloak the colour of wine;
A cambric apron filled with showers
Of fruit and birds and trees and flowers;
Neatly-fitting expensive shoes
With the highest of heels pegged up with screws;
Silken gloves, and myself in spangles
Of brooches, buckles, rings and bangles.
And you mustn't imagine I was shy,
The sort that slinks with a downcast eye,
Solitary, lonesome, cold and wild,
Like a mountainy girl or an only child.
I tossed my cap at the crowds of the races
And kept my head in the toughest places.
Am I not always on the watch
At bonfire, dance or hurling match,
Or outside the chapel after Mass
To coax a smile from fellows that pass?
But I'm wasting my time on a wildgoose-chase,
And my spirit's broken—and that's my case!
After all my shaping, sulks and passions

All my aping of styles and fashions,
All the times that my cards were spread
And my hands were read and my cup was read;
Every old rhyme, pishrogue and rune,
Crescent, full moon and harvest moon,
Whits and All Souls and the First of May,
I've nothing to show for all they say.
Every night when I went to bed
I'd a stocking of apples beneath my head;
I fasted three canonical hours
To try and come round the heavenly powers;
I washed my shift where the stream was deep
To hear a lover's voice in sleep;
Often I swept the woodstack bare,
Burned bits of my frock, my nails, my hair,
Up the chimney stuck the flail,
Slept with a spade without avail;
Hid my wool in the lime-kiln late
And my distaff behind the churchyard gate;
I had flax on the road to halt coach or carriage
And haycocks stuffed with heads of cabbage,
And night and day on the proper occasions
Invoked Old Nick and all his legions;
But 'twas all no good and I'm broken-hearted
For here I'm back at the place I started;
And this is the cause of all my tears
I am fast in the rope of the rushing years,
With age and need in lessening span,
And death beyond, and no hopes of a man.
But whatever misfortunes God may send
May He spare me at least that lonesome end,
Nor leave me at last cross alone
Without chick nor child when my looks are gone
As an old maid counting the things I lack
Scowling thresholds that warn me back!
God, by the lightning and the thunder,
The thought of it makes me ripe for murder!
Every idiot in the country
With a man of her own has the right to insult me.
Sal' has a slob with a well-stocked farm,
And Molly goes round on a husband's arm,
There's Min and Margery leaping with glee

And never done with their jokes at me.
And the bounce of Sue! and Kitty and Anne
Have children in droves and a proper man,
And all with their kind can mix and mingle
While I go savage and sour and single.

I think again of Yeats' Crazy Jane—an old woman who is a furiously articulate enemy of repression. She is perhaps wiser than Merriman's women, but she is their equal in anger.

A woman can be proud and stiff
When on love intent,
But love has pitched his mansion in
The place of excrement,
And nothing can be sole or whole
That has not been rent.

Nowadays, woman as critic is most obvious in the Irish novel; in the suffering heroines of Edna O'Brien, John McGahern, and Brian Moore. These writers may lack Merriman's comic spirit, but their insight into the plight of certain Irish women is genuine and moving.

There are many other aspects of woman that one might speak about in considering Irish poetry but I have tried to concentrate on those aspects which seemed to me to be the most important. There is an old Irish triad which says that Aristotle failed to understand three things: *saotar na mbeach, teacht agus imtheact no taoide, agus intleacht na mban:*—the labour of the bees, the coming and going of the tide, the mind of woman. We have discovered a little about the bees and the tide but, in all honesty, the mind of woman would, I feel, puzzle Aristotle as much today as it did in his own time. I know very well that these translations from the Irish have not clarified the mystery. But then since translation is, in any case, the art of fascinating failure—which is, nevertheless, a service, loving and illuminating —I am happy if these poems will manage to hold their readers' interest.

On Translating My Books

Isaac Bashevis Singer

I am often asked: "Why do you write in Yiddish?" and I want to try
to answer this question. My answer will be in the Yiddish style, which
means I will answer a question with a question: Why shouldn't I
write in Yiddish? Will I be able to express myself better in Turkish,
Chinese or Burmese? In Burmese how do you say: *Hak nisht kein
tschainik.* The literal translation of which is: "Don't beat the tea
kettle."

If I wrote in English, I would have to be not a writer but a translator, and a bad one to boot.

Some time ago a translator came to me all confused and perspired.
"What is the matter with you?" I asked, and he said: "How do you
translate from Yiddish, *a waycher mentsch diment* which means, a
man as soft as a diamond? In all languages a diamond is a symbol
of hardness but in Yiddish a diamond is soft. Should I translate:
soft like a diamond? Or soft like a Jewish diamond?" He seemed to
be in utter despair.

Those who count words assure me that English is the richest
tongue in the world. The Webster dictionary, like the Sunday *Times*,
becomes fatter from year to year. But I am convinced that the
richest language is Yiddish.

Take such words as: "A poor man". How many expressions are
there in English for poor? You can say: "a poor man, a pauper,

a beggar, a mendicant, a panhandler," and this exhausts all that can
be said about it. But in Yiddish you can say: "A poor shlemiel, a
begging shlimazel, a pauper with dimples, a schnorrer multiplied by
eight, a schlepper by the grace of God, an alms collector with a
mission, a perpetual needer, a delegate from the Holy Land, a messenger from a Yeshiva, a miracle worker without a following, a Rabbi
without a congregation, a poorhouse resident, a hungerman, a flying
wanderer, a warden for his own needs, a squire with a hole, a barefoot
count, an owner of a cabbage head, a bag carrier, a house-to-house
visitor, dressed in seven coats of poverty, a crumb-catcher, a bone
picker, a plate licker, a daily observer of the Yom Kippur fast" and
more and more.

This does not complete the list. When you say of a person that he
is a second Rothschild or a second Rockefeller and you wink, everyone will understand that he cannot make a living.

You can say about a poor man that he is broke, sunk, chews dirt,
keeps his teeth in his purse, penny pants, walks around with his
tongue sticking out, is a pauper with a certificate—and everyone will
know that he is constantly dreaming about rice pudding and chicken
soup.

In some towns in Poland when they want to say that a man is poor
they say: "He is as naked as a Turk." Why a Turk is more naked
than others I don't know. But it is the same as saying: "He suffers
like a saint on earth, like the wicked in heaven, he earns the water,
not the groats, or that for him the whole year is one long Passover—
no bread."

The writers' club in Warsaw used to be frequented by a poet who
was a hippie fifty years before hippiedom and when he wanted to
speak about a fellow poet in bad financial straits said: "We should
both have the money he is missing toward five guldens." How could
one translate all this into English?

To be serious, I happen to be one of those rare writers who works
with my translators and I'd like to share my experiences with you.

Number 1) There isn't such a thing as a good translator. The
best translators make the worst mistakes. I used to fight with my
translators and whatever fault the reviewers found in my works,
I blamed on the translators. But since I began to take part in the
translations, I developed a great compassion for the translator. However, no matter how much I love them, all translators must be
closely watched. If not, they are liable of making the most fantastic errors. I know of a man who translated a book from English into
Hebrew. When he came to a line which read: "She cried like a
woman in labor," he had a problem. He knew what a woman is,

what labor is, but somehow it did not occur to him that a woman in labor is a woman who gives birth, and since labor was associated in his mind with the labor movement, he translated it: "She cried like a woman in the Histadruth."

Number 2) A translation, like a woman, can be true and faithful and still miserable. What makes sense in one language may be utter nonsense in another. Some languages, like Yiddish, can take a lot of overstatements: mild exaggerations, terrible curses, nauseating blessings. Others, like English or French must be precise, logical, lean. What is a joke in one language can be sheer idiocy in another. What is dramatic in Russian is melodramatic in Swedish. Poetry and humor are almost untranslatable. The translator must be a great editor, a psychologist, a judge of human taste; if not, his translation will be a nightmare. But why should a man with such rare qualities become a translator? Why shouldn't he be a writer himself, or be engaged in a business where diligent work and high intelligence is well paid? A good translator must be both a sage and a fool. And where do you get such strange combinations?

Number 3) Translation can succeed best where the translator works with the author, or vice versa. At a lecture I was once asked: "What would you do if you were to meet God face-to-face?" And my answer was: "I would ask him to collaborate with me on some translations." I would not trust him to do it himself. I sometimes suspect that the Universe is nothing but a bad translation from God's original and this is the reason that everything here is topsy-turvy. My cabalist theory is that the Almighty trusted Satan to translate His Creation and it was published before He could correct it. I am not going to make the same blunder. I check my translators constantly—I mean those who translate me into English or Hebrew. What happens to me in Italian, Portuguese or Finnish I will never know.

Number 4) Not only is collaborating with the translator good for the translation, it also helps in editing the original. My translators are my best critics. I can recognize by their expressions when they don't like a story of mine or any part of it. Also translation undresses a literary work, shows it in its true nakedness. An author can fool himself in his own language, but many of his shortcomings become clear to him in another language. Translation tells the bitter truth. Unveils all masks. Nothing can prove the greatness of the Bible more than the fact that it has been translated into thousands of languages and it can be enjoyed in all of them. So great is the Bible that even a bad translation cannot damage it. The Ten Commandments cannot be misrepresented in translation because they are so simple, so clear and so eternally true. Many a writer should learn from the Bible what to do to assure his immortality. Writers about whom it is said that they cannot be translated at all because they play so much with language and are so ambiguous and obscure, do not deserve to be translated. My colleagues, it is my advice to you to avoid such works as you would the pestilence. A pun is clever in only one language and thousands of puns together are boring in any language. To our shame this century has produced countless writers whose works are nothing but puns and puzzles. Some critics and commentators consider this kind of stuff the most profound because it gives them a chance to write long guides and commentaries. Actually, neither the guides nor the commentaries can help the reader much.

By the way, Biblical scholars have been wondering why there are no jokes in the Bible. Many essays were written on it. One scholar thought he found half a joke in the Bible but he wasn't even certain that it was really a joke. Does this mean that God or the Prophets had no sense of humor? My own explanation is that God wanted the Bible to be understood in all languages and He knew that jokes would impede the translation. To translate a joke, a writer has to be a humorist himself. This is the reason why Gogol, Pushkin and Sholem Aleichem lose so much in translation. This is also the reason why it is so difficult to translate from Yiddish. Yiddish is a language with a built-in humor. Where in other languages are there words that do justice to such a situation?

Number 5) Since the nations did not accept Esperanto and since we are living in an epoch where old and half-forgotten languages are being resuscitated, translation is more relevant and necessary today than at any other time. No creation in one language can fill the cultural needs of a people. In literature, in science, in every field of human endeavor we are in need of translations and I sometimes think that in many cases the translator is more important than the original writer. Looking down on translators can be compared to looking down on women. We cannot do without them. The one who said that a translator is a traitor must have subconsciously compared the translator to a female. Translation must become not only an honorable profession, but an art. While I don't like bloody revolutions, I would love to see a translator's revolution. Translators are the ones who really should be liberated. In all of literature they have been the pariahs, suffering the scorn of the critics and seldom hearing a good word. When the book was good, the author got all the credit and when the book was bad, they blamed the translator.

Let this conference be the beginning of a rebellion, where ink instead of blood will be shed.

Many a prophet has prophesied that radio, movies and television would make language less important. Instead literature of every kind is becoming more important from day to day. There is a real explosion of publishers, writers, journalists. More typewriters are produced each year. Even the computers do a lot of writing. The less physical work people will do, the more they will write. There are entire buildings and even entire streets where the only sounds heard are the tapping of typewriter keys. We all know the expression: "In the beginning there was the Logos," but it seems that the Logos will even play a bigger part at the end. Allow me to quote a saying of one of my heroes: "Man will end up by eating words, drinking words, marrying words, getting drunk on words." The very essence of hypnotism is language, and since every language contains unique truths not to be found in any other language, translation is the very spirit of civilization. In my younger days I used to dream about a harem full of women, lately I'm dreaming of a harem full of translators. If those translators could be women in addition, this would be Paradise on earth.

Translation, Modernization, and Related Problems in the Spanish Language

Victor Alba (Pedro Pages)

I would like to speak to you, my colleagues of P.E.N., about three related subjects, three subjects which are not especially relevant to you as American translators but perhaps should be known to you all because they are a part of a very special situation of translators in other countries. These subjects are: translators under dictatorship; translators of very small languages; and translators in underdeveloped countries. In fact, all three of these can be related to underdevelopment because, of course, dictatorship is political underdevelopment, and a minor language is a kind of cultural underdevelopment. And these are basically not practical or tangible problems so much as moral problems for the translator.

*

For instance, what can a translator do under dictatorship in which there is: always a censorship system—and generally a very severe, very tight censorship, so that the translator has sometimes to traduce the author if he wants the work to be published? For instance, until recently in Spain, where censorship never accepted four-letter words (which in Spanish are much longer, and more picturesque and full of imagery than in English), he must forget about four-letter words—just fail to translate them—to get the book accepted. Or he must be faithful to the original in his translation and then risk that the book not be published.

115

In the matter of four-letter words it is not so important perhaps, but sometimes it is a matter of political vocabulary. I know some countries in which the censorship does not accept the word *citizen* and replaces it by *subject,* a very graphic and real word in those areas. What must a translator do? Accept the changes or give up translating books that can be useful to the reader. But, say, the problem for him is that he has to diminish the author in order to be loyal to the reader, or forget about the reader in order to be loyal to an author who will then not be published at all just because the translator has been loyal to him. And besides, in the countries concerned, translators are not in general professional ones; in underdeveloped countries there are no professional translators at all, they are people who write or people who teach and who translate besides. In many of these countries, translating has helped a lot of people to go on writing and keeping their manuscripts in the desk drawer. If they must remain absolutely faithful to the original text, I am sure that at the outside they will be permitted to translate a few mysteries, and perhaps some westerns; and then, of course, they will have to unlearn how to write their own works.

What is the solution? I have no answer and I'm sure you have no answer either. Nor can I even think about a question to my question; it is just an impossible situation which we have to resolve case by case and, of course, we cannot do any single thing about it but just fight against censorship in general.

Specifically in Spain, things are now—and I'm speaking now only about book censorship—a little better. For instance, we have grown in some way from the period of incest to the period of the triangle. Up to some years ago, in the movies and even in some books, it was impossible to speak of or to present an amorous triangle. Lovers did not exist, so the solution was that the lover became the sister or the brother. And you had a lot of movies which were a kind of propaganda for incest. Now we have the lover, we have the triangle, but still the bedroom doors are closed. My impression is that somebody in authority is just beginning to open the bedroom door, and that that is the next stage.

In politics—I mean in political literature—we can more or less assume that the evolution of the situation will be similar.

*

Another problem with which I have lived personally very closely, and which exists in many underdeveloped countries, is the problem of the very small languages. My language, for instance, is

Catalan not Spanish. When I write in Spanish, I translate my own language. Catalan is spoken by approximately five million people. There are other languages in a similar situation. And there are sometimes very good, outstanding poets and novelists, especially poets, who write in those languages. (For some strange reason, persecuted languages are much better at introducing poets than novelists or essayists or dramatists to a world readership.) I think it is a loss for the general culture, for the general intellectual life of the world if these people are not known simply because they write in, shall we say, very small languages.

When I was in France, and was discussing this with Camus—and Camus was a very generous man—he gave a lot of time to translate (with my help or just my knowledge of Catalan) some Catalan poets who were then published in France. But that is no solution to the problem. We do not have a Camus every day.

In helping to resolve this problem, you of International P.E.N. can be helpful. I don't know what the practical solution would be but, by experience, I would say that the best possible solution would be to work with somebody from the country. Normally, you will not learn Lithuanian or Catalan or some dialect used in the south of Italy, but you can find people there who know English well and who could work with a good English translator. For instance, a translator from Spanish could work in this way to translate some of the work of these people. This is admittedly not an ideal solution, but I have been thinking about this and, as I have said, it is the only practical solution I have found. Perhaps in this, P.E.N. could establish some kind of study group or something like it, a working group, to suggest some practical solutions, then something could be done, perhaps with the help of some foundation or even some publishing house. When you belong to one of the very small languages you cannot even submit your manuscripts or your books to anybody outside your small, small country. Because nobody reads the language! This is a major cultural loss that the P.E.N. could take steps to prevent.

*

The third problem, which is for me a very difficult problem to explain because I am passionate about it and cannot be objective, is the damned problem of the damned expert. *You* know what an expert is. Not a technician, an expert is a man who believes he has both common sense and experience, and he disguises his lack of common sense, his lack of experience, by using a strange, magical vocabulary. You find this kind of expert in any kind of

institution: foundations, the United Nations, and a lot of universities. It so happens that in underdeveloped countries—and I'm
speaking now basically about Latin America because that is what
I know best—the works of these experts are probably more influential than literary works in moulding the mentality and the
thinking of the people. Works on sociology, on economics, on
development, on any kind of such marshmallowish, polluting activity, are very, very influential. They are read by students, by
professors, by labor leaders, even by politicians, by a lot of people
who then think in terms of these works. But the works have
been written in English, or French, or whatever, for a readership
already familiar with this jargon, and because they are used to the
jargon the readers have stripped it of its magical content. But
these books, translated into Spanish or the language of any other
underdeveloped country, still keep their magical content. It's
like the Latin used by Molière's doctors: it helps to disguise a lot
of emptiness, or perhaps a lot of thought that the authors believe
should be disguised for a very good reason.

The result is that in the countries where students, professors,
labor leaders, and politicians are at a limited cultural level of
sophistication in which words still have this magical attraction,
this special vocabulary, this jargonese, is very useful to fool people, and as long as, in underdeveloped countries, the basic mission
of the expert is to fool people, not to solve problems, or not to
seek solutions to problems, translators—and I'm not speaking here
of literary translators but of the kind of slave who works in
international organizations and institutions and foundations and so
forth—are, in fact, becoming unconscious accomplices of this
fooling of the reader. For instance, you have a beautiful expression in English which says exactly what it means: *input-output.*
This in Spanish has become *insumo-producto*, which means
absolutely nothing. When you say *insumo-producto* you can make
anybody do anything in Latin America. It is like hocus-pocus.
And politicians speak about *insumo-producto* when they want to
justify upcoming increases in surtaxes, and architects speak about
insumo-producto when they want to justify slums, and economists
speak about *insumo-producto* when they want to justify whatever
economists try to justify, which is almost everything.

But things do not have to be this way. The language has a
choice of normal words, normal expressions, which can be understood by everybody, and which can very well be used to express
whatever the experts are trying to express with their magical vocabulary.

Since this is the case, I believe that there is a moral problem for the translator belonging to an underdeveloped country: his role is to refuse to translate the magic vocabulary, the jargon, and instead to put the magic vocabulary into broadly understandable words and expressions. This means a lot of work, a lot of knowledge; it means consulting people, discussing things, being imaginative and even learning from the common language of the common man. Because this common man will then be able to judge if the work is good or bad, if it is acceptable or not; *as of now,* the work of the expert must be accepted on the expert's own word, or on his magic word, if you wish.

Of course, one cannot force translators to follow a moral line, but I think that many translators are not aware of the jargon problem because they are working in a context which is far from the common people. I further believe that if the translator were aware of this, and if you gave him really straightforward solutions, he would use those solutions, because translators—even translators for international organizations—have some sense of the language and don't like to pollute their language with this kind of jargonese. Or to impoverish the language with this kind of translation! But, for this, somebody has to find the right expressions, the right words, to find the popular way of saying the pedantic thing. And in that I believe P.E.N. also can be helpful, perhaps looking for some money from foundations and putting some very small groups to work which will study this problem, which will find the popular version of the pedantic language, and then give these findings to translators in these big organizations so that they can use this straightforward vocabulary without having to squeeze their brains. (Literary translators like to force their minds because it is exciting and a challenge. Bureaucratic translators don't. We have to find somebody who can squeeze his own brains, enjoy it, and then give this ready-made solution to the so-called scientific translators.) In this way, we will be able to prevent the experts fooling the people and perhaps they will even come to enjoy this honest work enough to enable them to fool the experts themselves.

*

These are the three points that I wanted to make; two have some practical possibilities of resolution: the one on small languages, and the one on this magical language, jargonese; and I hope that you will take these two into account and study them in the near future. The third point, the one of censorship under a dictatorship, is just a matter of not liking dictatorships and saying so very clearly. And that, I think, is all.

Languages Are Comparable Yet Unique

Helmut Braem

I am glad—very glad indeed—that no dog happens to be listening to me right now. Only a few weeks ago, I mentioned in a little talk I was giving how difficult it must be to translate the various dog languages. I was, of course, speaking about German dogs, who must be rather simple-minded creatures, for all they manage to utter is *"wau-wau."* The average English dog's vocabulary however contains at least two expressions: *"bow-wow"* and *"wuff-wuff."* But if they happen to belong to the Establishment they manage *"yip-yip"* or even *"arf-arf."* During my German talk a Spanish lady was sitiing in the front row. Beside her sat a small black dog who was gazing at me attentively. His tail twitched just a little, and when I was barking away in German or English he put his head a little to one side but remained silent. He continued to do so as I went on to ask my listeners how they managed to convey in their translations that one dog's home was in China and that he would, therefore, bark *"wang-wang"* in contrast to another who came from Japan and would bark *"wan-wan."* The small Spanish dog listened attentively to all I had to say but grew increasingly restless as I began talking about the subtle differences between the Vietnamese and Spanish dogs' languages. In Vietnam, I maintained, all dogs bark *"gau-gau,"* in Spain, however, *"hau-hau."* As soon as I had mimicked the language of Spanish dogs, the little Spanish dog in the first row uttered a yowl, jumped from his seat, dashed to me and barked enthusiastically *"hau-hau, hau-hau, hau-hau!"* There was no stopping him. And why should he be stopped anyway? At last he had met someone in Germany who understood his language. He probably never understood why his happiness was so short-lived for he had to be taken out of the room so that I could continue with my talk.

Later, it occurred to me that there might have been a far greater commotion if there had been a Rumanian dog and an Arab donkey in the audience. For mind you: regardless of whether Arab donkey or Rumanian dog, they both talk to each other in the same-sounding language—both say *"ham-ham,"* and that is why no one can tell them from each other in the dark. But we must not forget that the Arab donkey and the Rumanian dog are at least separate entities as far as their different nationalities are concerned. Think of the poor German ducks, the miserable German frogs! Both hail from the same country, both say *"quak-quak,"* both sounds seem identical to the German child's ear, and the translator wrestling with a translation from the German might have the Devil's own time trying to determine whether the *"quak-quak"* in his text was produced by a German duck or by a German frog.

Why am I telling you all this? Only to remind you that all translation starts with a revelation: namely, the discovery that the structure of each and every language depends entirely on accidental circumstances. When, as a small boy, I first visited our neighboring country, France, I listened to the roosters' crowing near the frontier—German roosters to one side, French to the other. As a matter of fact, my ear couldn't tell the difference between the two sounds—both birds shouted *"kikeriki!"* But a Frenchman explained to me that in his country roosters shouted *"cocorico!"* At that I had to marvel a little, asking myself if the French maybe had other kinds of ears than myself? Up to this very day I have not found the answer.

As time went on I began to realize that things do sound differently in different countries and are, therefore, differently pronounced. And, furthermore, that it is mere chance which determines the phonetics of onomatopoeia. Let us assume that a Danish waiter drops a trayful of crockery in Copenhagen—the resulting noise is but a faint *"kling."* To judge from that, what he has dropped must have been very delicate porcelain indeed. The English *"crash!"* makes me think of rather coarse earthenware and the Finnish *"kratz"* surely denotes a very plain, rustic type of pottery. Perhaps we should attempt to render such sound-depicting words by employing a transliteration which is in fact "in tune" with their alien origin so that their Danish,

English, Finnish or whatever derivations are preserved. But just imagine the violent impact of genuine Chinese porcelain on a genuine Chinese stone floor! A Chinese would probably utter a melodious *"Hue-lala."* But in Germany we would most likely exclaim *"Püng-Krach-Klirr!"* Of such a nature are the two (sound) worlds that separate us. And they are as different from each other as the ears that perceive them.

But language also consists of sounds that are different—and individual—with each type of speaker. A narrator of prose, for instance, will talk to us in his very own voice. A poet, a dramatist will use another type of voice. Each of these writers has transformed his voice and made it into literature. And I believe that the translator's task consists first and foremost in his *perception* of that "literary voice" in the work of the author whom he has to translate. And only if that voice has found its echo in that of the translator can the dialogue between the two begin, and only then, I believe, can a basis be found, a common ground where the translator may eventually find his *mot juste.*

But what exactly is the *mot juste?* Is there in fact such a thing? When I am translating, that question worries me and my heart begins to flutter. You must forgive me, ladies and gentlemen, for having only a German heart. It happens to beat *"bum-bum"*—in a correct two-beat. But the Sanskrit heartbeat is a triad, a beautiful *"kikirá"* while the English apparently beats in four-four time with its *"pitter-patter."* Thus will languages and heartbeats differ from one another. Languages may be comparable yet they remain unique. Let me therefore briefly give you a few more instances of onomatopoeic expressions because they will, in my opinion, most clearly demonstrate the variety and diversity of languages. If, say, a German bee is busily buzzing around the blossoms, the German child's ear registers something like *"sum-sum."* Quite obviously the insect is meant to illustrate German diligence by humming *"sum-sum"*; in contrast to that, the British bee does seem somewhat lazy for it manages only just one syllable—*"ham"* or *"bas."* Or imagine the noise a pair of scissors make. A German one says *"schnipp-schnapp,"* a *small* German one might make do with *"schnipp-schnipp."* And since English scissors also make something like *"snip-snip"*—one could argue for a long time whether English scissors originally came from Germany or vice versa. Going further into this scissors business, it appears as if the noise they make might have something to do with their quality as cutting instruments. To judge from that, Greek scissors have no sharp edge—are, in fact, jagged. This is evidenced by their *"kritz-kritz."* Chinese scissors, on the other hand, must be so very delicate, so very tiny that they are only fit to pierce cartoonist's balloons or to impale paper tigers—they utter only a gentle *"su-su."* When it comes to Italian, Spanish, or Portuguese scissors, I suspect them to bear their name undeservedly and that we would do better in terming them saws—the Italian ones to saw off babies' knuckles *("kri-kri"),* the Spanish ones wrists *("ri-ri")* and Portuguese scissors could only be used to amputate legs above the knee *("terre-terre").*

All these splendid examples are proof of a fundamental misconception—namely, that word and thought are identical. If this were in fact the case, the same idea—or thought—would sound the same in every language, with the depressing result that we would all *speak* the same language. Allow me, at this juncture, to quote Mario Wandruszka, Professor of Romance Languages and Comparative Philology at the German University of Tübingen. By the way, he is also the very first philologist in our country who has made use of the work of established *literary* translators. Last year he published a brilliantly entertaining book: *Sprachen—vergleichbar und unvergleichlich.* The book's theme is the many possibilities of translation, but its title, I am sorry to say, is untranslatable. In English it may approximately be rendered: "Languages—comparable yet unique."

Mario Wandruszka says:

> "Our own language seduces us into taking the word for the thought. This is only natural, for we have learned to comprehend the world around us in terms of our native language, we have learned to express it, to talk to it. Therefore we are deeply convinced that our world can only be real in these very terms, that we possess it only in this our mother tongue. This is a pardonable error—even a necessary one, for how would we ever be able to talk seriously, convincingly, if we did not have the (deceptive) certainty of possessing this world in our words?
>
> "Only when we begin to familiarize ourselves with foreign languages do we learn to handle forms of speech for which there obviously are no exact equivalents in our own language. And it is only through this experience that we become aware of the existence of other worlds around us.
>
> "But the study of languages [and with it its university teachers] tempts us again and again to do just that: namely, to take the word for the thought. A philologist is taught to acquire his knowledge of any language by means of its poetic manifestations. He is instructed to detect and observe subtleties of style and expression and to

interpret them. The style of a language becomes part of his world, of his reality. The more passionately he devotes himself to the study of languages, the more easily he falls prey to the temptation to believe them to be *the* world. Thus languages become values per se, making even the comparable into a unique entity. Followed to its logical conclusion this would seem to be proof of the impossibility of translation as such. This, now, is the philologist's dilemma: he can't do without translation and translating—yet he is convinced that in fact no one can really accomplish it."

Thus far Professor Wandruszka.

You will no doubt all agree with me that the very essence of a people lies in *what* its language says. But does this also hold true for the *manner in which it says it?* For, unfortunately, ideas have a habit of changing, and language cannot keep up with this—in fact, sometimes it does not notice any change at all. George Bernard Shaw once said: " Thoughts die sooner than languages." Let me quote Mario Wandruszka once again: "Languages are a mixture of mental necessity and historical accident." And we are still somewhat laboriously trying to sort out which decisions have led to mental necessities and which were prompted by historical accident. "Only comparative linguistics can show us the amount of accidental insufficiency, incidental richness and linguistic surplus there is in our languages . . ." The French, for instance, possess two words for son-in-law; *le gendre* and *le beau-fils*. But this apparent oversupply is, in fact, the opposite, for *beau-fils* is not only son-in-law but stepson! A French acquaintance of mine once complained to me about his own situation as a twofold *beau-fils:* he had two *beau-pères* for whom there was no verbal French distinction—one of them was his wife's father, the other his mother's second husband. Only when talking in German—or English, for that matter—was he able to distinguish them by calling one *Schwiegervater* (father-in-law) and the other *Stiefvater* (stepfather). The Frenchman, therefore, can make this distinction only in other languages—not his own.

Just consider the simple sentence "I'm hungry." A Frenchman will merely say: *J'ai faim*. But what am I to say in German? *Ich bin hungrig? Ich habe Hunger?* It is obvious that we have a surplus in German, a shortage in English and French. Now if you happen to ask a German why he says *Ich bin hungrig* instead of *Ich habe Hunger* or the other way round, he will either not be able to reply at all or he will have to think about it for quite a while. I have asked among a large circle of friends in Germany if there was, in fact, any difference at all between those two phrases. We argued for a long

time and finally came up with the conclusion that *Ich habe Hunger*
was more emphatic than just *Ich bin hungrig.* But what is the poor
translator to do if even Germans themselves aren't sure about the
difference? And even if the poor translator from German does
realize that there *is* some subtle difference, how is he to convey it
in the target language? He can only do so by adding a word and
saying "I am very hungry." Let us assume I have to translate "I am
very hungry" back into German; I would have to write *Ich bin sehr
hungrig.* Now I simply don't believe that there are many German
translators who would think of translating "I'm very hungry" into
Ich habe Hunger. Far be it from me to attempt to cast a slur on
my German colleagues! I merely wished to show you how important it is for a translator who is worth his salt to query his own language continually, to examine again and again the sense, the exact
meaning he wants to convey. And at this point, I believe, is the
start of what I would call truly creative translation.

Just imagine your text mentions a child who has been playing
hard all afternoon. He returns home toward evening, walks straight
into the kitchen—exhausted, yet full of the vigor of youth, and ex-
claims: "I'm hungry!" And now imagine an elderly, refined couple
who have gone to a concert performance after an early supper. The
lady feels like eating a little something—"she is hungry." Lady and
child utter the same words, but what they *feel* is something different. The translator into German is aware of this—or at least suspects
it from the book's context. He will have to weigh facts against each
other, to try and put himself into the position of the characters to
be able to decide whether to add an emphasis or whether to leave
the text as it is. And most likely he will just let the child exclaim:
Ich habe Hunger. On the other hand, the lady will most likely say
to her husband: *Ich bin hungrig.*

A similar yet subtly different game could be played with the
phrase "I'm thirsty." In German we have the two modes of expression: *Ich bin durstig* and *Ich habe Durst.* A wanderer through
the desert is not "thirsty" after an endless exhausting march, but
instead he has *Durst.* "Thirsty"—that is a condition, a lesser type of
acute *Durst.* The distinction I shall have to make as a German translator parallels that applying to "I'm hungry." But let us go one step
further: say an American, French, Italian, Spanish translator finds
alternatively *Ich bin durstig* and *Ich habe Durst* in the same text,
he may be able to conjure up even the various *kinds of drink* though
these are not specifically mentioned in the text. When we encounter
the word *Durst,* we Germans think of water, Coca-Cola, beer, soda.
They are drinks to quench our thirst. But we are *durstig* for wine,

for our first Scotch after a tiring day at the office, for a pick-me-up
or a Martini. Two quite innocuous words, these, and only grammatically distinct from each other. But upon closer inspection they will
prove not that harmless after all because, on account of their different emphasis, they are able to convey different shades of meaning.
They are telling the translator from German what the author has left
unsaid. They communicate feelings. And if the translator from German is able to spot them and to translate them correctly into the
target language then he, too, is a creative writer—someone who,
though overshadowed by the original author, yet re-creates the
latter's work or even creates it anew in another language.

The translator as a creator—he can only be a creator if he is firmly
rooted in his knowledge, his perception of words. Let me give you
another example. Three years ago, the Polish writer Witold Gombro-
wicz received the International Publishers' Award. At the same time
his most famous tale, which had already appeared in a German translation, sparked a lively discussion. The English equivalent of its title
should have been something like "The Child in the Man named
Philidor"—admittedly not a very good title, for there is no exact
equivalent to the phrase *das Kind im Manne* in English. Suffice it
to say that this phrase stems from Nietzsche's "Thus Spake Zara-
thustra": *Im ächten Manne ist ein Kind versteckt: das will spielen./
Auf, ihr Frauen, so entdeckt/ mir doch das Kind im Manne!"*
Clumsily rendered, this means "In every real man there is a child
hidden who wants to play: Go on, you women, discover this child in
man!" Oddly enough, though, the German translator had rendered
this as *"Philidor mit Kind untern ächt"*—literally "Philidor, underpinned with child"—which sounds just as mad in English as it does
in German. What had happened? The unfortunate translator had
given a literal translation from Polish and neither the publisher's
reader nor the publisher himself had realized that this must have
been an obvious Polish idiom, a generally-used metaphor. If a Pole
wants to say that there is a child hidden in man, he says "He is
underpinned with child." If the translator from Polish does not
know this it may well happen—as in this instance—that an idiomatic Polish phrase becomes an idiotic one in any other language and
that no reader will ever know what is meant by this title.

Let us stay with titles for a moment. Some years ago Max Frisch,
the Swiss author, published his novel *Stiller*. The book was a best-
seller and became very popular reading but apparently was not read
all that much. After the book had been on sale for a couple of
years, a professor of languages decided to let his German students
translate a few pages of this book into English. He had the pages

duplicated and headed the extract *Stiller*—which was the name of the
novel's hero, Anatol Stiller. "Stiller—dammit, how did you translate
this?" asked one of the students after the course. "More peace," vol-
unteered another hesitatingly. The first one replied that he thought
this sounded a bit too full of bathos. "More quiet"—that was to the
point, that was closer. Then a third student chimed in: "No, no,
that won't do at all! STILLER . . . that's undoubtedly a challenge
and can only mean *Peace now!*"

You will gather, ladies and gentlemen, that the examining Professor wasn't a bit pleased with the various translations he had been
handed and that he asked himself how popular the hero of a so-
called best-seller would have to become so that even students of literature would recognize the fact that this Stiller wasn't a comparative
of "still" (quiet, or silent).

Such examples will no doubt provide an amusing topic for critics
of literary translations, and the supply of howlers committed by
translators is wellnigh inexhaustible simply because there are, unfortunately, quite a few translators who *will* take the word—in its
literal sense—for the thought. And if this word happens to be an
idiom, and he doesn't recognize it as such, he's just had it. I remember once reading a German translation of a slight, entertaining American story in the middle of which there suddenly appeared some
kind of surrealist vision. In a small snack bar, before the very eyes
of the cook and one of his customers, a raft was sliding or floating
across the quick-lunch counter bearing the first couple on earth—
Adam and Eve. I was fascinated—by the cook as well as by his
customer—neither of whom seemed to find anything extraordinary
in this. As it was the only truly surrealist scene in this book, I first
of all didn't believe my own eyes, then I wondered about the
author's and finally about the translator's. What had happened?
The cook had slid across the counter nothing more nor less than a
plate of bacon and eggs—known to the trade as "Adam and Eve on a
Raft"—and the translator, taking the author at his word, had come
up with this vision of our ancestors floating across the counter on
some kind of island made from tree trunks such as Mark Twain's
youthful heroes used to float down the waters of the Mississippi. And
all this, if you please—and to quote Hemingway— in "A Clean, Well-
Lighted Place"!

Let's return to comparisons. There are, according to my own
reckoning, sixty-one German slang synonyms for the word "money"
—that is, for both coins and notes. And, as regards money, I am convinced there are an equally great number of American slang expressions—if not more. I remember reading in the works of Sinclair

Lewis, and in some other fairly old crime stories, the word "bone" to indicate a silver dollar. Of course, I fail to see what a "bone," indicating a dollar, could possibly have in common with the human skeleton, but I can always tell without fail from the context whether a piece of a skeleton is meant or a piece of money. Yet it can happen that you read at one of the crucial points in a thrilling tale of crime and pursuit translated for the benefit of eager German readers: *"Die Dame in Schwarz im Taxi schob dem Fahrer fünf Knochen über die Schulter."* Translated back this would read approximately like this: "The lady in black was pushing five pieces of skeleton across the driver's shoulder." . . . Or five bones equalling five dollars. It would have been so easy to find an equivalent German idiom—*Mäuse* (mice) or *Müpse* (pugs).

It is extraordinary how the word "Geld" (money) can be multiplied in the various different languages. Linguistically speaking, there is an oversupply of "money"; unfortunately, it does not match the cash supply of the translator. And such oversupplies in several languages—especially in the linguistic underground—make me doubt that there should *always* be the *only* really matching, apt expression in the target language of the translator. Someone—I forgot who it was—once said: "The words offering themselves in the course of a translation can be compared to a bunch of keys to open a lock. Some don't fit at all, others slide effortlessly into the keyhole, but only *one* of them springs it in the end." This is a good, a very convincing simile. But I have long given up believing in any kind of rules while translating a text; after all, there are also exceptions to language rules and the 'system' of languages is, in fact, non-systematic.

It may be, therefore, that we have a great many words in our own language for the one we have to translate, or it may just be the other way around. Sometimes we have none at all. This is brought home sharply when we consider the ambiguity of many words. Think of the Romance languages which present, as far as blood relationships are concerned, such a very paternalistic type of image. In Spanish *los padres* (the fathers) can also mean the parents; *los hermanos* (the brothers) can also mean the 'community' of brothers and sisters; *los hijos* are the sons—but also the children—of both sexes. The same holds true for the Portuguese and Italian languages and, in part, also for the English language. None of them possesses a word for the unit *brother and sister* for which there is a German word *Geschwister*. If this word occurs in a German text, the English translator will have to say: *brother and sister* or *brothers and sisters* or *brother and sisters* or *brothers and sister*—according to the numbers and sexes of

each. The same difficulties are encountered by French, Italian, Spanish, Portuguese translators from German. I quote Professor Wandruszka once more: "Should there really be, in the imagination of the
English and French *no* conception at all of the *combined* image of
brothers and sisters as *Geschwister?* Or does perhaps this total picture in fact *equal* the phrase *brothers and sisters, frères et soeurs* in
the same way in which the Italians, Spaniards, Portuguese say *i fra-
telli, los hermanos* and *os irmãos* to include the sister or sisters? If
this is in fact the case—and everything points to it that, today, there
is no different conception of the thing as such in any of the modern
European languages, does this not also mean that what is called the
'verbal world image' does no longer convince us, if our ideas and con-
ceptions are so far in advance of our verbal expressions? Language is
the tool of the spirit, it is *not* the spirit itself."

Therefore, I see the modern translator no longer as a proponent
of Wilhelm von Humboldt's thesis that the diversity of our languages
is proof of a "diversity of *Weltanschauung*" (or world-image). This
thesis appears to me to be based upon a fundamental error, the
logical maxim "Who has the word, possesses also the thing, who
lacks the word, lacks the thing, who has no word for *Gemüt* (mind,
nature, temperament, heart, disposition, emotion, feeling), has no
Gemüt. Such a claim would be just as nonsensical as that he who
had no word for *Geschwister*(brothers and sisters) *had* no *Geschwister* (brothers and sisters)"—to quote Wandruszka once more.

Perhaps we should compromise and agree that no one language
discloses everything, that therefore most sentences need to be understood in their context. If there is no context, the translator is
either obliged to guess or to make use of his knowledge of the country whose language he has to translate. It is sometimes not easy to
distinguish between a translator's guesswork (maybe he was right
in guessing) or his creative translation. In one of Daphne du Maurier's novels there is a dinner party being held in an English castle.
It is the first dinner party after the death of the lady of the house
who had passed away four months previously. They had always
eaten very well when the lady of the house was still alive, and now, it
seems the culinary standard has not changed either. The late lady's
brother wants to compliment the host and remarks: "Same cook,
I suppose, Maxim?" Cook: male or female? The French, Italian,
Spanish, German translator must make a snap decision. The book's
context doesn't help him one little bit, for Daphne du Maurier never
mentions the cook again. The French and German translators
decided for *la même cuisinière,* the same (lady)-cook; they had
imagined the cook as being female. The Italian and Spanish transla-

lators plumped for a man: *lo stesso cuoco, el mismo cocinero.* I myself am on the side of the Italian and Spanish translators, because a male cook is more distinguished than a female one, and I, as a reader, could think of *him* rather than of *her* as being engaged in the kitchen of a castle and preparing such opulent meals.

In other languages than English, either the article or the ending tells me what gender we are talking about. But are those other languages therefore more exact than English? Are they perhaps not more cumbersome? Does not the context suffice, as a rule, to tell us whether we are dealing with a male or female person? *Cook,* as used in Daphne du Maurier's tale, poses the same question to every English reader as well. It is left to his experience to imagine a female or a male cook. In another novel of Daphne du Maurier's, *My Cousin Rachel,* which also features a cook we are not left in any doubt at all. A parson's wife complains to an acquaintance that her scullery maid is expecting a child from the gardener's boy: "What I cannot understand, Mrs. Ashley, is *where* it happened. . . She shared a room with my cook . . ." Now cooks are rarely found in rectories to begin with, and if there had been one, *he* would not have shared a room with the scullery maid. The translators interpreted the situation correctly and have written: *la cuisinière, la cuoca, la cocinera, die Köchin.* Language, therefore, implies by what it says that which it leaves unsaid; it rarifies, differentiates, modifies what is said by the unsaid. Or, to quote José Ortega y Gasset: ". . . the immense difficulty of translation: it is a question of saying something in a language which, as a rule, this language suppresses."

Therefore I am convinced that, apart from his languages, a good translator must also have a flair for what is left unsaid—what is merely implied—so that he can render what *is* said into his own language adequately. It is this special sense, or sensitivity, of the artist who is fashioning art with the tools of language—or who re-fashions it. I am fighting a bit shy of the term *creator*—an expression which has several layers of meaning in English; in German it points strongly toward *Schöpfer,* a term which hamstrings me a little. For *Schöpfer*—creator—in German implies a philosophical concept, with overtones of the Romantic Age, with metaphysical implications; and the translator is not a metaphysician but a craftsman whittling away at the hardwood of language. And sometimes he does this with great artistry, he becomes a creative craftsman. And this, I feel, should be his image in our world today.

I am certain you all know the simile coined by Cervantes, who once compared a translation with the reverse side of a beautiful carpet. This side should allow one to recognize quite clearly the mar-

velous texture, gorgeous pattern, magnificent colors of the carpet's
right side. This comparison has been out of fashion for a long time,
because people believed that a translation could only be good if it
did not appear to be one. Recently, however, there has been a rever-
sal of opinion to the effect that a translation must allow an alien element to shine through the fabric of language—the target language
should become richer, more expressive by our translation; that we,
as translators should not stubbornly cling to what just happens to be
"correct" at this very moment in our own language; that we should
make it up; that in a German translation from the American, the
Greek, Spanish, Italian, Polish, etc., the Polish, Italian, Spanish,
Greek, American should still be shining through the woof and warp
of our words. The same holds true for foreign slang. I feel I should
not translate slang into some regionally fixed dialect: a Negro from
Faulkner's Yoknapatawpha County cannot sound like a Berliner, and
a New York cab driver isn't working in Munich or Oberammergau.
When I translate slang I have to fashion a new, an artificial language
which has a slightly foreign tinge in my own language. Here we may
truly speak of a creative process: a beautiful carpet isn't just being
reversed, it is being woven anew according to the author's original
pattern. But, alas, it isn't always that you, as translators, will have
to reverse or re-weave beautiful carpets. Only too often books are
no more than coconut matting. And you can reverse and reverse
them—coconut matting remains coconut matting, no matter on
what side.

But if we *do* happen to handle beautiful and valuable carpets,
our translating becomes a task poised between science and art and
the result is artistic reproduction. We ourselves must be stylists
and be able to think of a number of things simultaneously and to
synthesize them. A truly gifted translator will be able to make an
instantaneous choice from a number of verbal alternatives. The
English and the German translator working from Romance languages must be able to differentiate, in his pre-conscious, if he will
have to translate *les fleurs, i fiori, las flores* with "blossoms" or
"flowers," with *Blüten* or *Blumen.* The same applies to the English
translator who is able to distinguish between "flesh" and "meat"
but who will find in his original text only one German word:
Fleisch. A translator from the Spanish will have to be on the alert
if the word "fish" denotes an animal swimming about *(el pez)* or if
it is ready to be eaten *(el pescado).* In each case, one language is
richer than the other. And while translating we often find that the
wealthier of the two enriches the poorer, enlarges it, extends it by
new words, new stylistic methods, in fact *coins* it anew.

And this requires that the translator keep himself au courant with each and every change in his "working" language, that he travel frequently in those countries whose languages he translates. Fortunately, in my own country, the Bonn Government has acknowledged this necessity by awarding grants to translators enabling them to spend some time abroad so as to deepen their knowledge of languages, to widen and modernize their vocabulary. There are about two thousand translators in Western Germany, and every year this grant is awarded to just *one* of them! We therefore have made sure that within the next two thousand years each one of our two thousand translators will have received a grant. I do hope Number 2000 will live to receive his traveling money. Ladies and gentlemen, now I am sure you can imagine how happy I am and how grateful to the American Center of P.E.N. not to have to wait fifty or five hundred years to be able to visit the United States.

Once back home, I shall take up my work again, eternally doubting, eternally hoping—just as you will. And maybe we shall all one day, seated at our writing desks, perish in the attempt to achieve the ideal translation. Perhaps we shall emulate the Chinese workman who wanted to smelt together two metals, two pure elements, into an alloy with entirely new properties and who ended up by throwing himself into the red-hot mixture so that the holy bond would be achieved.

Translating from Yiddish

Irving Howe

Together with a Yiddish poet named Eliezer Greenberg, a young man in his seventies, I have been occupied intermittently for the past few years in putting together a volume called *A Treasury of Yiddish Poetry*. It is perhaps the first effort to present modern Yiddish poetry, which begins in the late nineteenth century, in some sort of coherent scheme in English translation. I want to say a few words about the problems we encountered in this effort.

I would say that our problems fell into three categories: first, those which pertained to the formal nature of the genre, the distinctiveness of verse; secondly, those which pertain to special qualities of Yiddish, its syntax, vocabulary, grammar and sources; and thirdly, those which pertain to the special aspects of the culture in which Yiddish poetry was written, and then to the special aspects of the culture in which translations of Yiddish poetry are now being received. In my judgment, the greatest difficulties in translation, at least from the Yiddish, are cultural, rather than linguistic and formal, great as these latter difficulties nevertheless are. We had to try to work out some kind of collective policy concerning what kind of translations we wanted, and we could only feel our way into that policy.

Robert Frost says poetry is what disappears in translation. It is hard to fault this, except that empirically we know that some poetry

135

comes through in translation. Auden said that there must be some elements in poetry which are separable from their original verbal expression, and he lists technical conventions and devices and something that he said he can only describe as a tone of voice. He then goes ahead to say that to the degree that a poem is a product of a distinctive culture, it is virtually untranslatable into another culture, but to the degree that it is a product of a distinctive sensibility, it is translatable. This was one of our great—even insuperable—problems, in that the more distinctively and uniquely Yiddish was the cultural context and tone of a writer, the harder he proved to be to translate. Here the decisive case is that of the founder of modern Yiddish literature, Mendele Mokher Sforim, Mendele the Bookseller, who probably never has been or will be satisfactorily translated into English. Yet he is in some sense the quintessentially Yiddish writer. Among poets, one of the major Yiddish poets of the twentieth century, H. Leivick, seemed peculiarly difficult to translate partly because his "rhetorical quotient" is higher than one can readily adjust to in another language, and partly because his Messianic-sacrificial world-outlook is extremely difficult to make intelligible to English readers. Leivick himself is not at the center of the Yiddish world-outlook, yet he is a major schismatic figure in whom the stress upon the moral sanctity of suffering exceeds that common to Yiddish culture. The difficulty, then, is that we could not expect our English reader to know what the norm was from which this great writer was deviating, and to which he sometimes returned.

We had endless discussions among ourselves and our translators concerning whether we were going to move toward the literalism advocated by Nabokov, on the one hand, or toward the "imitations" done by Robert Lowell, on the other. We tried to steer a course between the two. We adopted rather the position of Dudley Fitts who I think was one of the great translators of our age, and who wrote concerning the Nabokov position which favors the thoroughly documented rendering:

> The trouble is that such a translation, though it gives the prose
> 'sense' of the original together with an explanation of whatever goes
> to lift the prose sense above itself and transmute it into a form of
> art, might also provide no evidence beyond the saying so that the
> art was art in the first place. We need something at once less am-
> bitious and more audacious: another poem.

That, roughly, was our view. For especially in regard to the translation of Yiddish poetry, of which there is very little in English, the

Nabokov position was impossible, since its whole premise is a high degree of familiarity with the culture from which the material is being translated. And for exactly the same reason, the method of Robert Lowell, if one can call it that, also proved to be impossible. Lowell's improvisatory and impressionistic method makes sense on two premises. First, that you have a poet of Lowell's genius who is doing it; we are not, in truth, very interested in the improvisations of less distinguished writers. Second, that there already is available a whole series of relatively accurate translations of the poem in question, so that even if we do not know the original, we have some rough sense of the standard norm of previous translations from which Lowell is deviating. But no such materials were available in respect to Yiddish poetry and consequently, we could not even conceive of using such an approach. We adopted the position of Fitts—that is, trying to render the poem in translation as *another* poem, which realistically means a different and inferior poem. No one would care to pretend that many of our translations are as good as the original poems, but we were concerned with communicating at least some of the prose sense of the originals; and this, it is worth remarking, often proved to be most workable with the more modernistic of the Yiddish poets. The older Yiddish poets, inclined as they were toward a folkloristic lyricism, proved to be extraordinarily difficult to translate; and the very first group of Yiddish poets in America— known as the sweat-shop poets—it was all-but-impossible to translate, since what came out in English often sounded like doggerel and exhortatory radical verse.

The second group of problems that we faced are linguistic, though it is hard to make a sharp distinction between these and the cultural ones. On the simplest but most exasperating level, there is the problem of a distinctive terminology associated with religious and cultural traditions for which English has no equivalents. Two examples: Cynthia Ozick did a lovely translation of a lovely poem by a Yiddish poet named David Einhorn. In that poem, the term *ba'al tefilla* occurs. I am not entirely sure how to translate this term except to say it refers to a rather commonplace version of a cantor, one who does a workaday version of the work of the cantor. Or he is the equivalent of a cantor in a very poor synagogue. In any case, there is no precise English translation, though there were plenty of didactic and explanatory terms for this word. But an explanatory phrase, which might go well in expository prose, obviously could not work in poetry. The only solution we could come to in regard to this crucial word upon which the original poem depended, was evasion. We cut past the impossible linguistic core of the original, and

looked for phrases of a suggestive kind. What we unavoidably lost
thereby was the distinctive cultural aura of that poem.

Another example is a poem by a very gifted Yiddish woman writer, Kadia Molodowsky. "God of Mercy" is a poem in which after
the holocaust she beseeches God to cease considering the Jews as the
"chosen" people: they've had enough of being "chosen." The very
last line, for anyone who knows Yiddish, comes with great rhetorical force. I happened to translate that poem, not terribly well, and
the final three lines of the English translation read "And God of
Mercy/Grant us one more blessing—/Take back the gift of our separ-
ateness." The last line is not a literal translation. I suppose a literal
translation would read something like this: "Take back from us
the holy spirit of our distinctive genius," which would be splendid
in a dissertation, but not in a poem. And so we had, as it were, once
again to engage in evasion, the evasion consisting in that there is not
available in English language the distinctive, precisely demarcated
vocabulary of the Hebraic religious tradition.

There were other linguistic difficulties. Yiddish is an unsettled
language, which reached whatever degree of stability in structure and
usage a living language can reach a good deal later in its development
than have most Western languages. It was constantly invaded by alien
vulgarism and constantly renewed by alien vitality, and it has therefore retained a greater freedom for verbal improvisation than has
modern English. There are various usages in Yiddish, such as playful
transpositions of parts of speech, that simply do not come across in
English. As a result, Yiddish poetry in translation tends to seem
less experimental and verbally fresh than it actually is in the original.

Another linguistic problem and perhaps the most serious of all is
that much Yiddish poetry is in effect bilingual—though even to put
the matter this way seems erroneous since it implies that a Yiddish
poet who employs a Biblical phrase in Hebrew is consciously turning
to another language. He is not, at least most of the time. He is
merely sliding, so to speak, by the most natural of processes, into a
Hebrew usage, perhaps drawn from Biblical association or memories of
prayer, that is just as much part of his experience as street Yiddish.
In effect, all writers of Yiddish, for the last hundred years, use a linguistic scale from street Yiddish on the one extreme to Biblical
Hebrew on the other. There are some Yiddish writers—for example
the religious poet, Aaron Zeitlin—of whom it is useful to think that
they write not in one but simultaneously in two languages. In the
work of some Yiddish poets now living in Israel there is likely to be
a heavy infusion of modern Hebrew, more so than with Yiddish poets
who come from Eastern Europe or who gained their education in

America. Now, for the translator, the likelihood of being able to render such linguistic shadings is very small, for even though he can fall back on the English of the King James Bible, he is in effect translating from two languages into one. This, I think, is one of the central linguistic difficulties in the translation of Yiddish.

In the end, however, the main difficulties were, I believe, cultural. Yiddish literature, especially in the classical phase that begins in the last third of the nineteenth century, carries a weight of historical associations and cultural assumptions that is not likely to be fully apprehended by the reader who is unfamiliar with the tradition of Yiddish, that is, with the whole Yiddish cultural milieu. Similar difficulties may no doubt arise in translating from any other language, but here the difficulties are especially acute because the culture of *Yiddishkeit* is at some considerable distance from that of the whole Western world. Modern English, French and Russian poetry may be packed with obscure allusions, but often these are no more obscure in translation than they are in the original. Their obscurity is, so to say, individual, unique to the particular poet; it derives neither from linguistic peculiarities nor historical particulars. By contrast, Yiddish contains allusions so deeply imbedded in the particularist tradition of Yiddish and the Yiddish world, as well as the more general Jewish tradition going back to Biblical Hebrew, that it seldom offers much guidance to the alien reader. So remarkably close-grained is Yiddish culture, that the writer in the original could assume that his reader is immediately prepared to grasp a Talmudic reference, a Hasidic refrain, an in-group witticism; and the greatest of all Yiddish writers, Sholem Aleichem, assumes that his mangling of Biblical quotations, a deliberate and playful mangling, will be caught by the Yiddish reader who has enough Hebrew to recognize the verbal and intellectual play that is involved. (If he isn't witty or learned enough to catch it, so much the worse for him.) The difficulty of reproducing all this in English is really beyond conception. In fact, it has never been done. A translator from Yiddish is therefore faced with the temptation, usually to be resisted, of weaving some commentary and gloss into his translation.

More starkly put: when you translate from French to German, or Russian to English, you are dealing with cultures both of which are fundamentally Christian. When you translate from Yiddish into any of these languages, you have a new and enormous cultural gap. Despite all the pieties about the Judaeo-Christian tradition, the truth of the matter is that we have two sharply different traditions at stake. Quite apart from the distinctive linguistic content, it is an enormous difficulty to communicate the cultural and historical aura of a work in one tradition into the language of another.

Now these differences make themselves felt on many levels. One
concerns the whole question of sexuality. There is a far greater degree of sexual reticence in Yiddish poetry and in most Yiddish prose
than is characteristic of Western writing at the present time. From
this the uninformed reader can form all kinds of mistaken impres-
sions, and in extreme cases may even wonder how the Jews perpe-
tuated themselves. At the least, he may wonder if there were romantic feelings among Jews in the old country.

Second and more important, the quotient of sentimentalism is
radically different in Yiddish from that of most Western cultures.
We tend to assume that there is a fixed conception of what sentimentality consists of, when actually the idea of sentimentality is
itself culturally formed and determined. The idea of the sentimental in Yiddish is radically different from that of Western culture.
As a consequence, something which suggests an element of restraint
in one culture will seem to lack it in the other.

Thirdly, and I think technically most interesting: there is in
general a higher "rhetorical charge" in Yiddish than in English or,
as far as I can see, in the other European languages. So that—I give
it away as a trade secret—all translators from Yiddish, good, bad
and indifferent, have somewhat to mute, to soften, to tone down
the original text. Yiddish seems inherently—or is it just a cultural
illusion?—more oratorical, more rhetorically charged than English.
There is a difference, so to say, in cultural temperature, and this
makes for enormous problems.

Fourth, another major cultural difference: Yiddish poetry seems
constantly to be approaching yet backing away from modernism.
To an English reader who has been brought up mainly on modernist
literature, that is, the school of Eliot, Yiddish poetry may at first
seem "old-fashioned," lacking in metaphoric innovation, deficient
in imagistic virtuosity, excessively rationalistic and didactic. In
part, such an impression would depend upon an insufficient familiarity with the historical conditions of Yiddish poetry; why it
constantly approaches yet can never entirely yield itself to modernism. A parallel difficulty arises in regard to the subject matter of
Yiddish poetry, indeed of all Yiddish literature, that is, the difficulty our imaginary cultivated reader finds in understanding why it
is that so much Yiddish literature deals with the fate, the collective
destiny of the Jews in general, rather than with the experience of
the Jew as an individual. Here too it is a matter of radically different
historical circumstances. At each point where Yiddish literature
began to venture into subjectivity, individualism and problematical
extremism, it was forced by historical circumstances to retreat, to
return to its earlier primary concern, the distinctive condition and
martyrdom of Jewish existence.

Finally, let me turn to another group of historical circumstances that make difficult the English reader's approach to Yiddish poetry— those having to do not so much with the culture in which it was written as the culture in which it is being received. The momentary interest in things Jewish which came over American culture at the end of World War II now seems close to an end. And the feeling toward Yiddish among American Jews is at the very least ambivalent. I am convinced that there is a deep resistance, which often takes the form of sentimental nostalgia, to the whole of the Yiddish experience among those who have emerged from it. What they want is to remember it while keeping it safely tucked away in memory; they do not want it to be a part of their living experience. And in Yiddish literature they have no interest at all, except insofar as it can vulgarly be misperceived as "Jewish jokes." This whole complex of feelings, so painful and elusive, obviously plays its part in the reception of translated Yiddish poetry.

A more serious response has been a complaint that our work has evoked among some more-or-less knowledgeable American Jewish reviewers. Their complaint, not without a certain justice, has been that we have given a kind of modernist emphasis to the history of Yiddish poetry, favoring those poets who are closest to us in spirit and tone. We omitted a number of the early figures, most of the sweat-shop poets, some of the nationalistic Jewish socialists, stirring lyricists as they used to be called; these are often the writers whom some of our reviewers read or heard recited when they went to the *Mittelshule,* the Yiddish schools in America, during their youth. These poets stirred them years ago with their noble rhetoric, and since then, it may be, they have not taken a close look at what has been happening to Yiddish poetry. What such reviewers wanted —and here nostalgia proves to be culturally crippling—is to have their memories stirred up once again yet not to be further troubled by the subsequent history, the inner transformation of Yiddish poetry.

This problem is intensified by the larger difficulties of Yiddish culture in America. Historically speaking, it must face the tragic possibility that, as a distinctive sub-culture based on linguistic attachment, it will soon be coming to an end. To say this does not mean that the Jewish experience or the Jewish community or the Jewish religion is coming to an end; not at all. It means only that a certain phase of the Jewish experience may be coming to an end: that phase in which the great majority of American Jews used Yiddish as their daily language, sometimes their only language, so that the culture they created from it arose organically and sponta-

neously out of their experience. A prominent force in that culture
was the literary criticism which, in the work of such gifted men as
Niger, Rifkin and Tabachnik, devoted itself with care and affection to
the work of Yiddish literature. Today, by contrast with thirty or
thirty-five years ago, there is not much serious literary criticism
being written in Yiddish. As a result, estimates of finished careers
and past work tend to become static and frozen, more a reflection
of received pieties than of living relationships. But when you edit an
anthology of Yiddish poetry, regardless of whether you do it well or
poorly, you must engage not merely with the problems of translation
but also with those of criticism. Choices signify judgments. This
poet deserves four pages, that one twenty pages, still another had
best be left out because he is mainly of historical interest to those
within the narrowing Yiddish cultural world, and a fourth should
be featured because his work happens to be of a kind that can be
successfully rendered in English.

I try to explain this to my Yiddish friends through an example:
If they had done an anthology of American poetry forty years ago,
they would surely have given a larger place to Longfellow, Holmes
and Lowell than would probably be the case if an anthology of
American poetry were translated into Yiddish at the present moment.
This is a change in literary estimate that seems not a mere fashion
but decisive and lasting.

The trouble is, however, that since there is not enough active
literary criticism and reconsideration going on within the Yiddish
cultural world itself, we were forced—not because we relished the
prospect or supposed we would be exempt from attack—to undertake a summary critical estimate of the various poets if we were
to have an anthology at all. And precisely those who know a little,
sometimes those who know a good deal, about Yiddish poetry
were the ones who found themselves disturbed, for in truth our
anthology did imply certain (not very radical) shifts in critical
opinion about the Yiddish literary past.

A final point. In working on our anthology, one of the main
things I learned was the extent to which translation from Yiddish
depends on far more than linguistic skill. It depends above all on
a command of what I can only call the cultural aura, the buzz and
hum of the implications of Yiddish. Sometimes we used a method
that in principle I cannot defend. We had some American poets of
considerable gifts who do not know Yiddish. Greenberg and I would
work out a very precise and literal prose translation and then we did
a great deal of notation, such as description of the syntax, the form,
the meter. Then these poets did an English version which we checked

back against the original Yiddish. We tried to be strictly accurate in these cases. We did not want "imitations," we wanted translations.

What we established here in effect was a cultural chain. First, from these translators to myself who am an amateur in this field, and whose knowledge of the Jewish tradition is severely limited and whose knowledge of Yiddish is fairly limited. Then, from myself to Greenberg, a veteran Yiddish poet, and then of course from Greenberg to the whole Yiddish tradition itself. This chain is terribly precarious. It can be snapped at any number of points. So that the problem for the future of Yiddish translation into English is not to find people who know the meaning of the words or can look them up in the dictionary, but to have available, at a time when most Jews are ceasing to use Yiddish, a corps of experts who would maintain the tradition, who would have a sense of cultural aura and of cultural associations, so that those who wanted to engage in the technical work of translation would have a resource to turn to for control and for check. Now in some ways of course, this is a tragic proposal but so too, it seems, is the situation that prompts it.

On Translating from Russian

Moura Budberg

I would like to start with a devastating quotation from the Book of
Genesis: "Go to, let us go down and there confound their language
that they may not understand one another's speech."

This was God's punishment on the people of Babel. And what a
punishment! The curse God put on Adam in the Garden of Eden
was nothing compared to that.

We, the translators, came along much later, in an ever-expanding
world, to reverse the trend, to make good the damage, to "un-con-
found" the language. We became the links, the liaison officers, the
treasure sharers, the reconcilers of the often irreconcilable, the
tearers-down of barriers. Fancifully, I see us as a vast army scrib-
bling away all over the globe and over all the years, a network of
industrious, often underpaid, much maligned working men and
women, holding the world together often against the will of
the world, fending off the ever-increasing confusion. *Traduttore*—
traitors—the Italians call us.

Much has come to be expected of us, often the impossible, and
much has come to be taken for granted. To look on the black side
first and get it out of the way, I will tell you what, to my despair,
John Lehmann says of translation: "To talk of translation is rather
like talking about the glass in front of a picture, when it is the picture itself that engrosses our attention."

145

A sad, very sad view, to my mind, when, in fact, without us the picture might rarely be seen at all! In fact, at this point, and in parenthesis, I shall read a little verse about the dead languages which
might have been much deader than they are if it hadn't been for us:

> We never read Euripides!
> Only Professor Murray
> Has time for such in days like these.
> We never READ Euripides,
> But sometimes in our hours of ease
> We skim through in our hurry.
> We never read Euripides,
> Only Professor Murray.

In fact, of course, we know the importance of what we do. A translator's reward is the pleasure that flows from the intellectual exercise
while his talents may not lie in the production of original literature.
The results can be breath-taking and not just any old scribbler will do.
The tools of the trade—linguistic knowledge and fluency of language
—are not the only qualities required. One needs knowledge, endless
patience, great scrupulosity, and a capacity for self-denial, a sense of
humor and an acute and sensitive ear.

In the Sunday *Times,* Raymond Mortimer has written about Arthur
Waley's remarkable translations from the Chinese and Japanese.
Waley maintained that the translator must be someone who delights
in using words and cannot rest until he has put the work that has
excited his imagination into a language comprehensible to others. It
was to match the monosyllabic verse of the Chinese that he invented
his rhythm.

Sympathy—even more, a familiarity with the subject—is essential.
Sympathy with the feelings of the author—for, in the absence of
such sympathy, why undertake the task? And also, most certainly,
a knowledge of the art of how not to use dictionaries. In that connection, I knew an enthusiastic Russian gentleman who got carried
away by his own self-confidence and translated an entire short story
into English without any knowledge of the language whatsoever,
solely with the aid of an enormous dictionary. I can't remember
the details, but the result was the most hilarious piece of work I
have ever read.

There are, of course, all manner of theories about how translating
should be done. All kinds of things have been said. For example,
a translation must give the *words* of the original; or that it must
give the *ideas* of the original; that it should read like an original work,

or that it should read like a translation; that it should read as being a contemporary of the original—*or* as a contemporary of the translator. On the one hand, some believe it perfectly legitimate to add to or omit from the original while others refuse to do so.

As far as theories go, I have always striven to give the words *and* the ideas of the original, to make the work read as a contemporary of the original, and only in very exceptional circumstances to add to or omit from the original. I have disciplined my usual lack of humility and, when I have found that a phrase of my choice has been properly used already, I have not tried to be clever or alter it in any way; if that is the correct phrase to use in that particular spot, that is good enough for me. On the contrary, it gives me one more reason for its retention.

One thing I have always felt is that the truest translation would obviously come from the author himself—as, in fact, Samuel Beckett has done, writing in French and then translating the work into English—and I think one can study Beckett as a lesson in how good translations work. Second-best can only be to try to get into the author's skin, to recreate his mood, to preserve intact his methods, to sense his driving force and harness oneself to that. The aim of a translation is to recreate. That is why, of all the arts, the one nearest to translation is, I believe, that of an actor, though the actor probably projects more creative talent than does the translator.

Some of the actual mechanics of translation come, I think, only with maturity. It is not enough to be perfect in a foreign language; there is an intuitive "feel" for language that a translator without such maturity will never acquire. For example, how do you re-create a *pun,* that most tricky of all forms of speech?

When Salvador de Madariaga, Spanish Ambassador to London, was on the point of retiring, a friend put it to him: "Are you going back to your pen?" And the reply came: "Do you mean the pen I live in or the pen I live by?"

It took me rather longer recently when I was working on *The Second Notebooks of Major Thompson.* Daninos is an incorrigible punster. He had written: *"La révolution que j'accepte est celle sans guillemets et sans guillotine."* I racked my brains over that one, and it came to me quite suddenly, as these things do, in the middle of the night: "The revolution I accept has a capital R but no capital punishment."

There is no doubt that the poorer the language, the more difficult it is to translate from it, for every word in it is so precise that only that one word can be used and the abundance of synonyms, both in English and Russian, make the choice sometimes a hazardous one.

As, for instance, the word "introspection" in French signifies merely the study of one's self and has none of the implications the word has in English. Of course, sometimes, the way a translation can be misleading is well manifested in the little synopses that are made of the songs of Raquel Meller, who only sang in Spanish. Here is one of them, *"La Guia,"* given to me when I was listening to her songs.

> It is the day of the bullfight in Madrid. Everyone is cockeyed. The bull has slipped out by the back entrance to the arena and has gone home disgusted. Nobody notices that the bull has gone except Nina, a peasant girl who has come to town that day to sell her father. She looks with horror at the place in the Royal Box where the bull should be sitting and sees there instead her algebra teacher whom she had told that she was staying at home on account of a sick headache. You can imagine her feelings!

I've never known what that song was about.

Vanessa Redgrave, the English actress, told me a story about a Hungarian journalist who was interviewing her and who said: "Everybody agrees that you are a revolting actress." She was slightly taken aback by such a frank appreciation of her art. Then he went on: "Will you explain, please, why you do revolt?"

The translator must be able to put himself in someone else's shoes and to *like* being there. Similarly, he must feel at home in any country and in any period of history. And it must all be done within the strictest, most frustrating of disciplines. He must be diligent, conscientious and intuitive.

I myself, after many years as a translator, have enjoyed it all immensely. It has always seemed worthwhile and I look forward to a good few more years of work ahead. My own great love, of course, has been my work from the Russian into English—and there, of course, I had a wonderful start. Although, as you will certainly be able to hear, I speak with a strong accent, my first language was English. I had an old-fashioned English nanny who was, in fact, a very cultured woman. Ours was a large Russian household, but the first language in which I learned to read and write was English. Translation from the one to the other became second nature. I have always read widely in both languages and have loved them passionately ever since.

I can never be grateful enough to Constance Garnett, without whose skill and perseverance Russian literature might have been known to the world only much later. She translated Turgenev, Chekhov, Tolstoy, Dostoyevsky. Good or bad, they introduced something of incomparable value to the western world.

Perhaps my greatest pleasure as a translator came quite late, when
I made a new version of *The Seagull* and of *Three Sisters* by Anton
Chekhov. Our estate was in the Ukraine and, at one time, Anton
Chekhov lived not very far away. I met him only once when I was
eleven years old, but I have never forgotten the man. I remember
being impressed by his penetrating eyes and his soft, gentle voice.
He treated me as an adult and that made me very proud. That one
memory has made my work on his plays particularly personal, a kind
of second meeting, as well as a vivid link with my own early life.

I think perhaps, too, it is necessary to translate not simply with
humility, perhaps nostalgia, but with love. When I have translated
Gorky, it has been like that. I keep remembering his deep voice, the
strong Volga accent, the way he used to talk for hours into the night,
drumming his long fingers on the table in front of him.

A few years ago I was asked to translate a novel called *Evgenia
Ivanovna* by the contemporary writer, Leonid Leonov. I had known
the author for a long time, I liked him and was lucky enough to hear
him read his book to me from beginning to end. It was a good story
with an original point of view, and deeply sad. I could hardly help
but do it justice, knowing, from his reading, the way the author had
felt about his work.

The English language lends itself brilliantly to translation into
Russian. I think, for example, that there is little to surpass Vveden-
sky's translation—in the last century—of Dickens. Alas, in the field
of poetry, there has not been such success. Everybody tells me that
Pushkin is untranslatable. It is difficult to imagine that this poet
who has already translated everything unsaid and unexpressed into
his own, all-human universal language, should be untranslatable.
Inevitably, in poetry, there will be loss, for to change the *sound* of
words, as, in translation, they must be changed, is also to change
their sensuous effect, and so to modify the vision that prompts the
poet's thoughts.

But, believe it or not, Shakespeare's Sonnets as translated by both
Marshak and Pasternak are as near perfect as one can imagine. By
some miracle—particularly, I think, in Sonnet 66—"Tired with all
these, for restful death I cry . . ." Pasternak has achieved the impossible, perhaps simply because, in his own right, he was a fine poet.
He seems to have combined Shakespeare's multiplicity of sense
with a clarity and simplicity of style, making one harmonious whole,
though sometimes his own poetical inspiration carried him away
from the original.

Marshak, on the other hand, seems to have married humility and
artistry in his rendering of the Bard. Another example: Ivan Bunin,

a Nobel Prize winner, translated Longfellow's "Hiawatha." He
devoted many years, 1896-1921, to it, and the result is light, poetical, and most successful.

Russian poetry, on the other hand, is remarkably difficult to translate—for very special reasons. It is earthy, permeated with sound
common sense and has a curious matter-of-fact quality. It is
plastic, adaptable, comprehensive. Russian poets don't use literary
or poetical expressions, but the poetry conveys poignant feeling
and consummate poetic art. In no other language do I believe this
is possible, because, if you translate the Russian by true literary
equivalents, you would have to say in a poem by Pushkin, for
instance:

> I want to be alone with you,
> A moment quite alone.
> The minutes left to me are few,
> They say I'll soon be gone . . . .

In English, you would have to say: "I would like a word alone with
you, old fellow (or old chap)." I know of no English poet who has
ever been able to deal successfully in poetry with the speech of
everyday life without slang or dialect. What is needed for this are
the Russian temperament and the Russian language. To translate it
is an art in itself, for poetic expression, as the English know it, is
rarely there and, if one were to translate too literally, there would
most likely be on the page a most unpoetic bald statement of fact.

And so to what I consider the translator's great despair: How do
you deal with the conversation of simple men, with the vernacular?
This was always a pitfall for me when translating Maxim Gorky, who
was one of the first Russian writers to write about the underdog, the
vagabond, the peasant. The directness and simplicity of the vernacular has been the rock on which many a fine translator has perished.
The way Russian peasants talk between themselves cannot be translated into colloquial English, any more than the talk of a Scottish
Gillie can be converted into English slang. This kind of translation,
too, is a special gift, a mixture of understanding of the thought
processes of simple souls and of inevitable compromise. The fact
that such compromise is worthwhile is illustrated by the immense
popularity in Russia of the poetry of Robert Burns translated by the
above-mentioned Marshak.

There are, you know, jokes without number about the traps into
which all translators are liable to fall. As I started with a piece of
robust Biblical exhortation, I would like to finish with a favorite and

getnle joke—in fact, I told it the other day to an earnest young translator I know who was taking himself a bit too seriously.

The late and incomparable James Thurber once met a fervent
French admirer. "I am fortunate," said the admirer, "because I speak
English well enough to appreciate—and to love—your stories. But,"
he went on, "I have also read them translated into French and, believe me, they are even better in French." Thurber, with his usual
modesty, gave an understanding nod. "I know," he said. "I tend to
lose something in the original."

On Publishers and Translators

Gerald Gross

I would first reflect on my colleague Joseph Barnes. I knew Joe for
many years and before then was aware of his pioneer publishing
contribution in making Russian literature available in translation in
America. This was something that he projected with considerable
distinction and more than the usual commercial success. A few years
back Joe was associated with me in what I think of as a significant
effort to merge the publishing community, the writing community,
and the world of translation—something I will talk about a little
later—The National Translation Center. Joe Barnes and I were involved in the work of the Center at the very outset, and I knew him
through the years as a publishing colleague for whom I had the
greatest admiration. I am most pleased that the meeting has taken
notice of the many memorable things that he was responsible for.
He did them with a quality that few publishers manage today.

Perhaps my talk could fall under the heading of "Notes on Translation as the Publisher's Disaster Area." I think we have all heard of
Hermann Broch, author of two works that have been hailed as
masterpieces: *The Death of Virgil* and *The Sleepwalkers*. I guess
it was about five years ago the Times Literary Supplement suddenly
stirred itself and did a lead article on Broch which commanded
our attention to his tremendous contribution, not only to German
literature, but to the world of letters at large. These works were

beautifully translated, *The Death of Virgil* by Jean Starr Untermeyer
and *The Sleepwalkers* by the Muirs. However, in a period of twenty
years each title had managed to attain a sale of only two thousand
copies. But book salesmen, these days, can go out and talk about
a new hot novel and get an advance laydown of twenty thousand
copies and the books go out—somehow they'll be sold.

Why such a difference? Our literate readers have, in a sense, been
conditioned by a kind of lack of national awareness of the foreign
work. In turn, recognition of the important role of the translator
has been very slow in coming—on the part of readers, critics, and
publishers. It must have been awfully sporadic in the nineteenth century when an interesting figure like Bayard Taylor was doing his
work in translation. In our century, there was a certain golden period
of which I think we are all aware: it started in the twenties, and came
to a head in the thirties and forties. In the twenties, when people
like Blanche and Alfred Knopf were signing up Gide, Undset, and
Mann, when Ben Huebsch published Feuchtwanger and Zweig at
Viking, and Proust was being published by the Bonis. And so on.
(Of course, Scott-Moncrieff was a British translator. We will be
coming to British translations and the problems they now present
to the American publisher in a moment.) But my point here is that
a certain *new* awareness of translation accrued out of the forties,
as one of the odd benefits for America of the Hitler scourge. The
intellectual migration which resulted led many foreign writers and
certain foreign publishers to take new footholds in this country
and brought us publishers like Gottfried Bermann-Fischer, Fritz
Landshoff, Jacques Schiffrin, Kurt Enoch, Willi Schlamm, Hanna
Kister, and Salman Schocken. Thames & Hudson had a branch here
for a short time during which it did some interesting translations.
And of course, there was Pantheon Books, the American home for
the great and ever young Kurt Wolff. Most happily, his work continues to be carried on, by Helen Wolff at Harcourt Brace Jovanovich,
and by André Schiffrin at Pantheon.

It was in the forties, then, that a new generative force developed
in translation because there was an influx of knowledgeable editors
to many publishing houses—editors with a fresh awareness of the
true worth of foreign literature and a verdant consciousness of
American reading habits. It is this consciousness of American reading habits that I think is really rather central to successful translation
as it can be executed in American publishing houses; Joe Barnes was
a perfect example of that kind of editor.

The difficulty of estimating American reading awareness and
tastes, and how best to connect with this awareness, is a part of our

constant problem as publishers. This judgmental problem exists clearly enough for us within our own native language. That is, we publishers often enough misjudge works and their levels of value and acceptance. We will sign up a novel or work of nonfiction for a heavy advance, somewhat tentatively confident that we may attain very good sales. And then we will discover that there are an insufficient number of interested readers and that no connection with the marketplace has been achieved. This kind of error occurs in an even more severe form with the foreign work.

The Pulitzer, the Nobel Prize, foster a certain sales impetus in this country, but it is most often not a sufficient amount in terms of turning over appreciable sales for the publisher. Many Nobel prize works, unfortunately, end up on the remainder counter. The reasons for this point to new directions that can concern P.E.N., American opinion-makers, publishers, and the other part of our structure: the world of booksellers and the world of librarians. They relate to ways that can improve the range of translation and have it make more commercial sense than it has made in the past.

It is a thankless problem for the publisher to attempt to have the bookseller understand why it should be in order for him to charge one or two dollars more for a novel by Günter Grass than he may charge for a novel by Saul Bellow. If it is difficult to get the bookseller to comprehend the reasons for this, you can imagine why it is even more difficult to get the reader to do so. And the problems that publishers face in dealing with the costs of translation are not minimized by the kind of increased international currency that is now taking place. By this I mean that there is an easier flow of information between foreign publishers and foreign agents and American publishers. This easier exchange and the consequent awareness of the American marketplace on the part of the foreign publisher and foreign agent result in new attritive demands on the American publisher. For example, on occasion we will now see the area of first serial rights become something of a foreign province, pre-exemptive claims and all. However, such first-serial sales are highly dependent on the translator and his American publisher. For this reason, it can make sense for the publisher if the translator is allowed to share in some of the first-serial income. Certain publishers recognize this, others refuse to recognize it. Specific adjustments can be made in negotiations to encompass this. However, what is now happening is that foreign publishers, also recognizing the first-serial market, will take a more proprietary position in that area, and will in turn cut out the translator's potential share. This is only one example of

the captious monetary side of agreements where translators can participate with the author in income from the sale of the book.

But I want to go back to the point I was trying to emphasize a little earlier, when I spoke of Broch and the sale of two thousand
copies in a twenty-year period. I also must refer to names like Goncourt, Straeger, Fromentor, Nadal, and so on. These are all awards
that have existed through the years for prize works in foreign letters.
They mean absolutely nothing in this country in terms of critical
response or in terms of remuneration for author and publisher. But
for the intermittent round-up article in The New York Times Book
Review, the reviewer is silent. There seems to be no way—and many
publishers have tried—to capitalize on the publication of a Goncourt
award novel. We can walk up Fifth Avenue and not find a bookseller who will recognize the Goncourt award. So that is an uphill
battle, and the publisher cannot think that by signing up a Goncourt
prize winner there is that much more money to be made, or that the
translator can ever hope to benefit from this. The money, the recognition, is simply not there. And, as I said earlier, we cannot get the
American book trade or the American reader to feel that it is in
order for him to pay a dollar more for a Günter Grass novel than he
may pay for the Saul Bellow novel. So then, how does the publisher
amortize his translation costs? Well, the customary way is to compensate on the terms to be granted to the original author. This is
certainly legitimate if one is prepared to recognize the true value of
the translation. Indeed, this is done when we see a review of a new
Grass novel focus on the tremendous contribution that Ralph Manheim has made to that text. And this brings us to one of our prime
critical points: how seldom we see a reviewer, who should certainly
be aware of its value, go out of his way to comment on the translation and work. If more reviewers would comment, more buyers
would be conscious. Publishers have tried to get this across to
reviewers in all sorts of ways. Now, it is just not working out well,
and part of the reason for this rests in the publishing community
itself. There are only a few publishers who do translations with any
degree of regularity. Of course, large firms like Doubleday or
McGraw-Hill will publish a fair number of translations, but I think
we can all name those few firms that seem to do it rather consistently. Pantheon, because of its European heritage; Knopf, doing less
because of the absence of Blanche Knopf; Simon Michael Bessie
at Atheneum; Helen Wolff at Harcourt Brace Jovanovich: these
firms are responsible for many of the best translations being published. There are comparatively few editors, then, who approach
translations with knowledge and conviction and concern for the

translator's contribution. I daresay this is true of England as well. We know those British firms on which we tend to rely for the best translations, and we know those others who, if we share the task with them, will do a terribly shoddy job, so that we will end up having practically to re-write the entire text.

One does not have to "have a language" in order to be able to deal satisfactorily with translations. I feel this quite strongly. If need be, I go to someone who knows the language to assist me, via readings, in checking out the translation. Quite apart from this, I am in complete agreement with W. H. Auden in his claim that the best translations are often those done by two people: a gifted writer in English, working with someone who knows the foreign language intimately. One cannot find a happier example of this than in Auden's own work with Elisabeth Mayer.

Publishers all too often have to grapple with poor translations. Good translators continue to be at a premium. They are heavily booked up. Publishers cannot stage their work over a period of time in order to commit a good translator for a varied and extended assignment of two or three years, which is what many a translator would prefer. If anything, it works the other way. As an example, let us consider André Malraux's *Anti-Memoirs*. Purchased for one of the highest advances that an American publisher ever paid for a foreign work, the $300,000 advance was most likely shared by Malraux and his French publisher, who had the rights to license the work in the world market. Now, a certain pressure develops as soon as a publisher pays out $300,000: he wants to earn it back. What to do then but obtain the quickest and best translation one can manage, and if it can be shared with or managed by the British publisher, so much the better. And so by rushing out the translation, what service was done for the publisher, or for Malraux, I wonder. Perhaps ten or twenty years from now someone will look at *Anti-Memoirs* and decide that it warrants a better translation. Lord knows there were sufficient agonies of this sort over the translation of *Dr. Zhivago*, both on the part of the translators and the American and British publishers. Once again, an urgent schedule had a bearing on the final editorial product.

Well, publishers' standards will vary in these matters. The solutions truly rest within the individual publishing offices. The problem of how best to earn out $300,000 is one that can be resolved any number of ways. And if there is an error that compels one to produce a poor translation, well then, the publisher will simply not get his money back as easily as he might otherwise.

In viewing American publishing, I think we are left with the rather firm impression that there are comparatively few publishers who care thoroughly and consistently about the way in which they go about translating works from a foreign language. When the other publishers do a good job, it is done inadvertently; that is, they will simply have engaged a good translator who happens to care and he does an excellent job. But no one in that office is really the wiser for it.

I have mentioned the lack of awareness on the part of critics, or at least, the lack of effort to comment on translations. And, as I said, this relates to apathy within the publishing community as a whole. An example: some years ago, someone made this point to the Ford Foundation out of a book called *The Craft and Context of Translation,* edited by two professors who have written and translated a good deal, William Arrowsmith, Professor of Classics at the University of Texas, and Roger Shattuck, Professor of Romance Languages there. The book is excellent. It has a rather interesting assignment at its end in the form of an agenda for translators and publishers. There, in brief summary, many key works of world literature still in need of a good translation are listed. That book was published about ten years ago, and I think that if we were to check the lists now we would find that very little has changed. And yet, out of that book a point of view was established and it was brought to the attention of the Ford Foundation. They cared sufficiently about the problem so that funds were set up for the formation of The National Translation Center. This was a five-year grant, to be administered by the University of Texas. It was to use the sum of $750,000 for furthering works of translation and for improving the criteria for translation in America. It had a rather prestigious board: Robert Lowell, W. H. Auden, and Joe Barnes, among other members. Although the work of the Translation Center began slowly, there was sufficient contact with the publishing community to emphasize what I mentioned earlier: the apathy that will exist on the part of most publishers to foster translations.

It was made abundantly clear to the New York publishing community that grants were available, via the Center, for worthwhile translations in all major languages, and minor ones as well. Well, the publishing community simply did not choose to apply for the grants. The money was never spent in full. Why? The bond of apathy runs from publisher to reviewers to readers.

This particular event could not be more symptomatic of the problems that continue to exist for translators and publishers. What more can be done? Something that will allow a publisher to do his new Broch, and not sell two thousand copies in twenty years, but at least two thousand copies in a single year—a reasonable figure to be sure. That kind of improvement for the publisher is bound to result in an improved lot for translators as well.

There are bodies of opinion in this country, fortunately, which help us to sell books. I have always been puzzled because it has appeared to me that there has been so little effort on the part of P.E.N. to mesh with these groups. I refer to the book-buying group that grows out of the American Library Association—the librarians themselves. The American Library Association *chooses* books—that is, they select the best books of the year in adult categories, in the children's book category, and so on. These books are then ordered in good quantity by libraries all around the country. There has never been any appreciable effort to relate the translated work of literature to the orbit of the librarian. Librarians wish to be concerned, and they want to be informed. Most happily for the publishers, they constitute an intelligent purchasing body and a stable audience. Many book publishers would be lost without them.

I propose that there be compilations of the best translations of the year. The ALA could administer this, perhaps jointly with a council out of P.E.N. This could deal with the major Western literatures and the Asiatic literatures, as well as some forms of technical subject matter. The Library of Congress listing of major works of adult literature and the best of children's literature amounts to about fifty titles for each year for each category. Those fifty titles, I assure you, *each* sell many more in one year than the two thousand copies of a Hermann Broch.

And so I think it is a question of getting out to the buying community. The stable part of one's readership for the publisher has to be the stable part for the translator; and that is the world of the American library, the college libraries and the school libraries. It is an extensive market, and it should be a fruitful one once again, once the war is over.

The ALA annual listing could stand as a most positive action, and there would be a positive response, I am sure. This has been proved in some degree by the establishment of the National Book Award for Translation; today, this and P.E.N.'s own award are the two going awards for translation. The initial grant for the National Book Award for Translation came out of The National Translation Center funding. That is how this important award got started. The publishers themselves were behind the other NBA awards, but they did not create one in translation. However, they have now recognized its value and they will continue to support it. Until the NBA award was instituted, the only award given for translation was, of course, P.E.N.'s very own, thanks to Harry Scherman.

I would like to call your attention to other things that continue to distress me. I continue to see college anthologies of modern fiction published for "comparative lit" courses with no credit for the translator. I check the beginning of the piece, I look at the back matter, I look at the front matter, I check the tail piece. All translations, and not a word as to the translators! Although this happens because one editor in a firm is not caring, there ought to be some way of getting to the publisher on this directly. For this situation is somewhat analogous to that of the reviewer who chooses to ignore the translator. However, these are college anthologies going into wide university use. If we cannot expect the comparative-literature teacher to be conscious of the translator, how are we ever going to move to subsequent stages of recognition? There are many ways in which our colleges can mesh with the writing community to think about translations, but it is most unfortunate if publishers themselves tend to denigrate the translator by a total lack of credit.

Another aspect of commitment to translation at the college level relates to the language curriculum itself. Foreign-language courses have a natural concern in the development of translators. And yet, this has never been adequately tackled in a direct fashion. Yes, there has been good activity at one or two campuses: the University of Iowa, Johns Hopkins, Texas. But I know of no other, even at Harvard and Yale. There is no concerted effort to have language courses move into the area of translation; but there is no reason why a graduate degree couldn't be given in translation, no reason whatsoever. Perhaps this simply has not been brought to the attention of our university presidents.

I don't mean to sound glum about the subject of translation. I think that the points I have raised in regard to the American Library Association and the university community are clear areas of involvement which can better the range of criteria and acceptability of translations. I see no reason why the literate reader of Bellow shouldn't be quite fascinated by the fact that Manheim has translated Grass, and that he is reading Grass through Manheim. There has to be some exchange along these lines in reading that translated page.

On the Poetry of Négritude*

Léon Damas

My choice of talking to you this morning in French in spite of the fact that in a few weeks I shall start a course in Afro-Latin-American literature, at an American university in English, stems from both tradition and gratitude. The tradition is of long standing in P.E.N. as is testified by the many congresses to which the International Secretariat has invited me, an honor which goes beyond my person to my country, Guiana, to Africa, and to the men of my generation—Césaire, Senghor, Alouin Diop—and to the literature which has come to be known as that of *négritude*. It is inherent in the P.E.N. tradition that, after many great presidents—including Arthur Miller, with whom I was able to establish a brotherly relationship at Abidjan in the Ivory Coast Republic—a member of the French Academy, Pierre Emmanuel, should become its head.

I have spoken of gratitude, and in so doing I am thinking of two men whose works remain examples of courage, honesty and self-sacrifice, examples which I shall never cease pointing out to those who follow. I refer in the first place to Langston Hughes, the friend and brother whose premature death shocked me all the more inasmuch as only two months before he had dined with me in Paris, where his publisher, Robert Laffont, was expecting him for an

* Translated into English by Frances Frenaye

161

autographing party, a French version of one of those "be simple" ceremonies. I am grateful to him for having pushed others along the path that he opened in 1925-26. It was at that time that he conceived and published, in the name of the "New Negro" movement, a manifesto which Jacques Roumain in Haiti, Nicholas Guillen in Cuba, Mario d'Andrade in Brazil, Albert Ortiz in Ecuador, Paulos Matos in Puerto Rico, Aimé Césaire in Martinique, Tirolien in Guadeloupe, Senghor in Senegal, and I in Guiana later made our own. Always in the forefront of battle at the four corners of the earth, Langston Hughes gathered in a rich harvest as our interpreter, publicizing in the United States and elsewhere writers of varied ages whose talent he was ready to back. He was, and will long be, a moment of our self-awareness.

My gratitude goes also to my compatriot René Maran, who died prematurely also, ten years ago. He went as he lived, quietly, without witnessing the victory of ideas for which he had fought so hard, often at his own peril. For he paid a considerable price for loving, defending and interpreting his race, and above all for having thrown his weight into the scale in its behalf. René Maran, whose Paris apartment was open to all, particularly to Americans, was the first to discover, in African, the French language, which we later made into a splendid weapon with which to carry on the driving ideas of Césaire. Batouala, who later received the Goncourt Prize, marked the beginning of a school of French literature that replaced the "travel" variety which had been based on preconceived ideas and prejudices, stupidly transmitted from generation to generation. For the first time, thanks to René Maran, Africa was seen from the inside, with one of its own sons as a witness in its favor, although this was at no small cost at a time when colonialism was in full swing.

Maran's testimony derived from a collection of facts, a testimony corroborated by André Gide. René Maran wrote of what he had seen and heard, of the sad, everyday realities he had experienced during a pilgrimage to the springs of his motherland, our Holy Land, where he rediscovered his human dignity, heretofore alienated, depersonalized, assimilated, and gallicized. His French life had, indeed, been but a shadow, a negation. In contact with his motherland, he saw, heard, felt, and finally spoke as no one else had spoken before him. By returning to the essence of drumbeat language, he detected and understood its soul, which he had to interpret to himself before he could bring it to light and translate it into another language (French) which he had made his and which *was* his, although at the same time it was not. But he paid dearly for his intelligence, courage, and unfailing honesty, until the day when such writers, as André Gide, Denise Maurand, and Victor Organieur bore witness, in their turn, to his foresight and lucidity.

As students in Paris, we discovered Maran, until then unknown to our generation, and we read his works, which were forbidden in our countries and even in his own Guiana, the birthplace of his parents. I owe my acquaintance with this great man to Mercer Cook, then working on his thesis at the Sorbonne. Under a distant and sometimes cutting manner, he had perfect integrity, an iron will, and humanity; his generosity, loyalty, and disinterestedness were unequalled. And to these qualities of the heart were added those of the intellect: open-mindedness, curiosity, and concern for the future of the new generation that intended to take over the struggle. He lives on in his work and his influence. The authority of his name and the impact of his signature continue to help us in our collective task; *négritude*'s debt to him stands beside those owed to Dubois and Garvey (two names which have become as one), to Price-Mars, Fernand d'Ortiz, Artur Ramos, Frobenius, Delafosse, and Herkowitz. René Maran proposed the line that it should follow—an onward march testifying to the movement of a race and a continent toward a meeting with other races and other continents, their cultures and civilizations, in which language was not to be used for retaliation but for dialogue. (I say this in contradiction to a certain traveler, or travelers, who have become not only linguists and lexicographers but professional pan-Africans as well and who confound language and retaliation despite the fact that the former works non-violently.)

It is a short step from the interpretation of gestures and events to their translation into another language. I remember the accusation brought by the French teacher of English, Georges Lafourcade, against inept interpreters, those whom the Italians say are not *traduttori* but *traditori* because they betray a meaning instead of conveying it, pull the wool over the eyes of uninformed readers, and lay claim to scholarship by translating languages of which they know nothing. (It is a good thing, in this connection that P.E.N., as a non-governmental organization, should support the action of the United Nations and of UNESCO in the realm of the rights of man.) Nevertheless, certain translators—or those who pass themselves off as such—must, from now on, give proof of some real ability and effort in the accomplishment of their task. How many times I have had to deplore the liberties taken with the texts of the poets of *négritude*! The translation into many languages of the works of Césaire, Senghor, Rabemanjara, Birago Diop, Frantz Fanon, and myself became mandatory after Jean-Paul Sartre had written his generous and brotherly preface to Senghor's *Anthologie de la nouvelle poésie nègre et malagache*. With French translations of the Harlem Renaissance, of the Afro-Cubans, the Haitians, the modernist School of Sao Paolo and the Puerto-Rican

Creoles, *négritude* continues to inspire original and critical works, theses and hotly debated anthologies, all of which show that the subject is marketable even if it does not always get the serious treatment it deserves.

Let us limit ourselves to the matter of translation. First things first: it was Césaire who invented, or first used, the word *négritude* in an article in the magazine *L'Etudiant Noir,* which we created in 1934-35; it was taken up again in the *Cahier d'un retour au pays natal,* which came out in a special issue of the review *Volonté* in 1935, because the Paris publisher to whom it had been submitted did not think it was saleable in book form. In the first English translation, made by Lionel Abel and the late Ivan Goll, in the United States during the war, *Cahier d'un retour au pays natal* became *Memorandum for my Martinique.* (Without wishing to put forward my own name, I may note that my collection *Poèmes nègres sur des airs africains* turned into *Songs of War, Grief, Love and Abuse,* not to mention the liberties taken with the text and the failure to heed my corrections of the translation.) Meanwhile let us consider Mercer Cook, former United States Ambassador to Niger and Senegal, who left the diplomatic service in order to teach French and French-African literature. Writing about the *Selected Poems* of Léopold Sédar Senghor, translated and introduced by John Reed and Clive Wake, he says: "Thanks to these two men, an important part of Senghor's poetic works is at last made available to us. Eleven out of twenty-five of his *Chants d'ombre,* ten out of twenty of his *Hosties noires,* seven out of his twenty-seven *Ethiopiques,* and eight out of twenty-two of his *Nocturnes* are presented to us in a translation which attempts to follow as closely as possible the particularities and the French meaning of the text in order to make it readable in English free verse." But translation was only the start—and not such a very great exploit—of putting across the poetry of Senghor, with its emphasis on rhyme, its choice of words, and its alliteration. In order to illustrate the difficulties, let us take two examples. The first line of one of his most famous poems, *"Femme nue, femme noire,"* is translated by "Naked woman, black woman." Although the meaning is there, the rhythm is different and the alliteration of *nue* and *noire* is lost. And, in the *Elégie de minuit* where the poet says: *"Je suis debout, lucide, étrangement lucide,"* we have: "I am standing up, strangely lucid." Here, too, the rhythm is broken and the repetition of *lucide* disappears. As a result, the translation is more pallid and prosaic than the original. In the last analysis, it is impossible to translate Senghor into English. This explains, to some extent, why his poetry met its first success in the German version, and also in

Italian, Czech, Russian, Japanese, and Chinese, before crossing the Channel. Mercer Cook finds the English translation praiseworthy because it is faithful to the French original, but there are interpretations that deserve reconsideration if there is a second edition. For example *négritude*, the key-word originated by Senghor, is twice translated as "blackness"; *croupe* is translated as "crest" and "hills", although in both instances the force of it comes from its original meaning; and there are other inexactitudes. Finally, as Mercer Cook says, we should have preferred to see "Negro" with a capital letter, and "negress" omitted.

I say quite frankly that our work deserves as much respect as any other and that a would-be translator must approach it seriously, with a real knowledge of the original language, intellectual honesty and, of course, a certain affinity; he must bring to the job genuine commitment. For what is translating if not carrying over the meaning and context of a work from one language to another, without the claim of making it a literary creation of the translator, as if his own language contained the sum of all wisdom? Men of all nations come together to build a temple to human knowledge. Those who aspire to be translators must never lose sight of two truths: first, that languages are constantly growing and, second, that other men before them have not hesitated to enlarge vocabularies with new terms. Most of the African languages were spoken before they were written, and the African peoples have constantly invented words proper to the genius of the vernacular.

Translating is important; it is a form of art, fraught with difficulties and pitfalls. To my mind, the translator must really be bilingual. To translate French or German into English calls for a German or French cast of mind. And, to say again what I really think, to translate from an African language when one is not African requires possessing the African spirit that stems from or is dominated by *négritude*. The words of one language do not necessarily have the same meanings or even equivalents in another. For, if we venture into the realm of thought and feeling, we see that these transcend the symbols which man has devised to express them. Words mean more to one man than to another, because they carry not just a literal meaning but a whole baggage of what they suggest to the imagination. Indeed, the literal meaning of a word is only a small part of its significance. Words have a power of attraction over the mind not unlike the power of music. And this the translator cannot convey because it defies analysis; its power is wrapped up with feeling, and that is the crux of the difficulty. African poetry, for instance, cannot be translated *effectively* without taking into account its poetical tradition, the fact that it is improvised, that it is never declaimed or recited but rather sung. I think I have shown this in my *Poèmes nègres sur des airs africains,* a collection of translated poems by Rongué, Fanti, Toucouleur, Bassato, and Bambara that represent the many aspects of poetry, Negro in inspiration and expression, which convey the feeling of *négritude.* Every circumstance of life, every event that draws public attention is the occasion for a poem whose language is the familiar one of everyday. The African is born a poet and is quick to improvise a song; he does not write for the benefit of scholars but in order to be understood by his people. This explains the puns, the plays on words, the humor, and the simplicity. In this poetry, rhyme and meter obviously have no part. The effect comes out of melody and cadence, out of rhythmical repetition, out of parallelism and antithesis. It is a poetry made up of balance and delicate shades of meaning, as Gide observed in his unforgettable *Journey to the Congo.* In so writing, the poets of *négritude* have maintained their inheritance, and in their name I am grateful in advance to future translators and interpreters who take it into account.

The Lot of the Translator

Guy Daniels

In one of his early sketches, the good Dr. Chekhov offers some useful advice on the handling of a newly-delivered baby. First, he says, you should spank it soundly, repeating each time you whack its behind: "Never be a writer! Never be a writer!" Now, this is excellent advice; but, as all of us here know, it lacks something. At some point the wee one's behind should be given an especially hard whack, accompanied by the admonition: "And above all, never be a translator!"

As a translator who has moonlighted as poet, critic, and novelist, I am of course aware that most practitioners of these different crafts are bedeviled by pretty much the same breed of *bêtes noires*: unfair contracts, little or no advertising, and everything else that comes from being crushed under the conglomerates' bulldozers clearing the way for mass sales of the latest cookbook, do-it-yourself sex manual masquerading as a novel, or whatever. But along with all this, there are certain scourges whose favorite victim is the translator; and the chiefest of these—the great *bich,* to say it in Russian—is blindness to the translator's very existence and function.

Nowhere is this kind of brutal indifference encountered so frequently as in reviews of novels—and not just run-of-the-mill novels, but major works of fiction. A recent and scandalous case in point (cited by Lewis Galantière in the first issue of *The American Pen)* was a review of Ralph Manheim's brilliant—and prize-winning—English

167

version of Céline's *De château en château* that managed entirely to
ignore Mr. Manheim. As the man said, "Up with this kind of treatment we should not put."

Of course the moment we raise the anguished question "What is to
be done?" we run smack into the much larger issue of book-reviewing in general in this country. To say that that issue is beyond the
scope of this paper and this speaker, is to put it mildly. It would require a whole team of economists to attack just one of the problems
involved: the ratio between the pages of advertising bought by a publisher in this periodical or that, and the dosage of reviews received
by his books, be they tremendous or trivial. And the other ramifi-
cations of the reviewing business (for such it is) are so far-reaching
that if, as Robert Payne has suggested, we form a P.E.N. Committee
on Reviewing, it will rapidly find itself in some very deep water
indeed.

Well, I think we should form such a committee; and the deeper the
water, the better. But even while still wading tentatively in the
shallows, it might splash about to some small purpose. It might, for
instance, help to discourage the lamentable practice of assigning
reviews of translated books to persons quite innocent of any foreign
idiom. It is a melancholy reflection that, at a time when American
translators are doing generally better work than their British colleagues, the reviews of translated books in the American press
should be so dismally inferior to those in the British weeklies. On
the other hand, it must be said that the strictly literary journals in
America serve the translating community fairly well. Also, that
their editors are less intrigued than are their British colleagues by
personal vendettas among translators. (Item: *Encounter* magazine
actually printed Vladimir Nabokov's bitter complaint that my—
shall I say "unflattering"?—appraisal of his *Onegin* was due to a
"sordid little grudge." Oh, Albion, Albion!)

The question as to how the translator of novels is treated in the
European press can best be answered by our distinguished foreign
guests. I should like, however, to mention just one curious case that
rather parallels that of Mr. Manheim and the Céline book. In the
past few months I have seen perhaps a dozen reviews, in the German
press, of Gil Orlovitz's formidable experimental novel, *Milkbottle H*,
translated by a little-known hero named Alexander Butenandt. I say
"hero" because extraordinary capacities are required merely to
puzzle out the original Orlovitzian text, not to mention translating
it. In fact, after a long struggle, the translator engaged by a French
publisher simply gave up. Whether his Italian colleague did likewise, I have not yet heard. But Herr Butenandt's German *Sitz-*

fleisch prevailed. And judging from the reviews—most of them favorable—he did a good job. Yet not a single one of the reviewers seems to have looked at the original English text. Because if he had, he would surely have realized—and told his readers—that Herr Butenandt had performed one of the most Herculean labors in the history of translation.

So far as prestige is concerned, the lot of the poet-translator would seem at first glance to be a good deal more enviable than that of his *prosateur* colleague. True, he is regarded by many as a professional despoiler of beauty—a notion given wide currency by Robert Frost's oft-quoted definition of poetry as "that which is lost in translation." But then this clever half-truth is easily exposed as such. Think, for instance, of that rather flat passage in Boethius where he tells us that past happiness recalled in present misery is a pretty painful business; then recall how it came out in Dante's translation:

> *Nessun maggior dolore,*
> *che ricordarsi del tempo felice*
> *nella miseria . . . .*

(Please note that in this case, the poetry was what was *gained* in translation. Also, that the translation is a close one, i.e., that the gain was not made by flinging fidelity to the four winds and calling the whole thing an "imitation.")

Certainly the poet-translator is largely insusceptible to that total invisibility which is so often the lot of fiction translators. In fact, I know of only one case where this kind of thing happened. And I know it well, because it happened to me.

Way back in 1960, *Poetry Magazine* printed a review of a volume of my poems that remains—the review, I mean—a literary landmark. The book was titled *Poems and Translations,* and about a third of it consisted of versions from Lermontov, Paul Fort, and Francis Jammes. When I first skimmed through the review I was astounded —and at the same time very much pleased—to see that the critic had concentrated entirely on my own poems. How flattering! I thought. Obviously, he considers me much more important than those other chaps. But then I went back and took a closer look at what he had said about those poems of mine. And . . . well, you know, he didn't think they were all that great.

But even if Daniels' poetry had not, after all, overwhelmed him, why had he completely neglected Lermontov, Paul Fort, and Francis Jammes? My first hypothesis—that the reviewer knew neither French nor Russian—I quickly rejected out of deference to *Poetry*

Magazine and its editor. (Also, because in 1960, ignorance of foreign languages had not yet become fashionable in poetic circles.) That left only one possible conclusion: that whereas Guy Daniels the poet, for all his shortcomings, at least *existed,* Guy Daniels the translator was an invisible man. (*Ipso facto*—and much more regrettably—Lermontov, Fort, and Jammes were also invisible.)

But if the translator of poetry is seldom invisible to reviewers, he is often well-nigh indiscernible to people of equal or greater importance: the editors, be they on magazines or in publishing houses. What has happened is that the poor translator has been swallowed from view in the horde of Imitators, Literalists, crib-makers, and crib-versifiers crowding the literary scene. And if he does briefly emerge into view, he has little chance of being recognized by the editors, most of whom have been so totally confused by the conflicting doctrines of Messrs. Lowell, Nabokov, et al that they haven't the slightest notion what a translator is—or whether he exists at all. Finally, of course, our humble postulant often goes unperceived because he is overshadowed by the big reputations of those poets—some of them very good poets, by the way—who are most active in practicing Imitation, Literalism, crib-versifying, and the other varieties of pseudo-translation that now represent the height of fashion—though, of course, they all date back to a not-so-honorable antiquity.

I take the position that each of these fads is, to one degree or another, prejudicial to the art of translating poetry. And I would warn both editors and translators against being too much swayed by them, lest they end up hopelessly adrift. The counts of my indictment are as follows.

First, against "team translation"—that procedure whereby a non-poet who knows a certain foreign language prepares a prose translation, or crib, of a poem in that language, which is then versified by a poet ignorant of the tongue in question. This procedure is vicious in several respects. *Primo,* the versifying member of the team, never having experienced the original poem as an artistic entity, is (necessarily) never animated by the prime mover of most good translations: the compelling desire to re-create, in one's own language, a beautiful thing one has come by *via* a foreign tongue. *Secundo,* being totally unfamiliar with the poetic corpus of which the original is a part, he cannot possibly—despite all the conscientious coaching of a Max Hayward (or the perhaps less diligent coaching of an Olga Carlisle)—be aware of the subtle rhythmic and other echoes of earlier poets of that particular culture; with the result that these echoes—and many other phenomena besides—find no place in his version. *Tertio,* as the practice of team translation is increasingly accepted, limitations of the kind just mentioned are increasingly taken for granted, and *critical criteria are accordingly relaxed. Quarto,* the growing popularity of team translation militates against the acquisition of linguistic culture on the part of poets. After all, if it is possible for Stanley Kunitz (or any one of a dozen others) to gain fame as a translator of Russian poetry without even bothering to learn the language, why (the young poet says to himself) should I take the trouble to learn any language at all? "Never mind the advice of that Fascist, Ezra Pound. Just give me a crib, and I'll make you a mind-blowing poem out of it." (And once the reader's mind has been blown, what cares he for Hecuba—or any other original creator?)

For all this, I think it must be said that team translation is the least noxious of the aforementioned fads; and that it has, quite improbably, given us a number of good poems. (I am thinking in particular of Richard Wilbur's versions from the Russian; but then they don't really count, since casual scrutiny reveals that Wilbur has cheated and actually learned some Russian.) Furthermore, team translation is sometimes the only possible way of getting at poetry in inaccessible languages; and it must not, therefore, be ruled out. It is, in short, an indispensable *pis-aller.* But the important thing to remember is that it *is* a *pis-aller*—something to which publishers should have recourse only when a genuine poet-translator is not available.

Imitation and Literalism are quite different phenomena altogether. That neither of these is translation in any acceptable sense was made everlastingly clear by Dryden in the year 1680. I refer to his *Preface to the Translation of Ovid's Epistles,* in which he depicts with devastating wit the perils of both heresies. That both Nabokov and Lowell should have chosen to fly in the face of Dryden's sage counsel is something that passes my feeble understanding of "anti" phenomena: anti-novels, anti-translations, and so on. But they did—and very deliberately. Thus the title of Nabokov's first essay, on translating Pushkin's *Eugene Onegin,* "The Servile Path," comes from a poem by Sir John Denham quoted by Dryden in the course of his exposure of the follies of Literalism. And Robert Lowell's term "imitation" comes, of course, from Abraham Cowley, to whom—and to whom alone, as a translator of Pindar—Dryden was willing to grant this kind of license.

Well, Dryden is not the kind of man whose advice should be taken lightly; and in the event, both Nabokov and Lowell have paid a price for flying in the face of that advice. Nabokov in particular

came a cropper with his glorified crib of *Onegin*. I was, I believe, the
first to point out (in a review published in the *New Republic)* that
not only was the emperor not wearing any new clothes, but that he
really didn't look very stylish that way. But nothing I or anyone
else (subsequently) said could equal Dryden's warning on Literalsim:

> 'Tis much like dancing on ropes with fettered legs: a man may shun
> a fall by using caution; but the gracefulness of motion is not to be
> expected: and when we have said the best of it, 'tis but a foolish task;
> for no sober man would put himself into a danger for the applause of
> escaping without breaking his neck.

This is of course a perfect description of Nabokov's erudite
pidgin-English version of *Onegin,* which abounds in what I have
called the "man-dog-bite" word order. Thus:

> Since plainly not always could he
> beefsteaks and Strasbourg pie
> sluice with a champagne
> bottle . . . .

(Want to know a secret? Pushkin didn't write that.)
     Dryden's characterization of imitation is equally applicable to
lowellization; i.e. distorting—very *creatively* distorting, of course—
an original beyond all recognition:

> Yet he who is inquisitive to know an author's thoughts will be
> disappointed in his expectation; and 'tis not always that a man will
> be contented to have a present made him, when he expects the pay-
> ment of a debt. To state it fairly; imitation of an author is the
> most advantageous way for a translator to show himself, but the
> greatest wrong which can be done to the memory of the dead.

Or, as Nabokov has said of Lowell: "I wish he would stop mutilating
dead and defenseless poets."
     At this point, a very intriguing question begs to be asked: Why
did Nabokov's pratfall, predicted by Dryden, finish Nabokovian
Literalism, while the twin heresy of lowellization has flourished?
     Well, I can think of a lot of answers to that question—the most
obvious one being that Lowell's anti-translations often "read well,"
whereas Nabokov's definitely do not. But my concern at the moment
is with the threat posed to the everyday, ordinary poet-translator
(like Dante in the passage quoted) by the various fads now predom-

inant. I have already discussed team translation; and I think we can agree that Nabokov's Literalism died stillborn. That leaves only Imitations. (With, of course, a certain overlap into team translations, since Lowell and the imitators of his Imitations insist on englishing poets whose language they do not know.)

First off, let's rid ourselves once and for all of the ploy that Imitations are the only way of reproducing the "true tone" of the original; that they are not really competitive with ordinary translations, from which they are radically different; and that, indeed, the master (Mr. Lowell)has disclaimed any such competition. In other words, let us have peaceful co-existence.

That they are radically different I will readily agree. Consider, for instance, the last line but one in Lowell's "imitation" of Pasternak's poem, "Hamlet." The original reads:

> *Vse tonet v fariseystve* . . . .
> Everything is sinking in Pharisaism . . . .

Lowell has:

> All's drowned in the sperm and spittle of the Pharisee . . . .

This is not only radically different from a translation: it is about as far as you can get from the "tone" of Pasternak's original, a poem light-years away from sperm and spittle—and, for that matter, from Mr. Lowell's characteristically spasmodic line. As Dorothy Sayers said of Congreve's Imitations of Horace: "If this is the impression which Horace produces on Congreve, then Congreve is altogether too impressionable." Examples could be multiplied *ad infinitum*, but it's not really necessary, to prove that imitations are most definitely *not* translations.

As to the master's disclaimer of competition, let me quote him: "I believe that poetic translation—*I would call it an imitation*—must be expert and inspired . . ." (Italics mine.) So much for peaceful co-existence . . . and inspiration.

It is my contention that the present vogue for imitations is a grave—and perhaps mortal—threat to the art of poetic translation. Consistent with the spasmodic nature of Lowell's reactions to life in general, all the emphasis is on *impact,* and none on fidelity to the original. (But then who cares about such trifles when the "in" thing is to "nowify"—and "subjectify"—the universe?)

Granted, as applied to the translation of poetry, "fidelity" is a very complex concept. Yet the poetic translation that is both *belle* and *fidèle* is not such a rarity as is sometimes maintained. The thing *can* be done (sometimes); and our first duty is to at least *try* for it, rather than to give up in advance. For most often imitation is, as Dryden said, "the greatest wrong which can be done to the memory of the dead."

Certain Difficulties in Translating Poetry

Ivan Elagin

For the past four years, I have been working on a translation of Stephen Vincent Benét's masterpiece—*John Brown's Body*. For those four years, I had the sensation of being besieged inside a fortress the walls of which were built of dictionaries; general dictionaries, technical dictionaries, Anglo-Russian dictionaries of every type and description. Surrounding these walls and swearing to "get" me dead or alive were the combined forces of all the Union and Confederate armies. How it all ended I do not know. It is possible that I was killed during an attempt to translate Negro dialect into Russian.

I should like to mention some of the problems I encountered in the course of translating Stephen Vincent Benét's poem into Russian. These are difficulties inherent in poetical translation. It is quite natural, of course, that a lengthy and complex undertaking should have its share of problems, but in my case, aside from all the occasional difficulties, the process of English-to-Russian verse translation contained one perpetually present difficulty. I am referring to the constant syllable discrepancy of Russian and English words. The trouble is that the English language is considerably more economical and concise than the Russian, and English words are for the most part shorter than Russian words. The brilliant translator and scholar in the field of literary translation, Kornei

Chukovsky, who died recently, once made the following remarks on the subject:

> On an average, a Russian word is almost double the length of the corresponding English word. This brevity gives English a particularly powerful and compressed quality: inevitably, in the course of translation into Russian, an energetic statement of seven lines is transformed into a limp, flabby one of some eleven or twelve lines . . . . Such a tendency is fatal for the language in which the word "crime" stands for *"prestupleniye"*, "bus" for "omnibus" . . . .[1]

In my opinion Chukovsky was wrong about the inevitable limpness of the translation. His own translations contradict this excessively pessimistic verdict. Chukovsky further cites a table which gives the comparative length of words in the English, German and Russian languages and which shows that, in a given text of one thousand words, the English version contains eight hundred and twenty-four one-syllable words while the Russian version has only three hundred and twenty-eight. In such a situation, it is natural that a verse translation into Russian should have "left-over" lines. Thus it is very difficult to preserve the equilinear principle according to which each line of poetry in the original must correspond to a *single* line in the translation. A translator of English poems into Russian who tries to abide by the equilinear principle feels like a zoo keeper whose job it is to take a cage where four contented rabbits live in perfect harmony, and place three giraffes and a crocodile into it.

Beginning literally with the very first line of Benét's poem I ran straight into a solid obstruction. The Invocation begins with the words:

American Muse, whose strong and diverse heart . . .

"American muse"—there are five syllables there. The Russian equivalent—*Amerikanskaya muza*—contains eight syllables and plays havoc with the rhythmic structure of the verse. Over these years I have tried to translate this opening line many different ways, but in every version something important had to be sacrificed. The worst of it was that in every one of the acceptable versions I had to speak of the American Muse in the third person for the sake of the rhythmic pattern. I realized however that in doing so I was

[1] Kornei Chukovsky, *Vysokoe iskusstvo*, Moscow, Iskusstvo, 1964, p. 173

distorting the author's intonation, which is one of direct address to
the Muse. Finally I adopted a compromise solution. Instead of translating the title "Invocation" by the Russian equivalent—which is
"Invocation to the Muse"—I entitled it "Invocation to the American
Muse," which in no wise contradicts the meaning of the original.
In this way I removed a five-syllable adjective from the opening
line and was able to preserve the form of direct address.

In translating rhymed verse it is sometimes necessary to make certain sacrifices, but when the poetry is rhymeless I always prefer to
add an extra line to the Russian translation if such an addition enables me to convey the sense and style of the original more fully to
the Russian reader. If this is to be considered an evil, it is yet the
least of evils. I think it much worse, again using Chukovsky's words,
to transform "a smoothly flowing narrative into a sequence of
convulsed short exclamations and sobs." A rigid adherence to the
equilinear principle inevitably brings about such convulsions of the
language.

Proverbs, sayings, songs, rhymes and abbreviations make up a
special category of stumbling blocks in a literary translation. Every
case in this category has to be solved individually. An abbreviation
like IOU, for example, is untranslatable because no such phonetic
coincidence exists in Russian. Thus a colorful colloquialism like:

> Saw that Sue had the finest hearse
> That IOU's could possibly drape her

is lost in translation. I had to content myself with a general Russian
phrase indicating that Dupre gave his wife the best funeral he could
manage on credit.

Authors often have a tendency—which is very irritating to translators—to throw about casual, fleeting hints in reference to well-known
sayings, nursery rhymes or popular quotations. Such a technique
works well when the author can safely assume that his readers are
familiar with this material from infancy; it proves however extremely
troublesome for the translator who has to deal with an audience
whose spontaneous responses are based on a completely different set
of childhood and cultural associations. I suppose I ought to thank
my stars that *John Brown's Body* had been written before the advent
of pop culture and television advertising, but even so I was often
faced with the necessity of either adding explanatory phrases to the
translated text or resorting to the ever-useful footnote.

There is for instance a scene in Book Three where a young man
and a girl are going off to fetch water. The girl's father watches them
go—and I quote:

The big pail clanking between them. His hard mouth
Was wry with an old nursery-rhyme.

Benét obviously has in mind the Mother-Goose rhyme which every
one here knows:

Jack and Jill
Went up the hill
To fetch a pail of water.
Jack fell down
And broke his crown
And Jill came tumbling after.

However, if I were to translate Benét's lines just as they stand, the
Russian reader—who grew up on different nursery rhymes—would be
left totally in the dark. It becomes necessary to supply the explanation omitted in the original by mentioning "the words of the old
nursery rhyme about Jack and Jill who went to the well with a pail."
Of course, since the Russian reader will not have the same spontaneous stream of associations connected with "Jack and Jill' as an
English-speaking reader, the difficulty cannot be entirely resolved.
In another example Benét also uses a nursery rhyme—this time a
re-phrasing of "Little Bo-Peep has lost her sheep." Speaking of the
disastrous situation of the Confederate troops toward the end of the
war, one of the characters, Wainscott Bristol, remarks on the dis-
appearance of uniforms, cavalry boots, supplies, recruits, and con-
cludes:

They all went home with their tails behind 'em."

In this case, one has to work out a compromise solution based on
the fact that in Russian there is an idiomatic expression connecting
tails and sudden departures, so that one can say something like: "He
went off with a flourish of his tail." Of course, such a translation
lacks the emotional impact of the original where the Mother-Goose
rhyme in the face of impending doom carries a tragic irony.
Fortunately, the problems are not always so complicated. When,
in describing the wartime population of Washington, Benét enumer-
ates:

Rich man, poor man, soldier, beggar man, thief—

he is using a children's counting-rhyme. Since Russian children also
play tag and use very similar counting jingles to determine who is
"it," the translation is quite painless.

Another category of references familiar to the English ear includes widely known prayers and hymns, usually Anglican or Presbyterian. In Book Two, when Carter, the drowsy telegraph operator, mumbles:

"Yes, Ma, I said 'Now I lay me' . . ."

it is obvious to the English-speaking reader that in his dream Carter is seeing himself as a little boy whose mother makes him say prayers before going to bed. This particular prayer which begins: "Now I lay me down to sleep, I pray the Lord my soul to keep" is probably the first bedtime prayer most English and American children learn. To a Russian reader, however, the words "Now I lay me" have no connotation with prayer or childhood. One possible solution is to give a literal translation of the line and then add a footnote, explaining that there is such a prayer. But there is also a second solution which appears to me more effective. Russian children at bedtime usually say a prayer which begins *Tsariu Nebesnyi* (O Heavenly King); so that in Russian, "Yes, Mama, I've said 'O Heavenly King' " sounds much more natural than an exact translation would have sounded.

There is a similar case later in the poem where the chapter about prisoners of war begins with the words: "For all prisoners and captives now." I translated this quotation from an Anglican prayer by using the closest analogy I could find in the Russian Orthodox litany: "And now for those imprisoned and held in captivity."

Benét often uses the texts of prayers, psalms and hymns. Speaking of the freed Negroes who followed the Union troops, he describes an old Negro slave's dream of a place where

All God's chillun got shoes there and fine new clothes,
All God's chillun got peace there and roastin'-ears.

Lines similar to these can be found in various Negro spirituals. Finding the right expressions in Russian poses a complicated stylistic problem. In dealing with it, I took into account the fact that in Russian writing, an exalted style—especially when it has religious or ecclesiastical overtones—is often associated with the use of Church-Slavonic or ancient Russian words instead of their modern equivalents. The Negro speech, in this case, is also rich with religious and Biblical overtones. For this reason instead of trying to translate "chillun" by distorting the Russian word for children, I chose the old Slavonic word which is used in the Russian Bible.

Among the toughest problems a translator faces is that of translating concepts which exist in one of the languages but not in the other.

In such cases, one usually has to substitute an explanatory phrase for
the non-existent lexical equivalent, that is, to describe an object instead of naming it. There are many instances of this in *John Brown's
Body*. Benét mentions for example: jack-o-lanterns, bounty men,
lagniappe days. Since none of these exists in Russian, I had to put
together descriptive definitions of lanterns made out of hollow
pumpkins, soldiers tempted into enlisting by government promises—
and to keep the descriptions both brief and clear. The idea behind
"lagniappe days" was perhaps the hardest to translate. It comes from
the Spanish *"la napa"*—a small gift which the merchant adds to the
the purchase. Benét contrasts the "lagniappe days" to the days of
wartime shortages in Richmond, creating the impression of security
and plenty with a single two-syllable word. In Russian the same thing
could be said only with the help of a long, cumbersome descriptive
phrase and an even longer footnote. I finally adopted a simplified
solution and translated the "old lazy lagniappe days" as the "old
carefree days of plenty." This is not an ideal translation but it
avoids clumsiness and retains the meaning of the original. There
was another, similar case involving a slang army expression. Sergeant Bailey says, recalling his friend:

> Ought to give him his old spread-eagle now.

The certificate given to a demobilized soldier had the image of the
American eagle with the wings spread out on it. Hence the expression. I could have, of course, said something like: 'He ought to
get the paper with the eagle" and send the reader off to the appropriate footnote. But I felt that a simple Russian army colloquialism,
"poluchit' vol'nuiu," even though it has no mention of eagles, would
provide a more accurate translation for the conversational tone of
Bailey's remark.

Translation of names and proper nouns into Russian can present
serious problems. Here, as in the other cases, there is no overall
recipe; the solution of each individual problem must depend on the
circumstances. The presence of a rigid rhythm pattern in the original complicates the problem greatly, while a looser rhythmic structure opens wider possibilities before the translator and makes the
finding of a lexical equivalent easier.

For example, the line

> So the slow blood dripped on the rocks of the Devil's Den

lends itself easily to translation because a name like "Devil's Den"

sounds perfectly natural in Russian. Explanations are unnecessary
and no part of the sentence needs to be omitted. But here is a more
complicated example:

> And the rocks are grey in the sun and black in the rain,
> And the jacks-in-the-pulpit grow in the cool, damp hollows.

A Russian reader will not know that jack-in-the-pulpit is the name of
a woodland plant which flowers in the spring. A literal translation of
this fanciful name might set the Russian reader imagining a real
hermit-like preacher living in a cool, damp hollow! It is, of course,
possible to refer the reader to a footnote. But this disrupts the reading process and kills the poetic effect of this colorful name. For this
reason I resorted in this case to a "hidden footnote"—an explanation
which is inserted into the text itself and which does not look like a
footnote although it accomplishes the same purpose: "And jack-in-
the-pulpit—wild flower—grows in the cool, damp hollows."

It is much more difficult to fit proper names into the framework of
a definite meter. The translator does not always emerge victorious
from these struggles, although there are occasional successes. It was
quite difficult, for example, to fit a full translation of the lines:

> Calling Blue Ruin and Georgia Lad
> With the huntsman's crotchet that sets them mad

into two Russian lines of the same meter, especially since the Russian
equivalent of "Blue Ruin and Georgia Lad" is four syllables longer
than the original. In this instance, I finally succeeded in rendering
both the meaning and the meter exactly. But one cannot have good
luck all the time. There are cases when something must be omitted
in order to preserve the metric limits. Some proper nouns can cause
total disaster. Here are four lines which ruined my peace of mind
for months:

> Winter walks from the green, streaked West
> With a bag of Northern Spies
> The skins are red as a robin's breast,
> The honey chill as the skies.

At first the image in the second line seemed to me quite clear.
A personified wartime winter carries a bagful of real spies working
for the North. And why not? There is nothing impossible about such
a poetical image. I was saved, however, by a deep-rooted streak of

caution. My daughter, to whom I turned for confirmation, told me
very confidentially that Northern Spies are a kind of apple that
grows in the United States. And then my sufferings began! I very
much wanted to include this name in the translation. But that meant
I must also include an explanation since no Russian would understand that the reference is to apples. However, the four short rhymed
lines are already so filled with images that it would be completely
impossible to find room for such an explanation. Making a footnote
was another possibility. But after many attempts I was forced to
give up and exchange the bag of Northern Spies for a simple bag of
apples. Those Northern Spies just would not fit into the rhythmical
structure of the verse. This is one of my failures.

An altogether special problem of translation emerges when the
original contains a play on words or a pun. It is a very complex and
sometimes insoluble problem since a pun that is possible in one language does not as a rule repeat itself in the other one and cannot therefore be translated. Here is an example of a difficult case in which
the play on words is based on the title of Victor Hugo's novel and on
the similarity between the surname Lee and the French definite
article. Speaking of the Southerners in defeat, Benét says:

> And called yourselves "Lee's miserables faintin' "

In another place Bristol makes an ironic comment on the sorry
state of the Black Horse Troop which, towards the end of the war,
has lost all its black horses and is now mounted on nags of sundry
colors. Bristol quips:

> Though the only horse you could call real black
> Is the horsefly sitting on Shepley's back.

The English pun on the words "horse" and "horsefly" is inevitably
lost in translation. On some occasions, however, it is possible to
translate a play on words to a certain degree. Here is an example
from Book Two. A member of the Confederate Cabinet, Judah P.
Benjamin, is wishing that his colleagues would admit

> The cold, plain Franklin sense
> That if we do not hang together now
> We shall undoubtedly hang separately.

The translator is here faced with a difficult choice: he can either
translate "hang together" by the correct Russian equivalent and

consequently abandon any attempt to translate the pun; or he can discard the correct idiomatic expression for "hang together" and make a suitable pun in Russian. I found that in this particular context it is more important to preserve the play on words, and I based the Russian pun on the expressions: to *draw* forces together and to *draw* a noose around a neck.

In English, as well as in Russian, there are idiomatic phrases which cannot be translated literally. They require either a descriptive translation or the use of a parallel idiomatic expression. An example of this is found in Book Four.

> Kiss the sweetheart before you're killed.
> She will be loving and she will grieve
> And wear your heart on her golden sleeve.

There is no Russian expression similar to "wearing one's heart on one's sleeve." I should like to quote here a manual for English-Russian translation, published in Moscow in 1960. It recommends the following:

> When a particular English idiomatic turn of phrase has neither an equivalent nor an analogous expression in the Russian language, while a word-for-word translation would result in a confusing literalism, the translator must give up the task of re-creating the imagery of the given expression. Instead he has to use a descriptive translation; that is, he must make clear the meaning of the English phraseological unit by mean of a freely chosen sequence of words.[2]

And further on:

> A descriptive translation always involves a certain loss.[3]

To return to the example I mentioned—it is of course impossible to translate the specific imagery of "she will wear your heart on her golden sleeve." One could insert a descriptive clause as suggested in the translation manual; but it seemed to me that this would interfere with the musical continuity of the lines—a thing especially to be avoided in a case like this, where the melody of the verse is itself

[2] V. N. Komissarov, Ia. I. Retsker, V.I. Tarkhov, *Posobie po perevodu s angliiskogo iazyka na ruskii,* Izdatelstvo literatury na inostrannykh iazykakh, Moskva, 1960, p. 60.
[3] Ibid.

a means of emotional expression. Therefore I used a Russian image
(one that can be approximately translated as "she will make a dis-
play of your heart") which differs from the original but is close to
it in meaning.

Sometimes, however, idiomatic phrases in one language correspond to similar idioms in the other language; then the translator's
problem is reduced to spotting the lucky find. For example, in
Russian common usage a Russian who "does not wear a cross" is
a dishonest scoundrel. (The expression probably came into being
because thieves and robbers of ancient times were pious enough to
take off their baptismal crosses before committing a crime.) I found
this idiomatic phrase very useful in translating a line of the Invocation.
Benét remarks that some less-than-virtuous first settlers had "neither
shirts nor honor to their back." In my translation this becomes:
"They wore neither shirts nor crosses." The meaning is exactly the
same.

Similarly close analogies may be found in the Russian language for
such expressions as: "geese flying in a narrow V" or "hell-for-
leather." Other idioms have no parallels in Russian—for instance,
"necktie party." In translating Jim Breckinridge's reproach: "Yuh're
always hankerin' after a necktie party," I considered inventing some
Russian phrase to denote "a hanging company" or "company of
hangmen," but found it much less contrived to use an existing Russian idiomatic expression "to prepare a rope necktie" for somebody.

The speech of Benét's Negro characters is a special problem in
translation. Biblical references, as we have seen, are constantly used
side by side with the most casual colloquial expressions:

> We'se loose in Freedom's land,
> Crossed old Jordan—bound to get vittles now

says Spade, the escaping slave.

I was very much tempted at first to translate all the peculiarities
of the Negro speech by means of Russian peasant idioms. I have
managed to resist this temptation, realizing that it would be as incongruous to represent nineteenth-century black slaves conversing in
Nijnii Novgorod accents as it would be to describe peasants in some
northern Russian village eating soul-food.

I was equally distrustful of another method of rendering Negro
speech, used in some Russian translations of American fiction. This
method consists in having the Negro characters talk with as many
grammatical mistakes as it is possible to fit into a Russian sentence.
I find it unsuccessful because, for one thing, the distinctive quality
of Negro speech lies in the pronunciation rather than in grammar.

So rather than translate the phonetically and grammatically distinctive qualities of Negro speech by means of distorting Russian grammar, I tried, in conveying the speech of Benét's Negro characters, to use some stylistic crudities, slang expressions, and colloquial idioms.

I should like to conclude this brief account of the problems of translation by adding that the very choice of the literary work to be translated is in itself a serious problem. Artistic merit is, of course, a primary basis for making such a choice, but when one is considering major works of epic literature, there is also another important criterion to be taken into account. and that is the value of the knowledge which the reader might acquire. Finally, the choice is determined to some extent by the literary preferences of the translator. The translator is not only a go-between but also an enraptured reader.

Many people have asked me why I undertook the translation of Benét's poem. Aside from its literary value, there was another reason. I do not intend to compare the Russian Civil War with the American Civil War. I know that these are entirely different phenomena. However, the historical events did have something in common. In both cases there was a national tragedy, a sharp split into two belligerent camps, bitterness and years of bloodshed. But, beginning with Lincoln's Gettysburg address the American conscience sought some sort of reconciliation. There was enough room on American soil for erecting monuments to both the victors and the vanquished. Almost half a century has passed since the Russian Civil War. Yet a spirit of implacable hatred still reigns both in Soviet literature and in the Soviet interpretation of history. To this day the Whites and the Reds are mortal enemies, and those who fought on the losing side are—with rare exceptions—depicted as villains by Soviet writers and historians. I hoped that a translation of Stephen Vincent Benét's epic poem might, to use Pushkin's expression, "awaken kindly feeling" in the Russian reader.

The Music of Translation

Muriel Rukeyser

Mr. Flood, Mr. Payne, translators, writers, poets: yes, it cannot be done, and yes we will go on doing it.

The matter of music and the matter of meaning—I think they are not opposed. I don't think the dualities are really opposed and I think the music here has a great deal to do with the meaning as it moves.

The movement of the meaning of what we are doing.

As children, it seems to me we have all come to translations in the same way that we came to the writings in English. Knowing indeed that the French works were against the French background. Feeling our way into something that had happened in France, knowing that the Asian languages were far outside and the collision of the strokes of meaning made as if pictures. All of these are "as if" because the physicality of what we are coming to is perhaps not a physicality as if we are coming to the work entire, to ourselves entire, and to something that is named. We have the "translator-traitor" name-throwing always behind us. And I think we might very well come to it openly.

Perhaps it is not so bad to be called traitors. Many of us have become used to this. We have to translate news; as the government says, to kill is to save, to go in to pull out, and so on. We have been translating all the time. And we are called traitors: many of us are called traitors for being against wars and so forth, because what treason is it to translate? It is some kind of mandarin thing to which we are traitors, but underneath that and I think—to get to the music here—one must dive far underneath into a place where we share experience.

I know in writing poems, the poems that I very often thought of not showing to anybody become the poems that are taken hold of later on. They are not in another dirty word they are not the obscure ones that don't go deep enough. For when you dive deep enough into experience you come to a place where we share our lives. And so in language there is something underneath our languages which is shared and this is curious, this is subtle, this is a secret and also this is known to all of us.

There is something under that. We make mistakes with it all the time. We work for perfection and we fall flat every three minutes. There is no perfection here and we want it.

We want to bring that over. Treason and resurrection and bring ing over, these are translations. It is a mythological effort to bring a music over into another life. And it involves one's own lost languages. As if we knew all languages. For example, I do not know Hebrew and when I hear the cantillation of the beginning of the Song of Songs and it says, *Shim ha-shirim* I know that means Song of Songs, there's something in me as if it were a lost language of my own. Well, is it? German was the private language of my parents and I flunked German in college because the taboo of not knowing what my parents were saying that they wanted me not to know was very strong. And it was not theirs. It was third generation. And you know what happens in this country. We're all translators.

We are the translated people.

And if we are third generation as I am, we know the second generation tried terribly hard to be everything they were not and bleached out all language, all poetry, all jokes *back there,* all cooking of *back there,* not to talk with your hands Muriel, only Mediterranean people do that. And the mistakes go back the other way. You can get awfully pretentious—sound awfully pretentious. I can sound awfully pretentious in France if Alain Bosquet does as he did translate a title of mine which was called *U.S. 1* which is a little too much of a national—it's a road, you know, it means a coastline to me. It means our conflict, it means my conflict, it means what happens on the Atlantic Coast, but when this comes out in France as *U.S. moi, U.S. 1* which came out as *U.S. I* and so on, that makes something one is not exactly. These things can all happen. All these mistakes, terrible mistakes.

A man cannot be translated, but it is possible through how you say a translator to have a child and certain things can be brought through. Again, every mistake, every ignorance, every falling flat on one's face comes through. It comes through in language. And here we are trying to bring over a significant music, signifying to someone un- known, to you my reader, unknown to me, that perhaps I'm born now, but what makes it significant. In the work entire, one modu- lated curve of emotion, as Lawrence said; curve of music in which the last word of the poem can sometimes show you where the tonic is, what lattice as in crystal structure this lives on.

What the poem climbs up to. Oh, take Milton's sonnet on his blindness which has all the waiting and losing and burying and hiding and finally comes to the one word wait: Not what they tell us in school, it isn't that at all. You come to the word wait, and on the word wait the marvelous structure of the sonnet is there, the fact that he is writing poems again is there, the whole thing comes through, absolutely before you. Well, it is that movement, that music, that has to be brought over. And it's a marvelous and ter- rible game. It can be done at times at which one is unable to write one's own poems and has something one cares for very much. Something marvelous. There can be set out before one and worked with. Not spun out of one . . . but in front of one.

And Nellie Sachs, tormented, pursued for the chimneys and the people like sand and the sand itself sharp and abrasive and beautiful and many-colored in her poems. And she believed, in Sweden, that the German police were after her. She asked to translate her poems and a publisher here said I must translate the whole book or none.

All these questions of the quests, one's absolute wish, they say it's going to be presented and then as I was saying before, the people to whom this is going to be significant. The one person, one's listener, to whom this is going to be significant. It doesn't happen often in bringing works entire through. It doesn't happen in bringing a word through. The example that Jespersen uses is "uncle," the Latin word *avunculus*—the root he says generally comes through. People remember the saying and bring this part of the word through. Not here, they remember the "dear little" as if it were a Russian "dear little uncle." We don't get *avus* except in the adjective. We get uncle, part of dear little. Our dear littles are the dead writers in this. My pleasure, my joy and my torture has been working with living poets so one has the frightfulness and blowups and marvelous letters and roses coming from other countries and a frightful letter from Paz came yesterday saying, "what do you mean you're going to

print a page of my afterthoughts in the paper edition of my selected
poems?" (It's a book we did ten years ago that was to come out in
a paper edition.) "I have no afterthoughts and by the way, could
you rewrite the book completely and could we change the name of
the book from *Selected Poems* to something else?"

But this thing of a living voice brought over where one possibly
can make a music, and one does not want a faulty music, one wants
the clear music, not of clarity, it was said yesterday when the thing
is not clear, it must not be translated as clear. But something of
the work entire, the word, each word, in itself whatever that is, and
with it suggestion, with it silence, with it potential, because it is
the thing at its potential.

What it gives us.

What we have in our early reading, this warming of an unknown
life present and entire as it all is. As these works in unknown languages are. I think of what must be a frightful translation of the
Vietnamese epic *Kim Van Kieu* and I puzzle that and puzzle that
with a script I can't read on one side of the page and a kind of
awful prose which cannot possibly be what it is, and now Cambodian
poetry. I don't know that I know a single Cambodian poem, and
they will be telling us all kinds of things about the Cambodians,
and we will not know a thing—could we have a project to translate Cambodian poetry? Could that be made now?

And other translations. I found a box, while in my nerves
before speaking I was pacing up and down and drinking water. At
the water cooler outside there is this, as an example of the kind of
translation that we have. Here's a box with a sign on it—Coffee
Stir Sticks. It sounds like a bad translation from the Chinese.
Well, what is it? Coffee Stir Sticks. I know what it is. It says
"300 count." You know, maybe it was made in Hong Kong, I
don't know. But here is the kind of translation that we have and
all our headlines say this all the time. But, when you go to each
word—I think of the story about Hans Christian Andersen who took
an awful lot of beating about everything he wrote and he liked to go
to houses and he liked to read the stories and he wanted grownups
there and children there and there was a critic there once—there
often is a critic, and this one did his job on the story and a little
girl looking at the work while the critic was going at it said, "Here's
one little word you didn't scold." The word was "and." You can
do that. But there is the work entire. In the translations of Hans
Christian Andersen, Rumer Godden speaking about them said they
don't come over clear. They have to be transparent, they have to be
wonderful translations and she said something, I don't know how you

would translate this. She said they come through as pawky. Now I suppose there's a word in every language that we have for pawky, but I don't know how to translate that. And yesterday when Isaac Bashevis Singer was doing that and we laughed and we clapped and he was doing all the words for poor in Yiddish and I thought of what we do. "I'm going where the climate fits my clothes" and "My pockets think I'm dead." We all have our ways of saying poor. But what he was saying was that the killed, the six million, his audience had been killed. His language has been killed. He didn't say that. He made jokes. That's the way he works. We laugh our heads off and yet an hour later . . . But this is a curious refreshment. This is visiting another culture. Boas used to say the only way to have a holiday really is to go to another culture. This is a holiday that brings something to us in the nature of finding. In the nature of discovery. This is us as translators, not us as readers because again, one is the twelve-year-old finding the things of the world and realizing in a curious way, a floating way, that these come from other people and other languages. Rilke said, "I believe that no poem in the *Sonnets to Orpheus* means anything that is not fully written-out there. Often, it is true, with its most secret name. All 'allusion' I am convinced would be contradictory to the indescribable 'being-there' of the poem." That "being-there" is what we are trying to bring over.

It can only be done by the *things*. It is working through the flesh. With all its mistakes, it's like bringing up a child. You know, one knows one's own howlers in doing the work and sees the howlers all around one very easily, more easily than one sees one's own often. But, it must be done, it can be done. There is only one poem in the world that I know that can really be translated. And it's the only abstract poem; when I was teaching, students would ask, would speak very often about abstract poetry, concrete poetry (what I think of as poured poems); but there is one abstract poem. It's Christian Morgenstern's "Fish's Night Song."

$$\breve{\ }\ —\ \breve{\ }\ —$$
$$\breve{\ }\ —\ \breve{\ }\ —$$
$$\breve{\ }\ —\ \breve{\ }\ —\ \breve{\ }\ —\ \breve{\ }\ —$$
$$\breve{\ }\ —\ \breve{\ }\ —\ \breve{\ }\ —\ \breve{\ }\ —$$
$$\breve{\ }\ —\ \breve{\ }\ —\ \breve{\ }\ —\ \breve{\ }\ —$$
$$\breve{\ }\ —\ \breve{\ }\ —\ \breve{\ }\ —\ \breve{\ }\ —$$
$$\breve{\ }\ —\ \breve{\ }\ —$$
$$\breve{\ }\ —\ \breve{\ }\ —$$

That can be translated, yes, you can do it by opening and shutting
your mouth or anything else you have. But that is it. And there are
these things that move from sound to the meaningless words. We
have them, we know what they are. We get them in the old days, a
few years ago a woman was not supposed to say it, but well, in the
early centuries and the nineteenth, you had O for a meaningless
space-holder or something to give it sound and exaltation, and then
you had ah—"Ah, what avails the sceptered race." That kind of
thing. We have something else now. Here is one example which
Frances Keene was good enough to show me in the translation that
Eshleman did of Vallejo, the line in the poem is *"Pero me busca y
busca. ¡Es una historia!"* and Eshleman has had the generosity to
translate it. "But she looks and looks for me, what a fucking story."
Well, that doesn't exist in the original, and it's a dishonor to the word
which is dishonored anyway as a kind of monkey insult or superiority
sign, but it is used as a placeholder, and we get an awful lot of that.
This in translation seems to me an abomination. And when you're
translating poems you long for something to solve your torment,
every few breaths. Because with almost any other language, you need
something for this place, and if it exists, it exists only by turning it
and putting in something which generally is not a good idea.

The things that one finds as solvings are generally not good ideas.
And you have to think how to bring over something that depends
on breathing, throwing against one's heartbeat, thrown against all the
muscles in one's body and this is only a way of speaking. What we
are talking about is something entire. One's self entire. Jespersen
speaking of languages says, you have to remember that it's the mouth
and the air passages and the lungs and the abdomen and the body
cavity. It's more than that. That's just a beginning. Collingwood
says it about painting. We say painting is seen through the eye and
done with the hand—nonsense. A painting is made by a man walking
up and down in space before another space and working on it and
turning his back on it and walking away and sleeping and doing all
this other thing, and it's seen in the same way. These are entire. The
movement in the Translation Bill of Rights from unit to unity is the
true movement here. And it is the movement in the translation of
poetry, and this is not to exclude prose. This is the total thing, and
it depends on every breath we take, and that is a figure of speech. So,
there is the thing of an equivalent music, and what is that? Do we
try to pull through the tradition in the translations of Emily Dickinson in Italian, the attempt is made to offer a hymn music because
Emily Dickinson's poems are based on a hymn music familiar to
New Englanders of a certain religion and a certain time. What is

that in Italy? What does that bring through? Is the Italian reader
like the general average man who forgot the stem of *avunculus* and
everybody knows the stem will be the part that's kept. But we have
received the word. The stem is the part that has been lost, thrown
away. We have to be willing to lose in this. We have to be willing to
see a great deal die. We have to trust our forgetting as we all trust
our forgetting. We know that these things are in us, somewhere. I
can't say that the tradition of China is in us somewhere, it has to be
shown to us. But there are correspondences and the work to
bring the music through counts on these correspondences and
counts on—I've heard people say instinct and intuition but I really
don't think there's any such thing. I think it's noticing, noticing
very much the thingy quality of poetry, these are physical things.
We are physical beings dealing with each other. Suzuki in answering
the question about the Buddha offering the lotus was asked, "Isn't
that fragile?" And he said, "I speak to you, you speak to me, is
that fragile?"

And these things have the tensile strength of a single life.

Now, Isaac Singer speaking yesterday was talking about his lost
language. His lost people. And when he said in a charming, hostly
manner, I will translate you, you will translate me, this is a deep,
deep urgent cry. I want to end with a poem called The Writer.
I wrote it, actually, for him, I don't know at all, really. But I read
that New Yorker review tearing him apart—his lost language and his
lost people and I thought of all of us and what music we are trying
to carry through and out of what and how we have been willing to
risk our terrible mistakes and our terrible failures all the time, and go
on making it and make it, knowing it is about perfection, knowing
that we cannot hope for it, it is impossible, but we will go on doing
it. The Writer. His tears fell from his veins, they spoke for six
million; from his veins all their blood, he told his stories but no one
spoke his language, no one knew this music. The music went into
all people, not knowing this language, it ran through their bodies
and they began to take his words, everyone the tears, everyone the
veins, but everyone said no one spoke this language.

Translation and Complicity*

Clara Malraux

As soon as one starts to reflect upon a subject, any subject, the whole universe seems to be obsessed with it. The most commonplace conversation opens up a new point of view; books and even newspapers provide sidelights. At least that is how it is with me and how it has been, in particular, since I learned of my invitation to come to this conference and began to focus my mind on the problems of translation. Truth compels me to admit that although I have translated for years and into three languages, I have, until now, thought very little about the problems involved, simply solving them as they came up, somewhat the way Monsieur Jourdain spoke prose without knowing it. But perhaps my unconscious was at work all along, for when circumstances caused me to put my mind upon the subject, everywhere, as I said above, I found grist for my mill—that is, I became aware of other people's ideas—I found plenty of my own ideas, for the most part in violent opposition.

But let us proceed in orderly fashion. A few days after receiving the letter inviting me to your meeting, I bought a literary monthly and a newspaper whose literary supplement came out on the same day. In both of them there were articles given over to the discussion between the translator of a successful book, whose translation was

* Translation by Frances Frenaye.

under attack, and two of our best translators, one of them from German and the other from English. The accused man said, not without humor, that "A sensible translator picks out a book to translate when he is fourteen years old and fifty years later is still translating it." To which one of his contradictors, actually a woman, retorted: "In theory, translation isn't just difficult; it's impossible," a statement which she later somewhat modified.

Stimulated by what I had read, I proceeded to question some of my friends, particularly those of foreign origin. Since Europe is such a fragmented continent, most of these friends came from small or smallish countries: Hungary, Yugoslavia, Holland, Israel. Never before had I realized in what isolation the best minds of such countries would live without translations and how necessary it is to carry out the "impossible" operation of putting what was thought and written in one language into another. Only a great power with a long past can live on its own resources alone; a lesser one would be bound to lose contact with the development of culture in general. I remembered the words of a Dutch friend, Eddy Duperron, one of the best representatives of a generation that almost entirely disappeared at the beginning of the last war: "It's tough to write in a language so little spoken and to know that there is no hope of finding more than a couple of thousand readers."

At this point I was struck by another and even more serious aspect of the problem: the possibility of a frightening impoverishment. I know that the important languages are widely known in small countries, but does this knowledge make for a better understanding of a foreign work than reading it in translation? I don't believe so, and I speak from experience, having read books in a language I don't really know well, Spanish, and then having re-read them in French. In short, I believe that it is better to read a good translation than to stumble through an original. People in the small countries seem to agree, since many of their important writers dedicate themselves for long periods to the theoretically impossible task of translation, which they consider a duty toward their fellow citizens.

I had a Hungarian friend, Ladislas Gara, who gave of himself unstintingly and successfully to the opposite mission, that of making the poets of his country known in France. He laid siege to the best French poets—all of them his friends—persuading the ones whom he thought most suitable to undertake such and such a translation. The translating process had several stages, with Gara in on them all, ceaselessly strengthening the ties between the original creator and his interpreter. The anthology of Hungarian poetry published at his instigation was a splendid success and an enriching contribution to our appreciation of literature.

I may say, at this point, that I heard André Gide observe that every writer should, in his lifetime, make at least one translation, that it was a fruitful experience to which he had, at one time, committed himself.

The translator, Marthe Robert, whom I quoted in my account of the newspaper and magazine discussion, voiced the following opinion:

> The impossibility of translation stems from the fact that there is no exact equivalent in one language for even the most concrete words of another. The word "bread", for instance, cannot be translated. In another language it has not the same weight, the same age, the same semantic frame, the same degree of expressiveness; it indicates the same object but without the same social and psychological connotations.

It is upon this last word, "connotations," that I should like to pause for a moment. Herein centers the great problem of all communication, whether between individuals or from one language to another. It is obvious that, at a certain level, communication is impossible, and I am glad of it. It is frightening to think of a world of total communication, with no unlit corners, no margin for dreams or interpretation. "It is only thanks to misunderstandings that we understand one another," said Laforgue, who after some years of eclipse, is coming into his own. And then words are never alone; they are joined to other words which define or, if I may say so, un-define them, whose vicinity gives them different shades of meaning such as those taken on by single notes in a context of music. The translator's freedom begins on what city planners call the "environmental" level, to which I might add that every work of art begins in the margin of possible interpretations. The fact that two and two make four leaves no margin for interpretation—there is nothing I can do about it—but outside of mathematics my manner of transmission modifies (while respecting it) what I transmit. There is the whole difficulty, to transmit something which originated with somebody else. This sort of marriage—for marriage it is—may be possible only between persons between whom there is a deep affinity. And, even then, we have to know at exactly what level the affinity lies.

In my view—and I don't want to shock you—the affinity is not at the level of knowledge of the language to be translated. Quite the opposite. This is obviously a paradox. Let us clear it up with examples from my own experience. I learned French and German simultaneously. When I am in German surroundings, I think and even dream in German. In making a translation, particularly a long one, from German into French, the German sentence before and inside me leaves its imprint on the French sentence which is yet to be born of it and has not yet acquired the independence of a true creation. There is only one way in which I can possess that which is trying to possess me: and that is to let it rest. When I return, after a matter of weeks, to this almost extraneous task words no longer concern me. What I try to seize, to adapt rather than to transpose it, is the rhythm, the underlying flow, like that of the blood in my body. There are books with which I achieve a real symbiosis, which welcome me as I welcome them; others remain permanently alien.

One day while I was working on Virginia Woolf's *A Room of One's Own* I realized that it was easier for me to translate a woman than a man. Virginia Woolf's long and sinuous sentences, her way of picking up and dropping a metaphor without ever abandoning it, fitted in with my capacities. Actually this discovery was not too surprising. Already I had conceived an idea—based, as usual, on my own experience and on that of literary friends—one which is perhaps oversimplified and exaggerated and which I beg you to consider simply as a directional sign; namely, that we write with our bodies, their motor impulses and breathing rhythms, their proportions and disproportions. Faguet, a critic—not a very great critic but one who influenced my contemporaries when they were in school—said, very convincingly, that he didn't believe that people who have never tried to write poetry can really love it. I wrote poems when I was a girl and most of them came to me (in an imperfect form) when I was walking. Those that came to me at other times had quite a different rhythm. Here I must say that the importance which I attach to movement has been recognized by other people of greater ability than myself. I shall quote the chief and most recent among them, Father Marcel Gousse, whose posthumous work (he died in 1961), *L'Anthropologie du geste,* has just been published. Jacques Madaule has said of this book—better than I could say it— "Isn't movement an epitome of man? Nothing is more human, especially in the broader context in which Gousse sees it, where movement is the basis of speech. For what does man do when he finds himself up against the universe? He mimics it with his movements or gestures; thus he becomes aware of himself and of the world. The fact that all his movements are eventually reduced to words does not permit us to forget their origin." And, in my opinion, movement and gesture imply rhythm. I may add that Gousse was a linguist and that today's scholars don't go along with his way of thinking; they are interested in structures rather than in

gestures or movements. But, since I belong to the generation of
Gousse, I may say that writing is often a question of mimicry, and
hence of rhyme, and that translation is likewise. Here is the level of
the creativity which I consider one of the most important components
of translation.

The experience of Marcel Proust, one of the greatest writers of the
first half of the century, is open to interpretation along the same
line. I should like, for the sake of my own reassurance, to examine
it with you.

Proust, as you doubtless know, made translations of Ruskin for the
purpose of getting to know him better. (Albert Béguin did the same
thing with certain German works, because he wanted to read them
and they had not been translated.) Neither one knew the language
of the original very well. Proust—whose knowledge of English was
slight—was helped by his mother, who wrote out a literal translation
for him in (so we are told) red, green, and yellow copy-books.
"How did you do it?" Constantin de Brancovan is said to have
asked him, "when you had so few notions of the language?" And
indeed, in his essay on Ruskin, Proust translated "living soul" as
"âme aimante—loving soul." In any case, after his mother had
made the preliminary motions, he found himself in the situation of
the translator who puts a certain distance between himself and his
first draft, or in that of one who enlists the aid of a compatriot of
the author whose language he does not know. With all of this
Proust achieved an historically remarkable translation or rather re-
creation, in which the long and sinuous sentences which envelop
Ruskin's thought are rendered to perfection. Of course, there is
an obvious affinity of rhythm and style between the two writers.
In his biography of Proust, Painter brings this out quite clearly:
"Ruskin's influence on Proust, that is, on his future works, came
not so much from Proust's wish to write like Ruskin as from his discovery that Ruskin wrote like him." Here we have an obvious case
of almost lover-like complicity, which is both clarified and further
complicated when we come to Proust's *Pastiches et mélanges.*

In short, what I am driving at is to prove that an underlying
tendency, a need of connivance and complicity, impels a writer to
make translations and parodies or, on a lower plane, verbal take-offs
—a game at which Proust, who was extremely sensitive to tones of
voice and rhythms, notoriously excelled. We have only to remember
how he rendered his characters' ways of speaking. Men and women
were, to him, essentially sounds and intonations. To return to
Proust's *Pastiches,* they were fantastically successful. He has told us
himself why he wrote them: "One must voluntarily undertake to

write parodies, in order to return, later on, to being original, in order
not to make an unintentional parody one's whole life long." Of
course, we must not go so far as to imagine that Proust was so pli-
able as to lose himself completely in the identity of another man; his
pastiches are born out of a deep understanding of both other writers'
capabilities and his own. Allow me, at this point, to quote him
directly: "As soon as I had begun to read a writer I made out, beneath his words, the underlying tune which is what distinguishes one
writer from another. This is how I was able to write parodies [let me
emphasize these words] because as soon as one has caught a writer's
tune, the words with which to imitate him come quite spontaneous-
ly." The "tune"—this is what I have meant when speaking of the
importance of rhythm. Elsewhere, in a letter to Robert Dreyfus,
where there is mention of Renan, Proust states even more clearly:
"My metronome was set to his rhythm."

Just recently there came out in France an anthology of Elizabethan
poets translated by Philippe de Rothschild. I must add, by way of
parenthesis, that the English writers of this period are, for the most
part, little known in France and that Philippe de Rothschild's translations are the work of a true pioneer. There are, naturally, omissions,
and a few errors, which critics fell upon with malicious joy. For my
part, I was completely satisfied, and a sentence in the translator's
preface added to my appreciation. Here it is: "A certain gaiety, a
dancing movement, is more important than unresponsive and pedantic exactitude." Yes, this sentence is really to my taste; it points up
what to me is the essential, an essential that can only be born of
a marvelous complicity.

I grant that this complicity—creative as it may be—is not, fundamentally, at the level of the original creation. I have never confused
my own writings with those produced in collaboration with an
author whom I was translating.

After this brief reference to my own work, I hesitate to quote
Proust again. Forgive me for what seems to be a sign of lack of
modesty; in reality, it is nothing of the sort. Here, then, is what he
says: "I have come to an end of the period of translations. When it
comes to the translations of my own works, I haven't the nerve."
The culmination of his activity as a translator was, indeed, left
behind; and, in spite of his deprecatory and pessimistic prophecy,
the translation of his own work had only begun. But the similarity
which he establishes between a personally creative work and a
translation is definitive. "The writer's task is not to imagine but to
perceive," he wrote. "The artist is essentially a scribe."

For Proust, then, artistic creation is to be achieved through sub-
mission to something that is already there. For me, this is self-evident. The same process, lower on the scale, is that followed by a true
translator. He must first lose and then gain his identity, submerge
himself completely in another's experience, and yet maintain his
own personality. This is a demanding task, and I say once again that
it cannot be successfully performed unless the two persons concerned
are creatures of the same universe, possessed of complementary sensibilities, and, above all, moving to common rhythms which well up
from the same depths of the unconscious.

New Aspects of Translation

George Quasha

Transformation: that is the key word in what I have to say. What little I've managed to do so far as poet, translator and editor has been done in the name of transformation: transformation of language as a way to transformation of self and civilization.

I regard translation as an extension of that which is being translated, not as a separate activity performed by a wise and disinterested craftsman. It *is* a separate activity but one which strives in the structure of its behavior to *re-perform,* within the materials of one's own language, the possibilities and special realizations which exist in a foreign work. The *necessity* for authentic translation is basically of the same kind as the necessity for poetry: that is, for real language, for language which serves deeper needs than we are normally able to meet. The meaning of the act of translation, as I understand it, is simply to say: look, this too is possible in American English, if that happens to be your language; in fact, not only is it possible, it is essential. This definition of meaningful translation will seem to some translators to be overly restrictive or perhaps a little romantic. Maybe. But, for me, it's all we have time for. The true craftsmen of language are asked to sign up immediately for the full-time (27 hrs./ day) job of making our language usable in a time of crisis—which time includes all of human history but especially Now; signed: W. Blake, E. Pound, R.M. Rilke, M. Rukeyser, and a host of other underground types.

203

So you see I'm making propaganda. I'm throwing my weight behind the hunch that what we really want to be doing is what is most deeply real to us as disciples of Earth and her various projections in the form of language. As translators we are among the privileged individuals who are devious enough to be able to relate to more than one of these projections; we want more than our share. That's fine, but the moralist in me says: twice as much fun means twice as much work in rendering our relationships authentic on all sides. No nonsense about double-standards: two mistresses mean twice as many wives. We must be faithful to both as though each were our only bridge between isolation and the great outdoors of human community. If we're lucky enough to be poets, fun and work are the same anyway. If we're just ordinary old superb translators, the journey is of a special kind: we have to keep reminding ourselves that our relationship to the language we're translating into has got to be as authentic as our relationship to the one we're translating from. Our responsibility is to make something as *real* as the reality that called us to this presumptuous business in the first place. It's one thing to say: look here, I've discovered how great Vallejo is and want you all to read him right away. And another to say: you unfortunate individuals who don't read Spanish can get the message with this brand-new substitute that I've cooked up. That sort of crazy self-assertion has to have something more behind it than a good dictionary, memories of a lively stay in Lima, and a noble desire to communicate using another man's words. In my opinion it's the culture snob, who won't admit that translation is communication in precisely the sense that language-art is communication, who has been causing so much trouble all these centuries. I mean there must be more than a few Rilke-loving young poets around who are victims of C. F. MacIntyre's brand of self-gratifying incoherence. Poets are teachers; historically and actually, they are teachers about what is possible in the way of genuine speech. In another language they're in the hands of the translators who more often than not are misrepresenting that message. Good intentions don't count.

But it isn't my purpose to come on as great reformer. My purpose here is to advertise the efforts of certain individuals to render translation an activity which bears close kinship to poetry in its unremitting struggle to renew human language. My version of the story is necessarily limited by what I'm prepared to admit as real. I do not apologize for that limitation; on the contrary, I believe it's a necessary admission, because I take it that no man without unbecoming hubris can claim or even desire to have a corner on reality. I grow more impatient every day with all manner of pretension about relia-

ble objectivity in the arts and in criticism of the arts. It would seem
to be an occasion for great rejoicing that here at least we are spared
the supercilious pose of always being right. I do not envy the critic
who feels it his obligation to do more than struggle for an active,
accurate and useful perspective. And here I give myself away: I'm
prejudiced in favor of the open-ended and the experimental in the
arts, a stance which says, "Today I'm doing it this way because all
the forces of heart and brain conspire to bully me into this solution;
thank God, I didn't sign any contracts to do it this way tomorrow."
I apply this to translation: by attending to the demands of Language
Now, we are free to give ourselves over to actual pressures to render
language functional; translation becomes part of a broader struggle
to launch our speech-boat on the troubled waters of experience; if
it sinks, tough, we pray for dolphins, or rather to them.

However, I don't wish to pretend to be advertising professional
modesty in saying that we must stay mainly in our own corners.
Modesty is a lovely quality but it doesn't respond favorably to being
sought, or advertised. Many of my heroes, like Ezra Pound, have
rarely been called modest. For example, I have no desire to be
modest about my personal outrage over the brutal American rape
of a small Indochinese country. And I am not among those who see
art as less serious or less responsible than politics to the fundamental
demands on human consciousness. On the contrary, art attacks the
disease at its root. If language is not itself the root, as Confucius and
Pound argued, it is at least the main stem of the plant growing there-
from—and our main link with the root. And one doesn't have to
listen to many speeches by certain high government officials to realize that Pound's concern for the connection between language (and
its art forms) and social history is relevant.

At the risk of appearing arrogant, I must continue to labor the
point that translation is serious business. Surely this is the point of
this conference, and surely everyone agrees: inauthentic translation
is worse than no translation. Our job is to transform language as a
way of transforming consciousness before it is too late.

Before the Southern preacher in me takes over, I want to get back
to what I was saying about the openness of art as an occasion for
rejoicing. I believe that genuine transformation of language accom-
panies those moments in our experience which strain our communication system and bring it close to the breaking point. The genuinely
new often appears first in the guise of a last-ditch, make-shift solution to an otherwise insoluble problem, and I suppose all translators
are aware of getting some of their best ideas at times when they seem
to have no ideas. The sheer fact of dealing with a foreign language

brings about a certain pressure on our own language to create space
for the perception that seems locked in the original. But our usual
bag of tricks for approximating the original reduces the tension; easy
solutions preclude new solutions. What is needed—even more than
increasingly subtle dictionaries to refer to—is a source of tension *outside* the verbal system in which one is working. The best source is
what might be called inspiration. A being called to the act of language by a sense of necessity that runs deeper than we can account
for. But it's pointless to try to discuss the felicities of inspired work,
unless there is someone present who knows where we can go load up.
Yet there are levels of being "called" which one can get in touch with
by means slightly less rarefied than incarnation. Means which have to
do with the root sense of "translation": relating across boundaries.
Ways of giving voice to deeper dimensions of our own language, so
that we "claim" a new linguistic function, we "transclaim" or "exclaim" from one language to the other. This genuine discovery is an
occasion for rejoicing because it has opened what Rilke called the
speech-seed. The translator has to have the patience to await the real
opportunities for discovery. He can't induce them. But he can go a
long way towards adjusting the circumstances so as to open the gates.

The best way of opening the gates is to keep one's mind attuned to
the needs of contemporary poetry. Ezra Pound is the hero of this
realm; as Hugh Kenner says in the introduction to that major work
of modern American poetry, *Translations:* "Ezra Pound never translates 'into' something already existing in English. The Chinese or
Greek or Provençal poem being by hypothesis something new, if it
justifies the translator's or the reader's time . . . . " I will not pre-
sume to add to the brilliant discussions of Pound's work as translator
which Mr. Kenner has offered in that Introduction and in a recent
series of articles which make up his forthcoming book, *The Pound
Era.*[1] And I would hope that any serious translator of poetry in
English is familiar with Pound's achievement. What might not be so
obvious is the way in which a translation like Pound's *The Seafarer*
from the Anglo-Saxon reintroduces musical possibilities into English
which the poetry has lost touch with; and, further, the way in which
that music partly becomes the basis for a major re-invention of
modern poetry as of Canto I of Pound's epic. More recently Basil
Bunting has extended certain of these Poundian contributions in a
long, musically structured poem called "Briggflatts" (Fulcrum Press,
London).

[1] A selection from that work appears in my magazine, *Stony Brook, 3/4, 1969,*
pp. 371-377, followed by a bibliography of other published sections. (See also
Wai-Lim Yip's recent study, *Ezra Pound's Cathay,* Princeton Univ. Press.)

A conventional definition of translation does not normally include the entrance of poetic possibilities into a poet's own work, and yet more and more one runs across young Anglo-Saxon scholars who are prepared to admit that Canto I is probably our best representation in modern English of the poetic meanings of Anglo-Saxon elegies. Canto I is also a retranslation of a portion of Andreas Divus' sixteenth-century translation into Latin of the eleventh book of *The Odyssey:*

> And then went down to the ships,
> Set keel to breakers, forth on the godly sea, and
> We set up mast and sail on that swart ship.
> Bore sheep aboard her, and our bodies also
> Heavy with weeping, and winds from sternward
> Bore us out onward with bellying canvas,
> Circe's this craft, the trim-coifed goddess.

Michael Alexander, in introducing his brilliant translations from Old English, published a few years back by Penguin Books *(The Earliest English Poems),* openly acknowledged Pound as the master. Scholarly carping about literal inaccuracies in Pound's versions, when heard against the music of the *Cantos* and of the best of that work which Pound's translations made possible, sound like the hollow voices of those condemned to hell in Canto XIV, "the perverters of language."

Ultimately, I would want to argue that even such works as Blake's *Milton* must enter our discussions of the meanings of translation: a work in which another poet in one's own language requires representation in order to resolve open poetic issues introduced by the original poet. Pound was constantly doing this sort of thing: testing, adapting, "making new" the authentic elements of past culture as part of contemporary consciousness. And contemporary poets like Robert Duncan have pursued this mission into the present, as when he musically "rescores" an earlier work in *Shelley's "Arethusa" Set to New Measures,* revealing musical meanings of Shelley which otherwise eluded us. Similarly, in a poem like "After a Passage in Baudelaire," Duncan takes a prose passage and makes it the basis for an original poem that, in some ways, brings us closer to the spirit of Baudelaire than most translations of that poet are able to do:

> Ship, leaving or arriving, of my lover,
> my soul, leaving or coming into this harbor,
> among your lights and shadows shelterd,
> at home in your bulk, the cunning
> regularity and symmetry thruout
> of love's design, of will, of your
> attractive cells and chambers

riding forward, darkest of shades
over the shadowd waters
into the light, neat, symmetrically
arranged above your watery reflections
disturbing your own image, moving as you are

    What passenger, what sailor,
looks into the swirling currents round you
as if into those depths into a mirror?

What lights in what port-holes
raise in my mind again   hunger and impatience?
to make my bed down again, there, beyond me,
as if this room too, my bedroom, my lamp at my side,
were among those lights sailing out
                away from me.

We too, among the others, passengers
in that *charme infini et mystérieux,*
in that suitable symmetry, that precision
everywhere, the shining fittings, the fit
of lights and polisht surfaces to the dark,
to the flickering shadows of them,
we too, unfaithful to me, sailing away,
leaving me.

L'idée poétique, the idea of a poetry,
that rises from the movement, from the
outswirling curves and imaginary figures
round this ship, this fate, this sure thing,

    est l'hypothèse d'une être vaste, immense,

    compliqué; mais eurythmique.

I think anyone familiar with Pound's versions of Cavalcanti's *Donna me priegha,* especially the one in Canto XXXVI, will hear clear echos here of such lines as:

    Where memory liveth,
            it takes its state
    Formed like a diafan from light on shade
    Which shadow cometh of Mars and remaineth

> Created, having a name sensate,
> Custom of the soul,
>   will from the heart . . . .

Both Pound and Duncan found in their confrontation with earlier
poets what Duncan calls, in a deliberate "mistranslation" of *L'Idée
poétique,* "the idea of a poetry,/that rises from the movement." The
idea of *a* poetry, and there are many poetries: it is our business as
poet-translators to render such an "idea" as reality "rising" from a
specific language "movement."

However, I do not wish to give the impression of caring little for
semantic accuracies in translation as we usually define it. But that
dimension of the serious business of translation is the one most
attended to, whereas the more illusive poetic qualities—the subtler
dynamics of a specific poetic system—tend to go unmentioned. The
translations which I admire most show a real struggle for semantic
accuracy. However, this sort of concern for literal faithfulness to the
original needn't be antithetical to the radical process of transposition
which I've been discussing. Certainly my own efforts in the Rilke
versions sought as much literal accuracy as I could manage. But I'm
thinking too of the job Clayton Eshleman did on César Vallejo's
Poémas Humanos (published by Grove Press)—one of the great poetic
works of the century which enjoys a reputation in Lima of being untranslatable. It is characteristic of a poet with Eshleman's sense of
the necessity for major risks and the need for profound transformation that he should take on a task which lesser men call impossible.
I cannot imagine any more urgent business than making Vallejo known
in English—particularly the major Vallejo of the later works. Eshleman
worked several years on the project: spending a year in Lima studying the language and Vallejo's papers (in the possession of the widow),
working with scholarly dedication toward establishing the first decent
text of *Poémas Humanos;* and setting forth on what was to take six
complete versions (or "strata," as he calls them) before he was satisfied. There remain inaccuracies, and I myself object to certain stra-
tegies which he uses to bring the Vallejo across. But these objections
are insignificant: Eshleman gives us a powerful image of Vallejo in
English and substantiates his claim that the Peruvian poet stands
beside Blake and Rilke as one of the major prophets of psychic transformation. In order to bring it off, Eshleman tells us he himself had
to undergo a measure of that transformation: he had to live the meaning of the poetry. His own important work as poet clearly begins
with his encountering Vallejo.

The kind of poetry which interests me most is that which puts
poetry in danger in an effort to expand it and renew it. The kind of
translation which interests me most is that which helps us to do this
by showing us what we haven't been able to do. In *Stony Brook* we
have presented a good deal of this sort of thing. Of special importance to me is the "ethnopoetics" work of Jerome Rothenberg, which
has appeared in each of the two double issues of *Stony Brook,* in his
anthology *Technicians of the Sacred.*[1] and in a new magazine,
Alcheringa, edited by Rothenberg and anthropologist Dennis Tedlock?
The central concern here is oral and performance-oriented poetry
derived from tribal practices around the world. This sort of thing
enjoys parallels in the whole range of modern poetries from Blake to
Pound to present. A number of contemporary poets—from the late
Charles Olson and other Black Mountain poets like Robert Duncan
to post-Beat poets like Ginsberg and Ed Sanders and then to experi-
mentalists like Jackson Mac Low, Jerome Rothenberg, Armand
Schwerner, Robert Kelly, Clayton Eshleman, David Antin, and others
—have sought to extend the Blakeian-Poundian tradition of revolutionary poetry. Rothenberg's *Technicians* provides the most comprehensive list to date of parallels between the translated works and
these contemporary tendencies in poetry. It is my belief that we are
approaching a period of radical transformation in our ideas about
poetry, translation, and language generally. I see my own work as
attempting to aid that transformation in every genuine way that I can.

*

In presenting these ideas before the Conference, I attempted a
performance of a Navaho chant-poem called "The Tenth Horse-Song
of Frank Mitchell (Blue)" (see p. 221) in Jerome Rothenberg's translation. Rather than attempt to discuss here, as I did in the presentation, an area of radically new methods in translation dealing with oral
poetries, I have decided simply to reproduce Rothenberg's own important statement on "Total Translation," from which I drew most of
my ideas. On the whole, I regard Rothenberg's work as the most significant addition to translation method in recent years. Extended to
its ultimate meaning, the method implies a reconstitution of the
"communal" meanings of poetry: poetry and translation as events
that bring us together in the rediscovery of our language.

[1]"A Range of Poetries from Africa, America, Asia & Oceania," Doubleday.
[2]Published by Stony Brook Poetics Foundation.

JEROME ROTHENBERG

TOTAL TRANSLATION

an experiment in the presentation
of american indian poetry

It wasn't really a "problem," as these things are sometimes called, but to get closer to a way of poetry that had concerned me from years before, though until this project I'd only been able to approach it at a far remove. I'd been translating "tribal" poetry (the latest, still imperfect substitute I can find for "primitive," which continues to bother me) out of books: doing my versions from earlier translations into languages I could cope with, including English. Toward the end of my work on *Technicians* I met Stanley Diamond, a good anthropologist & friend of Gary Snyder's, who directed me to the Senecas in upstate New York, & David McAllester, ethnomusicologist at Wesleyan University, who showed me how a few songs worked in Navaho. With their help (& a nod from Dell Hymes as well) I later was able to get Wenner-Gren Foundation support to carry on a couple of experiments in the translation of American Indian poetry. I'm far enough into them by now to say a little about what I've been doing.

* * * * * * * *

In the Summer of 1968 I began to work simultaneously with two sources of Indian poetry. Settling down a mile from the Cold Spring settlement of the Allegany (Seneca) Reservation at Steamburg, New York, I was near enough to friends who were traditional songmen to work with them on the translation of sacred & secular song-poems. At the same time David McAllester was sending me recordings, transcriptions, literal translations & his own freer reworkings of a series of seventeen "horse-songs"

that had been the property of Frank Mitchell, a Navaho singer from Chinle, Arizona (born: 1881, died: 1967). Particularly with the Senecas (where I didn't know in the first instance what, if anything, I was going to get) my first concern was with the translation process itself. While I'll limit myself to that right now, I should at least say (things never seem to be clear unless you say them) that if I hadn't also come up with matter that I could "internalize," I would have floundered long before this.

The big question, which I was immediately aware of with both poetries, was if & how to handle those elements in the original works that weren't translatable literally. As with most Indian poetry, the voice carried many sounds that weren't, strictly speaking, "words." These tended to disappear or be attenuated in translation, as if they weren't really there. But they *were* there & were at least as important as the words themselves. In both Navaho & Seneca many songs consisted of nothing but those "meaningless" vocables (not free "scat" either but fixed sounds recurring from performance to performance). Most other songs had both meaningful & non-meaningful elements, & such songs (McAllester told me for the Navaho) were often spoken of, *qua* title, by their meaningless burdens. Similar meaningless sounds, Dell Hymes had pointed out for some Kwakiutl songs, might in fact be keys to the songs' structures: "something usually disregarded, the refrain or so-called 'nonsense syllables' . . . in fact of fundamental importance . . . both structural clue & microcosm." (For which, see the first issue of this very magazine, pages 184-5, etc.)

So there were all these indications that the exploration of "pure sound" wasn't beside the point of those poetries but at or near their heart: all of this coincidental too with concern for the sound-poem among a number of modern poets. Accepting its meaningfulness here, I more easily accepted it there. I also realized (with the Navaho especially) that there were more than

*Reprinted from *Stony Brook 3/4,* © 1969, by permission of Jerome Rothenberg and George Quasha for The Stony Brook Poetics Foundation, Box 1102, Stony Brook, NY 11790.

simple refrains involved: that we, as translators &
poets, had been taking a rich *oral* poetry &
translating it to be read primarily for meaning,
thus denuding it to say the least.

Here's an immediate example of what I
mean. In the first of Frank Mitchell's seventeen
horse-songs, the· opening line comes out as
follows in McAllester's transcription:

dzo-wowode sileye shi, dza-na desileye shiyi,
dzanadi sileye shiya'e

but the same segment given "as spoken" reads:

dzą̄di silá shi dzą̄di silá shi dzą̄di silá shi

which translates as "over-here it-is-there (&)
mine" repeated three times. So does the line as
sung if you're accounting for is the meaning.
In other words, translate only for meaning & you
get the three-fold repetition of an unchanging
single statement; but in the Navaho each time it's
delivered there's a sharp departure from the
spoken form: thus three distinct sound-events,
not one-in-triplicate!

I know neither Navaho nor Seneca except
for bits of information picked up from grammar
books & such (also the usual social fall-out
among the Senecas: "cat," "dog," "thank you,"
"you're welcome," numbers one to ten, "uncle,"
"father," & my Indian name). But even from this
far away, I can (with a little help from my
friends) be aware of my options as translator. Let
me try, then, to respond to *all* the sounds I'm
made aware of, to let that awareness touch off
responses or events in the English. I don't want
to set English words to Indian music, but to
respond poem-for-poem in the attempt to work
out a "total" translation—not only of the words
but of all sounds connected with the poem,
including finally the music itself.

* * * * * * * *

Seneca & Navaho are very different worlds,

& what's an exciting procedure for one may be
deadening or irrelevant for the other. The English
translation should match the character of the
Indian original: take that as a goal & don't worry
about how literal you're otherwise being.
Lowenfels calls poetry "the continuation of
journalism by other means," & maybe that holds
too for translation-as-poem. I translate, then, as a
way of reporting what I've sensed or seen of an
other's situation: true as far as possible to "my"
image of the life & thought of the source.

Living with the Senecas helped in that
sense. I don't know how much stress to put on
this, but I know that in so far as I developed a
strategy for translation from Seneca, I tried to
keep to approaches I felt were consistent with
their life-style. I can hardly speak of the poetry
without using words that would describe the
people as well. Not that it's easy to sum-up any
people's poetry or its frame-of-mind, but since
one is always doing it in translation, I'll attempt
it also by way of description.

Seneca poetry, when it uses words at all,
works in sets of short songs, minimal realizations
colliding with each other in marvelous ways, a
very light, very pointed play-of-the-mind, nearly
always just a step away from the comic (even as
their masks are), the words set out in clear relief
against the ground of the ("meaningless")
refrain. Clowns stomp & grunt through the
longhouse, but in subtler ways too the encouragement to "play" is always a presence. Said
the leader of the longhouse religion at Allegany,
explaining why the seasonal ceremonies ended
with a gambling game: the idea of a religion was
to reflect the *total* order of the universe while
providing an outlet for *all* human needs, the need
for play not least among them. Although it
pretty clearly doesn't work out as well nowadays
as that makes it sound—the orgiastic past & the
"doings" (happenings) in which men were free to
live-out their dreams dimming from generation to
generation—still the resonance, the ancestral per-
missiveness, keeps being felt in many ways.

Sacred occasions may be serious & necessary, but it doesn't take much for the silence to be broken

by laughter: thus, says Richard Johnny John, if you call for a medicine ceremony of the mystic animals & it turns out that no one's sick & in need of curing, the head-one tells the others: "I leave it up to you folks & if you want to have a good time, have a good time!" He knows they will anyway.

I take all of that as cue: to let my moves be directed by a sense of the songs & of the attitudes surrounding them. Another thing I try not to overlook is that the singers & I, while separated in Seneca, are joined in English. That they have to translate for me is a problem at first, but the problem suggests its own solution. Since they're bilingual, sometimes beautifully so, why not work from that instead of trying to get around it? Their English, fluent while identifiably Senecan, is as much a commentary on where they are as mine is on where I am. Given the "minimal" nature of much of the poetry (one of its *strongest* features, in fact) there's no need for a dense response in English. Instead I can leave myself free to structure the final poem by using their English as a base: a particular enough form of the language to itself be an extra means for the extension of reportage through poetry & translation.

I end up collaborating & happy to do so, since translation (maybe poetry as well) has always involved that kind of thing for me. The collaboration can take a number of forms. At one extreme I have only to make it possible for the other man to take over: in this case, to set up or simply to encourage a situation in which a man who's never thought of himself as a "poet" can begin to structure his utterances with a care for phrasing & spacing that drives them toward poetry. *Example.* Dick Johnny John & I had taped his Seneca version of the thanking prayer that opens all longhouse gatherings & were translating it phrase by phrase. He had decided to

write it down himself, to give the translation to his sons, who from oldest to youngest were progressively losing the Seneca language. I could follow his script from where I sat, & the method of punctuation he was using seemed special to me, since in letters & such he punctuates more or less conventionally. Anyway, I got his punctuation down along with his wording, with which he was taking a lot of time both in response to my questions & from his desire "to word it just the way it says there." In setting up the result, I let the periods in his prose version mark the ends of lines, made some vocabulary choices that we'd left hanging, & tried for the rest to keep clear of what was after all his poem. Later I titled it *Thank You: A Poem in 17 Parts*, & wrote a note on it for *El Corno*, where it was printed in English & Spanish. This is the first of the seventeen sections:

Now so many people that are in this place.
In our meeting place.
It starts when two people see each other.
They greet each other.
Now we greet each other.
Now he thought.
I will make the Earth where some people
                              can walk around.
I have created them, now this has happened.
We are walking on it.
Now this time of the day.
We give thanks to the Earth.
This is the way it should be in our minds.

[*Note.* The set-up in English doesn't, as far as I can tell, reproduce the movement of the Seneca text. More interestingly it's itself a consideration of that movement: is in fact Johnny John's reflections upon the values, the relative strengths of elements in his text. The poet is to a great degree concerned with what-stands-out & where, & his phrasing reveals it, no less here than in any other poem.]

Even when being more active myself, I

would often defer to others in the choice of words. Take, for example, a set of seven Woman's Dance songs with words, composed by Avery Jimerson & translated with help from his wife, Fidelia. Here the procedure was for Avery to record the song, for Fidelia to paraphrase it in English, then for the three of us to work out a transcription & word-by-word translation by a process of question & answer. Only afterwards would I actively come into it, to try to work out a poem in English with enough swing to it to return more or less to the area of song. *Example.* The paraphrase of the 6th Song reads:

Very nice, nice, when our mothers do the ladies' dance. Graceful, nice, very nice, when our mothers do the ladies' dance . . .

while the word-by-word, including the "meaningless" refrain, reads:

hey heya yo oh ho
nice nice nice-it-is
when-they-dance-the-ladies-dance
our-mothers
gahnoweyah heyah
graceful it-is
nice nice nice-it-is
when-they-dance-the-ladies-dance
our-mothers
gahnoweyah heyah (& repeat).

In doing *these* songs, I decided in fact to translate for meaning, since the meaningless vocables used by Jimerson were only the standard markers that turn up in all the woman's songs: *hey heyah yo* to mark the opening, *gahnoweyah heyah* to mark the internal transitions. (In my translation, I sometimes use a simple "hey," "oh" or "yeah" as a rough equivalent, but let the movement of the English determine its position.) I also decided not to fit English words to Jimerson's melody, regarding that as a kind of oil-&-water treatment, but to

suggest (as with most poetry) a music through the normally pitched speaking voice. For the rest I was following Fidelia Jimerson's lead:

hey it's nice it's nice it's nice
to see them yeah to see
our mothers do the ladies' dances
oh it's graceful & it's
nice it's nice it's very nice
to see them hey to see
our mothers do the ladies' dances.

With other kinds of song-poems I would also, as often as not, stick close to the translation-as-given, departing from that to better get the point of the whole across in English, to normalize the word order where phrases in the literal translation appeared in their original Seneca sequence, or to get into the play-of-the-thing on my own. The most important group of songs I was working on was a sacred cycle called *Idos* (ee-dos) in Seneca—in English either *Shaking the Pumpkin* or, more ornately, *The Society of the Mystic Animals.* Like most Seneca songs *with* words (most Seneca songs are in fact *without* words), the typical pumpkin song contains a single statement, or a single statement alternating with a row of vocables, which is repeated anywhere from three to six or seven times. Some songs are nearly identical with some others (same melody & vocables, slight change in words) but aren't necessarily sung in sequence. In a major portion of the ceremony, in fact, a fixed order for the songs is completely abandoned, & each person present takes a turn at singing a ceremonial (medicine) song of his own choice. There's room here too for messing around.

Dick Johnny John was my collaborator on the Pumpkin songs, & the basic wording is therefore his. My intention was to account for all vocal sounds in the original but—as a more "interesting" way of handling the minimal structures & allowing a very clear, very pointed emergence of perceptions—to translate the poems onto the page, as with "concrete" or other types of minimal poetry. Where several songs showed a concurrence of structure, I allowed myself the option of treating them individually or combining them into one. I've deferred singing until some future occasion.

Take the opening songs of the ceremony. These are fixed pieces sung by the ceremonial leader *(hajaswas)* before he throws the meeting open to the individual singers. The melody & structure of the first nine are identical: very slow, a single line of words ending with a string of sounds, etc., the pattern identical until the last go-round, when the song ends with a grunting expulsion of breath into a weary "ugh" sound. I had to get all of that across: the bareness, the regularity, the deliberateness of the song, along with the basic meaning, repeated vocables, emphatic terminal sound, & (still following Johnny John's reminder to play around with it "if everything's alright") a little something of my own. The song whose repeated line is

The animals are coming by *heh eh heh* (or
heh eh-eh-eh he)
can then become

```
T                            HEHEHHEH
h                            HEHEHHEH
e                            HEHUHHEH
The animals are coming by    HEHUHHEH
n                            HEHEHHEH
i                            HEHEHHEH
m
a
l
s
```

& the next one:

```
T                            HEHEHHEH
h                            HEHEHHEH
e                            HEHUHHEH
The doings were beginning    HEHUHHEH
o                            HEHEHHEH
i                            HEHEHHEH
n
g
s
```

& so forth: each poem set, if possible, on its own page, as further analogue to the slowness, the deliberate pacing of the original.

The use of vertical titles is the only move I make without immediate reference to the Seneca version: the rest I'd feel to be programmed by elements in the original prominent enough for me to respond to in the movement from oral to paginal structure. Where the song comes without vocables, I don't supply them but concentrate on presentation of the words. Thus in the two groups of "crow songs" printed elsewhere in this issue, one's a translation-for-meaning; the other ("in the manner of Zukofsky") puns off the Seneca sound:

yehgagaweeyo *(lit. that pretty crow)*

&

hongyasswahyaenee *(lit. that [pig]-meat's
for me)*

while trying at the same time to let something of the meaning come through.

A motive behind the punning was, I suppose, the desire to bring across (i.e., "translate") the feeling of the Seneca word for crow *(gaga or kaga)*, which is at the same time an imitation of the bird's voice. In another group—three songs about the owl—I pick up the vocables suggesting the animal's call & shape them into outline of a giant owl, within which frame the poems are printed. But that's only where the mimicry of the original is strong enough to trigger an equivalent move in translation; otherwise my inclination is to *present* analogues to the full range of vocal sound, etc., but not to *represent* the poem's subject as "mere picture."

The variety of possible moves is obviously related to the variety—semantic & aural—of the cycle itself.*

[N.B. Behind it all there's a hidden motive too: not simply to make clear the world of the original, but to do so at some remove from the song itself: to reflect the song without the "danger" of presenting any part of it (the melody, say) exactly as given: thus to have it while not having it, in deference to the sense of secrecy & localization that's so important to those for whom the songs are sacred & alive. So the changes resulting from translation are, in this instance, not only inevitable but desired, or, as another Seneca said to me: "We wouldn't want the songs to get so far away from us; no, the songs would be too lonely."]

* For which see the author's complete version in his *Summoning of the Tribes* (Indian anthology issue of the *Buffalo Translation Series*, Volume One, Number One, 1969).

****

My decision with the Navaho horse-songs was to work with the sound as sound: a reflection in itself of the difference between Navaho & Seneca song structure. For Navaho (as already indicated) is much fuller, much denser, twists words into new shapes or fills up the spaces between words by insertion of a wide range of "meaningless" vocables, making it misleading to translate primarily for meaning or, finally, to think of *total* translation in any terms but those of sound. Look, for example, at the number of free vocables in the following excerpt from McAllester's relatively literal translation of the 16th Horse-Song:

(nana na) Sun- (Yeye ye) Standing-within (neye ye)
                                                        Boy
  (Heye ye) truly his horses
  ('Eye ye) abalone horses

('Eye ye) made of sunrays
(Neye ye) their bridles

(Gowo wo) coming on my right side
(Jeye yeye) coming into my hand (yeye neyowo
                                                        'ei).

Now this, which even so doesn't show the additional word distortions that turn up in the singing, might be brought closer to English word order & translated for meaning alone as something like

> Boy who stands inside the Sun
> with your horses that are
> abalone horses
> bridles
> made of sunrays
> rising on my right side
> coming to my hand
> etc.

But what a difference from the fantastic way the sounds cut through the words & between them from the first line of the original on.

It was the possibility of working with all that sound, finding my own way into it in English, that attracted me now—that & a quality in Mitchell's voice I found irresistible. It was, I think, that the music was so clearly within range of the language: it was song & it was poetry, & it seemed possible at least that the song issued from the poetry, was an extension of it or rose inevitably from the juncture of words & other vocal sounds. So many of us had already become interested in this kind of thing as poets, that it seemed natural to me to be in a situation where the poetry would be leading me towards a (new) music *it* was generating.

I began with the 10th Horse-Song, which had been the first one Mitchell sang when McAllester was recording him. At that point I didn't know if I'd do much more than quote or allude to the vocables: possibly pull them or something like them into the English. I was *writing* at first, working on the words by sketching-in phrases that seemed natural to my own sense of the language. In the 10th Song there's a division of speakers: the main voice is that of Enemy Slayer or Dawn Boy, who first brought horses to The People, but the chorus is sung by his father, the Sun, telling him to take spirit horses & other precious animals & goods to the house of his mother, Changing Woman. The literal translation of the refrain—*(to) the woman, my son*—seemed a step away from how we'd say it, though normal enough in Navaho. It was with the sense that, whatever distortions in sound the Navaho showed, the syntax was natural, that I changed McAllester's suggested reading to *go to her my son*, & his opening line

Boy-brought-up-within-the-Dawn
It is I, I who am that one

(lit. *being that one*, with a suggestion of causation), to

Because I was the boy raised in the dawn.

At the same time I was, I thought, getting it down to more or less the economy of phrasing of the original.

I went through the first seven or eight lines like that but still hadn't gotten to the vocables. McAllester's more ''factual'' approach—reproducing the vocables exactly—seemed wrong to me on one major count. In the Navaho the vocables give a very clear sense of continuity from the verbal material; i.e., the vowels in particular show a rhyming or assonantal relationship between the "meaningless" & meaningful segments:

'Esdza shiye'	e hye-la	'esdza shiye'
The woman, my son	*(voc.)*	*The woman, my son*

e hye-la nana yeye 'e
(voc.)

whereas the English words for this & many other situations in the poem are, by contrast to the Navaho, more rounded & further back in the mouth. Putting the English words ("son" here but "dawn," "home," "upon," "blown," etc. further on) against the Navaho vocables denies the musical coherence of the original & destroys the actual flow.

I decided to *translate* the vocables, & from that point was already playing with the possibility of *translating* other elements in the songs not usually handled by translation. It also seemed important to get as far away as I could from *writing*. So I began to speak, then sing my own words over Mitchell's tape, replacing his vocables with sounds relevant to me, then putting my version on a fresh tape, having now to work it in its own terms. It wasn't an easy thing either for me to break the silence or go beyond the narrow pitch levels of my speaking voice, & I was still finding it more natural in that early version to replace the vocables with small English words (it's hard for a word-poet to lose words completely), hoping some of their semantic force would lessen with reiteration:

Go to her my son & one & go to her my son &
   one & one & none & gone
Go to her my son & one & go to her my son &
   one & one & none & gone

Because I was the boy raised in the dawn & one
  & go to her my son & one & one & none & gone
& leaving from the house the bluestone home &
  one & go to her my son & one & one & one &
                  none & gone
& leaving from the house the shining home &
  one & go to her my son & one & one & none &
                  gone
& from the swollen house my breath has blown
  & one & go to her my son & one & one & none
                & gone

& so on. In the transference too—likely enough because my ear is so damn slow—I found I was considerably altering Mitchell's melody; but really that was part of the translation process also: a change responsive to the translated sounds & words I was developing.

In singing the 10th Song I was able to bring the small words (vocable substitutions) even further into the area of pure vocal sound (the difference, it it's clear from the spelling, between *one, none & gone* and *wnn, nnnn & gahn*): soundings that would carry into the other songs at an even greater remove from the discarded meanings. What I was doing in one sense was contributing & then obliterating my own level of meaning, while in another I was as much as recapitulating the history of the vocables themselves, at least according to one of the standard explanations that sees them as remnants of archaic words that have been emptied of meaning: a process I could still sense elsewhere in the Horse-Songs—for example, where the sound *howo* turns up as both a "meaningless" vocable & a distorted form of the word *hoghan* = house. But even if I was doing something like that in an accelerated way, that wasn't the real point of it for me. Rather what I was getting at was the establishment of a series of sounds that were assonant with the range of my own vocabulary in the translation, & to which I could refer whenever the Navaho sounds for which they were substitutes turned up in Mitchell's songs.

In spite of carryovers, these basic soundings were different for each song (more specifically, for each *pair* of songs), & I found, as I moved from one song to another, that I had to establish my sound equivalencies before going into the actual translation. For this I made use of the traditional way the Navaho songs begin: with a short string of vocables that will be picked up (in whole or in part) as the recurring burden of the song. I found I could set most of my basic vocables or vocable—substitutes into the opening, using it as a key to which I could refer when necessary to determine sound substitutions, not only for the vocables but for word distortions in the meaningful segments of the poems. There was a cumulative effect here too. The English vocabulary of the 10th Song— strong on back

vowels, semivowels, glides & nasals—influenced the choice of vocables: the vocables influenced further vocabulary choices & vocables in the other songs. *(Note.* The vocabulary of many of the songs is very close to begin with, the most significant differences in "pairs" of songs coming from the alternation of blue & white color symbolism.) Finally, the choice of sounds influenced the style of my singing by setting up a great deal of resonance I found I could control to serve as a kind of drone behind my voice. In ways like this the translation was assuming a life of its own.

With the word distortions too, it seemed to me that the most I should do was *approximate* the degree of distortion in the original. McAllester had provided two Navaho texts—the words as sung & as they would be if spoken—& I aimed at roughly the amount of variation I could discern between the two. I further assumed that every perceivable change was significant, & there were indications in fact of a surprising degree of precision in Mitchell's delivery, where even what seem to be false steps or accidents may really be gestures to intensify the special or sacred powers of the song at the points in question. Songs 10 & 11, for example, are structurally paired, & in both songs Mitchell seems to be fumbling at the beginning of the 21st line after the opening choruses. Maybe it was accidental & maybe not, but I figured I might as well go wrong by overdoing the distortion, here & wherever else I had the choice.

So I followed where Mitchell led me, responding to all moves of his I was aware of & letting them program or initiate the moves I made in translation. All of this within obvious limits: those imposed by the field of sound I was developing in English. Take the beginning of the 10th Song, for example—right after the chorus. The distortion of the word in the second position is very strong *(yii'naaya hye' ne yane)* & there are a couple of minor changes in the third & fifth position words, all before you get to the fixed vocables of the refrain. It's obvious too that the *hye' ne yane* substitute is drawing on sounds from those refrain voca. les *(nane yeye 'e)*, & that the other, minor changes (postpositional *ye* & medial *yi*) can also be linked to the refrain sounds. I translated, accordingly, for heavy distortion up front, lighter further along, linked to the key sounds of the refrain:

> **Because I was thnboyngnng raised ing the**
> **dawn . . .**

& the refrain itself:

> . . . NwnnN go to her my son N wnn N wnn
> N nnnn N gahn.

Throughout the songs I've now been into, I've worked in pretty much that way: the relative densities determined by the original, the final form by the necessities of the poem as it took shape for me. Obviously too, there were larger patterns to keep in mind, when a particular variation occurred in a series of positions, etc. To say any more about that—though the approach changed in the later songs I worked on, towards a more systematic handling—would be to put greater emphasis on method than any poem can bear. More important for me was actually being in the stimulus & response situation, certainly the most *physical* translation I've ever been involved in. I hope that that much comes through for anyone who hears these sung.

But there was still another step I had to take. While the tape I was working from was of Mitchell singing by himself, in actual performance he would be accompanied by all those present with him at the blessing. The typical Navaho performance pattern, as McAllester described it to me, calls for each person present to follow the singer to whatever degree he can. The result is highly individualized singing (only the ceremonial singer is likely to know all of it the right way) & leads to an actual indeterminacy of performance. Those who can't follow the words at all may make up their own vocal sounds—anything, in effect, for the sake of participation.

I saw the indeterminacy, etc., as key to the further extension of the poems into the area of total translation & total performance. (Instrumentation & ritual-events would be further "translation" possibilities, but the Horse-Songs are rare among Navaho poems in not including them.) To work out the extension for multiple voices, I again made use of the tape recorder, this time of a four-track system on which I laid down the following as typical of the possibilities on hand:

TRACK ONE. A clean recording of the lead voice.

TRACK TWO. A voice responsive to the first but showing less word distortion & occasional free departures from the text.

TRACK THREE. A voice limited to pure-sound improvisations on the meaningless elements in the text.

TRACK FOUR. A voice similar to that on the second track but distorted by means of a violin amplifier placed against the throat & set at "echo" or "tremolo." To be used only as a barely audible background filler for the others.

Once the four tracks were recorded (I've only done it so far for the 12th Song), I had them balanced & mixed onto a monaural tape. In that way I could present the poems as I'd conceived them & as poetry in fact had always existed for men like Mitchell—to be heard without reference to their incidental appearance on the page.

****

Translation is carry-over. It is a means of delivery & of bringing to life. It begins with a forced change of language, but a change too that opens up the possibility of greater understanding. Everything in these song-poems is finally translatable: words, sounds, voice, melody, gesture, event, etc., in the reconstitution of a unity that would be shattered by approaching each element in isolation. A full & total experience begins it, which only a total translation can fully bring across.

By saying which, I'm not trying to coerce anyone (least of all myself) with the idea of a single relevant approach to translation. I'll continue, I believe, to translate in part or in any other way I feel moved to; nor would I deny the value of handling words or music or events as separate phenomena. It's possible too that a prose description of the song-poems, etc. might tell pretty much what was happening in & around them, but no amount of description can provide the *immediate* perception translation can. One way or other translation makes a poem in this place that's analogous in whole or in part to a poem in that place. The more the translator can perceive of the original—not only the language but, more basically perhaps, the living situation from which it comes &, very much so, the living voice of the singer—the more of it he should be able to deliver. In the same process he will be presenting something—i.e., making something present, or making something as a present—for his own time & place.

May 25, 1969

JEROME ROTHENBERG
from the Navaho

THE TENTH HORSE-SONG OF FRANK MITCHELL (BLUE)

Key: wnn Ngahn n NNN

Go to her my son N wnn & go to her my son N wnn N wnnn N nnnn
  N gahn
Go to her my son N wnn & go to her my son N wnn N wnnn N nnnn
  N gahn

Because I was thnboyngnng raised ing the dawn NwnnN go to
  her my son N wnn N wnn N nnnn N gahn
& leafing from thuhuhuh house the bluestone home N gahn N wnn
  N go to her my son N wnn N wnn N nnnn N gahn
& leafing from the (rurur) house the shining home NwnnnN go to
  her my son N wnn N wnn N nnnn N gahn
& leafing from thm(mm) (mm) swollen house my breath has blown
  NwnnN go to her my son N wnn N wnn N nnnn N gahn
& leafing from thnn house the holy home NwnnN go to her my son
  N wnnn N wnn ( ) nnnn N gahn
& from the house hfff precious cloth we walk upon N wnn N nnnn
  N go to her my son N wnn N wnn N nnnn N gahn
with (p)(p)rayersticks that are blue NwnnN go to her my son N
  wnn N wnn N nnnn N gahn
with my feathers that're blue NwnnN go to her my son N wnn N
  wnn N nnnn N gahn
with my spirit horses that 're blue NwnnN go to her my son N
  wnn N wnn ( ) nnnn N gahn
with my spirit horses that 're blue & dawn & wnnN go to her
  my son N wnn N wnn N nnnn N gahn
with my spirit horses that rrr bluestone & Rwnn N wnn N go to
  her my son N wnn N wnn N nnnn N gahn
with my horses that hrrr bluestone & rrwnn N wnn N go to her
  my son N wnn N wnn N nnnn N gahn
with cloth of evree(ee)ee kind to draw (nn nn) them on & on N

wnn N go to her my son N wnn N wnn N nnnn N gahn
with jewels of evree(ee)ee kind to draw (nn nn) them on & wnn
    N go to her my son N wnn N wnn N nnnn N gahn
with horses of evree(ee)ee kind to draw (nn nn) them on N wnn
    N go to her my son N wnn N wnn N nnnn N gahn
with sheep of ever(ee)ee kind to draw (nn nn) them on N wnn N
    go to her my son N wnn N wnn N nnnn N gahn
with cattle of evree(ee)ee kind to draw (nn nn) them on N wnn
    N go to her my son N wnn N wnn N nnnn N gahn
with men of ever(ee)ee kind to lead & draw (nn nn) them on N wnn N go
    to her my son N wnn N wnn N nnnn N gahn
from my house of precious cloth to her backackeroom N gahn N
    wnn N go to her my son N wnn N wnn N nnnn N gahn
in her house of precious cloth we walk (p)pon N wnn N gahn N
    go to her my son N wnn N wnn N nnnn N gahn
vvvveverything that's gone befffore & more we walk upon N wnn
    N go to her my son N wnn N wnn N nnnn N gahn
& everything thadz more & won't be(be)be poor N gahn N go to
    her my son N wnn N wnn N nnnn N gahn
& everything thadz living to be old & blesst N wnn then go to
    her my son N wnn N wnn N nnnn N gahn
(a)cause I am thm boy who blisses/blesses to be old N gahn N
    nnnn N go to her my son N wnn N wnn N nnnn N gahn

Go to her my son N wnnn N go to her my son N wnn N wnnn N nnnn
    N gahn
Go to her my son N wnnn N go to her my son N wnn N wnnn N nnnn
    N gahn

Translation as Experience

George Reavey

Now, originally, I never thought I would be a translator or become
a translator or translate at all. I was primarily interested in history,
poetry, and literature, and began writing and being published myself
while still at the university. But then, knowing French and Russian,
I also began to study the "modern" French and Russian poets on my
own—not as part of the curriculum. Here we may feel a certain ear
for the rhythm of one's age; and the poets, the Russian poets, I began
dipping into while at Caius College, Cambridge, were Mayakovsky,
Yesenin and Pasternak. This was about 1928, a very long time ago
but only about ten years or less after these poets had drawn attention
to themselves in Russia. By 1930, I had written an essay called
"First Essay towards Boris Pasternak," which was published at that
time in "Experiment" (Cambridge). But, in it, I did not deal only
with Pasternak; I also discussed Yesenin and Mayakovsky. In France,
what attracted me soon, besides Baudelaire, Rimbaud and Apollinaire,
was the poetry of Paul Eluard and, very happily, I was to meet him
eventually in Paris. In 1936, I was also very happy to publish a small
anthology of his selected poems which I entitled *Thorns of Thunder*.
This turned out to be a really rare and, to me, very pleasing book
because of all the circumstances attending it.

    Not only did I select, introduce, partly translate, these poems of
Paul Eluard, but I also brought in other poet translators such as

Samuel Beckett, Denis Devlin, David Gascoyne, as well as Man Ray
and Eugene Jolas. In addition, Max Ernst did an original drawing
for the jacket of the book and Picasso a frontispiece drawing (a pencil sketch of Eluard). And, to top it, Eluard contributed an original
Picasso pencil nude of the Rose period. *Thorns of Thunder* was
finally published by my Europa Press where I had previously published Beckett's *Echoes Bones,* his first volume of poetry.

Now, on the Russian front, as I began living in Paris after the Cambridge days, in the early thirties, I began meeting not only emigré
Russian writers like Remizov, Berdyaev, Shestov, Bunin, but also
visiting Soviet novelists and poets, the writers of the new generation,
the generation that had emerged in the 1920's, after the Revolution,
writers like Isevolod Ivanov and Isaac Babel. Eventually, in 1935,
I also met Pasternak briefly in Paris. In 1931 I had already started
a correspondence with him, for I had sent him my essay and he had
replied. I was to meet him later at greater length. Thus, I was
being drawn into this peculiar association with writers who—although
the term did not exist then—were in a sense behind the Iron Curtain,
a curtain which we especially felt after the purges of 1936, '37, '38,
when I did not even dare to write of Pasternak. I remember translating a poem of his in 1933, which was published in the London
Adelphi, and sending him a copy of that. I was innocent enough at
the time to think he would receive it, but that issue of the *Adelphi*
happened to contain an article on Trotsky, and the copy was returned to me with a censor's stamp. It was nice to know it had
been censored; it was not just lost.

While I was having a fever over the weekend, an image suddenly
struck me—it might have been a nightmare. I said, everybody here
at this conference has already discussed the necessity for poetry—the
art of translating it, the art of translating as a necessity, and so on.
And I suddenly asked myself, what about the madness of translation?
What about this thing of seeing a body of work there, and suddenly
trying to get into it, surrendering oneself to it, and the whole process of transposition or transformation, a kind of dream process.
A process of surrendering oneself to a large work for days, hours,
and weeks, months at a time, and being at the disposal of this foreign
body. That needs a lot of thought and circumspection because it
is not every foreign body that one wants to surrender to necessarily.
Obviously, one has to pick and choose, and have a feeling for it. I
must say I certainly did have a feeling from the beginning for certain
poets like Mayakovsky, Yesenin, Pasternak, among the Russians, and
Eluard among the French. And, as a young man, I rushed in where
angels fear to tread. At the age of twenty-two, I suddenly translated

four Pasternak poems (I have since revised them), but still it is the kind of thing that possesses one, draws one in. But I did not necessarily think of myself as a translator, since I was writing and publishing my own poetry. Eventually, one got more and more involved—translations that are pushed on one, translations which possess one, translations which sometimes out of necessity one accepts to do. But living as we do in a particular era, in a special atmosphere of our age, our generation, our idea of the contemporary poet, we have our own ear to the rhythmic ground. Then one realized that communication was easy with Paris, but not Moscow. I first fell for the poets of an older generation, poets who were born—like Pasternak, Mayakovsky, Yesenin and Eluard—in the 1890's. Thus, one developed this personal involvement in certain poets whose way of using language, whose rhythms, whose images, whose metaphors, for some reason infected one; and, in the end, you could not somehow do without them and you had to do something about them. You had to write about them or to translate them, or both.

Now, I intend to speak of Pasternak especially. When one speaks of translating Pasternak, the question arises: which Pasternak? There are several Pasternaks. There is the poet, and there is the prose writer; that is one division. The other broad division is the early Pasternak and the later Pasternak. When we go into it more closely and meticulously, we become aware of many more stages of development—four or five; but I would say here that the first stage in Pasternak's writing culminated in *Sister, My Life* and the *Themes and Variations,* that is to say in 1922-23, when those books were published and when he became more widely known in Russia. Behind these books, there was still the old Russia and the impinging Revolution, and the civil war. Following this, we have a period of Pasternak's adaptation to the new form of life that was springing up—the everyday and ideological life of Soviet Russia; and there were several stages of that. There is the Pasternak of the 1920's, when he was still writing in his dynamic style, in which the verb plays such an important part while he is trying to deal with revolutionary scenes as in the long poems, *Lieutenant Schmidt,* and *The Year 1905,* which is rich in perspectives and has, indeed, some relation to the early chapters of *Zhivago.* But what attracted me most of all originally was Pasternak's early poetry. I had already acquired in Cambridge both of those very rare books, *Themes and Variations* and *Sister, My Life.* In his later years, however, Pasternak was moving towards a greater sort of gravity and purity, towards something like Pushkin's uncompromising clarity and Tolstoy's unswerving faithfulness to facts, when he affirmed: "What I have come to like best

in the whole of Russian literature is the childlike quality of Pushkin
and Chekhov, their modest reticence." By the 1940's, we have a
Pasternak who is purifying himself in the process. He purifies himself of those rich elements of verbal play, alliteration, assonance, all
the things which were so much a part of his early poetry. As an
example, I shall quote an earlier poem from *Themes and Variations*
entitled "Lines on Pushkin's 'The Prophet'." It is an evocation of
Pushkin writing that famous inspired poem:

> Stars were racing. Headlands seas embracing
> Salt was dazzling. And parching all the tears.
> In bedrooms darkness brooded. And thoughts were racing.
> The Sphinx to the Sahara turned its ears.
>
> The candles sighed. It seemed as if, meanwhile,
> The blood of the colossus huge congealed.
> And lips swam wide in desert's azure smile.
> With ebbing tide night evanescent reeled.
>
> Gusts from Morocco stirred the sea. Simoon
> Roared. Arkhangel snored in snows. Candles sighed.
> *The Prophet*'s lines, now roughly drafted, loomed
> Just barely dry. And Ganges' dawn was nigh.
>
> (1918)

Now where was Pushkin at the time he was writing "The Prophet"?
He was either in Petersburg or at his country estate. But here, in
this poem, in this fast-moving, dynamic, alliterative poem, Pasternak
sees Pushkin as a point in a simultaneous associative universe. Stars
and seas, the Sphinx and the Sahara, Morocco and Arkhangel, Pushkin's lines and the Ganges. A poem so full of alliteration based
mainly on the letters M, S, P, is not always easy to transpose into
another language, especially as each language has its own hierarchy
of letter sounds. Thus, the alliteration of that first line in Russian
is based on the letter "M", *"V móre mílys mísi."* In English, the
corresponding alliterative sounds tend to be "S". By contrast, we
have a poem of the early forties by Pasternak, "The Thrushes,"
where his style has greatly changed:

> A broody lunch-time silence reigns
>   About this station so remote.
> Close by the railway, in the lanes,
>   Greenfinches sing their lifeless note.

Sultry and boundless as desire
    Is this straight village road and space.
A lilac wood looks all on fire
    Beneath a grey cloud's hair-topped face.

Along a leafy road, the trees
    Engage in play a plodding horse.
In hollows, saying take me please,
    Snow and violets, mould and gorse.

It is from hollows such as these
    That thrushes drink, when in exchange,
With ice and fire in their knees,
    Of rumoured day they ring the change.

Here syllables, now short, now long,
    And here the showers, hot and cold;
Thus throats are fashioned like a gong
    Brass-lined with puddles' sheen and mould.

They have allotments on the stumps,
    Their games of peeping Tom, sly looks,
Their long-day fuss and rowdy romps,
    And chattering in airy nooks.

And dashing through their wide-flung chambers
    Enigmas dart in public rhyme.
Theirs is the clock of drowsy quavers
    And branches chanting quarter-time.

Such is the thrushes' shady bower
    They dwell in woods spared by the rake,
As artists should, tuned to this power,
    Theirs is the way I also take.

*Peredelkino (Early Trains 1941)**

In this poem, by contrast, everything is more localized. This is Peredelkino, Pasternak living in the country. The leafy lanes, the thrushes, the nearby station, and the many other poems where the

*Both the Pasternak poems here quoted are taken from *The Poetry of Boris Pasternak,* edited and translated by George Reavey. G.P. Putnam'S & Sons and Capricorn, New York, 1959 and 1960.

station comes in.   Observation of nature, very impersonal like most
Pasternak poems, and yet the Pasternak feeling without Pasternak
intruding his ego as Mayakovsky and Yesenin tend to intrude their
egos into their poetry. Pasternak hardly ever does. Yet this pastoral
poem is finally illuminated by this sudden assertion of artistic freedom: "They dwell in woods spared by the rake, as artists should,
tuned to this power. Theirs is the way I also take."

So far I have limited myself to Pasternak's poetry, but now a few
words about Pasternak's prose. The same thing is true of the development of Pasternak's prose, namely, its simplification and, as it
were, its movement towards a broader, more conscious reality than in
the earlier prose. On the other hand, there is the earlier Pasternak
prose, which includes novels such as *The Childhood of Lovers* and
The Last Summer (A Tale). All of these were written before 1934.
In fact, *The Last Summer* was the last of the early Pasternak prose
to be published before World War II. That was in 1934. What is
significant perhaps today is that, although most of Pasternak's work
has been republished in the Soviet Union, including most of the
poems of the *Zhivago* cycle, none of the earlier prose has so far been
reprinted. But V. S. Pritchett, in a review in *The New Statesman,*
affirms that the key to Pasternak was his prose. "Pasternak's idiom
was forged before. It grew out of the symbolist and imagery poets.
It puts poetic and popular speech side by side. In *The Last Summer
(A Tale)* one sees that Pasternak is one of the few writers in prose to
create a language close to the voice of our oral, visual and scientific
culture, whereas other writers are still writing in earlier and now
debased literary conventions. The whole work is less a story, though
it is poetic, comic, dramatic and full of movement, than a concerto
in prose."

After this, in the late thirties, Pasternak begins to attempt to
write in a simple, realistic view. As an example of this intermediate
style, one between *The Last Summer* and *Doctor Zhivago,* we may
point to the first chapter of a novel he was then writing, "The
District Behind the Front," which was never published. For example:
"I remember that evening as clearly as though it were confronting me
this very moment. It was my father-in-law's small mill house. That
day I'd ridden into town to transact some business for him." This
prosaic prose is very different from the type of prose he was writing
before such as, "After dinner, whole trays of smashed and broken
harmonies slid downstairs. They rolled and splintered in unexpected
bursts, more rude and remarkable than any waiter's clumsiness. In
between these turbulent falls spread miles of carpeted silence. That
was Arild upstairs, behind pairs of padded and tightly shut doors,

playing Schumann and Chopin on the grand piano. At such moments. more involuntarily than usual, one had a desire to stare out of the window. But no changes were observable there; the sky did not move or shimmer. It continued to stand like a sultry pillar, upon its fixed principles of rainlessness, while for forty miles around, beneath it, splashed a dead sea of dust, like a sacrificial fire simultaneously set alight from several ends by carters on the site of five goods stations and in the center of a brick desert beyond the Chinese wall of the city."*

When I asked Pasternak shortly before his death why he was writing in so different a style, he replied (I won't quote it all, just a few lines): "And then everything has been overturned. The society was abolished. The scheme of another order came next. The support had been taken out from under that modern artistic trend, wanting of self-reliance. It was, so to say, thrown into water—sink or swim— and how can I believe it should not have been drowned since then!! That is the reason I cannot acknowledge the lasting or remaining noteworthiness of my former books."** Here Pasternak goes so far as to deny his former books. "I deny them as being gone away along with their retired time." I mean his earlier poems and earlier prose. Well, I think he went too far there, because, since Mr. V. S. Pritchett, myself, and other people still have a feeling for his earlier verse and prose, these latter should not be so lightly dismissed.

Now, a word about *Doctor Zhivago.* I cannot go very deeply into this but I should like to focus attention on the opening lines of the novel. This opening line in Russian has a very pronounced, definite, poetic rhythm: *"Shlí i shlí i péli."* In fact, in Russian this line is a trochaic tetrameter. Translated into English as "On they went singing", which is good enough English and nicely brief, this rendering does not convey at all the rhythmic feeling of that opening, or the music of it. "Sínging, théy walked ón and ón" or "Walking on and on they sang" would be nearer to the rhythmical pattern of the original. Spiritually, there may be more than rhythmical significance to this trinity of verbs, *"Shlí i shlí i péli."* After all, the opening passage introduces us to a Christian funeral, and who knows but these verbs may be intended as a reference to the Holy Trinity. The wind that blows thereafter may suggest the Holy Ghost aesthetically; the trinity of verbs evoke the poet and set a rhythmical pattern for the novel.

*From *The Last Summer* (Avon, New York, 1959)
**Nine Letters of Boris Pasternak* (to George Reavey). Ed. Elena Levin, Harvard Library Bulletin (Vol. XV. No. 4) October 1967.

Thus, a translator may have more problems with Pasternak than with another writer, because of the change in style and this musical, poetic undertone, which we sense but do not always have rendered into English in *Zhivago*. What Pasternak was able to achieve after practicing, as it were, that simpler realism in the late 1930's (there were only about four short pieces published) was to extend his embrace of reality and character outside of himself as he does in *Zhivago*. In a sense, there are almost too many outside characters in *Zhivago* who do not have a fundamental part to play in the book. But, at the same time, Pasternak manages to incorporate his poetic rhythm with a broader realism, and in *Zhivago* both elements are united fundamentally.

The Teaching of Translation

Frank MacShane

The notion that translation is a teachable subject is likely to produce a sceptical response, as much so, perhaps, as the idea that the writing of poetry or of fiction can be taught. For that reason, I should like to begin with a disclaimer. I do not believe that writing of any sort can be taught in the same sense that dentistry can be taught, or carpentry or animal husbandry.

Nevertheless, there is a justification for having seminars or workshops in writing, including the writing of translations. In the first place, relatively inexperienced young writers can learn a good deal from working with older poets, dramatists, novelists and translators. They may not learn anything absolutely essential to their own work, but there is no doubt that they can use this experience to speed up their own development. In the seminar or workshop, the students also learn from one another. A group working together often generates a communal excitement, a generalized sense of urgency, which can encourage good writing and the creation of an art appropriate to its time. In this country, we have no literary cafés, no salons, no ateliers; instead, young writers create their artistic environment within the university.

While I cannot speak for others, what I have just stated is my own justification for the writing program that is now in its third year in the School of the Arts at Columbia University. As far as translation is concerned, there is another fundamental point to be made, explaining the presence of a translation seminar within the writing program; and that is my conviction that the first requirement for any translator is that he be a master of his own language, the language *into which* he is turning the foreign language. Our translation program has therefore been established in a school where the students are writers, rather than in one of the language departments where literacy in English is not always assured.

Beyond these observations, I have no generalized views about the teaching of translation. We are still at the beginning of our experience with translation seminars and have much to learn. What may be of interest, however, is simply to say why we decided to teach the subject and how we have been going about it.

Two years ago, when considering the needs of our own writing students, I conceived the idea of having a seminar in translation for those capable of taking it up, because I thought it might prove to be a useful additional skill for them to have as writers. Some writers find they do their best work when they are engaged in two or three projects at the same time. One cannot write poems all day long, or work on a novel more than so many hours, but it is often possible to turn to something else, like translation, that does not require the same expenditure of psychic energy. Moreover, translation may be useful to a writer in developing his own literary skills. He can concentrate on problems of expression without becoming emotionally involved in the work's structural and thematic problems, since in one way or other, these have already been solved by the author of the original.

In planning this course in translation, I realized that it might also serve a general literary and social need. This country has become involved with people all over the world, but we are ignorant of their arts and literatures, not to mention other elements of their consciousness. For this reason we tend to treat them as a lower order of human beings. It has become obvious that we can no longer afford the implicit racism that comes from associating with European works only; for the sake of our own humanity, we must experience the literature of Asia and Africa and Latin America as well.

With this double goal—of giving our own students another string to their bow and of encouraging the translation of little-known works—we began. We had no syllabus, no plan; we simply sat down together, about a dozen students who thought of themselves first as writers in English, and myself. The students varied a good deal in temperament and in language knowledge. Few of the poets intended to set themselves up as professional translators; however, they realized they should experience Baudelaire and Rimbaud in the original. To read them at all would require the help of dictionaries; in other words, they would have to translate them in one way or other. They believed, and I think rightly, that they could hasten this process by bringing their versions to the class, where they might be discussed and evaluated by others. The prose writers were more concerned with our second goal, that of translating out-of-the-way books. Some were quite accomplished and already had experience as translators; others were virtual beginners. I imposed no general standards of language competence because at the time I thought there was merit in the possibility that everyone could improve, regardless of the point where he began.

There was also considerable variety among the languages in which the students proposed to work in this first year, and this has continued in the second year. A number knew French, but there were also those who knew German, Modern Greek, Latin, Russian, Hebrew, and Yiddish. No one in the room knew all of these languages, but what united us was that the language into which the translations were being made was English, so that, at the least, the members of the seminar could comment on the works presented as though they were English poems, stories, or prose pieces.

For the first class I provided photo-copies of a short passage of the *Iliad* as it had been translated into English by a number of poets and prose writers from Chapman to the present day. None of us present knew ancient Greek, but we soon came to realize what I think is an essential truth about translating, that there is no final translation, that every translation is written for its own age. Chapman's Homer is the work of a Jacobean playwright; Pope transforms Homer into an eighteenth-century poet writing rhymed couplets; the prose versions of Samuel Butler and others convert the *Iliad* into a nineteenth-century novel, which was the predominant literary form of that period. Using the Butcher and Lang trot as a standard for literary accuracy, we could also see how the various verse translations, including those by Lattimore and Fitzgerald, illustrated the never-ending struggle between accuracy and literacy in English. We concluded with a look at Robert Graves's attempt, in *The Anger of Achilles,* to combine two forms in one work— narrative prose for the parts dealing with action, lyrics for the places where feelings are expressed.

This examination was amateurish in many ways, but it made us all aware of the ways in which the cultural climate of a particular time influences literary work. It also made us realize how important it was to be aware of what we were doing as translators. In an

effort to increase consciousness of this problem, I presented the
students with a number of ideas about translations of the sort collected and edited by Reuben Brower and by the National Translation
Center in Austin, Texas. We subscribed to the translation magazine,
Delos, so that students could be informed about new controversies
and concerns related to translation generally. We also took up in
the seminar some of the points raised in Stanley Burnshaw's book,
The Poem Itself.

For the most part, however, we were not interested so much in
the theory of translation as in the practice of it. I thought that such
general principles as there are would emerge more forcefully if they
came out of a visible problem in a student's work than if they were
considered abstractly. Accordingly, most of the classes were organized as workshops to which the students brought samples of their
work.

As the person in charge of this class, I could not possibly offer
instruction in all of the languages and literatures in which the
students were interested, and so I arranged to have a visitor come
in almost every week to give professional guidance in the language in
which he was an expert. Before the class meeting, the visitor was
sent both the original text and the student's version of it, so that the
seminar could be devoted to problems created by the translation.
The idea was that everyone present could learn by example, even if
he did not know the language in question.

As might be imagined, with a group of students who were writers
first and linguists second, the principal weakness in the various
works presented by the students was ignorance of the language. I
know that some of our visitors thought our exterprise somewhat
lunatic in view of the language limitations of some of the students.
Nevertheless, for the reasons I have already given, I believed the
seminar could be useful to people of various levels of accomplishment.

There is no doubt that the experience of hearing, week after week,
some of the world's most accomplished translators—such as Richard
Howard, Willard Trask, Cynthia Ozick, Richard Wilbur, Gregory
Rabassa, Jacques Barzun, William Jay Smith, Lewis Galantière, W.S.
Merwin, Edmund Keeley, and Richmond Lattimore—made the
students aware of the seriousness of the art of translation. The con-
secutive presence of so many different translators also exposed them
to a range of opinions concerning problems of translation. The question that arose repeatedly was the difficulty of remaining faithful to
the original while producing a readable English version. On the whole,
there was little theoretical disagreement on this point, since everyone
agreed that one should keep as close to the original as possible with-

out being stilted. In practice, however, the line was not constant, and the translators varied a good deal in the points they raised while discussing the students' translations. I remember a few points from the various visitors—for example, Lewis Galantière's insistence upon clear English expression sometimes at the expense of the French syntax. For what emerged was a curious phenomenon: in their own work as novelists or short-story writers, our students generally wrote a clear and effective prose, but when they took to translation, they often became stilted and wooden, writing sentences they would never allow to pass in their own work. Given the somewhat greater difficulty of translating verse, William Jay Smith warned the students to avoid an excess of monosyllables when translating from French poetry, while Richard Wilbur demonstrated the need for a thorough knowledge of the literature from which the poem is taken, so as to be aware of allusions and literary references, before undertaking a translation of it. Reverting to prose, Richard Howard stated his belief in the importance of trying to reproduce the complexity of the original text if that complexity embodies the thrust and meaning of the original. On the other side, the students heard John Hollander and Ron Padgett speak for daring and freedom in translation, including a conscious violation of meaning, in the manner of Ezra Pound, if it helped the English version.

These seminars were potentially useful for anyone trying his hand at translation, for they forced each individual to ask himself the questions that were being raised over each text so that he might deal with them in his own work. There were also questions relating to the implications of each student's work that were best answered by raising broad social questions. For that reason, even though none of the students was then working in Japanese, I asked Ivan Morris to tell them about some of the extraordinary problems that arise in translating from that language. I also asked Margaret Mead to come in and speak of another concern which may be of secondary interest to literary translators, but which is by no means an insignificant subject—that is, the need for a universal second language.

*

This, in brief, is what we did during the first year. It is hard to say what we accomplished, but we emerged with an undefined feeling that the translation seminar had been worthwhile and should be continued.

For the second year, I made a greater effort than before to get in touch with members of the various language departments at Columbia that were interested in translation. With the help of three or four generous foundations and individuals, I attempted to encourage

especially the translation of works from Asia and South America.
I spoke to publishers interested in translation and to students and
faculty members in the corresponding literature departments at Columbia. Unfortunately, despite expressions of interest and good will, few
students of Asian and Latin-American literature actually enrolled.
The difficulty lies in the nature of graduate education in the language
departments, which stresses literary history and scholarship. There
is only a peripheral interest in translation. This experience has rein-
forced my feeling that the first requirement for a translator must be
a commitment to writing in English.

Our seminar has, therefore, been made up mainly of our own
students with a few others from the language departments. Our
procedures have not changed a great deal from those of last year, although we have tended to break up into smaller groups of students
working all in the same language, and we have also introduced
individual tutorials for a few students. These changes were made
because a number of students found that the full seminar meetings
involved a certain amount of repetition and the discussion of points
only marginally interesting to many of them.

While emphasizing smaller group sessions, we also introduced a
greater number of sessions concerned with special problems in
translation. Let me give you a few samples of these. One of our
students was trying to translate medieval Japanese poetry, and when
his work was ready, I asked two translators to come in as visitors.
The first was Donald Keene, who is an accomplished and experienced translator from Japanese; the other was Mark Strand who
knows no Japanese at all, even though he has experience in translating from Spanish and, what was more to the point, is a poet in
English. The interplay between these two men, with their different
emphases—Keene feeling primarily responsible for fidelity to the
original, Strand concerned to make an English poem of the translation—was instructive. The gap between the two was wider than I
had expected. In a somewhat similar vein, we had a session in which
Stanley Kunitz spoke of his experience working in collaboration
with Max Hayward in translating the poetry of Anna Akhmatova
and Andrei Voznesensky. He brought in the various versions given
him by Hayward, first a word-by-word correspondence unrelated
to syntax, then a literal version with each word heavily annotated
for subtleties and complexities of meaning and literary significance,
then the later drafts as they went back and forth between the two
men, until the final, publishable version was written.

The difficulties involved in translating exotic languages were
revealed in another session in which Gregory Rabassa brought in

various drafts of his translations of Asturias' *Mulata,* a book which contains much Indian material and which in a sense is already a Spanish translation of Mayan legends. The trick was to put this into English without creating a false folklorical flavor. Rabassa also discussed the relationship of a translator to his author, when that author knows the language into which the work is being translated. He passed around drafts of his translation of Julio Cortázar's *Hopscotch.* for this purpose. Cortázar is himself a translator, and, when Rabassa sent his typescript to him for comments, the notes and suggestions and interlinear observations made by Cortázar became in effect an act of collaboration with Rabassa.

Two of our meetings were devoted to the problems of translating into English material that was not originally meant to be read privately as we read novels or books of poems. The literature of the American Indian is oral, and exists within a ritualistic framework, which means that along with music, dance, costume and painting, it is part of a total art. Jerome Rothenberg, who has done a considerable amount of experimentation in translating American-Indian texts, visited the seminar and demonstrated his technique, which includes an attempt to represent in his text many of the meaningless sounds that accompany most American-Indian songs.

A somewhat similar occasion was arranged by one of our students, an Indian from the Punjab, who was dissatisfied by the attempts that have recently been made to translate the Urdu poet, Ghalib. Some of these verses have appeared in *The Hudson Review;* they are the result of a collaboration between the Pakistani poet, Aijaz Ahmed, and several American poets, including Adrienne Rich, Mark Strand, William Stafford and W. S. Merwin. Our Indian student thought they were somehow inadequate, and he therefore arranged a program which included a film on the India that Ghalib knew a century ago, a recital (or rather, singing) of some of the poems in the original to give a sense of their musical quality, and the presentation of some dances that are intended to accompany the verses. Our student's point was that it is necessary to be aware of the whole cultural background of a work before translating it; and he demonstrated how very nearly impossible it was to put into English verse lines which came from a cultural pattern so different from our own, and which, as with the American-Indian poems, were part of a comprehensive art, not intended to be considered in isolation.

Yet another session was devoted to a criticism of some of the assumptions that have become so pervasive among contemporary translators into English. I mean, in particular, the view that the English of the translation should be colloquial and unaffected,

the English of contemporary fiction. This view has evolved from a
desire to avoid archaisms and artificialities that would place a barrier
between the original and the contemporary reader, but as our visitor,
D. S. Carne-Ross, pointed out, the translated text often reads so
plainly that it is not literature at all. The problem, briefly stated, is
how to create a contemporary style that corresponds to the quality
of the original, for after all, the style is what makes the original, not
merely the content.

These examples give a sense of what we have been doing in the
teaching of translation at Columbia. I have given this account in narrative form because we are still in the experimental stage and have
reached no firm conclusions about the project. My main concern for
the future is to raise the quality of work done in the seminar. I think
we have been a little lax in standards of admission; with a higher
level of performance, we can also serve as a means by which new and
interesting authors may be brought to the attention of magazine
and book publishers. In any event, I am convinced that this translation program is located where it should be within the University,
in the writing section of the School of the Arts rather than in a
language department.

This brings me to a final comment on the proposal to establish
professorships of translation in various universities. The president
of the P.E.N. American Center, Charles Flood, offered the services
of the Center in the hope of encouraging the training of young
translators. I understand that the initial reaction from the universities approached was disappointing. I am not surprised, because
I have long been aware of the hostility that some universities feel
towards imaginative writing and the arts in general. Nevertheless,
there are a few enclaves within American universities where this
activity is at least tolerated and even encouraged. The School of
the Arts at Columbia is one such place. Other writing programs
connected to English departments exist elsewhere round the
country. Here seminars or workshops in translation may be
established, and if that is done professorships will naturally follow.
But it is futile to operate the other way round, without a predispo-
sition towards translation among those responsible for the various
writing programs.

This brings me back to where I began when I spoke of the utility
of writing programs generally. No one can say what their ultimate
effect will be, but what we do know is that they constitute centers
of consciousness and of awareness about writing. The atmosphere
is at least potentially helpful to the creation of good work, including good work in translation. This may prove to be of crucial

importance, especially if we remember that the best translations into English have been made by men who were themselves writers in English—the translators of the King James Version, Chaucer, Chapman, Dryden, Pope, Shelley and so many others up to our own time. One needs to be a writer and to understand what that means before one can confront and handle the work of another. The translator must have the kind of sympathy a writer has, including a love for words and a delight in their possible combinations. These powers are unpredictable and mysterious, but without them no true translation can take place, nor can there be useful instruction in translation.

The World as Language

John L. Mish

By this general title I mean that human life as we know it is based on
our ability to communicate with each other—and that, despite mathematics, computers, and so on, still means language. But while we can
assume that human brains produce identical thought waves, the ways
in which these thoughts are expressed in actual language are of a
fantastic variety. It is this, mainly, which makes the translator's
task so fascinating but, at the same time, likewise so very difficult.
Even the best translation can never be philologically accurate; on the
contrary, if it is really good, it must be a compromise between the
original text and the language into which it is rendered. The Italians
with their usual grace express that succinctly by their saying
"traduttore—traditore" (translator—traitor). Yet translate we must,
today more than ever. Let us, therefore, cast a rapid glance at some
of the fundamental difficulties stemming from the very basic structural differences of languages.

A Chinese student of mine whose term paper, though otherwise
good, was written in ungrammatical English, said to me with a sigh:
"Why do you need tenses, numbers, and all the other grammatical
complications, when we Chinese have been perfectly able to express
our thoughts for over three thousand years without them?" An
American, trying to write correct Russian, is very likely to heave
the same sigh. To that dilemma there is no simple solution. We

must accept the fact that human speech has developed along infinitely different lines. How different, few of us realize.

Even among the nearest relatives of English, i.e., the Germanic branch of the large Indo-European family of languages, the differences are very great indeed. At one end of the scale is Icelandic, which is still on the level of Gothic or Old English, with almost as many inflections as Latin; at the other end, Afrikaans, which has abandoned even the few inflected verbal forms of current English, and has kept only an ending for the plural of nouns and a few others for the degrees of comparison. In between are the Scandinavian languages (Swedish, Danish, and Norwegian), whose grammar approaches that of English, and finally, Dutch and German, which retain more grammatical forms than English but fewer than Icelandic.

The same variation is more or less true of the Romance group. Italian has more "irregular verbs" than French or Spanish; Romauntsch, the smallest language of that group, has entirely lost the "historical past tense," which is restricted to literary writing in French, Catalan, and Rumanian, but is still alive in everyday Spanish, Portuguese, and Italian.

In the third large Indo-European group—Slavic—we have similar structural extremes—from Lusatian, on the one hand, with its inflections preserved from Church Slavonic times, synthetic aorist and imperfect tenses, and a complete dual, to Bulgarian on the other, where the synthetic declension of nouns has been given up entirely and replaced by analytic constructions, much as in English. The most important Slavic language, Russian, is between these two extremes, although most English speakers will find it almost as complex as Latin.

But these are minor differences. When we come to non-Indo-European languages, the varieties of structure become more startling. The Semitic languages, like Arabic and Hebrew, attach so little importance to the vowels that they do not usually express them in their writing, because the sense of a word is determined primarily by its consonants. In English, "last, lest, list, lost, lust" have totally different meanings, whereas the Arabic *"Katab, Kâtib, kitâb, kutub, kitâbah"* all have something to do with the idea of "writing." Actually, no two Arabs pronounce the vowels in exactly the same way, because they are felt to be of secondary importance.

The differences between languages may go far deeper. In Turkish, there are no relative pronouns and no conjunctions introducing dependent clauses; subordination is expressed by an astonishing variety of special verbal forms. Translating from Turkish is therefore particularly difficult. "I beg you to reply to my letter" (eight words) becomes *"Mektubuma cevap vermenizi dilerim"* (four words). The possessive "my" and "your" are expressed by endings, as in Arabic, Hebrew, Hungarian, Finnish, and other languages.

We are all familiar with the differences between transitive and intransitive verbs. But Hungarian makes a further distinction between definite and indefinite objects and has two systems of verbal forms to express this idea: *"Látok embert"* = "I see a man;" but *"Látom az embert"* = "I see the man."

In Basque, the subject of an intransitive verb takes one ending; the subject of a transitive verb, another. For instance: *"Gizona etorri zan"* = "the man came," but *"Gizonak umea ikusi zuen"* = "the man saw the child." This particular case—elsewhere known as the ergative —plays an important part in some Caucasian languages, e.g., in Georgian. There, a further fundamental distinction is made between voluntary and involuntary actions. A Georgian speaker does not use the same construction for "I love the dog" and "I beat the dog," since the former action is independent of his will but the latter must be willed.

Most people are aware that many languages have grammatical genders and express grammatical relations by different endings. But the languages of the African Bantu group (e.g., Swahili, Zulu, etc.) use so-called "class prefixes" and express the number of nouns, tenses of verbs, etc. by prefixes, not suffixes. Thus, *"Watu wadogo wawili walikuja wanione"* means "Two young men came to see me," where the syllable *"wa,"* repeated five times, is the plural sign of the first class (human beings).

At one extreme of human speech are the so-called polysynthetic languages, which endeavor to make single words of very complex ideas. To this group belong many Amerindian languages and Eskimo. In Aleutian, for instance, *"kamgasigatasadalik"* means "having prayed more intensely than possible for a human being;" or *"amanuyakuq"* = "he sets himself the task of expelling him." Fortunately for the translator, these languages are not represented by important written literatures.

In some of the outstanding languages of civilization, such as Chinese and Japanese, pronouns are used very sparingly; and as there is nothing in their verbs to indicate the person, their sentences would seem to us incomplete. Yet the sense is usually clear from the context, although this places additional hurdles in the translator's path. Japanese—and Korean, too, for that matter—has, in addition, a bewildering variety of endings which serve only to express different degrees of politeness, e.g., *"Kita – kimashita – oide*

nasaimashita," all of which simply mean "came," but the first is
plain, the second polite, and the third deferential.

In one known instance of an old literary language, this has led to
the creation of two distinct languages, namely in Javanese. There
"ngoko" is spoken to and among inferiors, and *"Kromo"* to and
among upper-class people. Even the grammatical particles are different. Thus: *"kowé lagi apá?"* and *"sampejan sawég poenápá?"* both
mean: "What are you doing?"

The most subtle and therefore the greatest difficulty lies in seman-
tics. No word corresponds exactly to its lexical equivalent in another
language. English "to take" is French *"prendre,"* but in French you
do not "take" a walk, you "do" it *(faire une promenade)*. On the
other hand, one "takes" patience *(prendre patience)* in French, but
in English one "has" it. "To make love" is not the same as *"faire
l'amour."* This leads us to the enormous variety of idioms, which
require special care of the translator. I remember how hack translators of English detective stories into Polish regularly translated
"clean-shaven" literally, which came out as "cleanly shaven," whereas the corresponding idiom is "smoothly shaven." For me, one of
the most difficult languages is ordinary—i.e. non-scientific—Japanese,
just because of its innumerable idioms. It is not enough to have
acquired an adequate Japanese vocabulary of single words; you must,
in addition, learn several thousand idioms. Two examples: *"o ki no
doku desu"* = "it is poison for your spirit" = "I feel so sorry for you."
There are other ways for saying "I am sorry" or "sorry for myself."
Or the common phrase: *"hajimete o me ni kakarimashita"* = "for the
first time stuck to eyes" = "glad to make your acquaintance."

However, the insidious difficulties of translation reach to an even
deeper level. Basic concepts are often fundamentally different in
different civilizations. When the first European missionaries in China
began to translate Christian concepts into Chinese, they found no
exact equivalent of our "sin" with its purely Western metaphysical
undercurrents. They finally followed the earlier Buddhist missionaries in adopting the Chinese *"tsui."* But to the majority of Confucian Chinese, *"tsui"* means simply a "crime," that is, a violation of
the criminal law or of the socio-political code. The Buddhists had
used it in the sense of hurting one's own karma, since in their religion there is no God to be offended. Now the Christians gave it
their meaning—but you had to be a Christian first to understand its
metaphysical implications. It was even worse with translating "God"
in the monotheistic Christian sense. To this very day, Catholics and
Protestants use different terms in Chinese for this fundamental
concept: "Lord of Heaven" (Catholic) and "Superior Ti" (Protestant):

in the second case, the meaning of the word "Ti" has varied greatly in Chinese philosophical literature from "imperial ancestor" to "emperor." Again, the non-Christian Chinese cannot understand this term without first being taught Christianity.

And so it is everywhere.

When translating from ancient Greek, you must remember that *"tyrannos"* is not the same as "tyrant"—any usurper of political power was so called, although he might be mild, progressive, moral, and extremely popular, as some of them were.

Language is the outward expression of people's thinking; but this is always colored by individual history and spiritual development. The translator faces the formidable task of conveying to another culture the intricacies of the original, but to do that accurately would require innumerable footnotes and make the translation unreadable for the average person. So the translator must try to transpose the meaning and underlying thought of the original into another language and cultural background, which ideally cannot be done. However, by its very definition, an ideal cannot be reached. The achievement is in the striving, not in the perfect result.

The Old Man's Toys

Richard Howard

Originally I was to speak on the relation of the writer to the translator within the same person and, as I began doing that and thinking
about all the writers who have been translators and all the translators who have been writers, I found—thinking about it as broadly as
I could—that there was inherent in that enormous body of texts (I am
only talking about Western literature), in that enormous body of
achievement, there was a genre, a secret genre that I began to unearth,
and I would like to propose it to you. I am trying to formulate it,
not to justify it. But I believe that if we discover a genre it helps us
think about literature in a firmer and more feeling way. Genres
emerge not because literature changes, but because our attitude
toward literature changes; for example, in a sense there have always
been novels, but we only discovered the novel at a certain point in
the development of literature. And that is why I call my talk, *The
Old Man's Toys.*

In order to explain the genre, I merely have to define two things.
What an old man is, and what a toy is. By old, I mean that when a
man—or a writer—no longer writes in order to explore or discover
who he is, he has become an old man. Old, in other words, means
self-recognizing. A toy is the one thing we play with which is not
a part of our bodies. A toy is the one thing which is not ourselves.
So that the old man's toys, in other words, would be precisely
those objects or things which we play with, recognizing ourselves as

247

ourselves, which we yet know to be *not* ourselves. Now, there is, in
translation , a kind of response to the literature of others which
becomes *the old man's toys*. And I am going to talk about that
genre, and I will give you a number of examples of it, some of them
very questionable. But I think you will see what I am proposing and
formulating, not justifying. Old men, George Bernard Shaw said—
who ought to have known—old men are dangerous because they do
not believe in the future. The old man's toys are a matter of immediacy. They· are a matter of instant playfulness, and of final fooling.

I would like to tell a story here (and I shall try in my remarks to
mention only writers who have been translators)—there is a wonderful
story that H.D. tells in her little book about being analyzed by Freud.
In 1937, H.D. was being analyzed by Freud, and she was astonished
during one of the more difficult early sessions to discover the short
old gentleman get up from his chair behind his desk and come around
to the couch on which she was lying and pound furiously on the head
of the couch and say to her, "You will not form a transference to me
because you do not think it is worthwhile falling in love with an old
man!" One of the most extraordinary stories in the history of
psychoanalysis, and a splendid example of what I am talking about
in terms of the old man's toys: to symbolize this story, let us simply
say that it is the muse that is being addressed, the muse does not
think it is worthwhile falling in love with an old man, and the old
man must therefore make a toy out of the muse.

Now let me give some examples first of what is *not* an old man's
toy. I am going to list some great writers in the West who were
translators and whom I do *not* mean. I do not mean a translator
like Luther, who translated a book because he was in jail. I do not
mean Freud who translated a book because he was a young man in
need of money. I do not mean the kind of translating that was done
by *hommes de lettres* who ransacked literature for possibilities both
characterological and literary—Rilke translating Elizabeth Browning,
Gide translating *Arden of Feversham*. Those are not old man's toys.
These writers translated books all their lives. It was a natural and
indeed an incremental activity. I do not mean a translation (although
here we come closer to what I mean) like Proust's translation of
Ruskin. I was very struck with Madame Malraux's points on the
subject, and it is true, as she says, that Proust became more Proust
after he had translated Ruskin. And that is closer to what I had in
mind, but at the time Proust translated Ruskin he had not yet
arrived at self-recognition, which is my definition of old age. By the
way, I of course do not mean the biologically old. The three figures
who characterize best what I call the style of old age had all stopped

working at 46: Shakespeare, Schiller, Nietzsche would be characteristic of what we may call the style of old age. But we are more likely
to think of someone like Verdi, or Monet, or—let's say—Titian.
Titian is a very nice example, and those of you who are familiar with
a wonderful play written by the twenty-year old Hugo von Hofmannsthal called *The Death of Titian* will remember an extraordinary
scene in which the ninety-nine-year-old man on his deathbed, painting still, starts up and then asks for his early pictures to be brought
to him and, Hofmannsthal says, "insists that he must see them, those
old pale ones, must now compare them with the new ones he's
painting. For now, he says, things hard to grasp are clear to him. He
understands as earlier he never dreamed he could, that up till now he
was a feeble blunderer." That is what we ordinarily think of, of
course, as the style of old age. It is the style we acknowledge in the
celebrated remark of Hokusai who said that "At seventy-three I had
come to understand something; if I live to eighty, I shall have made
further progress, and if indeed I live to be a hundred and ten, then
everything that I do, even if it be no more than a stroke or a dot or
a blot, will be a masterpiece."

Now that is the style of the old man's toys, and it has nothing to
do with being a hundred and ten as Hokusai suggests. It has to do
with some kind of self-recognition—and now I'm going to give some
existing examples of the old man's toys. My favorite one, and the
one that I treasure the most and was therefore most charmed to
hear adduced, is Dryden—it was very touching that Guy Daniels
used Dryden critically (and he is indeed a great critic) to dispose
of certain heresies in modern translation. Dryden's last book of
verse came after what his readers all thought or certainly had every
right to think was "all passion spent". The career was over, the
work was done, the famous translations had been made, in fact:
the Virgil, almost all the other things, the Horace, the Ovid, the
Juvenal, the Persius. Nonetheless, this old man at the very end
published a book called *Fables,* in which alternately and indiscriminately and without any specific differentiation, he offered great
poems which were sometimes translations, sometimes work of his
own. We are no longer able to tell, unless *he* tells us or unless the
scholars tell us. The late Dryden is the perfect example, in other
words, of the old man's toys. I am going to read you one brief
passage of this old man's toys. It is actually a translation, but it is
a translation which by this—by what I call this sort of final fooling,
this extreme commitment to alterity as playfulness, has been
absorbed, assimilated, accommodated and has become part of the self:

The day already half his race had run
and summoned him to due repast at noon.
But love could feel no hunger but his own.
While listening to the murmuring leaves,
he stood more than a mile immersed within the wood.
At once the wind was laid. The whispering sound
was dumb, a rising earthquake rocked the ground;
with deeper brown the grove was overspread.
A sudden horror seized his giddy head
and his ears tinkled and his color fled.

It goes on for hundreds and hundreds of lines—it is great poetry,
and it is great poetry arrived at by, as I call it, toying. Dryden says,
in the introduction to the *Fables*, "For this last half year I have been
troubled with the disease, as I may call it, of translation. The cold
prose fits of it, which are always the most tedious with me, were
spent with the history of the League. The hot, which succeeded them,
in this volume of verse miscellanies."

Other examples of the old man's toys are certainly and preemi-
nently Valéry's *Virgil*, Goethe's *Divan*, Baudelaire's Poe, a good deal
of the late Browning, Karl Kraus, Offenbach and—to adduce a very
slight example but a very beautiful one—our greatest American poet,
Wallace Stevens' Fargue. At the end of his life (he lived to be seventy-
six) Stevens gave a reading here in New York. I am sure some of you
were there for that occasion. I was very much there, and I remember
he turned to the audience suddenly, in that very grand and imposing
and almost preposterously composed manner of his, and said:
*"I should like to close this program by turning now to the work of
someone else."* That is the old man's toys. He is closing the program
by turning to the work of someone else. "For a very few minutes,"
Stevens said, "I shall read paraphrases. I call these translations paraphrases because in order to carry over the sense of cadence, paraphrases seems more useful than literal translation." And then he
read what I thoroughly recall were some perfectly wretched versions
of Léon-Paul Fargue; but it was the first time that Wallace Stevens
had ever translated or paraphrased anything, and he felt the need to
do so because, as he said, he wanted *"to close this program by turning
now to the work of someone else."* There comes a time in the life
of great writers when they need "to turn now to the work of someone else" in order to complete the recognition of themselves. Both
William Morris and W. H. Auden seem to have endured and indulged
this need with the Northern literatures. With the Germanic; in fact,
quite literally with the Icelandic both of them have had a kind of

autumnal—or wintry—romance with Icelandic literature. Morris, like
Auden, did not really know Icelandic; he worked with a scholar who
did—but both men found a kind of completion to their own already
considerable *oeuvre,* a kind of ultimate playfulness; and if you look
at Auden's translations from the *Elder Edda* that are just out now,
and at Morris' late translations of the sagas, you will see that there
is a kind of self-recognition which is half accusation, half indulgence.
Yeats (who quite late in his life worked from the literal Jebb translation of Sophocles' Oedipus cycle)—Yeats has a wonderful remark
on this subject which helped me a lot to see that it *is* a subject:
"to make one's creativity by turning from mirror to meditation upon
a mask." That is the old man's toys: turning from the mirror, which
is our own work, to meditation upon a mask, which is translation.
My notion of the genre can be summed up nicely by a remark (which
I take very personally) from Thomas Hobbes. Thomas Hobbes, when
he was a young man, translated, as you know, Thucydides entire.
When he was an old man, when he was eighty-six, he published a
verse translation of the *Iliad* and the *Odyssey.* Because, he said, he
had nothing better to do.

There is one other remark about Thomas Hobbes I would like
to quote, and then you will see why I take him so personally. It
comes from Aubrey's *Brief Lives:* "In his old age he was very bald,
which claimed a veneration. Yet, when indoors he used to study and
sit bareheaded and said he never took cold in his head, but that the
greatest trouble was to keep off the flies from pitching on the bald-
ness. He was wont to say that if he had read as much as other men,
he should have known no more than other men."

Now, I'm going to give you a few more examples of old man's
toys, and I want you to think about them . . . charitably. Think of
Henry James in 1911 in his home in Rye, working away on a translation which strangely enough no one has ever seen, which allowed him,
I think, to complete his work in the novel, though he had never been
able to fulfill his work in the theater. Henry James' translation of
John Gabriel Bjorkman. Think of Virginia Woolf's translation (which
strangely enough none of us has ever seen) of the Fragments of Heraclitus. That would have been an old man's toys. Think of Emily
Dickinson's translation (which strangely enough, none of us has ever
seen) of the Elements of Euclid. That would have been an old man's
toys. Think, almost finally, of Ronald Firbank's translation of *The
Pillow Book of Lady Sei Shonagon;* and finally—so that you see
exactly what I mean—think of Ernest Hemingway's translation,
probably completed up there in Idaho just before the end, of *The
Princess of Cleves.* Those are the old man's toys. None of them

exists, but they are the fulfillment of my genre. It is a way of thinking about literature, a way of approaching that final alterity, that
final otherness which translation, in the case of certain great writers,
can give us. I would like to cite two other examples, real ones this
time. One, the case of Nabokov's impossible *Onegin* which nevertheless released him—he was only sixty when he finished it. He is
now only seventy—but producing that monstrous translation and
even more monstrous commentary upon it released him to write his
real masterpiece which is, as you all know, a kind of satyr-play or
parodic version of it. We would not have *Pale Fire,* Nabokov's
masterpiece, if we did not have that other work of translation, so
that in this case the old man's toy allowed him to produce what is
not at all a toy, but the central work of his canon.

My final and closing instance is the last two operas of Giuseppe
Verdi, operas based on plays of Shakespeare, and provided with
brilliant libretti which are indeed translations by the young Boito,
a man who was himself a composer and had previously written all
kinds of other libretti (including by the way, the one for *La Gio-
conda).* Verdi, at the age of eighty-three, transformed himself and
wrote the two operas, the two works which as a man who had already
recognized himself were not himself—and therefore were most
himself.

Re-Creation of the Chinese Image

Shih-Hsiang Chen

Image-making, a major concern of all poetic creation of the world since high antiquity, now particularly prized in modern criticism, has for at least a half century been thought of abroad as not only the mark of the native talent of Chinese poets, but the natural gift of the Chinese language. The duty of the translator from Chinese, then, would seem to be to re-create the richest imagery. And if the translator is regarded as creator, he would seem to have the amplest supply of material and inspiration. But by the same token his task is all the more arduous, his responsibility all the heavier.

At this point I may say the question of the translator as creator can be somewhat clarified, if only because, in the case of translations between Chinese and western languages, the problem is magnified. It should be obvious that the more divergent any of the two languages are, the greater the challenge to the translator. Furthermore— though indeed there may seem to be more room and opportunity for him as creator—the greater demand on him to realize the optimum amount of the rich properties, from one totally different language into another, restricts rather than increases his freedom, if he is to be a responsible creator or re-creator, and not a carefree inventor. We are aware of his difficulties, but neither are we to exaggerate them. We want to see how his work can properly be done.

It may be helpful here to observe really how different Chinese is
from Western languages in general, and from English in particular; and
to see in the process some larger implications of the question of the
translator as creator than it may offhand appear to have. In terms of
languages, we might think of the question as a merely technical one.
But in a broad, long-range historical view, I believe the question
should be considered for its large cultural, or intercultural, significance as well, though we may not have all the time to go into it here.
Let us for the moment assume that it is true, though admittedly
simplistic, that Chinese is an imagistic language, so inherently apt
for image making. Its counterpart or opposite, then, an Indo-
European language, say English, would by contrast be more discursive, hence felicitous for logical presentation and conveyance of
idea. But it does not follow that all Chinese poetry is imagistic poetry.
And even though it ever were, not all imagistic poetry can be *ipso
facto* good poetry. On the other hand, when Mr. C. Day Lewis says
that an image, a poetic image, is "a picture made out of words," he
is not thinking of Chinese "words." He is surely not thinking of
such word-pictures of the Chinese script as have been indiscriminately
called "ideographs," but is referring to such a marvelous image as
was made in English words by Meredith:

> Dark grows the valley, more and more forgetting,

or another one just as familiar and admirable:

> A rose-red city, half as old as time.

Of cities and time the Chinese genius has produced equally memorable poetic images. The T'ang poet Wang Chien, whose date is 750-
835, has left us this one:

> *T'ien nan to niao ming*
> *Chou hsien pan wu ch'eng*

And much earlier, in the fourth century B.C., Ch'ü Yuan in his *Li Sao*,
known as "Encountering Sorrow" in English translations, which is
perhaps the most celebrated work of all Chinese poems, presented at
the climatic point the unforgettable image of irrevocable time experi-

enced in utter despair:

Shih ai ai ch'i ch'iang p'i

時 曖 曖 其 將 罷

Now we may consider, is it a sensible question to ask whether the Chinese couplet by Wang Chien and the line by Ch'ü Yuan are more imagistic, or imagistically more effective, than the English lines earlier quoted? At this very moment, I think it is safe for me to assume that among this distinguished international audience, no matter how enthusiastic about Chinese poetry, few would really feel the Chinese lines imagistic at all, not to say more imagistic than the English lines. I can imagine the polite murmur: "Despite the sonorous pitch accents and distinct cadences, we do not understand what they *mean*." And it would not improve matters much, if I wave at you, or even project on a screen for you, thus to see the manuscript on which the sixteen Chinese characters are written. The characters, the word-pictures as "ideographs," bless the heart of Mr. Pound, just do not perform instant magic. Through the language barriers, poetic images, or poetry for that matter, cannot just *be*, but, in due respect to Mr. MacLeish, must *mean*, as they cross the cultural and linguistic border. It is the translator's task to make them mean as they *be*. And if he brings them into being, into such being as poetry must be in another language, his process, whether through hard labor or inspiration, is not short of the creative.

Let us see how the Chinese couplet and line, so beloved of their native sensitive readers as unforgettable, soul-stirring poetic images, can be re-created in translation; and how the results can make them stand beside and emulate their peers in English originally created. Along with

A rose-red city, half as old as time,

the Chinese couplet says, through Arthur Waley:

In the southern land many birds sing;
Of towns and cities half are unwalled.

And the line of Ch'ü Yuan, through much of my hard labor, now can mean as well as be:

Time, pallid and opaque, soon will be setting.

This, I hope, may find kindred company with the lines of incomparable "melancholy beauty" of Robert Burns praised so highly by
Yeats:

> The white moon is setting behind the white wave,
> And Time is setting with me, O!

I do not know, of course, the exact process of Waley's inspired
translation, but I can tell his way of discrimination, though subtle
and slight, elimination and addition, not being at all bound by
Poundian popular etymology or the grammarian's literalism; but,
more important, his sense of the wholeness of the relationship
among all the words, which would only fall apart through etymological reproduction, or would become through the overplay of the
word-pictorial, "ideographic" fancy only a puzzling heap of broken
images of a mutilated kaleidoscope after Christmas day. Last but
not least is his sense of euphony of the original as well as in his
translation. We know it is but a vain hope to reproduce the exact
sounds of one language, including even onomatopoeia, in another.
But the quality of the euphony in the original, especially when it
subtly contributes to the poetic expression, giving it such a total
sensation of sound, form, sense and feeling as any successful
poetic image must have, can and should be grasped by the translator
in his most sensitive and alert reading. And when he is able to
reproduce that quality, his simulation transcends the mere sounds,
but carries over or distills parts of them to fit the total effect in
another language for its feeling and sense, as well as the euphonic
expressiveness that is transformed. In such an instance of intense,
complete alertness, resulting in successful imitation, the translator's
state of mind as well as his accomplishment deserves to be called
creative. It is no less than genuine mimesis of high order.

For a good reader of both Chinese and English poetry, trained
to be sensitive about imagistic effects, and I hope for the good
audience now, somehow tuned up, as it were, to the fusion of
sound, sense and vision,

> *Tien nan to niao ming*
> *Chou hsien pan wu ch'eng*

is quite like

> In the southern land many birds sing;
> Of towns and cities half are unwalled.

If the English lacks the melodic sonority of the Chinese pitch accents, it compensates by a greater number of nasal consonants to echo richly the original symphony, and just enough additional light sibilants and open vowels to vivify and modulate it. We are aware that the analysis of sound effects on the expressiveness of poetic sense is often a tricky game, and may be only an appreciative afterthought. The inspired translator, in this case Mr. Waley, might be, most likely, not at all conscious of these phonological counterparts when he re-created these lines. But while sound and its literal meaning in linguistic convention must be exclusive to each language, we may believe with Sir Richard Paget that there is the universality of language as gesture in its primary or primeval expressiveness, which is shared by all human races despite latter-day cultural differentiations. (This I think is precisely at the basis of what Muriel Rukeyser calls, in her brilliant presentation from this same platform, the "equivalent music," the thing that she says is "beneath" all languages.) National linguistic habits, having largely to cater to the workaday humdrum business communications, would tend to blind and deafen the user to the primal vivid expressiveness of language as gesture, which should have universal appeal. A translator at his happiest moment can prove this, by taking the best expressions of one language and empathetically making them ring again with fresh vitality in another tongue. In doing this the translator restores, in fact advances, a new consciousness among all readers, including both foreign and native, of the pristine quality and power of the literary art, which basically share universal principles; and which, through him, can overleap linguistic boundaries and unite more peoples among humanity in the finest thoughts and feelings. To this extent, his responsibility, as well as his achievement, is that of a creator.

If he happens to be working between Chinese and English, the two languages which are not only so vastly different, but of which the one is so old and conventionalized, and the other so full of wears and tears by the widest use of the modern business world, the challenge to him is all the greater, and his accomplishment is the rarer feat. He has to know all the old Chinese conventions, but be able to see the poetic image afresh. His English rendition would be with a sense of rediscovery, a new sense of identification of the poetic mind, over and above all the apparent dissimilarities of the languages and the remoteness of cultural traditions. I think I can fairly assume that Mr. Waley had experienced the music of "La Belle Dame Sans Merci" as well as the image of

A rose-red city, half as old as time,

when he rendered

> In the southern land many birds sing;
> Of towns and cities half are unwalled.

A thrilling sense of identification is there, with some of the Chinese
musical thought carried over as well as that of English revived, but
he copied none. For he, as a translator of unfailing fidelity, thus
created. And I can certainly confess that, in my humble effort of
rendering Ch'ü Yuan:

> Time, pallid and opaque, soon will be setting,

I was very conscious of Burns:

> The white moon is setting behind the white wave,
> And Time is setting with me, O!

Yet at the same instant, I was deeply affected by the melodic sound
of despair of the Chinese original, as much as by its vision and feeling of melancholy beauty that constitutes the poetic image:

> *Shih ai ai ch'i chiang pi*

Hence

> Time, pallid and opaque . . .

is the mimesis in result. I must say also that at the moment my
attention was raised above the word-pictures, or individual "ideographs," and even the original grammatical construction, though my
comprehension had initially been firmly rooted in them. Now looking back, I see that the original word-order is preserved, and the
sense of every word reduplicated. But this was not my real concern
in translation. I read the line until I saw before me the poetic image
of Time. There appeared the eerie vision of dimming but ever-
haunting light, as if also audible with the mocking voice of irrevocable fate, distant but distinct, which the poet at the climactic
moment of his lament recognized, when in deep anguish resounded
his outcry. For *ai ai,* my choice of "pallid and opaque" with the
suggestion of a slight internal rhyming effect, as if in mimicry, was
not a foremost conscious phonological design when I was translating.
But I was most conscious of the poetic image, as a total fusion of

sound, vision, passion and even intellect, and let the appropriate words spring up in mimesis. From this experience as a translator to re-create a poetic image, whether the result is complete success or failure, I may suggest that Mr. Lewis' definition of the poetic image be slightly modified to read: The image is a picture made out of *word-music*. This, I believe, is at least of special benefit to advise on translation from Chinese into western languages. When Lewis spoke of "words," he could take for granted that words in western languages are presented in phonetic scripts mainly, if not merely, as auditory properties. Words when they make poetic images, therefore, presuppose word-music. What I want to emphasize is that Chinese words, despite the peculiar fact that they are represented in character scripts, properly called logograms, are no less auditory properties. Their word-music may be even more evident, because of the inherent melodic quality of their tonal or pitch accents to differentiate meanings. What may be less evident, but perhaps even more important, is the fact that the famous "isolated" nature of the Chinese language, its totally uninflected monosyllablism, and its sparing use, if not thorough avoidance, of any grammatical connectives, make the sense of a Chinese sentence or poetic line more dependent on the rhythm, cadence, and sometimes even rhymes and assonances modulated according to something like the principles of counterpoint and harmony in its phraseology, to determine meanings in the whole symphonic context.

I stress this point because the Fenollosan exotic approach, armed with Ezra Pound's inventive genius of popular etymology, has actually mistaken the Chinese script by illusions of the eye for the Chinese language whose real expressive power lies in the arrangements of the musical syllables on the tongue. Indeed the script of any language could have visual attraction. If a Chinese were indoctrinated to believe that the English script were all that visually symbolic, he might see in

> The white moon is setting behind the white wave,
> And Time is setting with me, O!

that the round-shaped O stood for the full setting moon, and so many w's and m's were pictures of the wave. Maybe Burns had all that imaginary Chinese genius! A Dostoyevskian character says, "Without God all is possible." We might say, too, for an imagined language without natives all is possible. Mr. Pound's great achievement in his *Cathay* is because of his universally admired, incomparable lyrical gift to make the Chinese poems sing in English as few

other translators can. His translation of the *Shih Ching,* or Confucian
Odes, later, where I sense he is even less preoccupied with his popular-
etymological fancy, sometimes produces the most effective mimicries
of the pristine ancient Chinese lyrical voice. Of his inserted drawings
of Chinese characters in his Cantos, I will say nothing. For the
Cantos are not translations. He is free to invent, and with his genius
he can make any chimera look a normal animal in his fabulous zoo.
A man of such singular genius can do anything and be justly celebrated for his accomplishments, including his inventive Chinese etymology
for his creative translation. But such innovation, once welcomed as
ingenious and original, can be done only once by one man. He must
not be copied, and one would hope his popular etymologism will
never be imitated.

I may seem to be stressing, or overstressing, the importance of the
auditory, phonetic, euphonic and musical quality of the Chinese
language for semantic as well as aesthetic understanding. If so, it is
because I wish to balance—or somehow to correct if I may—the
impression of the Chinese language owing to the Fenollosa-Poundian
infleunce, which is still felt among other translators, and still fasci-
nates western creative writers. Let me say that truly scientific analysis of Chinese etymology is of immense value and of indispensable
service to the profound understanding of the Chinese language. But
even then, it must be remembered, as serious philologists have long
since agreed, that it is the phonetic parts or phonetic cognates, not
the radicals or so called signifiers of the characters that reveal the
primary etymons of the words. The pictorial-ideographical aspects
of the character script serve at best for the native writer and reader,
and should for any translator, therefore, only as reminders of certain
associative meanings, most often only on second thought. We note
them, for all practical purposes, in the *décor*, not in the core, of the
essential meaning. It is how the words sound, especially how they
modulate in relation to the rest of the sentence or the whole work,
and not how they picturesquely look when each is visually isolated,
that really matters to the intended creative or mimetic sense. The
characters can, of course, help etymological research. But because
of the many long centuries of continual vulgarization of their forms,
they must undergo the most intricate retrieving process of analysis,
to the last minutia, to yield authentic fragments of information. And
fragments they must remain, glimmering particles able to illuminate
the nation's social. psychological or literary history when detected
and used wisely. We are in grateful debt to erudite men of imagination and strict discipline in philology. Nuclear philology is what
I might call this honored field of etymological study. But it is like

nuclear physics, where the application of its theories, and of its passion for ever so refined technique of fission, must be kept within bounds as it affects our life and work. Nuclear matter, in life or in language, must be carefully guarded against the temptation of its overplay. For to break down a Chinese poetic line or prose sentence to its minuscule etymological raw elements and try to reproduce their senses in translation actually defeat the purpose. It may happen as Bernard Berenson said, I think, of some nineteenth-century critics that they break a watch into its microscopic tiny parts and want to hear how it ticks. Of course it won't.

We recognize that in the general field of translation, even though we confine ourselves only to speaking of translations between Chinese and western languages, or merely English, there could be endless arguments about theories. Each one's persuasion may be regarded as a bias, influenced by his upbringing, professional habits and personal experiences with specific materials. When we can and perhaps do agree, it may be on principles so broad and obvious that they may not actually get us far enough. However that may be, let us try at least for a moment to pursue the broad area of agreement and see how or whether it may possibly be made somehow to work in practice. And my emphasis is on practice. Thorough comprehension of the original, we say, and perfect representation of it in translation can certainly be agreed on as our ideal. But this proposition we may find to be not only utopian as all ideals are, but on close examination to be antinomous. This antinomy, I hope, will be instructive. For thorough, or nearly thorough, comprehension of any great work may be much better represented in a huge volume of analytical criticism than in translation; and perfect representation in at least the material sense is as impossible for any creative artist as for the translator, unless it be an entire replica. Here the consideration of the translator as creator, again, may become relevant. The antinomy reveals his limitations, restrictions as well as his special privileges and possible distinctions. Unlike the critic, of whether textual, philosophical or aesthetic concern, the translator cannot discourse, but must imitate—though he must have implicit understanding of all these concerns. More like the creative artist, he in his mimesis must necessarily transform, but for him there is the additional discipline required—that of fidelity to the original voice, idea and imagery. He has his work cut out for him. He, a somehow predestined Sartor Resartus, must sew a garment of essentially exotic pattern, yet he must domesticate it so that it not only becomes acceptable, but also distinguishable as new fashion. He must have painfully studied every stitch and hem of the original

article, but must in his production show the least of the seamy side
of his learning. He has to appear innovative for his new public, but
he had better know well how the foreign model has been enjoyed by
the best of minds among its original admirers, so that the new taste
he introduces be not spurious. Sometimes this knowledge helps a
good deal. Here I might state an experience of a reversed situation,
of my translating from English into Chinese. It was a passage from
Ben Jonson's *Alchemist*. I was deeply struck by the biting force of
outrage in the dramatic speech and its tremulous emotion. But, too
engrossed by the strong diction, I was at a loss how to produce it
in Chinese without some good native guidance. I needed the help
of those who were brought up with the tradition, and who must
have read the original much better than I. Then I noted Mr. Ivor
Winters' admirable analysis of Jonson's "careful manipulation of
iambic and trochaic feet," and his occasional "trisyllabic substitu-
tion, which," says Mr. Winters, "effects a nervous leap, as suddenly
stilled as it was undertaken." My appreciation of the significance
of the meter led me to understand better the power and meaning
of the passage:

> Thou vermin, have I ta'en thee out of dung,
> So poor, so wretched, when no living thing
> Would keep thee company but a spider or worse.

Accordingly my Chinese version tries to render the "nervous leap"
toward the end:

> *Ni tu ch'ung, kang ts'ung fen li nieh ch'u lai ma?*
> *Ni pei pi han ts'eng, mei yu tung hsi ken lai*
> *Yu erh wei wu, chih chih yu chih chu yao pu hai keng tu!*

I had heard a suggestion among an admiring British circle of early
sophisticated readers of *The Waste Land*, that a most ironic effect
was achieved by Mr. Eliot's using the word "nevertheless" to simu-
late a heavy sneeze amidst carefully measured iambics in

> Madame Sosostris, famous clairvoyante
> Had a bad cold, nevertheless,
> Is known to be the wisest woman in Europe.

This helped my translation to be able to imitate it:

> *Soso-tui fu-jen, chu ming cheng fa yen*
> *Te le chung shang-feng la, en k'e shih ja,*
> *Wu jen pu chih hsiao, chih hui chia yü chuan ou.*

瑟 索 兌 夫 人， 著 名 "正 法 眼"
得. 了 重 傷 風 啦， 嗯 可 是 啊，
無 人 不 知 曉， 智 慧 甲 於 全 歐.

　　Too easily engrossed by the literal meanings of the powerful diction of a foreign masterpiece, especially when it is in Chinese characters, of which each individual one could be visually and intellectually so fascinating, the translator is often too spellbound, clinging to a tree, a twig or a leaf, and forgets the woods. He thus often fails to hear the sounds of the words together, their intervals and phrasing, in relation to the rest of the line. But that sound relationship is after all what makes real meaning. And, if a precious good image is present, that relationship is what really conjures the mental image for him to convey in another language, not the individual pictorial shapes, nor the isolated ideographic elements with so many dazzling and puzzling free associations. Miss Louise Bogan once told me that, after much of their shoptalk about the secrets of poetic composition, T. S. Eliot came to a simple conclusion, that "to write poetry, we must know how to breathe." I think it is the best advice for translators, especially to translate from Chinese. Chinese literary theory began, in fact, with the notion of *ch'i*, which has been later interpreted in general art criticism to mean "spirit" or "vital force," but by which, when Ts'ao Pei first used it in the third century for literary composition, he meant precisely "breathing." Now it often happens that after deciphering each individual character with bated breath, at last a translator may, as if by afterthought, string the words together, grammatizing the sentences somehow in another language. He resorts to an over-abundance of expletives, superfluous participles, prepositions and adverbs, showing all his stitches that manage to hang the new garment together. Piously or proudly he may show all the seamy side in full view, revealing hard labor which he has gasped through; drawing, however, anything but admiration for the workmanship. In fact the over-abundance of apparent grammatical tags, and superimposition of personal pronouns, so alien to the Chinese, distort rather than communicate the original meaning. They fail both the sound and the sense. I understand this process, and I feel great sympathy for the translation of a productive scholar, published not too long ago in a sumptuous volume of a prestigious series. The following example is two lines of Chinese verse, of some fifteen modulated monosyllables, or characters, each. Here goes his English:

> This was the way of it:
> He being immersed in phrases painfully consenting, it
> was like darting fish with the hooks in their
> gills, dragged from the depth of an
> unplumbed pool;
>
> He being shrouded in beautiful language,
> all aflutter, it was like
> birds on the wing and the arrow
> strung to the bow—down they drop
> headlong from out of the cloud.

The two Chinese lines, long, to be sure, according to Chinese prosodic norms, are

> *Yü shih,*
> *Ch'en tz'u fu yueh, jo yu yü hsien kou*
> *erh ch'u ch'ung yuan chih shen;*
> *Fu tzao lien p'ien, jo han niao ying chiao*
> *erh chui tz'eng yun chih tzun*

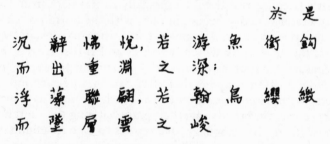

And my version, published in a small volume, is

> Hence,
> Arduously sought expressions, hitherto evasive, hidden,
> Will be like stray fishes out of the ocean bottom to
> emerge on the angler's hook;

And quick-winged metaphors, fleeting, far-fetched,
Feather tribes while sky-faring are brought down
from the curl-clouds by the fowler's bow.

This is about one-third shorter than the other version. The alliteratives came rather naturally to me, when the euphony of the original verse echoed in my mind with clear cadence and thought. The images might have thus become more vivid, I hope, and more direct, when they are not interfered with by the personal subject which is superimposed by the English translator and is not in the Chinese original. The frequent absence of the personal subject in Chinese does, we must admit, often cause great difficulties in translation. But it has to be handled with great caution when it has to be inserted.

This may appear to be a small technical point. But it may conveniently lead us to some general conclusions about the Chinese language and translation, pertaining to my subject. It may be true after all that the Chinese language is more apt to create images and effect more direct and concrete appeal in its way than the inflected languages. But this, as I emphasized, is not so much because of its pictorial-ideographic script, as its isolated, monosyllabic, hence inherently terse nature. Furthermore its pitch accents add a melodic dimension, which, however, is no mere ornament but an integral part of the total semantic property of the language in its expressiveness of meaning. Consequently, the arrangement of the various tonal monosyllables to make sense is heavily dependent on the right rhythm, which, again, is not for mere musical effect but for literal meaningful signification. The terseness of the language makes it necessarily more suggestive than indicative or discursive. The suggestive quality is, moreover, many times increased, owing to the fact that the language has been too long cultivated. It has thus accumulated through thousands of years allusions in words and phrases, taken for granted in the native tongue but often utterly untransferable in another language. This suggestiveness also, while it may put off the foreign reader, often—like that of household jargon or college slang—effects an intimate tone of irony, piquancy or humor by the native user of the language. The translator from Chinese, therefore, must first of all have the acutest inner ear for a picturesquely represented tongue, of which extraordinarily rich musical patterns of suggestive phrasing, cadence and modulation are actually semantic determinants of meaning. He must, of course, have implicit understanding, penetrating as well as comprehensive knowledge. But he must be undeceived by the appearance of the script, and, more important, unhampered in his breathing by the isolated monosyllables or characters. Then with his acute inner ear and mental, emotional and intellectual perceptions for imagistic effects, he can breathe the meaning and rhythm, so to say, and compose, re-create and transform, without losing fidelity. His problems, we realize, may not be so basically different in kind from those of his colleagues in other languages. But the high degree or large extent of the challenge to him may be remarkably more obvious, hence perhaps somehow more revealing when so discussed as we did. If it is not too presumptuous to claim a position for the translator as creator, the translator from and into Chinese would aspire after it with a tremendous sense of difficulty. But considering the ingenuity, cultivation and sincerity demanded of him as of any creative artist to overcome that difficulty, he aspires also with a sense of desert.

On Translating Genji

Ivan Morris

I shall try to avoid making generalizations about translation, and I
shall try to be specific. I want to discuss the opening sentences of
The Tale of Genji, the novel written at the beginning of the eleventh
century by Lady Murasaki, and I am distributing a kind of analysis.

Let me describe this analysis* to you. On the first page you see
the opening sentences written in my execrable calligraphy. On the
second page are the same sentences in a Romanized version. About
the only easy thing about Japanese is that it is pronounced more or
less as it is written in the Romanized version, the vowels being pronounced as in Italian and all of them enunciated, so that you can in
fact read this passage fairly reliably. There follows a detailed analysis, which those of you who are interested in such things can study.
The analysis explains what each word in these sentences means, what
its grammatical function is, and it also explains some of the more
complicated syntax. This goes on for several pages; in fact, it goes
on to page 277, word by word. I may say that this is more or less the
approach I use in making my own translations from classical Japanese,
so it will give some idea how time-consuming the work is. I find that
to translate a page of Japanese and to arrive at a version I consider
publishable takes about five times as long as to write a page of my
own work, and it is far less satisfying. Why one goes on doing this
I cannot imagine.

*Reprinted on pages 273-279.

One reason, of course, why it is so time-consuming is that it is
essential to do this kind of analysis as the first stage. I find this the
most tedious and unpleasant stage, but it has to be done if one is to
have a serious translation.

After this I give my literal translation at the top of page 278.
It is an almost word-for-word translation, as you can see if you compare it with the analysis. The additions in square brackets have been
introduced so that the sentences will make sense. Classical Japanese
has virtually no pronouns; English requires many personal pronouns.
Classical Japanese has no tenses; English requires them. Above all,
classical Japanese has no punctuation whatsoever—no commas, no
inverted commas, no full stops, nothing. So we have to add a good
deal to make a barely understandable translation.

Often I find it necessary to have an intermediate stage between
the literal and the free versions. When I translated *The Pillow Book
of Sei Shonagon,* I did the entire work first in the way you see it on
page 278. Then I did a freer version, an intimation of what the
finished English translation might be, and then I put it aside for
about six months to get as far away as possible from the details. Then
I came to it again and produced a finished version, and then as the
last stage I went back and compared this final version with the original Japanese to see if I had gone too far away from it. As you see, it
is immensely time-consuming.

In the next section (page 278) I have copied out the opening lines
of Arthur Waley's monumental version of *The Tale of Genji.* His is
very much better than mine because he happens to be a very much
better writer than I am. It is also rather freer than my version, not
a great deal, but somewhat, and it is very much more rhythmical,
very much more readable.

After this comes what I consider to be the worst possible type of
translation, and I shall be as frank in giving my views about my
fellow translators here as I hope they would be about me. Number
7 is to me the nadir of translation. It was done by a very eminent
French scholar, probably the most distinguished expert on classical
Japanese, Professor Haguenauer of the University of Paris. Finally,
I have provided a recent translation by Oscar Benl into German, and
I would say it is somewhat less free than my finished version or
Arthur Waley's finished version, and obviously a good deal freer than
Professor Haguenauer's version.

Let me say here that I have no intention of translating the whole
of *The Tale of Genji.* I think it would be rather pointless to do it at
this stage. Twenty years from now maybe might be time for a new
version. What I am doing is translating certain parts which appear

in the text of a twelfth-century scroll, a magnificent work called the
Genji-Monogatari-Emaki, which includes passages from the earliest
extant text of *The Tale of Genji.* This does not mean to say that it
is the most accurate text. It is not, by any means. It is a very special
sort of text designed to accompany the scroll paintings.

We are dealing with a single passage, the opening words of *The Tale
of Genji.* One of the advantages of taking a passage like this and
examining it in detail is that it allows one to test general statements
about translation. I have been reading the excellent P.E.N. Manifesto
on Translation this morning. On the second page it says that a sentence in Japanese has to be broken up into its separate parts and then
refashioned before it can be expressed in English. Absolutely true,
and this is also true of all Oriental languages. Then it says: "The
translator may spend hours unraveling and re-creating a single paragraph." Certainly this accords with my own experience. Then it
says: "He must somehow suggest the rhythm and structure of the
original, and write in a style that conveys the style of the original."
This sounds unexceptionable, and of course that is what he should
do. But I suggest that it is often completely impossible. Arthur Waley
has not been able to do it. In his translation given on page 278 he has
not in any way suggested the rhythm and structure of the original,
nor has he written in a style that conveys the style of the original.
If he had, it would probably have been as unreadable as the Number
Seven version.

It is very nice indeed if these things can be done, and occasionally
Waley was able to do it, but I think normally we have to resign ourselves to "translator's despair," and we must realize that the style of
the original is among the things that have to be jettisoned if we are
going to produce works of translation readable as literature. I challenge anyone in the world, however well he knows Japanese or English, however well he writes in English, "to write in a style that conveys the style of the original," when translating *The Tale of Genji.*

You will see that there are numerous footnotes in Professor Haguenauer's translation (page 278). In fact he provides six footnotes for
the first two sentences of the book. This goes on all the way through.
Waley has virtually none. Oscar Benl has, in the same passage, one.
I have nothing in principle against footnotes in translations from
classical Japanese. I do think, however, that they are terribly off-
putting for most readers. If I were to read a work of Turkish literature, for instance, which I know nothing about, and found that
half the page consisted of footnotes, I think I would be instantly
repelled. Nevertheless, there are many times when one does need
to know certain specific facts if one is to understand what the passage
means. I think that trying to work the facts into the translation is
not the best solution, because the reader does not know whether he

is reading what the original writer said or whether it is what the original writer said plus explanation. And often he may be struck by the question: Why did the writer bother to explain that So-and-so was an Emperor who lived in the ninth century? Wouldn't his readers know? In fact, the original writer did not explain it and the fact was worked into the translation to help the reader. I do not think this is a satisfactory solution. I have tried it, and given it up.

I think the best solution—obviously I think so, because it is the one I now use—is to have as many notes as one considers necessary, but to put them at the end of the book, where they do not have to be seen, but where they are readily available. An ideal solution, if the publisher agrees, is to have a separate volume of notes. That worked with *The Pillow Book of Sei Shonagon,* which is provided with a volume of notes so that the reader can read the main volume without looking at the notes at all. A reader who wanted to find out more could have the second volume open next to him, and he would not have to look back all the time to find the right page for the notes, and he could refer to them easily. Certainly it is not the ideal solution, but I think it is better than the others.

Now I go back to Professor Haguenauer's translation. Some twenty years ago, he started out with the intention of translating the whole of *The Tale of Genji,* but of the fifty-four chapters he completed only one. I think the reason is obvious—he would have gone insane if he had kept it up. Not to mention what would have happened to his readers, if any. It is unreadable. You see all the square brackets. He believes—and this is typical of the French school of translation from the oriental classics—that everything that is added should be put in square brackets. The trouble is that he is not consistent. He has added things which he has *not* put in square brackets, so that even according to his own principles it does not work. For instance you see question marks, full stops, and three lines from the end there is the definite article *le.* Well, there is no definite article in Japanese, and that *le* was added by him. He simply forgot to put the square brackets in. Lucky for his sanity that he did, because if he had really been consistent he would have had to put square brackets round each of those full stops, colons, commas, and inverted commas, and what use would it be? The only people who could get any possible benefit out of this are scholars and students, and presumably they can read it in Japanese anyhow. I see no purpose in this type of translation except as a scaffolding, which is quite essential to the translator himself, but serves no other purpose. Arthur Waley produced a scaffolding and threw it away. Professor Haguenauer produced a translation that is all scaffolding, and we do not see the building.

One depressing thing about producing this sort of translation is that very soon it will be possible to do it by machine. Machines will probably do it very much better than we can. The machine won't leave out the square brackets round the full stops, and they certainly won't leave them out from the definite article. These machines exist, as you know, and by a hideous irony Arthur Waley was evicted by a machine from the house where he had lived for so many years in Gordon Square. He was told to leave by his landlord, the University of London, for whom he had done so much good work, in order to make way for a computer which was going to translate Russian. It does translate Russian. It is sitting there at this very moment, translating Russian into non-English. He pleaded with the University to let him stay for a few more years. He knew he did not have long to live, and for an old man to move with all his books and papers was a horrible ordeal, but they were adamant. The lease had expired, the machine had to come in. Now such machines can do this type of translation very well, and I imagine they may be helpful for translating certain scientific and technical material. A machine-made translation from a Chinese work on nuclear physics would be useful to an American nuclear physicist. But the machines won't help those of us who translate literature to avoid the tedious first steps we have to go through in order to understand what the text means. It is only when we really understand the text that we can start being free. We cannot take liberties with it until we really know it. Only because Arthur Waley knew Japanese and Chinese so very well, so accurately, was he able to permit himself the great freedom he took.

Here is what Arthur Waley wrote in his *Notes on Translation:*

> "A French scholar (whom I greatly admire) wrote recently with regard to translators: *'Qu'ils s'efface derrière les textes et ceux-ci, s'ils sont été vraiment compris, parleront d'eux-mêmes.'* Except in the rather rare case of plain concrete statements, such as 'The cat chases the mouse,' there are seldom sentences that have exact word-for-word equivalents in another language. It becomes a question of choosing between various approximations. One can't, for example, say in English, 'Let them efface themselves behind the texts.' One has to say something like, 'They should efface themselves, leaving it to the texts to speak,' and so on. I have always found that it was I, not the texts, that had to do the talking."

Now comes the magnificent sentence which I think about so often when I am working. Arthur Waley continues:

"Hundreds of times I have sat for hours in front of texts the meaning
of which I understood perfectly, and yet been unable to see how they
ought to be put into English in such a way as to re-embody not merely
a series of correct dictionary meanings, but also the emphasis, the tone,
the eloquence of the original.

" 'Toute recherche esthétique,' the French scholar continues, 'va contre
la bonne foi du traducteur.' I would rather say that the true work of the
translator begins with 'recherche esthétique.' What comes before that—
knowledge of the foreign language—is of course essential as a foundation,
but it is a matter of linguistics and has nothing to do with the art that
I am discussing. There do of course exist texts in which only logical
meaning, and not feeling, is expressed. But particularly in the Far East
they are exceedingly rare. The appeal, even in philosophical texts, has
always been to emotion rather than to logic."

As for Arthur Waley's translation of The Tale of Genji, one can, if
one wishes, call it a paraphrase. But that is simply a quibble, and we
have to conclude that the only translations worth doing are paraphrases, if Waley paraphrases, and if Haguenauer's translations are
regarded as correct, then translations are useless for literature.

This is what I wanted to say. I hope you will have a chance to
study classical Japanese literature. As Arthur Waley said in the
introduction to his translation of Japanese poetry, it is really quite
simple and a few weeks suffice for mastering the basic essentials of
classical Japanese.

The Opening Passage of *The Tale of Genji*

I In the Japanese script:

いづれのおほむ時にか女御更衣あまた侍ひ
給ひける中にいとやむごとなき際にはあら
ぬがすぐれて時めき給ふありけり
はじめよりわれはと思ひ上り給へる
御方々めざましきものに貶しめ嫉み
給ふ同じ程それより下﨟の更衣たちは
まして安からず

II Romanized Version

izure no ōmutoki ni ka nyōgo kōi amata saburaitamaikeru naka ni
ito yamugotonaki kiwa ni wa aranu ga sugurete tokimekitamau
arikeri/ hajime yori ware wa to omoiagaritamaeru onkatagata
mezamashiki mono ni otoshimesonemitamau/ onaji hodo sore
yori gerō no kōitachi wa mashite yasukarazu/

III Analysis

1. izure
    interrogative pronoun: *which?*

2. no
    possessive case particle.

3. ōmutoki
    ōmu: honorific prefix;
    toki: (noun) *time, period.*

4. ni
    conjunctive particle, functioning as the *renyōkei* of the copula,
    nari, 'to be'.

5. ka
    adverbial particle indicating doubt, uncertainty.

6-7. nyōgo kōi
    nouns: Imperial Concubines (the *nyōgo* being of higher rank
    than the *kōi*).

8. amata
    adverb: *in large numbers, numerously.*

9. saburaitamaikeru
    saburai: renyōkei of *saburau, hagyō* verb meaning 'to be in
        attendance'.
    tamai: renyōkei of *tamau*, an honorific auxiliary *hagyō* verb.
    keru: rentaikei of *keri*, a past or affirmative verbal suffix.

10. naka
    noun: *middle, midst.*

N.B. *nyōgo . . . saburaitamaikeru* is a subordinate clause modifying
    naka.

11. ni
    case particle: *in, on.*

12. ito
    adverb: *very.*

13. yamugotonaki
    rentaikei of *yamugotonashi* (literally 'cannot be stopped'):
    impressive, dignified.

14. kiwa
    noun: *social level, status.*

15. ni
    same as no. 4 above.

16. wa
    case particle marking the emphasis inherent in a word or
    phrase (here it emphasizes the negation contained in *aranu*.
    no. 17 below).

17. aranu
    ara: mizenkei of *ari, rahen* verb meaning 'to be, exist'.
    nu: rentaikei of *zu*, negative verbal suffix.

N.B. the *rentaikei* is used rather than the *shūshikei* because the word
precedes *ga*, no. 18 below.

18. ga
    particle creating a phrase having the property of an independent
    substantive (N.B. the word *hito* or *mono*, 'person', may be
    understood between *aranu* and *ga*).

19. sugurete
    sugure: renyōkei of *shimonidan* verb *suguru*, 'to excel';
    te: renyōkei of verbal suffix *tsu* (affirmative, emphatic, past)
       used adverbially.

20. tokimekitamau
    tokimeki: renyōkei of *kagyō* verb *tokimeku* ('to flourish,
       prosper').
    tamau: rentaikei of *tamai* (no. 9 above).

21. hajime
    noun: *beginning, outset (renyōkei* of *shimonidan* verb, *hajimu,*
    'to begin').

22. yori
    case particle: *from, since.*

23. ware
    personal pronoun: *I, myself.*

24, wa
same as no. 16 above.

25. to
conjunctive particle marking the end of a subordinate clause:
that.

N.B. *ware wa* is an elliptical subordinate clause meaning 'I (indeed)
shall be ahead of the others.') The verb modified by the *to* clause
is omitted and some word like *kangaete* ('thinking') must be understood; the *omoi* in *omoiagari* (no. 26) must not be taken to govern
the *to* clause.)

26. omoiagaritamaeru
omoiagari: renyōkei of *ragyo* compound verb *omoiagaru* ('to
be proud, haughty, conceited');
tamaeru: rentaikei of *tamaeri*, the *-eri* (progressive) form of
tamau (no. 9 above).

27. onkatagata
on: no. 3 above.
katagata: duplicated (plural) form of *kata* (noun meaning
'person, lady').

N.B. *hajime yori . . . omoiagaritamaeru* is a subordinate clause
modifying *onkatagata*.

28. mezamashiki
rentaikei of *shikukatsuyō* adjective *mezamashi* ('vexatious,
provoking').

29. mono
noun: *person.*

30. ni
equivalent to the phrase *no yō ni* ('in the manner of', 'as if')
no: no. 2 above.
yo: noun meaning 'manner, fashion'.
ni: same as no. 11 above.

31. otoshimesonemitamau
otoshime: renyōkei of *shimonidan* verb *otoshimu* ('to despise');
sonemi: renyōkei of *magyō* verb *sonemu* ('to be jealous');
tamau: shushikei of *tamau* (no. 9).

32. onaji
rentaikei of *shikukatsuyō* adjective *onaji* (used here in an
exceptional *wabummyaku* form): *same, identical.*

33. hodo
    noun: *extent, degree; rank.*

N.B. a coordinating case particle *to* or *ya* ('and') is to be understood between *hodo* and *sore*.

34. sore
    personal pronoun: *he, she.*

35. yori
    case particle (see no. 22 above) with extended meaning of *more than.*

36. gerō
    noun: *low-ranking person.*

37. no
    see no. 2 above.

38. kōi
    see no. 7 above.

39. tachi
    plural suffix (mainly honorific).

40. wa
    see no. 16 above.

41. mashite
    adverb: *all the more, still more (renyōkei* of *sagyō* verb *masu,* 'to increase', followed by *-te* as in no. 19 above).

42. yasukarazu
    combination of *yasuku* and *arazu*
    yasuku: renyōkei of the *kukatsuyō* adjective *yasushi* ('calm, at ease')
    arazu: ara (no. 17 above)
        zu: shushikei of the negative verbal suffix *zu.*

Inserendum

20b. arikeri
    ari: renyōkei of *ari, rahen* verb meaning 'to be, exist';
    keri: shushikei of *keri,* past or affirmative verbal suffix.

N.B. *mono* ('person, one') is to be understood between *tokimeki-tamau* and *arikeri: ito yamugotonaki . . . tokimekitamau* is a subordinate clause modifying this *mono*.

IV Literal translation (essential additions in square brackets):

Which honourable period [was it when] in midst of Imperial
Concubines (of different ranks) [who] were in attendance in large
numbers there was [one] who (certainly) not having a very impressive social position flourished outstandingly. Honourable ladies who
from beginning had continued to be haughty [thinking] 'I (indeed)
[shall be ahead of the others]' [regarded her with] scorn and
jealousy as vexatious person. Imperial Concubines of same rank [or]
lower than her were still more uneasy.

V Suggested free translation (Ivan Morris, 1966):

It happened during the reign of a certain Emperor that among the
many Imperial Concubines there was one who, though she did not
enjoy a very impressive position in society, was held in particular
favour. The great ladies at Court, who had all been proudly looking
forward to securing first place in the Emperor's affections, regarded
this vexatious rival with scorn and jealousy. Still more disgruntled
were the women who ranked as her equals or inferiors.

VI Translation by Arthur Waley (1925)

At the court of an Emperor (he lived it matters not when) there was
among the many gentlewomen of the Wardrobe and Chamber one,
who though she was not of very high rank was favoured far beyond
all the rest; so that the great ladies of the Palace, each of whom had
secretly hoped that she herself would be chosen, looked with scorn
and hatred upon the upstart who had dispelled their dreams. Still
less were her former companions, the minor ladies of the Wardrobe,
content to see her raised so far above them.

VII Translation by Ch. Haguenauer (1959):

En quel Règne [était-ce]? [Toujours est-il qu'] emmi Dames du
Gynécée, Chambrières qui, en nombre, servaient [aux Appartements
impériaux], il y [en] avait [une] qui (2) n'étant point en [une]
situation fort insigne (3), [l']ayant emporté avait [son] temps (4).
Les Personnes [de qualité] (5) qui, d'emblée, [se sont] monté [la
tête] – [chacune] avait pensé: "[Ce sera] moi" (6) –, [y voyant]

l'être qui [leurs] yeux décille, [la] ravalent, [la] jalousent. Les Chambrières, d'un rang à peu près égal [au sien, ou] inférieures [à elle], sont [,elles,] encore plus inquiètes.

(2) Kiritsubo est le nom de la chambrière en question: l'auteur ne le donnera que plus loin (ici, p.45, 1.9 et la note 5); ce silence a pour objet de piquer la curiosité des auditeurs ou du lecteur. Pour ce que est de l'interprétation de la fonction du complexe . . . *aranu-ga . . .,* cf. ci-dessus, p. 34, 1.29 et suiv.

(3) *Yamu, goto naki,* "il n'y a rien qu'on ne puisse achever," a dû signifier ici, à peu près, "qui ne le cède en rien" — "insigne, suprême". Il faut comprendre que la naissance ne plaçait pas Kiritsubo à un rang insigne, tel qu'elle dût ne le céder en rien aux autres Dames, en matière de préséance; en fait, sa naissance ne lui donnait pas droit aux plus hauts privilèges, à commencer par l'honneur d'être la favorite exclusive du souverain.

(4) *Tokimeku.* Kiritsubo était la favorite du moment; elle avait dès lors accaparé la faveur impériale.

(5) Il s'agit là exclusivement des concubines impériales de haute extraction aristocratique.

(6) Chacune d'elles a pensé en son for intérieur: 'La favorite ce sera moi, et pas une autre''.

VIII Translation by Oscar Benl (1966):

Unter welchem Herrscher geschah es wohl?—da war unter den vielen Nyōgo und Kōi (1) eine, die war aus nicht allzu hohem Hause stammte, aber die kaiserliche Huld am meisten genoss. Die Nyōgo, von denen jede von Anfang an und selbsbewusst die höchsten Erwartungen für sich selber hegte, standen ihr mit Verachtung und Missgunst gegenüber, und erst recht waren die Kōi, die gleicher oder geringerer Herkunft als sie waren, verbittert.

(1) Kaiserliche Nebengemahlinnen Ersten und Zweiten Ranges.

On Translating from Sanskrit

Raja Rao

I am really not a scholar of Sanskrit, though I love and enjoy Sanskrit more than any language in the world. And I will tell you why my insufficiency is so great as we go along, if you will bear with me.

About the beginnings of the nineteenth century—that is, during the Napoleonic wars—an Englishman was caught by the events, in Paris. He just could not go back to his own country, or proceed to India where he had his job. He had, while in that strange and rich and corruptible oriental country, however, learnt a language that seemed to him as to a few others, quite extraordinary. And as it often happens with the Indians, they tried to claim for it (as for many other things in India) such superior qualities—of course the oldest, the richest language of the world, called Sanskrit, which in the language itself meant the together-perfected or the totally-refined—and this Englishman, like a few others, was marveled with some of its great virtues but could not, of course, endorse all the magnificence the Indians claimed for it. And Goddess Saraswathi or (maybe) the Englishman's Karma, or both together, had decided that this was how it should be, that is, this Englishman would for historical reasons be caught in Paris and be unable to proceed on his journey. And he took the opportunity offered him to go and talk to the scholars about this extraordinary language, and the news caught fire. Scholars began to come and listen to him with

281

much eagerness and care. It was also, one must not forget, the time
when German romanticism had its first echoes, and the myth of
India, as everybody knows, played a decisive part in feeding the imagination of German intellectuals. (Certain texts from Tamil were
translated into Latin, and they were printed in Holland—these were
the Upanishads, themselves originally composed in Sanskrit, and so
on.) Thus the European mind was, as it were, in its karmic necessity
fed by an imaginary India—and then came Sanskrit itself on the
scene.

The discovery of Sanskrit was so revolutionary that scholars could
not believe their eyes. Here was an ancient language which seemed
linked with their own Greek and Latin, and perhaps older than both.
This came as an intellectual shock to the proud European. And when
they started learning the language more (it was in Paris that the
European school of Sanskrit scholarship first started) people came
from Germany and England, and even from Italy, to learn this
ancient language. The more they learned it the more enthusiastic
they grew, and simple translations now began to appear of some of
the well-known Sanskrit texts. By the middle of the nineteenth
century, the reputation of Sanskrit literature had grown so immense
that few of the French or, for that matter, the English poets failed to
hail Saraswathi or Lakshmi, Shiva or Rama. (Hugo, Leconte de
Lisle, Lamartine, and, of course, Shelley.) Some scholars by now
concluded the discovery of Sanskrit to be the greatest event in
European cultural history since the discovery or rediscovery of Greek
in the fourteenth century. Sanskrit had by now become a major
language of the world, because of its subtlety, its exquisite riches,
and its extraordinary philosophical traditions.

By the third quarter of the nineteenth century Europe discovered
Indian philosophy, and through Deussen and Schopenhauer it was
to enter the main stream of European thought. (Nietzsche, as one
knows, at the moment he lost control of his mind, in Turin, was
discovered reading a Purana. And, of course, Schopenhauer had acknowledged what an influence Indian philosophy had had on his life.)

While this discovery of Indian thought was continuing, sometimes
through pure scholarly works like those of Max Müller's and sometimes through sentimental and theosophical interpretations of Indian
philosophical traditions, politics suddenly came into the picture,
somewhat delaying this Indo-European cultural communication.
Later still, the two great wars occupied the world to a degree that
made further exchange at the deeper levels somewhat difficult. However, after the last war, Europe discovered the marvels of Indian
music. And its discovery, musicians both in Europe and America tell
me, is of great technical significance—apart from the sentimental

intervention of the sitar amidst the picturesque customs and costumes of modern young America, and England.

I have said all this only to come to my central theme—which is that when European writers (and linguists) discover the metaphysics of the word, the Sanskritic tradition of it, they will realize what a magnificent treasury of human achievement lies buried in these texts, and that nowhere else (not even in Chomsky's dreams) perhaps, was the word analyzed to its roots in a manner which is at once masterly in its imaginative adventure as well as logical in its structure. The day the Western world discovers the Indian science of the word will perhaps lead modern literature to other possibilities—apprehended by Mallarmé first and then followed partly by Joyce, but without the philosophical background that the Indian tradition offers—and thus make the origin and effect of the word something more than an experience of linguistic adventure or an intellectual accident. The word as such would become, properly understood, the very means of liberation. The writer here becomes not merely an aesthete (in the real sense of the word) but one dedicated to the search of the Ultimate Truth (Brahman)—and the precision of the word therefore becomes a *sadhana*, a spiritual exercise. The magic of Mallarmé would still have its wonders, the Joycean invention would still have its rich immediacy, not by a horizontal statement as it were, but by a vertical one, something that Valéry was trying to perform. The Sanskrit writer knew the word had a finality that only a free man could name. Thus Mallarmé's ideal poet and the poetic language of *Le Livre* would be shown to have already existed in Sanskrit. And the key to it all was there for any serious poet's discovery—and practise.

What then is the word? In Sanskrit we call *sabda* both sound and word. In a small dictionary I have, it says: "*Sabda*, sound. The object of the sense of hearing; and property of *akasha*—ether. 2. Note (of birds and men, etc.) Noise in general. 3. Sound of musical instrument. 4. A word, sound, significant word, a title, an epithet, a name, etc." From where does the word arise? It arises of course from silence. For, before the word was, was silence, and after the word is, is silence again. And now from silence arises an intimation of some feeling as yet nameless. (And of course this would apply to all words and of whatever nature.) The nameless feeling which silence seems to have pushed up now enters into the realm of the mind—here it becomes a picture. This picture, then, is articulated as sound-silence which finally the tongue postulates as a flowing (short or long) note. And again this note is heard by some one through his ear. The ear takes the message through the brain into the realms of mental awareness from where it again descends into primal silence, dying where alone is understanding an experience. That is to say, where the sound

of the word has died into silence, it is from here that understanding
arises. In silence therefore is a word understood. From silence has
the word arisen. So it is from one silence to the other that the communication is made. Here we have to be very subtle. The question
to be asked is: Is there anyone, anybody there—any person, I mean—
where there is absolute silence in one? Could there be two ultimate
silences? Since where there is silence there could be no formulation
of thought, all silence is impersonal. Hence there is something but
no one there, there where the sound first emerged as a possibility.
That *something* where there is no one could not be different for
different people, for differentiation is itself the result of the person,
of the mind. There where there is no one, but isness is, then, is the
origin and end of sound—and of the word.

Let us look at it from another point. Just as form goes into the
very make of seeing (as the great Sage Sri Atmananda has said) and
seeing into the make of form—in fact since nobody can cut one from
the other—that is to say, there is no seer separate from the object
seen; so it is with sound; there is no hearer separate from the sound;
so the hearer and the sound are one. Therefore how could one say,
one has seen an object, one has heard a sound? (Hence the dictionary
meaning of sound as the object of the sense of hearing.) In fact, in
Indian tradition, the object is defined as that which comes into
being because of the act of seeing and has no independent existence
as such: *Drishyam.*

What then is the world: The world is just a playful division, for
one's enjoyment of one single experience. The *rasika* is the one who
enjoys *rasa*, the flavor—the enjoyer of artistic experience is he who
has the taste of the Absolute. Hence sound is nothing but the
Absolute Itself, and therefore is the Absolute in terms of the poetic
experience called *Sabda Brahman* (The Absolute as sound-word).

If then the Absolute is the origin and end of the word, both the
grammarian and the poets are *sadhakas,* men who practice words as
means to liberation. Bharthrihari our great poet, therefore, not
only wrote some of the most exquisite verse ever written in any language, but also wrote a textbook on words, and showed the way of
liberation *(moksha)* through the Word. Here we meet Abbé Bre-
mond's demand of *prière et poésie,* except that there is no God in
our outlook on poetic experience—Brahman is none other than oneself as silence. I enjoy the Word for myself, and this enjoyment is
poetry. If you have the intellectual maturity and artistic sensibility
to enjoy it, then we both enjoy the same thing—except that there
is never any two. There is ever and always a not-two. Do not even
say one, for that would be blasphemy.

The word therefore, at this level, is naturally magical. The real
name of anything is its vibration in pure silence (in ether, in *akasha,*

if you will). The perfect word then is the vibration of the object by
itself in itself and about itself where no one hears, sees, smells, or
touches. And the perfect word rightly pronounced would then have
the power (at a slightly lower level) to create the object itself. No
word that is not a natural name (of any object, thought or experience) could be its precise definition. Poetry than is that magical
link of precise names only to be understood when you have the
possibility of that silence in you wherein the word goes back to its
silence as it were, and you enjoy, if one could say so, Brahman.
That is to say one enjoys oneself, which is, of course, saying there
is just Joy and no one there to enjoy it. Joy joys Itself. And Brahman is of course *Ananda,* joy. Such is the origin and aim of
Sanskrit poetry. Our first Vedic texts tell us from the very beginning that our poets were sages—*rishis, kavis*—and it is the Vedic poets
who laid the foundations of Indian civilization. The *kavi* was the
seer. Hence wisdom and poetry were one. The word became *mantra,*
sound as incantation.

A very ambitious tradition indeed, and one could boldly say the
Sanskrit poet kept this tradition till at least the seventeenth century
(from two, three or four thousand B.C.) and has enriched the world
with some of the most astonishing combinations of sound and meaning strung together that man has ever discovered. Kalidasa, our most
important poet, coming almost two thousand or more years after
the Vedic *rishis,* commences one of his most famous poems with the
verse:

> *Vagaartha vivasamprukthauvakartha pratipataye*
> *Jagathah pitharau vande parvathi parameshvarau.*

He says that just as sound goes into the make of meaning and meaning
into the make of sound—so are Shiva and Parvathi, Shiva being the
masculine principle and Parvathi the feminine. But then without
Shiva there is no Parvathi, just as without the word there is no meaning.

The word made concrete, then, is the object, the woman. Hence,
padartha—the meaning of the word, literally, but which to this day
means just an object. That is to say, any object, an eggplant at the
market or the stone on the street or a complex trichuration of a
doctor. The sound made object is the world.

But as there are so many objects, and of such complex natures,
what does one do to achieve the naming of objects? For this the Vedic
poets—the seers—had already shown how the elements had primary
sounds or root sounds—*ra* for fire and so on—which means that every
one of the elements has its own particular vibration (that is, when you

take the world as a possible reality, which is always the problem with
the Indian) and each sound has its own color, its own geometrical
form: color, sound, and form, going together, the word must structurally represent the whole of the object's qualities. This would mean
that a root-sound or *bijakshara* is added on to another root sound
(since there are so few primary elements) and these again with
another root sound, and thus you compose an object. The composed
object then composes itself with other objects or actions (which
again are objects, as you *see* activities) and so you make a whole
phrase. And again as no phrase can stand by itself because of its
associative value, and since one group of root sounds join with
another group of root sounds, you have a whole picture painted in
one sentence, and the sentence could, sometimes, as in Bana (the
eighth century) be two pages long. (Joyce, as you see, would not
have had to invent his very private language had he known Sanskrit.)
The root word joined on to another root word, a whole book, *Le
Livre* of Mallarmé, could be but one sentence. This has not been
achieved so far. But someday someone could still do it.

From the structure of so complex a philosophy of the word,
writers developed many theories of poetics, the most important
being the schools of *rasa* and *dhvani* and *sphota*. The word *rasa*
means flavor or enjoyment. *Dhvani* means sound suggestion,
aura. And *sphota*, the quantum of any word—it explodes. The poet
through a complex organization of his sounds—sounds that could
create objects, as it were—works up an associative structure of
images and vocables from level to level which when rightly pronounced and rightly heard (from silence to silence) leads you to
ultimate joy which is the Absolute itself. It does not matter
whether the mood is hate or love, tenderness or heroism (there are
eight *rasas* in all—sometimes they are believed to be nine) you can
reach the Absolute through any of these modes of being. Total
hatred leads to the abandonment of the world as such, total love
to the surrender of the ego, and so on. Every emotion leads one to
the Absolute, for it is to Brahman that every gesture and sound is
directed, hence all poetry is worship made to the Absolute, to Shiva
himself, who is none other than the Ultimate "I." Thus all words
are worship done to oneself. And *mantra* or incantation is nothing
else than supreme worship done to the One and One thing which is
truly to be described as Not-Two, *ekam, advaiyam*.

Having come so far, you will realize how impossible it is to translate Sanskrit prose or verse into any language. The vocabulary in
Sanskrit is so rich that some words like *rainbow, king* or *mistress*
have over two hundred synonyms, and Shiva, Devi or Krishna over

a thousand names. And since the language is so supple in structure, you could begin your sentence almost anywhere and yet your sentence would be tight, precise. I say translation from Sanskrit to any other language is almost impossible, but this is not true. If all words are worship, and since true worship is universal, any language could lead one to this ultimate experience, and there is no doubt that he who could come to the silence within himself could find the proper equivalents for each of the Sanskrit words in any context. The world is rich enough and man inventive enough to find multiple combinations of sounds to say the same thing over and over again, but each experience is ever unique, differentiated and new, and as such the majesty of all true poetry in any language. Indeed, if Sanskrit poetics could rightly be understood and applied by critics, it would open a new field in the understanding of any book of prose or verse, from the inside as it were, from the very depths of being.

Therefore, going back to Kalidasa's simile that word and meaning are as Shiva and Paravathi, and as Paravathi, the meaning, arises from the word to go back to the root of the word, which is Shiva's silence, the Indian poets have played a grand game of sounds and of sound combinations. I have myself found nowhere the flavor of poetry as in our Sanskrit poets. The ends of poetry are stated to be profit, pleasure, virtue and liberation.

Let us take a few samples:

> *Devi sureshvari Bhagavathi Gangé.*

Devi means she who is a goddess. *Sureshvari* comes from the words: *sura* meaning a higher being; *ishwari* implies the head, but a woman chief, as it were. *Bhagavathi:* she who is ever-generous, and therefore blessedness as such. This verse literally translated would read as: You the chieftain or queen of all the superior beings (or gods) and blessedness itself—You the Ganges.

> *Tribhuvana tarani taralata range.*

Tribhuvana: the three universes, the three fields, the three gardens.
Tarani: heaven, but also means the sun, a ray of light, a raft, a boat. It is also close to *tarangita* which means waving, tossing with waves. Also, overflowing, tremulous, for *taranga* means waves, or a leap, or (flowing) clothes.
taralata: trembling, waving, tremulous, fickle, libidinous, sparkling.

ranga: color, hue, dye paint, the theatre, arena, dancing, singing, nasal modifications of a vowel, etc.

Which combined, as you can see, could have no real translation, for
each word has several meanings, and any single level of meaning
leads one to one proper statement only. But you could have four or
five statements without difficulty, and I am sure some could make
more combinations of meanings. But word to word at a single horizontal level, as it were, one could translate the verse as:

> O Goddess, queen of superior godly hosts,
> blessedness as flow, O Ganges.
> O you flowing, floating, shining, through the three universes
> and making the space, the arena, to dance on, flow on. . . .

> *Kashi kshetram shariram, tribhuvana janani vyapini gyana ganga.*

Kashi is Benares. But it comes from *Kash,* to shine, to be
brilliant, beautiful. Also, to see, to appear. To banish, to open,
to bring out, to bring to light, etc. Benares then is when one is
brought out, that is, you are shown in your true nature, and
Shiva, the Absolute, and the Lord of Benares, who is yourself,
the Self, shines in his true splendor.
Kshetram means field, ground or soil. Place, abode, repository,
sacred spot. Place of pilgrimage. A sport's ground (for Shiva
dances here). The body (as the field where the soul works), the
mind, the house, a triangle, a diagram, etc.
Shariram: a body. The constituent elements. That which is
made of all the elements.
Tribhuvana: the same as before: three universes, three gardens
or fields.
Janani: Mother, mercy, compassion. The great Mother.
vyapini: Pervading, filling, occupying—coextensive, invariably
concomitant, etc. It is also a name of Vishnu who sustains the
world by pervading it.
Gyana: Supreme knowledge. Knowledge for Liberation.
Ganga: The Ganges.
This verse may be translated as:

> In the shining field of the body
> flows the triple-universe-pervading Ganges-as-knowledge.

The last example I give will be from Bharthrihari again, prince, grammarian and poet, who has been outshone in brilliance only by Kalidasa.

> *matar medini tata maruta sakhe jyotih*
> *subandho jala*
> *bhratar vyoma nibaddha esha bhavatam*
> *antyah pranamanjalih*
> *yusmat sangavasopajata sukrtodreka sphurannirmala—*
> *jnanapasta samasta moha mahima liye*
> *pare brahmani.*

Matar: Mother.
medini: the earth, land, soil, place.
tata: Father, someone worthy of respect. Also said in affection, as papa, but never familiar.
maruta: air, relating to *maruts,* the spirits of the air. Breath, vital air, etc.
sakhe: friend, *copain,* companion, soother of pain, one on whom one could fall back for help or enlightenment.
jyothi: fire or light. Light of Brahman, the faculty of seeing, etc.
sabandho: duly bound together or well bound or fraternally united, a father, a husband, charged with fragrance, etc.
jala: dull, cold, frigid, water, libation, etc.

The first line therefore could read as follows:

> O mother earth and father air
> O friend fire, great kinsman water etc.

And I could conclude this talk with nothing better than to quote a rough translation of the whole verse in full and you can see how poorly it translates.

> O mother earth and father air,
> O friend fire, great kinsman water
> brother ether—to you all
> in final parting, I offer reverence.
> Through your long associations
> Have the right deeds been performed.
> Through you I have won pure shining wisdom,
> Unweaving the sweet delusions of the mind.
> Now I merge in the Supreme Brahman.

And Brahman, as we have seen, is pure shining silence.

The Flight of Dragon-Cloud
in the Land of Morning Calm:
The Poetry of Han Yong Woon (1879-1944)

Younghill Kang

We have at hand the completed work of Han Yong Woon's NIM E
CH'IM-MUK or Dragon Cloud's *Meditations of the Lover,* one of the
most highly regarded books of poetry among the modern generation
of Korean writers, and the first Korean poet, ancient or modern, to
be translated as a whole. This work will be published this fall by
Yonsei University Press, Seoul.

First, if you are of those who seek for a hidden meaning in names
—though this is not considered polite in the Far East where you may
come upon some celebrated scholar unjustly styled "Asses' Bray"—
the Korean Zen Buddhist monk, Dragon-Cloud, has been aptly
named. That name would indicate some big shifting cloud in dragon
shape—rapid changes from light to darkness, from darkness to light—
the supernatural mystery in the natural elements. Dragon-Cloud is
his Buddhist name, carrying symbol suggestion. His pen name,
Manhai, was also Buddhistic and signified Ten Thousand Seas.

Korean readers need no introduction to the poetry of Han Yong
Woon. Western readers unversed in Korean hardly know his name.
This is a pity. He should be an international as well as a national
poet. In the first quarter of our turbulent century Han Yong Woon
was one of the famed "Thirty-three," martyrs all, signers of the
Korean Declaration of Independence in the peaceful revolution
against annexation of their country by Japan. This document was

read aloud in Pagoda Park, Seoul, March 1, 1919. One of these translators, Younghill Kang, being a student in Seoul at the time, was in
the vast crowd of onlookers, greeting the sonorous words with wild
acclaim. Han Yong Woon also made a speech in Pagoda Park that
day. He had insisted that the term "Peaceful Revolution" be incorporated in the Declaration of Independence.

Han Yong Woon signed his name in behalf of all Korean Buddhists.
He was a Zen Buddhist, and he was a scholar. He was forty years old.
Since the age of sixteen, he had meditated and studied in many mona-
steries, among them the famous ones of Diamond Mountain commem-
orated by him with a poem by that name. Like myself, he came from
a poor but scholarly family; but he was from the south, whereas I
was born up north. In spite of the greatest poverty, his mother and
his father were from high families who had contributed many scholarly officials to the country. He spent three years in prison for signing the Korean Declaration of Independence under Japanese Military
Government. On coming out, middle-aged and in poor health, he
persisted in peaceful revolution, both by research and by his writings.

Meditations of the Lover was published in Seoul in 1925, and I
got a copy of it before it was forced underground by the Japanese
Military Government. I was even then greatly impressed by this
revolutionary, but highly eastern work. It was couched in the form
of love poems, a bold stroke in a country at this time still ruled by
families and clans and family-arranged marriages.

But what a learned treatise could be written on WHO IS THE
LOVER? He or She—and there are two voices, male and female—
are the truest of true lovers, forced into a perennial cosmic parting
in which dark forces of the world have taken a seasonal hand. There
is sorrow hardly to be endured, and tears. But tears are not "idle
tears" as to the Victorian poet, Tennyson. Tears have their own
cosmic purport and meaning. In Han Yong Woon, tears are dynamic.
They are going somewhere.

> "Ah ah when do we create
> a world of love
> and fill up time and fill up space with
> tears?"

A Korean commentator has counted up the voice parts, male and
female, in these poems, although I have not done so myself. The
female voices are said (by him) to predominate. Still, the guide
across Ten Thousand Seas of Sorrow seems to be the poet, Manhai,
himself. Yet all the poems read as related one to another, and in
each is the authentic personal ring.

The learned treatise which I mention, perhaps to be written in the future, might claim that THE LOVER here is the same as that celebrated by Rilke, T.S. Eliot and even St. Teresa of Avalon. But this might be rather stretching the point. God is nowhere mentioned. In place of God is the Emptiness. Infinity, eternity, and highest of all, THE LOVER.

Being in the first place a Korean nationalist—indeed it might well be argued that an undivided Korea is THE LOVER—Han Yong Woon may seem content to sing of the Karma of some earthly love, under the odong tree and in the hibiscus shade. But here we point to Max Müller, the great German scholar of comparative religions, speaking on eastern Sufi mystical writing: experiencing God in the soul being inexpressible, only the language describing the union of earthly lovers can be analogous.

T.S. Eliot, that grand Middle Westerner of the U.S.A. turned Tory, was quite a Confucian. He believed in transmitting, and he held that great poets and thinkers should be re-transmitted, every generation. As the world grows smaller and smaller, other translations of *Meditations of the Lover* may make up for shortcomings in our own. Surely there must come a time when English literati visiting Seoul, in heady symposium with cosmopolitan scholars and poets of the town, will not confine their talk to Yeats, Pound, Eliot, Lowell, Ginsberg etc. To be uncognizant of big modern poets in the Far East is to become a Hermit Kingdom in reverse.

Han Yong Woon was well in advance of his time, whereas T.S. Eliot was exactly contemporaneous. As far as these translators are concerned, both have been moving forces. But it is the Easterner, Han Yong Woon, who should now disclose himself and come into his own as a worldwide figure. If he was for Korea as a modern revolutionary poet and a great patriot, it still should not be lost sight of that he was of that small body of mystics with the same message throughout the ages: immortality, fraternity, love. It is time that he should travel an international path like his friend, Tagore.

THE LOVER ORIGINALS

Who were they
the lover originals
how did they meet
and when?

Who were they
the lover originals
where did they meet
and how?

The lover originals
did they invent parting
or did some other lovers
invent the original parting?

I only know
the lover originals
even they knew
about parting.

No lover parts
not to meet but only
in order to meet so parting is
just a way taken by love.

Once having known the meeting
we weep to consider the parting
so make our vows at parting
to love meetings ahead.

Here we step in
hereditary footprints
left by the lover originals
we meet we part
just as they too have done.

As no lover parts
but to meet so no lover
meets but to part meeting is also
just a way taken by love.

The meeting of lover originals
made the original joy
the parting of lover originals
poured the original tear.

Tears of parting
more than all joys of meeting
then again joys of meeting
more than all tears of parting!

Ah ah lover
after our tears
when is to be our joy
of long ago?

(Translated by Younghill Kang and Frances Keely)

Russian Poetry and Methods of Translation

Helen Muchnic

The term "translation" is large and loose. At one end, it is equated with communication as such. "Each of us translates everyday," says Auden. "Whenever we speak to each other about anything but the most impersonal matters, the listener has to translate into terms of his own experience what the speaker utters in terms of his." And Tolstoy, sensing the enormous gap between life and talk about life, almost despaired of communicating at all. "I was just now lying down behind the barracks," we read in an early entry in his diary. "Wonderful night! . . . I thought, I'll go and describe what I see. But how write it? One must sit down at an ink-stained table, take a sheet of gray paper, ink, stain one's fingers and draw letters on the paper. The letters will form words, the words sentences; but how is it possible to transmit an emotion?" From this awareness evolved the unique perception that formed Tolstoy's style, an endless attempt to bridge the gap between living and writing, to translate experience into words. And in Tyutchev's "Silentium"—wonderfully translated by Nabokov—there is the celebrated line: "A thought once uttered is untrue." *(Misl' izrechennaya yest' lozh!)* At the other extreme, we have machines that are capable of such logical translations as "The spirit is willing but the flesh is weak" into *"Vodka khorosha, no myaso plokho,"* i.e. "The vodka is good but the meat is bad."

But whatever his concepts, however profound or superficial his
aim, mechanical or personal his approach, a translator interprets,
transmutes, transports; there is no such thing as a completely objective translation. Even attempts at literalness vary. Here, for example, in *Eugene Onegin* (Chapter III, Stanza 16), is Pushkin's sad
Tatyana:

> *Toska lyubvi Tatyanu gonit,*
> *I v sad idyot ona grustit'.*

Dimitri Obolensky translates: "Love's anguish impels Tatiana, and
she goes into the garden to abandon herself to sadness," and Vladimir
Nabokov:

> The ache of love chases Tatiana,
> and to the garden she repairs to brood.

When the translator is engaged in shifting a work of literature from
one language to another, his task is even more formidable than when
he is transferring his own emotions from the realm of the unspoken
to the spoken, for he must now cope with the silences as well as the
words of another. He must contend with a recalcitrant being that
resists transportation, and he succeeds only if he knows how to perform a feat of almost complete identification without, however,
losing touch with his own soil and tongue. This requires, in addition
to perfect command of the language into which he is translating, a
rare endowment of emotional and intellectual flexibility. Unfortunately, many of our translators are not so endowed; too many, lacking patience and seriousness, proceed with hasty violence and,
instead of bringing home intact the living being they had pursued,
manage only to drag in a maimed body or a corpse.

The crucial matter of seriousness and ability aside, a translator
has three methods to choose from. These have long been recognized,
and more than two centuries ago John Dryden discussed them in
nearly the same terms we use today. "All translations, I suppose,"
he wrote in a *Preface to Ovid's Epistles* (recently reprinted in *Delos 2*),
"may be reduced to three heads. First, that of metaphrase, or turning an author word by word, and line by line, from one language into
another. . . . The second way is that of paraphrase, or translation
with latitude, when the author is kept in view by the translator, so
as never to be lost, but his words are not so strictly followed as his
sense; and that too is admitted to be amplified, but not altered. . . .

The third way is that of imitation, where the translator (if now he
has not lost that name) assumes the liberty, not only to vary from
the words and sense, but to forsake them both as he sees occasion;
and taking only some general hints from the original, to run division
on the groundwork as he pleases." The first of these Dryden com-
pares to "dancing on ropes with fettered legs: a man may shun a fall
by using caution; but the gracefulness of motion is not to be expected; and when we have said the best of it, 't is but a foolish task."
It is the way of pedantry; "too faithfully," he says, "is, indeed,
pedantically; 't is a faith like that which proceeds from superstition,
blind and zealous." The second method, "paraphrase," is the one he
favors. As for the third: "To state it fairly . . . imitation of an
author is the most advantageous way for a translator to show himself,
but the greatest wrong which can be done to the memory and reputation of the dead."

Today all three methods are used, and each has its advocates. Of
the third category, Edmund Wilson, in reviewing Robert Lowell's
Imitations, remarks, by contrast to Dryden, that he himself has
"always said that the best translations—the Rubaiyat, for example,
are those that depart most widely from the originals—that is, if
the translator is himself a good poet; otherwise the result is fatal."
Had Dryden seen Lowell's work might he have changed his mind
about this freest of all methods? Robert Conquest would doubtless
say no. In the May 1970 issue of *Encounter,* he takes Lowell to
task for his renditions of Akhmatova and Pasternak, citing mistranslations, and arguing that Lowell misses the "tone" and "personality"
of the Russians. Since Lowell was writing independent poems, which
made no claim to accuracy, it seems to me beside the point to blame
him for mistranslations. The second charge, however, does have some
relevance, for unless the spirit of the original is preserved, why make
an imitation at all? As for results, though, judgments are bound to
differ, and I, for one, cannot agree with Mr. Conquest's strictures.
Despite some obvious misreadings in "Requiem" and some lines in
"Hamlet" that may strike one as inappropriate—"take me off the
hooks," for example, in Hamlet's plea to the Lord—Lowell's imitations, to my mind at least, show a remarkable feeling for the essence
of Akhmatova and Pasternak; and, most importantly, they are very
good English poems. Nor am I offended in the slightest by his putting together several of Pasternak's lyrics to form his own "Hamlet
in Russia, A Soliloquy." Mr. Conquest finds this unpardonable.

The second category, the most tempting and most perilous, contains the greatest number of practitioners and the highest incidence
of casualties. This is the category of translation proper, an attempt

at accuracy in both letter and spirit; and because such accuracy is
extremely difficult to achieve, the field is strewn with the maimed
and the dead. Nevertheless, however difficult, the task is not impossible, as witness Richard Wilbur's renditions of Molière, and in the
Russian-English department, the few pieces from Pushkin, Lermontov and Tyutchev once done by Nabokov, as well as Pasternak's
Shakespeare and Shelley and Marshak's transmutations of Shakespeare's sonnets and of Robert Burns. Of the latter Tvardovsky has
said that they are poems in their own right, as if "Burns himself had
written in Russian," which sounds like an answer to Auden's remark
that "The perfect translation, an unrealizable ideal, would be one in
which the reader heard the foreign author speaking as a unique person with a unique perspective on the world and a unique tone of
voice, yet was persuaded that he thought and spoke, not in his own
but in the reader's tongue." How is this done? Differently, of
course, in each case, but never slavishly. Marshak takes many liberties with Burns's text, does not try to reproduce, or even suggest, the
dialect of the original, changes words, transposes lines, but retains
the gist, and so fashions a masterpiece of what Belinsky called
"assimilation." As for his way with Shakespeare translations, consider, by way of illustration, Sonnet 30. The whispered sibilants
of its opening lines.

> When to the sessions of sweet silent thought
> I summon up remembrance of things past,

are changed by Marshak to sighing palatals and glotals:

> *Kogda na sud bezmolvnykh, taynykh dum*
> *Ya vyzyvayu golosa bylovo . . .*

The sounds are different, but the contemplative sadness of the lines
is perfectly conveyed. So is the wide-voweled mourning of the fourth
line:

> And with old woes new wail my dear time's waste

in

> *I staroy bol'yu ya boleyu snova,*

and the painful shrillness of the ninth:

> Then can I grieve with grievances forgone,

in the grating *zh* sounds of:

> *I uzhasayus' vnov' potere kazhdoi.*

Marshak follows the original line by line and almost word by word, without, however, falling into literalism. His is not a mere "tracing" of the words, as the Russians call it, not a carbon copy of the poem, but a re-creation of its mood by means of the original poet's own devices. The same miracle is achieved by Nabokov in such pieces as Lermontov's "Farewell":

> Farewell! Nevermore shall we meet,
> We shall never touch hands—so farewell!
> Your heart is now free, but in none
> Will it ever be happy to dwell

is very good in itself and an almost word-for-word rendition of:

> *Prosti! — my ne vstretimsya bole,*
>   *Drug drugu ruki ne pozhmyëm;*
> *Prosti! — tvoye serdtse na vole . . .*
>   *No shchast'ye ne syshchet v drugom.*

This is the kind of thing Nabokov alone among modern translators might also have achieved with *Eugene Onegin,* had he so chosen. But he chose otherwise, preferring, on grounds of faithfulness, to "dance on ropes with fettered legs." In the preface to his pedantic version he explains his choice: there are three ways of translating a poem: the "paraphrastic . . . a free version of the original," examples of which are "unfortunately available to students"; the "lexical (or constructional)," which "a machine can do under the direction of an intelligent bilinguist"; and the "literal," the "only . . . true translation," like his own. And the result? I select for comparison—any stanza, of course, would do—Pushkin's description of the ballet in Chapter 1, stanza 20:

> *Teatr uzh polon; lozhi bleshchut;*
> *Parter i kresla, vsyo kipit;*
> *V raike neterpelivo pleshchut,*
> *I, vzvishis', zanaves shumit.*

The first three lines reproduce the noisy excitement, expectation, and impatience of the audience in a full house just before the curtain is raised; the last, is the awaited moment: the curtain swishes up. Here are four 'paraphrastic" translations:

> The house is full, the boxes glitter,
> The pit is like a seething cup.
> The gallery claps with loud impatience,
> The curtain rustles—and goes up.
>
>   (Dorothea Prall Radin)

This is simple, accurate—and unexciting.

> The theatre's full, the boxes glitter,
> The stalls are seething, the pit roars,
> The gallery claps and stamps, a-twitter;
> The curtain rustles as it soars.
>
>   (Babette Deutsch)

This is patently a translation. "A-twitter" is unnatural and clearly chosen for the sake of rhyme.

> The house has filled; the boxes glisten;
> Pit, stalls, are like a seething cup;
> The restless galleries clap—and listen!
> The rustling curtain has gone up!
>
>   (Oliver Elton)

Like the previous one, this is also obviously a translation, with "and listen!" a gratuitous intrusion for rhyme's sake.

> The house is full, the boxes gleaming,
> Orchestra, pit, all is astir,
> Impatient clapping from the teeming
> Gallery—then the curtain's whir.
>
>   (Walter Arndt)

This is awkward. The rhythm stumbles, and the enjambement at the end spoils the effect completely. Not one of the four does justice to the original. But is Nabokov's any better?

> By now the house is full; the boxes blaze;
> parterre and stalls—all seethes;

> in the top gallery impatiently they clap,
> and, soaring up, the curtain swishes.

The next quatrain is a breathless stillness. The stage has been revealed, and at its center, exquisitely posed, stands the prima ballerina, Istomina:

> *Blistatel'na, poluvozdushna,*
> *Smychku volshebnomu poslushna,*
> *Tolpoyu nimf okruzhena,*
> *Stoit Istomina. . . .*

According to Nabokov:

> Resplendent, half-ethereal,
> obedient to the magic bow,
> surrounded by a throng of nymphs,
> Istomina stands.

And one's reaction is: so what? The lines that follow are a magic re-creation of Istomina's performance: the perfect balance of her tiptoe stance, her suppleness, lightness, and grace. They are more than a picture; they are the sound and rhythm of her dance: the slow circling, the swift leap, the adorable entrechat—and the whole stanza shimmers in the aura of Pushkin's delight in the dance and in his stanza. There is no delight in the "paraphrastic" translations of it I know; they are too strained for anything but anxiety. And whatever delight Nabokov may have experienced, he has kept under wraps.

His translation, he tells us, was initially undertaken as a teaching aid. But teaching is meant to generate enthusiasm for the subject taught, as well as to inform. And I find it hard to believe that his "trot," as he himself takes pleasure in calling it, would induce any one to learn Russian for the sake of reading Pushkin, though it might indeed be of help to a student already well on his way. Out of intense devotion and profound understanding, deliberately, idealistically, Nabokov murders Pushkin—an amazing literary crime. And knowing what he has done, he himself begs Pushkin's forgiveness in a lovely lyric done in the difficult Onegin stanza—a characteristically ironic performance, a virtuoso piece, that shows his mastery despite his abdication—a graceful wreath laid on the body of his victim:

> What is translation? On a platter
> A poet's pale and glaring head.

His own version is

> honest roadside prose—
> All thorn, but cousin to your rose.

It is, he tells Pushkin,

> The shadow of your monument.

The murderer's excuse is that translation is murder by definition.
The "only true translation" is the literal, and even at its best, what
does it come to but decapitation: "On a platter/a poet's pale and
glaring head"? Nabokov's is a counsel of defeat. To follow him,
better give up: stop all translation and avoid general slaughter. Yet,
it has happened that even inferior translations have inspired great
poetry. Matthew Arnold did not think well of Chapman's Homer,
but Keats, too ignorant to know that "between Chapman and Homer
there is interspersed the mist of the fancifulness of the Elizabethan
age," was moved by it to write a glorious sonnet. "On First Looking
into Chapman's Homer" is vindication enough, were vindication
needed, for the serious enterprise of translation.

There is nothing in the structure of the Russian language or its
prosody to make its poetry intrinsically untranslatable. Oliver
Elton said so in a preface to his *Eugene Onegin,* and Nabokov has
implied as much in the brilliant discourse on prosody which he
appends to his own version. But unquestionably Russian poetry—
and especially Pushkin, the source and exemplar of all Russian literature—is excessively difficult to turn into another language. One
reason for this, I would suggest, is the special characteristic of
Russian writing, that "earthiness," as Maurice Baring called it,
which is its native and distinctive trait. It is a literature with a
marked predilection for directness and simplicity, and such distate
for the elaborate, the grandiose, the abstract, that rhetorical devices,
large concepts, grand emotions, all are muted in it. However poorly
translated, Shakespeare, Dante and Goethe remain impressive
because of their rich metaphors, cosmic symbols, historic fantasies.
But in *Eugene Onegin* there is none of this; its language is simple,
its tragedy subdued, and its philosophy is a kind of playful wisdom
that permeates the whole and comes through in ironic hints. Instead
of striking verbal effects, intellectual disquisitions, extraordinary
events, there are implicit meanings, unexpressed emotions, an ever-
present, deeply integrated perception of life that is always understood but never explicitly given, and a human drama, the depths of

which evolve in silences. Robert Frost's definition of poetry as
"what gets lost in translation" could have no better example.

Small wonder that here angels fear to tread. And maybe Pushkin
is doomed to remain forever the exclusive property of Russians.
Nevertheless, is it too wild, or too reprehensible, to hope that some
day a translation of *Eugene Onegin* will appear of which it might at
least be said, in paraphrase of Bentley's classic comment on *The Iliad*
of Pope, "A very fine poem, though you must not call it Pushkin"?

The Problem Seen from England

George Astley

Each night of this Translators' Conference I have rewritten my paper striking out material that has already been said and putting in a few new, clear and concise thoughts which are at once uttered by the next day's speakers in rather better form than I had put them. Thus, in a state of confusion I thought of a phrase—surely it must be by Oscar Wilde—"I don't know what I think till I hear what I say," and that is how I feel.

Many distinguished people here have given illuminating facts on nearly every aspect of this difficult and testing profession. So, from the sublime verse quoted by Brendan Kennelly, I shall turn to the ridiculous but inescapable fact that the translator must *eat,* a function daily becoming more costly.

Behind this historic meeting lies a particularly vital fact. What are we about? What has the P.E.N. Translation Committee been trying to accomplish? To me it appears that, at last, one of the most important literary organizations in America is coming to grips with the protection of the translator and I say *protection* advisedly.

So many of you, intellectually occupied with turning out brilliant work, if possible on time, will sign, without sufficient study, contracts, letters of agreement, and even make verbal gentlemen's agreements; then, if any dispute arises, you are left not only with time-consuming worry, but often with the expense of fighting the matter out on your own with no intermediary to turn to.

I would like to tell you, very briefly, of the form and modest achievements of the British Translators' Association and why, with respect, it is a much more effective organization in the literary field than its nearest counterpart, the A.T.A., over here.

To begin with, it has always had the full backing of the British Society of Authors, which with its four thousand members is, as you may know, a very powerful organization in the United Kingdom.

When I formed the Translators' Assocation in 1958, we already had some forty to fifty literary translators within the Society's membership with which to set up a hard core. To these, and about two hundred others, we sent out a detailed questionnaire. The returns were truly appalling, in that the average fees were 30 shillings, i.e., about $3.50 per thousand words, with no continuing interest of any sort.

As a result of these figures and other information, the Association was formed as an integral part of the Society, but with an Executive Committee of well-known translators entirely responsible for its affairs. A meeting of a number of prominent English publishers was arranged at which they agreed that the Association would be beneficial first to themselves and then to the translators. However, when I suggested £2.10, about $5.00, as a minimum fee, some of them threw up their hands in horror and said that I would price translations out of the business. And they were *all* adamant about *any* encroachment on subsidiary rights on which, with some justice, they said they made their money.

I resolved then and there to pursue a policy of "softly softly catchee monkey," and the British publishers can be a very shrewd lot of monkeys. They had to be educated, cajoled and pushed into a position of offering £2.10 per thousand words. As soon as this became common practice, we upped the minimum to £3, continuing to apply the same process until we reached the present £5.10, approximately $13.50 per thousand words. This figure is more in line, though you may consider it low. In this connection one must bear in mind that the cost of living is rather lower in England than over here.

Time and time again I have had tactfully to restrain my committee from raising the basic uniform fee by too much too fast, pointing out that they, as top members of their profession, could and should, for the benefit of all, stand out for top fees but that we had to consider the younger and less experienced members who, however clever, could not expect to obtain the same compensation.

The daily work goes on steadily: vetting contracts; advising on fees; intervening in disputes; giving names and specialist qualifications, all cross-referenced, to publishers; administering prizes; chasing after monies due to members; arbitrating, and so on. On the last point, a recent arbitration set up by the Association, based on a complaint by a publisher that a member's work was unpublishable, resulted in the complete vindication of the publisher. I found this very satisfactory, because these things get round and help to establish a reputation for absolute impartiality.

You may think from the way I have been talking that we regard publishers as enemies. Believe me, this is in no way the case. In my capacity as Registrar of the Society of Authors, I count many of the English publishers as great personal friends and, although we sometimes fight on matters of principle, this personal relationship can frequently help to take the steam out of matters which might otherwise end in litigation. The publisher takes the major risk and without him we should be nowhere.

I was happy to note that all three publishers who have spoken at this Conference appear to appreciate, at least in principle, the importance to the translator of a continuing interest in his work, and will give their attention to the ways in which this can be achieved—a rather more liberal attitude than that taken in England at present, although we are beginning to see the light.

Mr. Gross's clear explanation of costing is, I know, correct, but could we not make a start by, at least, taking "participation in success" as our watchword and go on from there? The 1969 summer issue of The American P.E.N. bulletin found our recommendations of sufficient interest to print in full. We feel these to be reasonable and are grateful that they did so. Mr. Helmut Braem now wishes to translate them into German and I hope they will be of use.

I do not know why work in translation does not sell as well as original work in most countries. And few translations reach the heights. For instance, a series of six immensely accurate historical novels on medieval France by Maurice Druon, the youngest member of the Académie Française, under the title of *Les Rois Maudits,* very well translated by my late brother-in-law Humphrey Hare and published by Hart Davies, all neared, but never broke through the ten thousand mark while selling by the hundred thousand in France. Full of blood, thunder, rape and witches, one would have thought them excellent film material, but no! Nevertheless, they are steady bread-and-butter money for the English publisher.

Now to the thorny problem of copyright, on which I have had a number of abortive meetings with our Publishers Association. We do not see why the translator should not be able, as the author does, to have an exclusive license to publish in volume form, with agreed

language, territorial and other limitations. The British custom of
outright assignment of copyright to the publisher has grown up over
the years for no particular reason. A matter of prestige, some may
say, but *not* always so. Film rights, for example, should never be
included in a translation contract but sometimes are. I know it only
occurs in rare instances that a film is made based on a translation,
but note the following case.

A work of Max Frisch, in translation, published ten to twelve
years ago and on which, for some unknown reason, the copyright
was left in the hands of the translator, was made into a film. For
this the translator received £3,000. Another work, same author
same translator *but* copyright registered in the publisher's name,
is now being filmed. It may produce £500 for the translator, or
maybe nothing at all. I have obtained the agreement with Penguin
Books that, in the case of film rights, under these circumstances,
they shall receive 10% and the translator 90%. They contend, however, and rightly, that it is probably due to their publication that
the attention of the film producer was drawn to a possible script.
In this day and age there are ever increasing ancillary possibilities
for the copyright holder, and I have no doubt that publishers are
well aware of this.

I have been told that translators are getting very "uppity," the
inference being no doubt that this, in England, is due to my own and
the Association's activities. I can only say that it is a good thing
that they should be so, as there are plenty of people who try to slap
them down and it is quite time that all these years as the Cinderella
of the literary profession should be put behind.

Naturally, we disapprove of the hack translator, and every effort
is made to ensure a high standard, which is not easy to control.
There appears to be far too much sub-editing of a good translator's
work in the publisher's office which is, to say the least, unfortunate
and usually very irritating for the translator.

I do not believe the original author should have the overall right
of vetting a translation of his work. It often happens that he is
unable to speak English himself, let alone criticize good English
prose.

Personal relationships with the literary editors of the major newspapers are helpful to translators in obtaining proper credit for their
work. I complain in a friendly way every time I catch a reviewer
ignoring a translator's existence. I note every case and I see those
drawn to my attention by members where no credit is given
in reviews. We take the line that although, for better or for
worse, there may not be space to criticize the quality of the transla-

tion, at least the translator's name *must* appear in the heading, adding that it is also unfair to the public not to make it clear that the work is a translation. The English papers—with the notable exception of *The Observer,* whose literary editor is himself a translator—are on the whole very good about this.

We advocate that the translator's name should appear on the title-page of the work and in all publicity connected with that work, which I see shows as Clause 7 of the P.E.N.'s recommendations, all of which I think are admirable. Perhaps Clause 3 should be amended to ensure that the flat fee per thousand words is accepted as a non-returnable advance [see Appendix, p. 376].

Some contracts provide for a payment on signature, a further payment on delivery of the manuscript, and a final payment *on publication.* The latter should be avoided at all costs, as a dubious publisher can delay publication indefinitely. Insert instead, "final payment on publication or within two months of delivery of the manuscript, whichever shall be the sooner." Most of you here will be aware of these and many other points, but you would be astonished to know how many translators are not.

The translator is the catalyst between the cultures of nations and as such is becoming an even more essential figure in a world of rapid communication. Nobody can afford to do without him, and he must therefore receive a just but not necessarily excessive reward for his labors to enable him to live without the pressures of taking on too much work to the detriment of his standards. More and more publishing houses are coming under the aegis of vast industrial concerns, and one hopes that, even if books do not make money—which they do—there will still be men of integrity who are prepared to divert some of the profits from the manufacture of paper knickers to the production of works of importance which may even show a a loss.

If I can be of use to any American translator, published in England, with the exception of involving the Association in legal expense, I should be very happy to do so.

*

The three translation prizes we have established are included in the P.E.N. List of Grants and Awards to Writers and carry a cash value, but—alas—I fully corroborate Mr. Gross's view that, despite our efforts, a nominal publicity value goes with them so far.

Finally, as an aristocratic old Englishman who, by the accident of fate, has become a sort of Trade Union Leader, I say to you in all sincerity:

TRANSLATORS OF THE WORLD, UNITE!

On Translating from Bengali*

Amiya Chakravarty

I am speaking mainly from notes, and I apologize to you for the
paucity of the materials that are available in translation from Bengali
into English. I do not have access to any Eastern literature on translations as such. Tagore easily dominates the literary situation in the
East. He translated himself and he hit upon a happy moment when,
not so much because of literary reasons but because of the need of
some kind of reciprocity between East and West, he was able to
strike the imagination of both civilizations. He touched the mind of
an England which occupied India but really did not know her culture. He also influenced Europe by bringing a cargo of verses which,
along with the power and the sensitiveness of his personality, made
for some transference of Bengali poetry and acceptance of it by
some of the poets and writers of that time. And yet his translations
did little justice to his original poems.

The problem lies very deep in the nature of the Bengali language.
I am sure it is the same in other cases. We use a lot of saturated
words, and even now keep rather close to the spirit of Sanskrit where
each word was charged with a rather high cosmic significance: profound metaphysical concepts, associational phrases which are

*The revision and preparation of the taped speech for publication has been made
possible by the assistance of Kay Bierwiler (M.A.) of the New York State University at Albany.

redolent with the monsoon rain or, later, the legend of Radha and
Krishna. The great Indian epics also are in the background. It is
so difficult to know what to do with such situations. If you added
footnotes, it would betray the whole meaning of a proper creative
translation. If you cut them out, it would be very bare and obvious. If you tried to transfer these concepts into equivalent English
concepts, you would be inviting tragedy.

Before I go into a short history of our efforts, I should tell you
how Tagore struggled when he wrote the English *Gitanjali*. He has
a number of wonderful rain songs where the key word could be
Srāvana. Almost anything you want to do with the rain will cluster
around that word: the call of the blue sky, the infinitude which
brings out the light on a tryst. From a cosmic background it became
the story of particular lovers: Krishna always painted with blue skin
and Radha, fair. Then it became a part of the associational complex
of the tradition of lovers meeting down the corridor of time. If you
say that these words and concepts are too narrowly Indian or foreign,
what are you going to do with them? You can say July is the month
of rain, but quite obviously July will bring pictures of umbrellas, wet
pavements, rubber shoes. It is hard to get to the cosmic-canopy of
clouds, the thunder and lightning. As in the sudden awakening of
nature in the Spring here or in Europe, fields and valleys of Bengal
put on a sheen of green. Millions of blades of grass come out because
of the monsoon rain, the touch of the first drop of rain. All this is
part of a total concept. In the English translation, July has to acquire
the deep shadows and silent steps of the monsoon. Before it has
ushered in this drama of rain there is the hush in the earth.

Tagore is trying to give that suspense along with the oncoming
rain. Thunder and lightning are part of the great event. He sat down
and said, I can't put in the word *Srāvana* then I'll have to add the
footnotes. If I mention July, that too is a very difficult situation.
So he tried to convert the English July into a symbol of the Indian
or Asian monsoon. But he knew he could not go on doing this just
for one translated word or concept. His translation does get something across:

> In the deep shadows of rainy July with silent steps thou walkest.

Then the poet addresses the spirit of the silent witness:

> Do not walk past my door, it is open.

But there is nobody in the street, all the shutters are drawn and the
guest has come. The arrival. All these dimensions have rain clouds
and much more even than that.

Parallel to this lies the fact that some of Tagore's best poems are regional. They are agricultural as well as cultural. Millions of Indian peasants look at the sky for a hint of rain. The ground is parched. It makes a difference between life and death—the coming of rain. Tagore evokes the aching, thirsty earth, wishing for rain. He is speaking to the condition of the actual, the regional or natural situation as well as to the condition of the human heart. All the overtones are there. Perhaps this is too rich, but it discloses the futility of translation, excepting for the purpose of communication.

We gained a lot because of the fact that Tagore opened many doors between England and India, West and East. We are very grateful. But he had to pay the price for it, a quick saturation came to Western readers as they read the same type of translation—a kind of prose form, some of which is very good. But there are no surprises of rhythm, of colored words, associational phrases. Phrases and cadences had to be stripped bare. They come out of the sausage-machine where the whole poem appears as neat little packages, all looking more or less the same. You can imagine how acutely Tagore felt the inadequacy of what he was doing. How can I betray the Bengali language? he queried.

Many people say that Bengali is such a melodious language, therefore it loses so much in translation. But Tagore did not think so. Each language he once remarked has its own secret resources of music, and he added that perhaps English was the most musical. The clash of consonants and the delicate use of the nuances of syllables in English verse bring out the deepest music. Not the kind of onomatopoeia or the easy music like the murmur of innumerable bees, the cooing of doves in immemorial elms. This is good, clever, Tennyson. There are many other passages, but when you come to "After life's fitful fever, he sleeps well," you have Shakespeare. The fitfulness and the feverishness of the f's and v's suddenly glide into l's and the soft s's. We reach a shining level. The deepest context is both hidden and explicit. It is not death; he sleeps well; there is something more. A great poet brings out the highest resources of a language to express his experience. Bengali has a melodic element which we use. It has a Sanskritic ontological background, the key word, the phrase, the "tone" have to be brought before the reader to initiate the climate as well as the concept.

A great ode-like poem of Tagore illustrates how the language suffered from translation. It is not that his best work is ornamental, but he could draw upon the sonorous and the sacred sources of the Vedic verses from ancient India or the lyrics and dramas of Kalidasa as he wrote his Odes. He did translate into English a few of his own

"classical" lyrics. There is one on the evening. The darkening sky is
before us, the sea is heaving under the sunset covers, and a lonely
bird is on its wings, flying to its distant nest. The poet, in his translation, simply gives the picture of the evening and says,

> *Bird, oh my bird, listen to me. Do not close your wings.*

His "message" is given. As long as we are using the wings, we shall
fly beyond this gathering darkness: somewhere, to our distant nest.
But the picture of the evening, the sunset cover, the slow steps, the
"feel" of loneliness rather than the idea of it—that is what composes
the intangibles of music and assonance, feeling tone, pictorial element.
Take them away and you still have something. Because he was a man
of thought, Tagore could say:

> *Though the evening comes with slow steps, and has signalled*
> *for all songs to cease. Bird, oh my bird, listen to me. Do not*
> *close your wings.*

But in the Bengali original you can see and sense this and hear the
silences and the internal rhymes while moving toward the "wholeness" of the poem. The reader is held in a state of intense experience. There is a suggestion of possible impending tragedy, and yet
we are sustained by an inevitable pitting of the human will or the
will of nature against what we call, loosely, destiny or fate. The
entire evening and the picture of a throbbing life give meaning to
this poem. I remember Paderewski playing *"Das Abends"* on the
piano and slowly building up the steps of the evening. How to do
this in translated verse?

One says that we will never look at the translation again, never
believe in it. People complain that the Bengali language is so delicate
and so fragile that you cannot get anything across in any other language. We have not claimed anything exclusive for that language, but
we are conscious of the inheritances coming to each language through
two main sources. One, the musical resources; the other, the ontological (primary thought or experience). This is our problem. Tagore
did many fine things in his early English translations but soon he gave
up, and most of his major poems, particularly of a later period, were
untouched. And yet there is an even richer music in his later, barer
Bengali lyrics, because the musical orchestration yielded to the conversational beauty where you hear the whisper of the word, the delicacy of a lover's pleading, or a word held back because of the sum
of emotion.

The same happens in one of his early lyrics, actually a song. The poem brings us to a lover on the road; he meets his beloved as they pass. He could not say what he had to say. Their eyes met. As they passed each other without having exchanged a word, he found that what he had to say had been said and was being said by the new spring flowers, by the blue horizon.

Tagore uses words and music so delicately as to make them seem almost casual: to us, that is the richer thing. We can take one of his last poems which he wrote when he was on his death bed, a poem on the last evening. The primal morning had come with the question "Who are you?" No answer. The sun had traveled from the eastern horizon to the west, crossing the meridian of the sky, and the question is repeated, "Who are you?" As before, there is no answer. This is all. Twelve lines. The question, as it were, brings its own answer. Who are you?

Tagore confronts us with the mystery of the original and the problem of translation which is also mysterious. Translations, I believe, can still be valid if they are done in the language learnt by a poet at his mother's knee, a poet for whom it is the language of his subconscious. Not the kind of language—and I am not being modest—that we Indians use as a workhorse for purposes of lecturing or teaching or talking or even expressing ideals. But a far deeper sharing can only come to those moments when a language leaps into life. It is an ignition, a luminosity which happens when the translator is a genius and also is a master of his own language. Few of us can claim this. We do not have an Arthur Waley in Bengal. We do not have a Donald Keene. We do not even have an Edward FitzGerald. We Indians had to go across the ocean to prove that we existed. Crossed over to the golden streets of "London town" to say that some Indians are still alive. And we are still doing this crossing by translating ourselves, hoping however that some real translator-artist will come along. That somebody, if he is conscious of his responsibility, will consult others. He will need insights, above all, from those who are familiar with the originals. We from India can be of some help. Bengali poets who know their language well and who can point out where the translation does not seem to get to the original, are needed even by a translator who speaks and writes in flawless English. But the main initiative and the artistic discipline have to be wielded by an artist-translator.

We are building up an Indo-Anglican (perhaps also an Indo-American) literature. A few of our truly gifted Indian writers write directly in English. Raja Rao is here at this Conference—a great novelist, a master craftsman. R. K. Narayan is known all over this

country and, of course, all over the West and in India. But I am not
enumerating; there are other remarkable novelists. If I had to name
some one novelist from Bengal, it would be Bhabani Bhattacharya,
an outstanding contemporary writer: a creative artist. I wish they
would translate from their own mother tongue, but they don't.
I wish we could put them back to their own language and then make
them translate a bit! But I must not be small-minded about it,
because a real Indo-Anglican literature is growing; but I must also
confess that I have not read a single poem written in English by an
Indian writer which is great poetry.

Some writers' and translators' workshops have arisen, mainly in
Calcutta, but also in other Indian centers. This is a very hopeful, a
creative emergence. Thought transference, trans-creation, transliteration. I would rather use Robert Lowell's phrase—imitations. A translation can be the shadow of the original. And yet it can be a faithful
shadow rather than a deviational translation. Sometimes the literary
and the literal elements can coincide, though rarely. That would be a
happy event. Let us welcome this period of experimentation and
achievement.

As you can detect, I am not yet fully convinced, but also I do not
wish to be unduly critical. There have been fine attempts here and
there. Successful English translations, particularly from ancient
Indian texts, have been and are being published. Bengali is rich in
short stories. Excepting for a few stories of Tagore, no one volume
has yet gained Western acclaim. A volume named *Tales from Modern
India* (edited by Natwar Singh) is altogether fine both in its range
and quality, and I commend this collection of modern Indian short
stories. But is it not a pity that we Bengalis—let us say we Indians—
and the English-speaking world have been close to each other for
a hundred and fifty years and more, and yet our total production
performance in translation is very inadequate. We should come to
look at this problem and find out some means to award scholarships to new writers and translators. Let us get some writer, young
or older, to attempt to understand Bengali, Hindi, or any other major
Indian language and to do the translations in a very proper way.

To come back to Tagore, we owe much to him for his English
writings, and we are also thankful that he realized the enormity of
his undertaking and the part failure of his enterprise. He knew it.
He disappeared from England when he felt he was being lionized
and heard a rumor that he might even be invited to Buckingham
Palace because he had written in English. He thought the bubble had
almost burst. It was time to go to America. Not as a poet, but as a
man among men, with Robert Frost, Sinclair Lewis, and Carl Sand-

burg and others. He was not in the United States speaking as a poet,
not interpreting himself at all. He became unconsciously the spokes-
man for Indian ideas, and philosophy. He lectured at Harvard and
other intellectual centers of learning. But this was not an artist
speaking about his art. There are some elements which got involved
in it, but he very quietly left his field of art and creative writing.

What remains of a poem when it is translated? I have two illustra-
tions. The first, Robert Frost, said that poetry—the best part of it—
is the fragrance, the aroma, and it is the first thing which disappears
in translation. The petals of the flower may be cut up and dried but
the flower is gone. The other poet was Boris Pasternak, who was also
a great translator. I do not know Russian, but I am told that many
of his translations of Shakespeare were excellent. However, when he
looked at English translations of his poems, he just groaned. He said,
Look what they have done. They got one line, perhaps a good one,
but the rest, the poem, isn't there. When we urged him to translate
Tagore into Russian, he said: I did that once. I'll never repeat that
mistake. I know the crime I perpetrated. Now the State comes and
asks me to translate from Tagore as part of a collective enterprise. We
must resist this process and I have done so. I'm not going to attempt
a single Russian translation of Tagore for the Centennial, but you
won't misunderstand. We appreciated his reluctance and his refusal.

Let us have really gifted and sensitive translations. Let us have
some Indians who are knowledgeable enough to catch the overtones
or the subtle tones of the English language. I go to Oxford and hear
undergraduates talk, and my heart is filled with despair. I could never
achieve their level of inevitable speech. They could almost get an
idea across in a casual way because it is their language, it runs in their
bloodstream. They are not thinking of translations but they are re-
creating a sensitive feeling. In some of our Indian films, we have gone
to the limit. All of our major actors and actresses, at one time at
least, had to sing. And if it is an English version, they were footnoted
in English. Even if they were jumping into the ocean or committing
suicide, they had to bother about English prepositions. If they used
the word *not only* they had also to put in *but also*. With half a *but*
and an *also* they were jumping into the ocean. I can remember Yeats
telling me " . . . we have at last taken revenge on you. We are making
you dream in bad English."

Modern Translations into Italian

Fernanda Sottsass Pivano

One of the very first things I noticed long ago as a young translator, was that no translator is ever completely satisfied with other translators' translations; therefore, I started quite early wondering what it was to be wrong in this strange *métier,* this strange profession. Was it because someone wanted a sentence to be translated word-for-word, while someone else wanted to change it a little or much or very much following his inclination or mood or taste? Or, was it because someone wanted an ancient language to be re-created in a fake ancient language, while someone else wanted to create the flavor of other times through modern words? Or was it because someone wanted a foreign-language rhythm to be destroyed and turned into another language rhythm, while someone else wanted to try as hard as possible to invent a non-existent rhythm to face this weird hospitality problem?

I found out that, more often than not, each translator had his own very strong opinions about what he was doing and most of all about what other translators should or should not have been doing. This confused me a lot.

When I talk of translators, I am referring to the literary ones; but among these I am not referring to the highly skilled technicians who dictate translations of three different books to three different typists at the same time, after changing the typewriter keys to humor the

321

different editorial practice of such-and-such a publisher. The translators I am talking about are the silent, patient, hardworking research-
ers who write and re-write a sentence over and over again to reach
whatever dream they have about that sentence and, if this kind of
research can be called a creation, then I myself surely have my own
very strong opinion, which is that a translation can only be a creation.
But my own very strong opinion is also that a translation should by
no means destroy the original texture and flavor, let alone the original rhythm and style; because by this the author's reality—and I
don't mean his way of writing but the writing itself—would be destroyed as well.

Whoever might mistake such a technique for a word-for-word
translation would be severely baffled at his very first attempt at
achieving it. It is clear enough how different is the consciousness of
any author from anyone else's consciousness; but it seemed unthinkable to me the way the various translators' approaches could differ
for the same words being translated into a different language. This
sounds like an old Mr. Lapalisse's statement, but it was for me the
very beginning of a technique that kept my work going for decades,
with no feedbacks of bad conscience since I knew that I was doing
my best to try to have my authors understood in a very different
language from a very different consciousness and I was doing my
best to keep them safe in their own inventions and fantasies.

It is probably through this approach to translation that some of us
in Italy started "discovering" authors as the simplest way to "invent"
another way of life, during the faraway decades of Mussolini's un-
mild literary dictatorship. I assume that many of us have read
Donald Heiney's book *America in Modern Italian Literature,* the
most accurate and sharp portrait of those Italian literary decades
I have come across so far; and someone probably recalls with respect, as I do, the work done by two Italian writers, Cesare Pavese
and Elio Vittorini, who "created" American literature for Italian
readers and by so doing created a new generation of writers and a
new consciousness towards literature.

I suppose everybody knows what the cultural basis of those Italian decades has been. Our Undersecretary of Fine Arts declared in
1926: "Artists must prepare themselves for the new imperialist
function which must be carried out by our art. Above all we must
categorically impose the principles of *Italianità.* Whoever copies
a foreigner is guilty of *lèse-Nation* like a spy who admits an enemy
by a secret doorway." This rule was very strongly enforced, together with a typical censorship against any creativity aimed at
making the very narrow channels of political and moralistic propaganda overflow.

Writing in Italy during those decades without incurring censorship meant either fulfilling the cultural autarchy by singing in a peculiar, rhetorical language the values of classical imperial images and stifling by the sounds of ever-ringing brass bands the daily brainwashing of everybody's consciousness; or, escaping into poetry and its so-called obvious lack of directness or straightforwardness or clearness, since at that time our poetry was mostly labeled as metaphysical and hermetic. A creative writer had to be very careful about whatever he was writing, if he did not want to end up in confinement in some secluded village of our deep South (which was really deep at that time) or maybe in a jail quite more unfriendly than any jail designed for non-political crimes; and the 1931 law that required the *tessera* of the Fascist Party for professors did not derive much help from the Academies.

OK, you all know what I am trying to get across, and I don't even want to make you believe that everybody in Italy was unhappy. The very first time I saw Pavese after the so-called "Liberation," with the last Fascist *Cecchini* still shooting in the streets, he threw me off balance by saying: "No one but a fool would think that all Italians were anti-Fascists. Only a very few of them were." He was probably right, I don't know; but Fascist or un-Fascist or anti-Fascist as they might have been, the system was so strict that I think we might safely say that a general alienation from real human values was suffocating our public and private consciousness to death.

Unless this is clear it is really very hard to understand the work of these writers, Pavese and Vittorini, who devised the trick of translating books where suggestions of freedom were bursting off like ripe fruits on a rich tree, as a way of expressing themselves; and by freedom I don't mean any already ambiguous political freedom but literary freedom, the freedom of a prose or poetry written in a new language in order to express new feelings about new things, where traditions might be respected but might also be discussed or ignored. It was mostly the American naturalists who were translated in Italy during the thirties: Caldwell, Steinbeck, Saroyan, and Sinclair Lewis were the most popular, but even Melville's *Moby Dick* was translated by Pavese, who also wrote the first Italian temptative essay on Walt Whitman, by whom he had been turned-on to the American mingling of life and writing, as opposed to the Italian idea of immaculate pages of a *Turris Eburnea* where prose and poetry were fleckless—or to modernize it all, stainless, unpolluted—by such a supposedly dirty thing as everyday reality and life. Hemingway, who was severely forbidden by our censorship, had to be read in English or French translations; the lack of communication and knowledge led

to mistakes, and mistakes have been made, for instance, in preferring
James Cain to Faulkner. But anyway these authors were read in an
atmosphere of conspiracy that gave the books an unpredictable,
what's-next flavor; more or less, maybe, the flavor that the classics
had when they were discovered in Italy in the early Renaissance. One
of the most outstanding examples of this sort of attitude was the
enormous success of the *Spoon River Anthology*—yes, I really mean
Edgar Lee Masters' *Anthology,* which in Italy, during the Nazi occupation, was a kind of underground safe-conduct or pass, such as to
give its fans or even just its readers the features of something
between a conspirator and a new-style-of-life adept.

How much has all this to do with translations? Vittorini and
Pavese and a little later I myself were called *Americanisti,* which
did not only mean that we were translating American authors but
that we were suggesting that particular approach to literature that
American literature seemed to us to embody at that moment to the
Italian consciousness. In the frame of such literary choice, many
problems had to be faced, and I am not referring to the practical
problems like obtaining from our Minister of Popular Culture permission to publish the books we wanted to publish. I am actually
referring to the technical problems of translating new ideas expressed in a new language (as the American language was or seemed
to be when compared to its English great-great-grandfather) into our
very old Italian language built up through very old centuries to
express very old ideas.

This is what I mean by "translation as creation." When I started
in Pavese's wake, or footsteps if you prefer, doing my own work
(of whatever significance it might have been), I learnt most of the
technical approaches to a page to be translated from him. I learnt
the very first rudimental practice of underlining all the unfamiliar
words and all the slang words, to read aloud a sentence trying to
reach whatever rhythm the original sentence seemed to have my ear,
to try hard to forget our Italian so-called formal elegance, by which
what was actually meant was a French-like sonority or roundness of
sound—a rotundity, if this makes any sense. And right away our
"cross and delight" problems sprang out from those pages: the problem of occasionally understanding American slang and always of
inventing an Italian slang, and the problem of shifting pages which
were rhythmically flowing away on mostly monosyllabic or bisyl-
labic American words to pages slowed down and made heavy by our
long plurisyllabic words.

The problem of understanding American slang sounds now quite
meaningless to our young translators, who have at their disposal

numberless dictionaries and vocabularies and varieties of specific slang glossaries; they can also meet numberless English-speaking tourists in Italy or they can eventually take a plane and fly to America or to England for help. We all know how fast times are a-changing and I see someone around who might remember that all such chances were not given to the *Americanisti* of the decades I am talking about; and that, rather than disheartening us, the tantalizing difficulties were fascinating us, as if the obscurity of a word were stimulating to the discovery of an all-clear but quite new language. The discovery of the American language through reading a book was very much connected with the discovery of a book through the discovery of its language; and this gave the translations from American done in those decades a particular kind of enthusiasm, of commitment: the Italian *Americanisti* of the thirties and forties have been as *engagés* as the political writers in the fifties.

Such a commitment is what I consider a creation in a translation. But from the moment of discovery, the creation was mostly tied down to our endless attempts, our never-ending efforts to find non-existent Italian language fit to create a vicarious fiction or poetry such as we were not allowed to write of our own, while the all-Italian classical tradition was imposed on our consciousness. American slang was in itself a specific problem, of course, and one that was never actually solved. There was no such thing as slang in Italy, except for a few technical slang words, like the thieves' or the beggars' or the football slang; and the cartoon magazines approved by the Establishment and its censorship were offering a middle-class slang, mostly derisive of any attempt to escape from the portrait of a tough, bullying, patriotic, reckless, no-time-for-nonsense youth on which the future of our so-called empire was resting. Needless to say, we carefully avoided such slang; and when I was talked and talked and talked into using it in Fitzgerald's *This Side of Paradise* translation, I didn't have to wait very long to see how foolish I had been when I finally used even just a couple of words of it: that particular Italian slang died out after a very short time, completely erased from language and consciousness probably because of its lack of reality, of its being born from a propagandistic program put into being on a cartoonist's drawing-table rather than from spontaneous talks and inventions of people in the street.

The only way out of the problem of slang seemed to be our dialects, and this was for a moment the solution chosen by Pavese, who was born in a section of North Italy called Piedmont and who was very much involved with this. His using of his dialect was a whole lot more than a sentimental choice for him: besides believing very much in his birth as a country boy, he was quite aware that putting a stress on the agricultural, little-town life was already showing a symbolic choice between the overimposed imperialist pattern and the forbidden human dimension of an un-heroic reality. But his experiments of using Piedmontese words while translating Faulkner did not seem to be very profitable to him; and he gave them up and kept using his dialect in his own prose as soon as his prose was allowed to be published.

As for my own experiment on translations of slang, what I tried to do as hard as I could was to turn it into peculiar ways of our spoken language, which was quite different from our literary language and supposedly improper for a good book. Starting as it did as a solution of the slang problem, this experiment widened to the whole stylistic texture of the books I translated, but of course I couldn't hold on to such a solution whenever I was working on old traditional authors—which actually I accepted to translate only under a very typical pressure of those decades: publishers were most unwilling to publish American authors for fear of having the books seized by political anti-foreign censorship, even though their reputation as literary publishers was actually helped a great deal through such publications. Bompiani started in 1929 and published Cain, Caldwell, Steinbeck, and Vittorini's *Americana Anthology* (1942); Frassinelli started in 1932 by publishing Melville and Anderson, Einaudi started in 1933 and introduced Gertrude Stein, Masters, and Hemingway in Italy, and Mondadori in 1933 started a competitive literary series of "foreign" authors which included Sinclair Lewis, Dos Passos, Faulkner and Saroyan. Publishers were usually blackmailing the *Americanisti,* by expecting them, whenever they wanted very hard to have an American author published, to translate it more or less free, (Pavese translated *Moby Dick* for 1000 lire, about one-dollar-fifty, and I really mean one-dollar-fifty, and for the same fee I translated Masters' *Anthology*) and by expecting them to reciprocate the favor by translating a "traditional" (beyond censorship) book for a normal fee.

That's how I happened to translate a book by Jane Austen and one by Charles Dickens; and from this moment my problem was to get out of using colloquial contemporary Italian. Therefore I found myself re-reading half forgotten Italian books of my scholarly education, trying to capture their rhythm and their texture. It was at that moment that I found out how strictly connected with contemporary life a really good book is for all its universality and how hard it is to re-create an ancient rhythm and texture without making a fake reconstruction, not very unlike the wax statues of Marie Tussaud.

I worked very hard before giving the problem up. I still have big, huge index books where I used to collect any word which had been used in the same book more than once with the same or a different meaning, each word with the number of the page where it was used. The idea was to be sure to make exactly the same number of repetitions as the author, which—together with the attempt of producing a more or less similar rhythm based on accents, on the general cadenza—was my suggestion to turn the old style of a language into an old style of another language *without* using ancient, lifeless words.

I am not sure that my attempts reached their aim: I gave up translating old authors as soon as I could. But while translating the new ones, I went on using the technique of recording all repetitions and of never forgetting the original rhythm. This was a hard enough job in itself, but it was a real drudgery when it came to the editors' revisions, with their opinions about how to make our translations "pretty" or "likable" or even just "correct". Their first idea of prettiness was usually that any repetition at all had to be avoided, whenever they noticed one; and the easiest ones to be noticed, of course, were the "he (or she) said" in our beloved modern-American dialogues. It was typical, much later, to read a young man's criticism where he blamed Pavese for not respecting those repetitions.

Anyway, the easiest, most rudimental attempt to keep up with the original rhythm seemed possible to me by respecting the original punctuation, of course, I grew a deep dislike for the French craze of those years, of turning whatever paragraph of whatever language into the breathing of the French literary, traditional paragraph; and I was aghast when I saw this same technique applied in an Italian pirate (and later to be rescued) translation of *A Farewell to Arms:* Hemingway's beautiful, inimitable sequence of very short sentences, three-four words each, was drowned into long, eighteenth-nineteenth century paragraphs, complete with colon and semicolon. What had this to do with the prose that had turned some of us on to a new style of writing long before we came to know about its author's new style of life? I was more and more confused.

Later, with the mythical discovering time gone into the postwar flooding rivers of Coca-Cola and economic imperialism—I mean, after America had become a physical reality with not so much to be dreamt about and after our champions of clandestinity were accepted by the Establishment—I kept translating for a while simply because this had become my profession; but my approach to translating didn't change as far as my attempts of turning the American authors' rhythm and style into Italian were concerned; and the weird disguisement of Hemingway prose in that Italian translation disturbed me a lot. I was wondering, while doing the authorized translation of *A Farewell to Arms,* whether my reaction was just a sentimental one, or whether I was undergoing the professional distortion of refusing another translator's way of translating, or whether I simply believed quite strongly in my own technical devices. The Last Judgment Day came for me while translating Faulkner's *Intruder in the Dust,* when I found on my table a paragraph about twenty pages long without a period, where the thoughts and images and actions were linked by numberless gerundives and present participles: a form which I could not possibly use in Italian in that sequence without sounding like an untalented primary-school pupil doing her homework. It would have been easy, so easy, to break the paragraph, as was usually done in European translations, and to make several Italian-sounding sentences out of that long wave of breathing; but I chose to work seven months trying not to break it, and I will never know whether my dedication rewarded me with a practical achievement or not.

My anxiety, my eagerness to be true to my authors' styles, led me to write to them and ask for explanations and advice; their kindness and patience provided me with the most precious experiences of my life as a writer and as a human being. As soon as my passport was granted to me, I went to Paris to meet Alice Toklas, and she gave me precious information on her fabled Gertrude Stein, on whom I had written a long essay while translating one of her books. When Richard Wright came to Paris after being invited by Jean-Paul Sartre, I went to tell him about a never-to-be-published book called *Uncle Tom Is Dead* which I had written half-fanatically during the war.

Then Ernest Hemingway came to Italy and by giving me his generous friendship he made up for whatever dedication to his books I had committed myself to. He hated to talk about what he had written and couldn't stand explaining the meaning of some of his colloquial expressions which I was foolish enough to call slang. He flatly stated that he never used slang in his books, that any word in his books might have been used by Shakespeare and might anyway be found in a dictionary. Next morning, under the shining sun of Cortina d'Ampezzo, while pulling a little sledge up the hill where Tiziano was born or maybe had just lived, he insisted that he never used slang; and it wasn't until much later that I learnt about such prose rules of his Kansas City *Star* as: "Use short sentences. Use short paragraphs. Use vigorous English. Be positive, not negative," or: "Never use slang, which has no place after its use becomes common. Slang to be enjoyable must be fresh," or: "Avoid the use of adjectives, especially such extravagant ones as *splendid, gorgeous, grand, magnificent, etc.*"

Whatever influence such prose rules had on his formation as a writer, they surely relieved me of my worries about keeping or not keeping his short-sentences rhythm in my translations of his books or looking for intensity rather than for sensation in the choice of the Italian adjectives to mate the original ones. Listening to him while he was telling a story which he would have written next morning, after getting up at sunrise before the visitors' trickle (soon to become a flood) would start, and standing up in front of his typewriter to type down deliberately the story which he had warmed up by telling it at the dining-table—listening to him telling that story at the dining-table was more useful to understanding his writing than reading thousands of words of criticism on his technique of writing. And I remember a happy day in his open car, Mary hidden under a blanket, Hemingway drinking from a few bottles of gin which he had taken with him, when I suddenly understood the real sound of his fabled dialogue, just by listening to his answers to Mary, his breathtaking gambling with the use of that "to do" which is, really for ever, impossible to translate into Italian.

My next flesh-and-blood discovery was William Faulkner's sarcasm. His prose had mostly meant a very interesting stylistic tantalizing trial to me, when I happened to translate it; and when I first met him I was mostly impressed by his silence and his chivalrous ways, like catching hold of my arm when crossing a street, the way men used to do with ladies during the Golden Age (at least in Europe). But when I saw him later and his silence was not so defensive and his ways were not so stately anymore, I found in some of his answers, in many of his remarks, a sarcastic way of eluding some unpleasant reality, some reluctant statement. This sarcastic key came out over and over again, while making fun of a lady—who very much wanted to have a Nobel Prize at her dining-table and, who, Faulkner said, had spent three days choosing a menu, hiring servants, mailing invitations, setting the table, going to the hairdresser and finally shining the silverware without knowing that actually he had already chosen not to attend her dinner; or while walking slowly in the dusk (or, as he would say, in the dust), pretending to look for a phantom window shop where that morning, passing by car, he had seen a very beautiful necktie, which he very much wanted to buy, and stubbornly going up and down the same street as if he wouldn't see that all the shops were closed anyway. I could go on and, somehow, the Biblical oratory and the Joyce stream of consciousness acquired a new light for me, and I started looking through his pages, to find out when his images were true and when they were disguising his discontent.

I don't know, maybe I am all wrong. I had spent years looking for a connection between fiction and reality, between a book and its reality, between an author and his reality, all of which had very little to do with French or American or Italian or whatsoever literary "naturalism" and which only concerned my eagerness to find, if not a blueprint, at least a tentative way out of our Italian attitude towards literature as an abstract tournament where the "Queen of Beauty" could be reached only by giving up any connection with so-called "vulgarity" and so on; yes, like the old British Victorian days, except that not being vulgar at that time for Italian Establishment meant being a Fascist.

What a confusion. Now—I mean, after the war, in the fifties—those times had been swallowed up by a large tide of tragedy and disaster, of forgiveness and grief, with all the hatred drowned in blood and too much blood to have mercy on. Our principle of *Italianità* was there, like a tiger made of paper, as Mr. Mao Tse-tung would say, and some of us were too tired to find out for whose fault it all had happened and too wise anyway to think that finding it out would help anyone. There we were, with the American authors of our dreams of liberty —which we had translated for no tangible advantage, surely not for money, even more surely not to get any academic honor out of it, sometimes getting jail or confinement sentences and always public disgrace for it—all of them suddenly being very popular, with publishers contending for their copyrights and exploiting whatever celebrity had come out of the *Americanisti* myth.

That myth had lost most of its meaning for some of us; and after having checked my interpretations by personally meeting my authors, or their wives or daughters when my authors had died, there seemed little more for me to do, since I was not particularly interested in an abstract, purely formal critical research.

It was more or less at that time that Allen Ginsberg's *"Howl"* blew my mind out when I read it in that *Evergreen Review* special issue on the San Francisco scene. OK, maybe I have been all wrong again, but in his attitude during those McCarthy days, I rediscovered some of the emotions which I had shared at his age with some Italian writers while looking for that unclear something that might turn a brainwashed consciousness into a living one; and by "his attitude" I mean of course what *I* thought his attitude was at that moment, what his attitude seemed *to me*. I insist on the relativity of my personal interpretation because, much later, he severely complained about my stereotyping him, and I remember him in Florence, in a very crowded movie theatre where we went to see a Pier Paolo Pasolini something, when an American boy asked him: "Are you Mr. Allen Ginsberg?" and he answered flatly, "One of them." Whatever he really meant at that time, what I thought I saw through his lines, was a proposal of a full-time frankness or truthfulness or whatever you want to call it, a suggestion of total directness and of searching into one's own consciousness as a first step to try to find the core of anyone else's consciousness and start a new, unmanipulated communication between human beings, a suspicion about bureaucracy as one of many alienation sources, a revival of a human dimension as based on spiritual values versus the materialistic values born from the gradual mechanization of souls.

It sounded a little like our old non-Fascist story, except for the image of the "mechanization," which for us had been "Fascistization" of the souls; but it was the first time that I saw it written down so clearly and with such unaggressive effectiveness, and anyway it showed me a way out of the intellectual sclerotization that was stifling Italy during the sixties. It seemed natural to me that I close my profession as a translator by translating his poetry. And by doing so, I unexpectedly happened to be involved with the Italian public consciousness again, much as twenty years earlier I had happened to be involved with it while dealing with our myth of the fabled American democracy and literature.

Translating became creative again to me. Once again, I was facing a language which was born from reality rather than from scholarly learning, and I was able to check again how far from banal reality a poetical reconstruction of reality is. When I heard of Jack Kerouac's technique of taping and typing real people's talks, I listened carefully to Neal Cassidy's monologues, to see how much of Kerouac's creativity had worked on Neal's words to reproduce his rhythm, his cadenza. The problem was a fascinating one to me, because, although I didn't translate Kerouac's books, I was constantly looking for the connection between a colloquial language and a literary language, and, anyway, the difference between the real way of speaking without being self-conscious and a written colloquial language. (Please notice that I said *written* rather than *literary*, because a literary colloquial language would be like wax statues to me again, like Minstrel-Show Deep-South dialects).

So there I was again in front of a book of poems, with another unseizable Moby Dick luring me from those long, urging lines, and, when the first shock was over, the technical problems started: how was I to keep that rhythm with our slow, always too slow, too slow for ever, Italian-language rhythm? How was I to contract our long

words into short, sometimes snapping monosyllables? How was I to
work out those clicking genitive inflections built up as they were in
a vertical crescendo with our unruffled extensive sequences which
were built up with endless "of" and "of the" and heavy syntactical
constructions? How was I to invent an Italian way for those
sequences of nouns-used-as-adjectives to build up a running-shot
image large enough to include everything, really everything, really
all the ugly-beautiful ecological reality of whatever was rising up
from those lines?

I found a way to turn the running-shot descriptions into Italian
by following my old trick of just being faithful to the original. I was
typically criticized for it: a young man wrote that my translation
was just what we call *interlineare* or *bigino*, one of those word-by-
word translations used in Italy by lazy pupils who don't feel like
working on their Latin or Greek homework; an old man wrote that
I hadn't worked hard enough on it. After all, times had not changed
so much as far as criticism was concerned; and I have not been very
discouraged, because I still feel some connection between those all-
including images and my attempts to make them understood in
Italian or at least to give our readers a feeling about them as they
have been originally written down.

But there were other problems, sometimes easy problems due to
my ignorance of Ginsberg's environment (and Michael McClure
helped me a lot, going for hours through Ginsberg's book with me
while Ginsberg was in India); sometimes technical problems, like
how to avoid our censorship wrath and seizing of the book. (When
Ginsberg refused to let his so-called daring lines be translated by
half-scientific words which would baffle our censorship, he threw me
into deep disaster but gave me a clear evidence of what *real* spoken
language meant to him). I got more and more involved, and I will
never forgive myself for the weeks I stole from Allen Ginsberg's
life while trying to learn from his voice how to capture the Moby
Dick of his poetry. His patience and his scholarship are known to
whoever has had a chance to work with him; and for future scholars
I taped eight four-track tapes, recording our attempts to translate
his "TV Baby Poem" into Italian, with each word discussed and
scrutinized and peeled off in an effort to find an Italian word as
close as possible to it and to all the possible meanings of it.

Now, is this a creative translation? Maybe it is.

I might go on; but I already have to apologize for talking too
much and for talking mostly of my personal experiences, rather
than attempting a theoretical critical research on the problem of
translating. My poor casual story probably doesn't mean much to

a formal history of translation, of criticism, and of criticism of translation; and I find myself still clinging to human relationships rather than to rational theorization as I did in my girlhood. I don't even wonder if my translations have been good or bad: what I know is that I always tried to guess, as much as I could, what my authors had tried to mean in the books I was translating; and, by so doing, I was rewarded with personal involvements that took me close to some writers' techniques and sometimes to their inspirational feelings. Their beautiful pages and their beautiful minds, their written and spoken, literary and non-literary words, sometimes crowd my mind maybe far beyond some technical translation problem. Under the large gliding wings of their images and creativity, of their knowledge of human suffering and joy, of their respect for death and life, I found a reason for my quiet, patient, stimulating, most enjoyable work.

"Traduit de l'Américain"

Pierre Brodin

Because of my interests and work, which can be described as bridging two civilizations and cultures, I have read a good part of the recent crop of American novels, both in the original and in their French translations, and I would like to offer a few casual remarks on my experience in that field.

I have sometimes been pleased, more often irritated, and frequently scandalized by the books *traduits de l'américain* (a relatively recent expression substituted, about twenty years ago, for the traditional *traduit de l'anglais*).

The people chiefly responsible for my anger are, of course, the French publishers. Too many members of that businessmen's club are running too hard after fast money. They choose books, not for their literary values, but for their chances of becoming *best sellers*. They draw heavily upon *names* of well-known writers, upon lists of popular books, and discard artistic and experimental literature as unremunerative. Even such enlightened publishers as André Bay, of Stock (a delicate poet and essayist in his own right) left lying in a drawer, for three or four years, Anais Nin's novels and *Journals* because they did not seem to carry enough appeal for the general public.

A second calamity lies in the way translations are chosen by the publishers. Most translations are entrusted to people who do not know enough about the American language, literature and civilization.

Most publishers also want books to be translated too quickly. They frequently set unreasonable deadlines—three months, for instance, for a 300-page novel.

Lastly, they have been paying translators very poorly, which, of course, may be justified in the case of slipshod work, but is less so when the translators have worked very hard and delivered a creditable piece of writing. As of today a recognized translator receives an average of 10 F. to 12F.50—that is, less or a little more than $2.00 —for one typed 25-line page of the English text. This meager salary has been more or less standard since 1957 and it does not take into account the rising cost of living.

There is, also, the problem of censorship. Books can be censored, in France, for reasons of obscenity and pornography and, just as in some American States, the definition of those terms is open to question and frequently varies. Henry Miller's *Tropics* were translated completely and adequately (by Henri Fluchère) long before they were authorized in America. But the French translation of Burroughs' *Naked Lunch* contains a certain number of blank pages, representing passages which the publishers did not want or did not dare to have translated. There are, however, also non-pornographic pages which have not been translated, and I strongly suspect the publisher and/or the translator of having found in censorship an easy excuse for not translating difficult passages. (There are many painful, almost untranslatable paragraphs in Burroughs' novel, and one sympathizes with the translator!)

In dealing with the *traduit de l'américain*, we must now examine the justifications of the French translator and his special problems.

Unfortunately, no particular talent is generally required, except some knowledge of English and French. No academic degree, no previous experience is asked. Some of the translators, unfortunately, are mere hacks or rank amateurs.

I will include in the category of hacks most of the translators of detective stories (with the possible exception of Marcel Duhamel of *La Série Noire*). In a novel by Uta Donella published by Presses de la Cité and entitled *Oublie si tu veux vivre (Forget if you want to live)* the translator culminated an unintelligible sentence with the following, in which he confused *closed* and *open: "Karl, les yeux fermés, nous toisa l'une après l'autre,"* which means once re-translated: "Karl, with his eyes closed, gazed at each of us in turn". A difficult trick, indeed! Another hack confused, in a novel by J. D. Salinger, "horse race" and "race horse" and translated the former by *"cheval de course"* instead of *"course de chevaux"*!

The problems of the translator *from the American* are, of course, quite complex and specific. He must, first of all, beware of *cognates,* and then, be familiar not only with English but with American, and not only with the American speech, but with the American slang and brand new American terms. Otherwise, how many mistakes he can make!

Let us, first, take a look at *cognates.*

The book by John Updike, *Of the Farm,* was translated into French as *La Ferme,* an unfortunate expression which carries a quite different meaning. (*La ferme!* in familiar French means *Shut up!*) Besides, this *farm* is not a *ferme.* It is a large rural estate, where neither agriculture nor breeding is practiced. *La ferme française* evokes something quite different and the whole book will probably be misunderstood because of this initial, perhaps unavoidable, mistranslation.

Another example of *contresens*—the French word for misinterpretation or mistranslation—can be found in the translation of Salinger's *Catcher in the Rye,* a title translated, God knows why, by *L'Attrape Coeur,* which means the *heart snatcher.*

The translator of *L'Attrape Coeur* evidently did not know all the meanings of "figure," nor those of "terrific." Therefore he translated "She had a terrific figure," (which, in conversational French could be expressed as *"Elle était vachement bien roulée"*) by *"Elle avait un visage terrible,"* which means "She had an awesome face"!

In another passage, the words "What are you majoring in?" becomes *"Qui est en majorité là-bas?"*, that is, "Who holds the majority there?"

Funnier still is the translation of ". . . And run around the goddam house, naked", which becomes: *". . . Et puis courir à poil autour de . la maison",* which means "and run, naked, *around the house"*!

These are only a few examples of the way Mr. Salinger's work was translated into French. One of my younger colleagues, D. E. Schlesinger, found more than one hundred *contresens* in the one volume of *L'Attrape Coeur.*

Puns are extremely difficult to translate, and titles are often based on this type of play upon words. It is occasionally possible to explain this in a footnote, but such an explanation, particularly on the title page, would seem heavily pedantic.

Among the bad or unsatisfactory titles of recent years, I would like to point out a few. The most ridiculous, in my opinion, are the following:

—*Le Cow Boy de Charme,* for *Midnight Cowboy (Le Cowboy du macadam,* title of the French version of the movie, was a slight improvement).

—*L'Attrape Coeur (Catcher in the Rye)*, already mentioned as one of the worst.

—*Couleur de Tendresse (The Color of Darkness*, by James Purdy), which is a heavy *contresens*.

—*Frankie Addams (Member of the Wedding*, by Carson McCullers), a total elimination of a beautiful image, replaced by the name of the heroine.

—*L'Homme de Buridan (Dangling Man*, by Saul Bellow), a kind of bad pun which evokes *L'Ane de Buridan*, the donkey of Buridan, an argument proposed by a Scholastic doctor of the fourteenth century and a symbol of the inability to make up one's mind.

Among the good or satisfactory titles *traduits de l'américain*, I will report:

—*Les Domaines Hantés (Other Voices, Other Rooms*, by Truman Capote), which strongly suggests the haunted, supernatural atmosphere of Mr. Capote's early stories.

—*Savannah (The Fair Sister*, by William Goyen), because this word in French immediately conjures the Old South and the Negroes of the *Savane*.

—*MOM (A Mother's Kisses*, by Bruce Friedman), because the word *momism* is just as well if not better known in France, than in America.

*

The translator has not only to come up with a good title. He has to keep up with the times. He has to realize, for instance, that *pot*, which used to be a container for plants, is now a drug, and that *grass*, *turn on*, etc. are no longer what they used to be.

It is often necessary to study in depth the technical vocabularies and to come to the United States to hear them and understand them properly. Such was the case for M. Rambaud, the translator of John Rechy's *City of Night*, who acquired the language of the drug pushers and users and hustlers by frequenting for a period of several months the milieux of *junkies (camées), fairies (tapettes), gays (folles), pinkies (pédalettes), drag queens (reines des tantes)* and *connections (contacts)*.

Other special jargons, which are not usually included in dictionaries are those of the *hips*, the *squares* and the *cool cats (les mecs qui ne se laissent pas démonter)*; those of the religious and ethnic groups: Jewish or Yiddish terms (a *chaver* is a believer, *ur*—*camarade*); those of sex. How many French translators know that *hamstring* means *enjarnaguer* and *to turn on* is *"s'envoyer en l'air"* or *"se mettre les veines en fête"*?

A serious and paradoxical problem, for the French translator, is what to do about words that the novelist has written in French (or pseudo-French). When there are bad mistakes inserted in the original novel, must one attribute tham to the printers, to the character created by the novelist, or to the novelist himself? I am afraid that James Baldwin's French (in *Another Country*) is quite rusty, whereas Mr. Updike's is probably better, even though his characters, in *The Centaur* and *Couples* sometimes speak in funny but atrocious French or "franglais": *huile étendarde* for *Standard Oil*, *dorme-t-elle?* instead of *dort-elle? trois heures c'est trop beaucoup*, etc.

Another difficulty for the translator is to try and write approximately the same number of lines as in the original—an often difficult, almost impossible task. Looking at a translation for a bilingual edition of the poetic novel *House of Incest*, by Anais Nin, I found that, on pages 62-63, the English text has 21 lines and the French translation more than 27. It is quite frequent that the translator cannot put in one page what should be one page and what is paid as one page!

*

Then, who is the ideal French translator and what is the ideal French translation?

Mr. Nabokov once said something to the effect that the best and only translation is a "literal translation with commentary and abundant footnotes." I don't entirely agree. The literal translation may be useful in science and, generally speaking, in non-fiction, but it falls short of creative work.

It is reasonable to state that a good translator must be not only an expert but a man of imagination, judgment and taste, and, of course, a *creator*.

A good translator must have mastered not only two, but possibly three or four languages. Maurice Edgar Coindreau, an *agrégé d'espagnol* and a former Princeton professor, is equally at home in Spanish and in English and his knowledge of French, Spanish and English is an invaluable asset for all his translations.

The good translator must be able to realize that the English spoken at Montreal may not be the same as the English spoken in New York or London. Let us take, for instance, the word *bluff* which may mean, in French, *bluffer* or *bosquet d'arbres,* or the word *riding* which may apply to a horse or to an electoral division.

A good translator from the American must understand thoroughly the structure of both languages and realize how important word *position* is in English. The difference between a *race horse* and a *horse race* has already been mentioned and is an example of this.

Very often *humor* is based on this type of shift of meaning. For instance, when the elephant jokes were going around, they told you: "What is more difficult than getting a pregnant elephant in a VW?", the answer being: "Getting an elephant pregnant in a VW."

English sentences can be extremely ambiguous, with the meaning of a chain of words apparent only when the sentence is completed. There can, in fact, be situations where the meaning is pinpointed only when another sentence makes it clear. Take, for instance, those words: "Time flies. You can't. They fly too fast," which were used in a test for candidates to the United Nations Interpreters' Section. The crucial word *they* comes only in the third sentence and eliminates the possibility of *flies* as a verb. The right translation of the first sentence being not *"Le temps fuit,"* but *"Chronométrez les mouches."*

One must also keep in mind the effect of the French work upon the subconscious of the readers. The name of the heroine of William Goyen's *The Fair Sister* is Savatta. This name, in French, would be ridiculous: *une vieille savate,* not only means an old shoe, but a decrepit has-been, whereas Savatta is a young, beautiful woman. The translator, rightly, had the imagination to change Savatta into Savannah.

Another example, in that connection, is to be found in the translation of a novel entrusted to M. E. Coindreau. M. Coindreau had to translate, within a very poetic context, the word *meadow lark*. The meadow lark, in French, is *le pipi des prairies*. M. Coindreau used his judgment and taste and found something much more harmonious than *pipi des prairies.*

I have already mentioned that M. Coindreau is a man of many cultures. I believe that the good translator must be a man of culture, actively engaged in improving his knowledge and taste. He should prepare his mind to translate by reading books written in the style which is the nearest to that of the original. For instance, reading Marcel Proust may help a translator of Henry James or William Faulkner, even though James, Proust, and Faulkner has each his own mannerism.

Another important point. A good translator should not undertake to translate a book he does not like. Translating should be a pleasure and give its author the impression that he is creating a great work of his own. Among the French translators of American novels who sympathized with their subject and took pleasure in translating, I will again mention M. Coindreau and a few of his colleagues of Gallimard who personally choose all the books they translate.

Time is of the essence. There are no shortcuts in translating. One must never hurry. There may be three or four different drafts. And a 300-page book will demand at least six months of toil.

Finally, I would like to mention that the translator should try to suggest, in one way or another, the literary implications of the American title of a novel. Take, for instance, John Steinbeck's works. His titles are borrowed from Milton *(In Dubious Battle)*, from Blake *(Burning Bright)*, Robert Burns *(Of Mice and Men)*, Shakespeare *(The Winter of Our Discontent)*, from "The Battle Hymn of the Republic" *(Grapes of Wrath)*. It is evident that *La Flamme* is a weak translation for *Burning Bright* and that even *A l'Est de l'Eden*, for *East of Eden*, does not have the same impact for a nation like France, where knowledge of the Bible can be scant. It is a notable fact that there is often a fundamental difference underlying the choice of titles by French and American authors and that this very difference makes for major if not insurmountable difficulties in going from one language to another. Whereas the French are fond of linguistic allusions, plays on words recalling proverbs or well-known phrases (for instance, *Le Chemin des Ecoliers, Les Enfants du Limon,* or *La Symphonie Pastorale)*, American authors favor literary allusions like those already mentioned à propos of Steinbeck. An interesting example of this fundamental difference is Vercors' *Les Animaux Dénaturés:* the French title is a play on words. It was translated into "You shall know them," an expression which refers to the Biblical "By their fruits you shall know them."

In conclusion, may I suggest that critics should be more aware of the problems faced by those who do the difficult but often rewarding work of translation? They should realize the creativity involved, the constant need for judgment and good taste, as well as for sound linguistic background, and therefore they should give the translator his due, naming him almost as co-author of the work they review, for in a certain fashion, he is. Such a recognition of the true nature of this literary category would certainly give the translator the incentive he needs, particularly if it brings the *éditeurs* to be more careful in choosing those to whom they entrust a work and to be more generous in their treatment of both the time element and the financial remuneration involved.

Translating into Polish

Krystyna Tarnowska

I will try to give you what is my very general view on translating and on the role of translators. I will begin at the beginning, my personal beginning, even though they say that one of the surest ways of making a bad speech is to begin with history. I hope you will forgive me.

Almost thirty years ago, in 1943, the Gestapo came to my house to arrest me. In the course of their search they came across the manuscript of my maiden effort in the art of translation. During my investigations, they kept coming back to those papers and I had a really hard time trying to convince them that they were not some kind of a code giving information to the allied forces of the German troops' allocation, but simply an innocent attempt to translate an English classic into Polish.

The reason I recall this experience is to show the way in which I was first drawn into what was to become my full-time occupation. I began translating as a very young girl during the war, when the Germans occupied my country, partly as a form of escapism and partly out of defiance, since the Nazis had forbidden us to have any books in English, which had either to be destroyed or turned in to the authorities.

So it was then that, more by accident than design, I began to translate the letters from Yorick to Eliza by Lawrence Sterne, whose

Tristram Shandy I undertook many years after the war. This proved
to be one of the most satisfying jobs a translator can hope for. Even
the critics liked it.

At this point I owe you an apology. I would have liked much
better to discuss some specific aspects of translation, for instance, to
tell you something about my work on Sterne, but unfortunately my
invitation took some time to arrive and what with other delays,
there was simply no time for me to work up the subject in an adequate
and interesting form.

For this reason I decided to confine myself to saying a few words
on what I feel about the art of translation and the role of the translator in contributing to the creation of national culture. This may
sound a little bit pompous but, in fact, all you are in for is a handful
of observations by someone who has devoted many years to what is
genuinely a labor of love. Goethe said—and what a profound and
forceful observation it was—that every literature finally gets bored
with itself if it is not refreshed from some foreign source. Even in
the richest literatures we can find countless examples of the fertili-
zing influence of fine translations. Without going too far back into
history—though we could recall that, as long as four thousand years
ago, accomplished translations were made of the Gilgamesh epic from
Sumerian into Accadian—we need only point to the momentousness
for French literature of the appearance of Baudelaire's translation of
Poe, or to the way in which FitzGerald created a whole trend in
English literature and even thinking with the *Rubaiyat of Omar
Khayyam*. In Polish literature similar events were the translation of
Byron's *Giaour* by our great poet Adam Mickiewicz or the version of
Calderon's *El Principe,* by our other great romantic poet, Juliusz
Slowacki, which was as original a work in Polish as Calderon's was in
Spanish. We all know the importance for national cultures and liter-
atures of the art of translation, the more so in the case of smaller
literature as that of my country. The theory of translation has been
the subject of hundreds of books and treatises and thousands of
comments, words of wisdom, even jokes. But it was not until the
Renaissance that wider attention was given to translation when Latin
ceased to be the *lingua franca* of Europe and it was a time to render
the classics into national languages. It was then that two opposite schools of thought came into being. One maintained that translation should be as faithful as possible; the other preached that translators should be free to transplant to their own literature whatever
was beautiful and instructive in the classics with complete liberty.
The translated work was regarded only as a collection of material,
as food for thought. This principle, very useful for its time, but in

consequence simple devastating, was given various names: tapping the classics, borrowing from them, or more bluntly, robbing them. What was important was not the relationship between the translation and the original, but whether it added lustre to the native literature and stimulated the development of the language. The boundaries between translation, paraphrases, imitation and original writing were fluid and immaterial. In the eighteenth century, more translations were made than ever before and considerably greater attention was given to the theoretical side. Gradually there crystallized a new belief: that the original should not be simply an excuse for the translator to enrich his own literature but that his duty was rather to give as good an account as possible of the work he was translating. Eighteenth-century ideas on this subject were epitomized by Alexander Fraser Teitler in his essay on the Principles of Translation, which appeared at the end of the eighteenth century. According to him, there are three basic requirements of good translation: 1) that the translation should give a complete transcript of the idea of the original work, 2) that the style and manner of writing should be of the same character with that of the original, and 3) that the translation should have all the ease of original composition. Almost two centuries have passed since the appearance of Teitler's book and in that time writers, linguists and philosophers all over the world have turned out no end of tracts on the art of translation. Nevertheless, all the problems raised in Teitler's essay, written with an admirable eighteenth-century clarity, remain relevant to this day, and most of his judgments are still valid. I have dwelt on Teitler's book because I would like to use his very simply-phrased principles as a frame of reference for the question: who and what makes a good translator—in general terms, because such statements are also needed—and when does the translator become a creator? What is the lesson of Teitler's first principle? That the translator must have a good command of the language he is translating from, of course—though, luckily for me, not necessarily the *spoken* language—and he must have a thorough grasp of the subject of the original. This might seem to be a simple requirement, yet the translator cannot be satisfied simply with the knowledge of the language. He must also be familiar with the country and the people, its history and its customs, its culture, its literature. Furthermore, with every new project, the translator must acquaint himself with new areas of life, new problems, new themes and backgrounds. After all, even the simplest book about another period requires research: costumes, household articles, customs, have to be carefully studied and visualized if they are to be

adequately rendered. Of course there is always something you don't
know and even the best translators have dropped some astounding
bricks. But this is rare in the case of a responsible translator, except
perhaps in moments of strain, when the instinct which warns him of
lurking danger goes to sleep. This alarm bell is a kind of distrust and
suspicion of apparently innocuous and familiar expressions which
suddenly spring a new meaning. In this case, the translator consults
dictionaries, lexicons, reference books, other people—and often life
itself is his adviser. Well, this alarm bell once didn't ring for me.
I was translating a selection of Evelyn Waugh's short stories, and I
put into the mouth of a girl—an English girl, visiting Algeria—the
astonishing statement that Algeria, though beautiful, is simply
infested by frogs. Of course, what the girl meant was there were too
many French people for her. (A very British attitude then.) But I
translated it literally and then, reading and realizing, visualizing real
frogs jumping about the place, I simply wished I were dead. But
faithfulness in rendering the content of the original and even in
conveying what is vaguely called its "spirit" is not the only thing
expected of the translator. The second of Teitler's principles
declares that the style and manner of writing should be of the same
character as that of the original. We know that every writer
represents some kind of separate style, a pattern of distinctive
ways of expressing himself. We expect the translation to follow
this pattern as closely as possible, to present the work in its proper
idiom. This is a much more difficult requirement than faithfulness.
In order to assimilate not only the content but also the style of the
original, the translator cannot rest content with only understanding
the work. He must burrow into it, somehow he has to try to step
into the author's shoes, spy out his most personal techniques,
pilfer and digest them, and, on top of all that, still have the gift of
rendering them in a different language medium. Finally, Teitler's
third principle: the translation should have all the ease of original
composition. This is the hardest rule of all for the translator to
observe. For, as Teitler says, it is not easy for someone in fetters
to walk with grace and ease. And fetters are what he has put on the
translator with his first two principles. To achieve the same effect
with different means and method is a formidable proposition. The
only way of handling it is through a creative linguistic talent and an
intuitive sense of language and style. I have tried, with the help of
Teitler's close on two-hundred-year-old principles, to present the
most general view of what the art of translation involves, and—in
very general terms—the requirements placed before a good translator.

Let me now say a few words on the question of who a translator is or should be as I see it, and the role he plays in the artistic and intellectual life of his country. I think that in drawing a strict distinction between translation and original writing, we should be very careful not to exclude the work of the translator from the more general concept of artistic creation and lose sight of the crucial, social significance of this art. I say social because, after all, what are involved are not two elements, the original and the translation, but three. The original, the translation, and the reader.

Let me go into this a little deeper. The first question that suggests itself is: whom are we translating for? The simple answer imposes a whole series of rules governing this difficult and noble art. In addition to the original work and its translation there stands the reader, and translation is therefore a social activity to the same—if not greater—extent as any other endeavor in literature. The wish to make known the thoughts and feelings of foreign writers is perhaps more altruistic than conveying one's own thoughts and feelings. The translator does not express his views, although in choosing something to translate he turns above all to works that suit him best artistically and philosophically. Only then can he be certain that he will translate them better and more aptly.

The reader, the third side in this triangle, does not, it has to be assumed, know the original or the language from which the translation is made or the rules governing this language. He wants to be given a good book in his own language, trusting that in content and style it is a complete equivalent of the foreign work, just as the concert-goer trusts that the orchestra or soloist is playing what is written in the score.

The failure to appreciate the independent creative role of the translator—and we all know that up to now it very often is not appropriately appreciated—is still accompanied by an underrating of his social function, and this seems to be the logical consequence of the fairly widespread treatment of this art solely as a trade to which anyone can turn his hand. It might be said in answer that this is true to the same extent that anyone can in principle become the author of an original work. After all, craftsmanship is as essential an attribute of original writing as of good translation. But in both cases, apart from skill, it is necessary to have talent.

I feel that in the broader aspect, the worth of a translator's work can be measured not only by the degree of its formal excellence, but also by its import for national culture. It is only by meeting these two demands that the translator's work becomes meaningful and he can expect to be admitted as a full-fledged creator to the

literature of his country. By fulfilling the requirements of formal
excellence, he becomes the author of new language and stylistic
values and so he acts like an original writer. A gifted translator, with
as perfect a command of his native tongue as the original writer has
of his, enriches the language and imagery of his country, and by
communicating foreign ideas and situations enlarges its knowledge
and awareness. I would hazard the statement that all debates on
translation are reduced, if stripped of this broad perspective of
social significance, to a more or less academic discussion of whether
a work in itself can be expressed a second time as another work in
itself.

We need only remember the chapter on the impossibility of translation in Benedetto' Croce's *Aesthetics*. The theory of the "irrepeat-
ability" of the aesthetic experience is only tenable if we treat the
work in a vacuum. Obviously, the very fact that the audience appreciates and understands and is moved by it, indicates that aesthetic
experience is repeatable. We know that Hamlet or Cid excites
audiences in the same way whether they deliver their speeches
in French or English or in languages into which a genuinely artistic
translation has been made. And an Englishman or a Pole is equally
prompted to reflection over the affairs of the world when he reads
in *The Tempest* in Prospero's dialogue with Miranda: "We are such
stuff/As dreams are made on, and our little life/Is rounded with a
sleep." Or is prompted to reflection over the affairs of men when he
listens to King Lear. The Polish and Russian reader responds in the
same way to Bolkonsky's thoughts in *War and Peace* when, wounded
on the battlefield, he muses about the ultimate verities. We close
Don Quixote no less wise and rich for the experience than are the
Spaniards themselves.

So let me once again say that the social humanist factor plays
perhaps an even greater role in the work of the translator—a responsible, creative translator—than in the case of a writer. By this I mean
that the translator is all the time conscious of the reader, that he is
with him always and that finally he himself is a reader, the first
reader, meticulous, searching, intuitive, assessing the rises and falls of
his author. He is his author's severest judge and closest friend who
does not gloss over his errors but is proud of his virtues. But he is
also the pupil of the great writers of his own country from whom he
learns how to wield his language confidently, and tries to possess
their secret of arranging words and phrases in such a way as to find
the most perfect form for the work translated by him.

At the same time the translator is an explorer of foreign languages,
foreign literature, customs and history. He travels to other centuries

and other countries, observes their inhabitants, studies the minutest details of their existence. In other words, he is under a twin obligation: continuous prospecting of the area of his native literature and repeated expeditions into the heart of foreign life and language. The literary gifts essential to the translator's work need, I think, to be supported to an even greater extent than in the case of original writing by enormous culture and knowledge. The translator must be not only an artist aware of his task in assimilating a foreign work, but also an informed reader of the literature of his own and other countries.

Before I end these brief remarks on the art of translation and the role of the translator, I would like to emphasize once again that only by appreciating the importance of his work can he make proper use of his gifts. The awareness that this work is both an enrichment of national culture and a bridge to other peoples imposes on the translator the obligation above all of adopting a personal attitude towards the work which he is proposing to translate. This same awareness prevents the dedicated translator from shrinking from any challenge. And the challenge is truly rewarding. To immerse oneself in the work of a man from another nation, perhaps another age, to catch the rhythm of his thoughts and then to track their course through words and phrases fashioned by other laws and customs and tuned to other melodies—it really is a fascinating adventure.

The distinguished Polish writer, Jan Parandowski, President of the Polish P.E.N. Center, has said: "The translator attains the highest dignity when he is aware of his mission as an honorable intermediary in the exchange of goods which the centuries and the nations have bestowed upon each other, when he understands his importance in intellectual life, when he is guided by the same loves and ambitions, the same hesitations, reflections and anxieties to which the author is subject, and when he has the same belief that he is working on something indispensable and indestructible that is worthy of respect—and fame."

Translation in Russia:

the Politics of Translation

Mirra Ginsburg

In my talk I will depart from the general tenor of the conference and speak, not about the intrinsic problems of the craft of translation, but of translation under the pressure of external forces. I suppose this talk might be titled "The Politics of Translation," since much of the time translation in Russia has had to function in a situation of stress and under pressure of conditions that had nothing to do with literature or translation as such.

In the field of translation, as in so many other fields, the situation in Russia is quite unique—deplorable in some respects, enviable in others. There has always been great interest in foreign—particularly European—cultures in Russia, perhaps partly as a result of Russia's relationship with the West. Russia has never really been viewed, either by herself or by Europeans, as a European nation, but as a kind of cross between Europe and Asia, or, by some Russians, as an entity entirely apart, with its own culture and its own inimitable destiny. For some reason—perhaps because of industrial lag—Russia, that giant country, has been afflicted with the psychology of a small nation. In relation to the West, there has been a constant interplay of arrogance and a sense of inferiority, admiration and hate, attraction and fear: constant attempts to compare and compete, and a constant struggle between those who would turn West and bring the West home and those who would turn inward and develop Russia's

351

own uniqueness, often preached with a mystical sense of messianic mission.

I experienced a good deal of this myself as a child. My family emigrated from Russia to Canada when I was very young and one day at school a teacher referred to Russia as a semi-Asiatic country. Typically, I was offended and protested that we were Europeans. I remember, it rankled for days.

When we were still in Russia, friends of my parents would speak approvingly of a man they respected as "a European," as though being merely Russian was equated with "primitive" and "provincial". One of my father's friends nicknamed him a "Scandinavian gentleman," and this was taken as a great compliment.

Among the pre-Revolutionary gentry, Russian was vulgar. They spoke French, and some affected an "English manner" to stress their superiority. Even Yevgeny Zamyatin, when he returned to revolutionary Russian after two years in England during World War I, cultivated the image of "an English gentleman" despite the fact that he wrote scathing satires on what he thought to be English life.

This conflict seems to persist to this day. Just recently a friend who had escaped from Russia less than two years ago spoke to me of a literary scholar we were discussing as "a man of European caliber" —"a European mind".

Historically, the political efforts to "open a window on the West" affected literature as well. In the seventeenth or early eighteenth century, the jester of Peter the Great translated Molière for presentation at court. Ambassadors to foreign courts brought home texts of plays they had seen performed, and these were kept in the archives of the central administration of foreign embassies.

In nineteenth-century Russian fiction, we often encounter well-born young ladies reading gallant and sentimental French romances. In the eighteenth and nineteenth centuries, Russian scholars—Lomonosov, Karamzin, and others—translated La Fontaine, Homer, Pope. Great Russian poets—Zhukovsky, Pushkin, Lermontov—made brilliant translations of English and German poets including Southey, Walter Scott, Byron, Uhland, Goethe, Heine and Schiller. Zhukovsky translated *Undine* from the German of Lamotte Fouqué, and made free translations of the Persian and Indian epics *Zohrab and Rustem* and *Nalas and Damayanti* from the German translations by Rukkert. He also did a translation of the *Odyssey* on the basis of an interlinear translation done for him in German by a German scholar.

Nineteenth-century fiction, predominantly French, German, and English, was widely translated, as were the foremost writings of Italy, Spain, and the Scandinavian countries. This was also true of the works of the ancient world. The literate Russian had access to the best, or much of the best, of the world's literature. It was this that made it possible for a man like Gorky, who knew no foreign languages, to have a close and extensive knowledge of foreign literatures.

As for the quality of the translation, that is another matter. Much of it was extremely bad. Much was bowdlerized in conformity with Russian puritanical standards, and also, perhaps, in order to pass the censors.

Material for translation was chosen more or less haphazardly, as it usually is in commercial publishing. Attempts to systematize the choice and improve the quality of the translations came later, after the revolution.

*

The revolution in Russia signalled an extraordinary liberation of energies, especially in the arts. At a time when the country lay in ruins, when supply, transportation, and other economic activities were all but paralyzed, there was a sudden burst of cultural activities and a proliferation of schools and movements in all the arts, including literature.

Zamyatin* describes the situation in Petersburg during this period. It was, he says, "the merry and grim winter of 1917-1918, when everything broke from its moorings and floated off somewhere into the unknown." "Streets without streetcars, long lines of people with sacks, miles and miles trudged daily on foot, improvised stoves, herring, oats ground in the coffee-mill. And, along with that, all sorts of world-shaking plans: the publication of all the classics of all periods and all countries . . . the staging of the entire history of the world in a series of plays." "Petersburg, swept out, emptied; boarded-up stores; houses pulled down bit by bit for firewood . . . Frayed cuffs; collars turned up; vests, sweaters . . . Fevered efforts to outstrip want, and ever new, transient, precarious plans." "In frozen, hungry, typhus-ridden Petersburg there raged a veritable cultural-educational epidemic." "We hurried to meetings, one meeting overlapping another." And always the same people, Gorky, usually the initiator and chairman (he was the veritable patron saint of literature in those days), Chukovsky, Blok, Zamyatin, Gumilyov, and others, less known in this country.

"It is difficult," says Zamyatin, "to repair plumbing or build a house, but it is very easy to build the Tower of Babel. And we were building the Tower of Babel."

*The quotations from Zamyatin are from *A Soviet Heretic: Essays by Yevgeny Zamyatin*. Edited and translated by Mirra Ginsburg (The University of Chicago Press, Chicago & London, 1970).

Part of this Tower was the World Literature publishing house, founded by Gorky in Petersburg in 1918, under the People's Commissariat of Education. And to quote Zamyatin again, "As though recalling its role as a window on Europe, Petersburg flung this window wide open, and European works, in the excellent translations provided by World Literature poured out in editions of many thousands to all ends of Russia."

Russia was exhausted and starving after years of war and revolution, but this almost fanatical band of writers and poets threw itself into the work of saving and expanding the cultural life of the country. Books were to be made available to the widest circle of readers, old and new. These were to be given the best of world literature in the best translations. The preparatory work was placed in the hands of a "learned council of experts," under Gorky's chairmanship. The literatures of various countries were entrusted to specialists in their fields. Indian, Chinese, Arabic and Mongolian literatures were represented by academicians. German literature was entrusted to Blok and two professors. Gumilyov was on the committee for French literature. Korney Chukovsky and Yevgeny Zamyatin were responsible for the English and American literatures. Each group drew up long lists of books, which were then discussed by the council. Among the writers considered were such diverse figures as Carlyle (*Sartor Resartus,* later rejected), Thackeray, Hawthorne, Oscar Wilde, Shaw, Jerome K. Jerome, Hall Caine, Barrie and Rex Beach.

Earlier translations were carefully evaluated and often found unacceptable, and the problem arose of finding good translators and establishing standards. The office of World Literature was besieged by hungry ladies and gentlemen, members of the dispossessed gentry who knew foreign languages and thought that this was enough to qualify them. They were asked to submit sample translations, and the results were invariably disastrous. Attempts were made to draw established writers into the work—Kuprin, Merezhkovsky, and others. Nothing came of that either. Chukovsky and Gumilyov were asked to formulate the criteria for translation of prose and poetry. Soon after that, Chukovsky wrote a small book, *The Principles of Literary Translation,* in which he attempted to define the problems and develop some basic principles. He was actively helped in this by Gorky, Blok, and others. This book was later expanded and went through many editions under the title, *The Noble Art.* It was a pioneering work in a field which later received a great deal of attention and study.

With few exceptions, the translators of the time were, as Chukovsky describes them, a "gray mass"—hacks, without any conception of literary values or the problems and responsibilities of translation.

This "gray mass" had to be trained and educated. This was not to be an academic exercise, but an urgent task, and it was launched with great energy and dedication.

A Studio of Literary Translation was organized in connection with World Literature, where lectures and courses and workshops were conducted by Zamyatin, Gumilyov, Lozinsky, a philologist who became one of the most brilliant translators in Soviet Russia, and others. The students were both practicing translators and newcomers, as well as some writers who learned a great deal about their own craft by analyzing that of translation.

World Literature planned to publish two series, a standard edition of some 1500 titles and a popular one of 2500 titles. The publishing house existed until 1924, and in that period it issued about 200 titles. The lists were later taken over by other publishing houses.

The Anglo-American section prepared the works of Byron, Coleridge, Jack London, Joseph Conrad, Poe, Southey, Walter Scott, Upton Sinclair, Mark Twain, Whitman, Wilde, Wells, Shaw, O. Henry and others, all of them with introductions analyzing the work and the background of the given author.

Interestingly enough, the World Literature publishing house was very soon put to the service of the Soviet regime's propaganda abroad. In 1919, at a time when paper, like everything else, was scarce and everything was done on a shoestring, a most magnificent catalogue was issued. Gorky's introduction concerning the significance and objectives of World Literature appeared in it in Russian, French, English and German. The books to be published were listed in Russian and in the given language. This catalogue was to be distributed in all the major countries of the world.

At the end of the 1920's came a new period. Political considerations became dominant in the choice of material for translation, particularly with regard to contemporary writers. This meant rigid selection, controlled by definite criteria. Translation was often used as a bribe "to win friends and influence people" and as a reward. During the thirties and forties particularly, this meant that only "friendly" writers were to be translated: those who expressed themselves publicly in terms favorable to Soviet Russia and the Soviet regime; those who supported the Communist movement abroad; those who exposed the evils of capitalism. Sometimes mistakes were made. Friendly writers were invited to Russia, where they were often appalled by the disparity between propaganda and reality. Those who wrote damning reports when they returned were immediately attacked and ostracized. When André Gide wrote a critical report on what he had seen in Russia, he was immediately dropped and attacked. When Hemingway, a great favorite in Russia, published *For Whom the Bell Tolls,* which did not flatter the Communists in the Spanish Civil War, he instantly became *non grata.** To a considerable extent, this is still true today, although the choice of material is now much broader.

Not only was the material for translation carefully controlled, it was also "edited," often severely. In this, the Soviet period continued the traditions of the eighteenth and nineteenth centuries. Early Russian translators of Shakespeare, for example, turned *Hamlet, Lear,* and other plays into propaganda for the divine right of the monarch and the glories of serving him. In one case, Lear's madness was altogether deleted, for how could a royal personage be mad? Care was also exercised to protect the delicate sensibilities of the reader from such vulgarisms as "marriage bed" or any references to the sensual passions. Zhukovsky, whose translations were excellent, nevertheless modestly transposed all physical references in the *Odyssey* and in the ballads he translated to a properly delicate spiritual sphere. In extreme cases, such words as "pants" or "breast" were deemed inadmissible, and you might read of a lady feeding her infant with her "bust," which for some reason was considered more delicate.

In Gogol's story, "The Nose," Major Kovalev wakes up one morning, looks into the mirror and discovers, to his horror, a smooth empty place on his face where the nose should be. In Russian literature, there is still an empty place where the genitals should be. And translators still dutifully castrate the texts they are working on to avoid shocking the reader with the vulgarisms of decadent Western literature.

I remember when Arthur Miller spoke here about his trips to the Soviet Union, he mentioned attending a Russian performance of *Under the Bridge,* which he could with difficulty recognize as his own. The family relationships of the leading characters were changed to eliminate the more "shocking" aspects of the erotic involvements.

This, of course, seems totally ludicrous, if not outrageous to us. Yet, in its less extreme form, it does reflect a valid problem that arises before the translator. In many cases, for example, we find ourselves compelled to modify the emotional tone of a passage because of a difference in the level of expression acceptable in the cultures concerned. What is dramatic in one language, may seem melodramatic in another. This is also true of the number or strength of adjectives one can use. The area of sexual explicitness is even

For Whom the Bell Tolls was not translated into Russian until a year ago. Today Hemingway's collected works are being published in the Soviet Union in Russian translation.

more sensitive. It seems to me that bringing to the reader material for which he is entirely unprepared might, perhaps, do more violence to the work than deletion or toning down. In any case, the answer is not too simple. I recently saw a Russian translation of Henry Miller's *Tropic of Cancer,* published in the United States and evidently held in stock for the day when it may be possible to bring it to Russia. The translation was pretty bad. But even apart from that, in Russian the four-letter words which we don't even notice any more because they have become a matter of daily usage are neither startling, nor revolutionary. They are so incongruous, so outside the normal experience of the reader that they are simply funny. And I am sure Henry Miller never intended that.

There has also been a good deal of mutilation of texts for political reasons. Points emphasized, changed, deleted, passages and chapters dropped, and so on.

In areas of no interest to the censors, however, translation has served a very useful, if not directly relevant function, and still does so to some extent. It became a refuge for writers who could not write without violating their conscience. This was especially true of poetry. Pasternak is an outstanding example. So is Zabolotsky, a fine, though lesser poet, and an excellent translator. So is Akhmatova. Just as some writers turned to historical fiction, often writing about the present under the guise of the past, so translators turned to fields where they could function without compromise. Pasternak translated Shakespeare, Goethe, Verlaine, Byron, Keats, Rilke, and Georgian poets. Zabolotsky translated *The Tale of Igor's Host,* Georgian poets, old and modern, and German poetry. Akhmatova translated Oriental, West-European , Latvian and Jewish poets. She also edited a collection of Korean classical poetry. It must be said, however, that politics were not the only reason for their doing this work, since the translation of poetry by poets is an old tradition in Russia. And it was not for political reasons that Samuel Marshak, who was not a great poet himself, produced his excellent translations of Shakespeare's sonnets, of Blake and Burns, or that Chukovsky translated Whitman and Kipling and children's verse.

Another political fact has influenced the field of translation. Russia is a multi-national state. The number of ethnic groups in Russia is estimated at anywhere from one to two hundred. Some of them, like the Georgians, Armenians, Tadzhiks and others have old cultures and rich literatures. A large number of others, especially in north Siberia and the Soviet Far East, had no writing and no written literatures. An intensive effort was made under the Soviet regime to develop alphabets and writing for these cultures. Again, a good deal of the motivation has been political. Ideology cannot be instilled without the written word. The government's campaign to extirpate religion, to compel nomadic peoples to a settled existence, to collectivize even the native fishermen and hunters of remote areas, and to destroy resistance to change in the traditional ways of life could not succeed without written means of communication. And so writing and literacy became a major goal.

In this case, as in many others, literacy was often of dubious benefit. Many of these peoples had magnificent oral literatures which, of course, were directly bound up with their religions. The forcible destruction of religion and the "modernization" of "backward areas" meant the loss of enormous literary wealth, which ethnologists and folklorists today are hurriedly trying to minimize by recording what is still remembered by the old. The younger people have been to school. Some have had secondary and higher education. Many have become doctors, teachers, scientists. Some have become writers, to whom the Soviet regime points with great pride. Unfortunately, in this area the spiritual impoverishment is especially glaring. What these ravished cultures were given was reason—a very crude kind of reason— in place of wisdom; facts—or what pass for facts—in place of truth; and dogma in place of imagination. And it was now Lenin and Stalin in place of the Upper Spirit Topal Oyka, and Trotskyites and foreign imperialists in place of the man-eating Ninwits. Most of the new writers, with very few exceptions, turn out the dreariest and crudest kind of obedient socialist realism. But the poetry is often better than the prose, perhaps because the sources of poetry are so much closer to the sources of folk literature.

The new writers are widely translated into Russian. There are translations from Kazakh, Tatar, Chukchi, Bashkir, Kirghiz, Yakut, Ossetin, and other languages. Russian works, new and old, as well as foreign works, are translated into these languages. Some of the national works are translated into the languages of other nationalities. The Soviet Literary Encyclopedia boasts that more translations are published in the Soviet Union than in any other country in the world. Translation in Russia is done from and into more than one hundred languages, and more than half of the books published in Russia are translations.

There is an increasing amount of translation from African and Asian languages into Russian, and often from Russian into these languages, though mostly of political literature. A tremendous number of dictionaries is constantly being published in the languages of Russia, Europe, Africa and Asia.

Sections on translation exist in a number of colleges, usually in the foreign-language departments and sometimes in departments of fine literature. The study of languages generally has expanded since Stalin's death. The number of contemporary European and American works translated has also increased, and while the choices are still governed to a large extent by political considerations, they are somewhat more liberal and flexible.

And so, for a variety of reasons, first cultural, and then political, and lately, whenever the pressure relaxes, cultural as well, translation has become an enormously important area of literary life in Russia. During the past two decades, particularly, the problems of translation have received increasing attention. Linguists, literary scholars, writers, and translators have written widely about various aspects of the field. The theoretical work which began with the little book of principles by Gumilyov and Chukovsky has grown far beyond the original expectations of the founders. Dozens of works have been published in various languages and various parts of Russia, examining the many problems of language, communication, meaning, and various methods and approaches to re-creating a work in another language. Chukovsky continued to write in the field until the end, expanding and revising his book on *The Noble Art*. There have been numerous collections of essays on problems general and specific. One series is titled *The Craft of Translation,* another, *The Translator's Notebooks.* In addition to the work done in European Russia, individual studies have appeared in the Ukraine, Byelorussia, Georgia, Armenia, Kazakhstan, Tadzhikistan, Uzbekistan and Azerbaidzhan.

Various schools and theories of translation have come and gone.

Some of the important things that have come out of all this are a consciousness of craft, a considerable body of fine translators, a large and often excellently-rendered literature in translation, and, perhaps as important as all these, an attitude toward the translator as a valued creative artist.

Lest all this sound much rosier than the facts, let me add:

— despite the emergence of a corps of excellent translators, the mass of translations is still quite gray.

— translators are respected, but poorly paid. Like original writers, they are paid not by the size of the book or by royalties, but by the size of the printing. An easy little book printed in large quantity will pay more than a very difficult work issued in a relatively small edition. (And their editions run from ten thousand anywhere to two hundred thousand.)

— while the choice of works to be translated is somewhat broader, it is still severely limited by political considerations—especially with

regard to modern works. Here, too, the size of the printing is manipu-
lated at will, so that some works are sure to reach a small audience.
"Moral" censorship is still in force, and works are still severely edited.

— just as many writers have written "for the drawer," so translators
also translate "for the drawer"—or, in recent years, for underground
publication by "Samizdat"—the "home publishing" so widely current
today. A work is typed in several copies and distributed among
friends. They in turn produce more copies, and so on—in a geometric
progression. And so, many works officially unavailable actually gain
a large circle of readers. The works of Ezra Pound, Allen Ginsberg,
Ferlinghetti and others are circulated widely in "Samizdat" editions.
So is Orwell (*1984* and *Animal Farm*); I have found (unacknowledged)
quotations and ideas from *1984* slipped into a science-fiction story
by a writer not particularly notorious for opposition moods.

On the whole, despite the continued restrictions, censorship, and
manipulation of availability, more and more contemporary literature
is being translated and published officially in Soviet Russia. In the
last ten or fifteen years, Russian readers have gradually been allowed
access to a wide range of foreign writing, including works by such
diverse writers as Joyce (early works), Kafka (in infinitesimal doses),
Mauriac, Hesse, Camus, Sarraute, Böll, Grass, Golding *(Lord of the
Flies)*, Graham Greene, Faulkner, Robert Penn Warren, Capote, Salinger, Updike, Cheever, Vonnegut, Carson McCullers, Chinese and
Japanese writers, new and old. Some of the choices are easy to understand, some rather surprising. (Among the latter—the large and numerous editions of what is essentially non-ideological literature of play
—science-fiction and detective and murder mysteries by American
and other writers, which are enormously popular in the Soviet Union.)

It will be interesting to see what effect this expansion of the literary horizon will have on technique, approaches, and range of subject
matter if and when the Russian writer ever regains the opportunity
to learn to write again. The translator may then prove to have been
an important factor in helping Russian literature find its way back
to itself.

On the Impossibility of Translation

Robert Payne

It seems to me that the world's languages all resemble infinitely complicated grids, and the basic patterns of these grids scarcely ever coincide, and even the units that make up the grid—the words and the silences—for it is worth remembering that all written languages have words and spaces between the words—even these words and these silences never or very rarely coincide. If a word in one language appears to correspond to a word in another language, then we should be on our guard. And it can be taken almost as a general rule that coincidence does not take place, that something else, something other, takes place.

Let us pause for a moment at the concept of coincidence. "Dog" = *Hund* = *chien* = *sobaka,* equals, and one can go on for ever. There should be an ideal platonic dog just as there should be an ideal platonic God, but it is not easy as all that. When a German thinks of a dog, *Hund,* he is not necessarily thinking of the same kind of an animal as a Frenchman when he thinks of a *chien* or a Russian when he thinks of a *sobaka.* The shape, the general picture he forms in his mind is quite different. The fox terrier, the dachshund, the borzoi, the pekingese are very different, and the general concept of dog is so broad that it has to be reshaped every time we think of it except on those comparatively rare occasions when we talk about dogs in the most general terms, when we make generalities about them; thus:

361

all dogs are carnivorous. All dogs are not carnivorous. All cats eat
fish. But this is not true either, for cats exist in certain parts of Per-
sia where there are no rivers, no streams, and therefore no fish. The
world is made up of particulars, and language itself is the human
response to all these particulars, a response accumulating over thousands of years and coming to a point every time anyone opens his
mouth and says anything at all about these countless particulars.

Or let us take another tack. We were talking about coincidence,
and I have suggested that "dog" = *Hund* = *chien* = *sobaka* are not
coincidental. Even when the words are alike, when they coincide
exactly in the shape of their letters, it happens very often that they
do not coincide in meaning. The French *conscience* does not mean
conscience, though it is spelt in exactly the same way and derives
historically from the same roots. *Conscience* is like one of those
colored balloons filled with many other balloons of different colors.
No coincidence there. Or if we take the hieroglyphic languages
like Chinese and ancient Egyptian. In ancient Egyptian there is
a little drawing of a man kneeling and raising his arms, and this
quite obviously means prayer. A drawing so similar that it might be
taken for coincidence occurs in Chinese, and this also means prayer
or a man praying. But there exists demonstrable evidence that when
an Egyptian prayed, his prayer, the nature of his prayer, was very
different from the prayer, the nature of a prayer, of a Chinese, for
the Egyptian invariably worshipped the sun in one or other of its
aspects, and the Chinese had no particular feeling for the sun. What
they worshipped above all was Heaven, *Tien,* which was a considerably more complex idea. The coincidence is accidental. The Chinese
character for growth was a plant pushing its way up through the
ground; so it was in ancient Egyptian, and here, I believe, the coincidence is *not* accidental. Some symbol, some word for growth is, in
a very real sense, common in all languages. We know what growth
is. We translate the Chinese symbol into the Egyptian symbol or
even the English symbol "growth," but are there any other coin-
cidences? Birth and death, perhaps, though I suspect that the associations of death, its shape, its energy, its colors, are inevitably
different in different cultures.

What I am suggesting is that whenever we translate exactly and
accurately, it is a coincidence, not in the way we have been using
the word coincidence, but in the sense of the purest accident. And
the task of the translator is to move sure-footedly among these
accidents. He cannot do this logically. He cannot assert that a
grammatical construction in one language corresponds to a gram-

matical construction in another. They don't. *Parce que* does not
quite mean "because," but it is near enough. We have in English only
the most rudimentary conception of the subjunctive; the French are
born subjunctivists. A great deal of French is quite simply untranslatable in English. Each language arises out of a different experience,
and if they overlap, that is another accident. It would be perfectly
possible to imagine two languages which do not overlap: incommun-
icable to one another, untranslatable into one another. This can, of
course, happen with dialects of the same language. A man from
Brooklyn may speak an English which is totally incomprehensible to
you and to me. Or one can imagine an anti-language made up of the
shapes of the silences enclosed between the letters, and how would
you translate into that?

All we have learned from the grammar-books is wrong, and deadly
wrong. We all know now that language is fluid, living, changeable,
turbulent and untameable as life itself. It is not there when you
look at it because it does not keep still; the river of Heraclitus pours
forever through our mouths and our pens. The word I uttered a
moment ago in a language known to us is already in process of
becoming another word; it is dying, or changing. Ripeness is all.
Growth is all. When a word dies, another word does not always take
its place.

I once used the phrase "a scurry of snow," and my father, an
inveterate reader of dictionaries, discovered that the noun "scurry"
never had any existence until I invented it, for it is credited to me.
But I did *not* invent it. It was a slip of the pen, or I thought the
word existed as a noun, and anyway it was the merest accident,
and though I am pleased that the word is now and forever henceforth credited to me, it is for the basest of reasons: I had always
vaguely hoped to get into the dictionary somehow. But the phrase
"the scurry of snow" raises many questions. How many words are
invented by a slip of a pen, or because a man thought the word
existed, or simply by accident? I suspect that all words began
accidentally and continued to go on living by a series of accidents.
When Adam first said the word "apple," did he know what he was
saying? He may have meant something else altogether, he may in
fact have meant: 'Look out, that's dangerous." Instead he said
"apple," and we know what happened.

Another problem. I shall probably use the words "a scurry of
snow" again in a book that will be translated. What is the equivalent,
the coincident, of "scurry of snow" in Russian, Greek, Hebrew,
Chinese, Danish? Translators will have a good deal of trouble. It is
a very new word, and does not appear in foreign dictionaries, at

least not yet. I shall look very carefully to see how they translate it
—this word, this obstinate ghost, the only word in the dictionary
which is mine, even though it does not really exist.

We have said that the words and the silences do not coincide except for a very few words like *growth,* and perhaps the parts of the
body, like *face, hands, feet, shoulder, tongue, hair, heart,* though I am
somewhat doubtful about all of these. *Sky,* too, in whatever language, is suspect, for each culture seems to have a different concept
of *sky.* Sky, which seems to be common to all cultures, is in fact
colored by each culture, by its history, by its myths, by its very location. A Russian sky is not an English sky; a New York sky, those
three or four inches which you are permitted to see between the sky-
scrapers, is not the same as the wide arching sky seen over the deserts
of Arabia, or by a man standing on a small ship in the Pacific.

I think this is important: we are so accustomed to the illusion
that words mean what they say, or seem to say, when in fact they are
continually changing their meanings, skipping round corners, altering
their shapes, gathering weight or losing weight according to the
emphasis of the words near them, and offering to translators the
impossible task of rendering one word by an equivalent, which simply
is not an equivalent. This is commonly known as torture.

In spite of this quite intolerable burden imposed on translators,
I believe that on some rare occasions translation does succeed brilliantly, beyond all expectation, and sometimes even beyond all
possibility. The impossible becomes possible only because the problem contains its own solution. Ivan Morris has pointed out that, in
the *Manifesto on Translation,* we had written that the translator
should somehow suggest the rhythm and structure of the original
and write in a style that conveys the style of the original. He pointed
out that Arthur Waley's translation of the *Tale of Genji* was not following the structure or rhythm of the original. I think he was being a
little pedantic there because it does seem to me that one thing that
Waley did absolutely superlatively was to suggest the illusion of an
original. This is obviously true, since Japanese sentences are laby-
rinths which have to be unravelled while Arthur Waley's English
sentences are always very clear. But I am quite certain that Waley's
English is not ordinary English. Clear, yes; but there are subtleties
and echoes and the sense of another language. We have the illusion
that we have been given a Japanese work which has mysteriously
elected to be written in English. From this point, it just becomes a
magician's game. You can only do it by magic. Certainly there is
very good evidence that Waley was a magician. Waley would read a
whole paragraph (except there are no paragraphs in Japanese), and

then he would forget the text and reconstruct the feeling and the imagery in English. Occasionally a word got left out, occasionally a little bit was put in, but what he did in effect was a kind of transformation act. He read it, he absorbed it, he dreamt it, he felt it, and then having absorbed it, an hour later he disgorged it. And the point is that it works and it probably is the only way it does work.

APPENDIX

Biographical Sketches

VICTOR ALBA (PEDRO PAGES) was born in Spain and educated at the University of Barcelona. He is now a citizen of Mexico, where he makes his home, and is the author of many books on Latin American history and politics. He is also a Lecturer in Political Science at Kent State University. Since his native tongue is Catalan, he takes a special interest in the problem of getting translations made from the "small languages."

SIDNEY ALEXANDER is the translator of Guicciardini's monumental *History of Italy,* for which he won the P.E.N. Translation Prize in 1970. His own books include *The Hand of Michelangelo, Michelangelo the Florentine* and *The Celluloid Asylum.* His short stories and articles have been published in dozens of magazines and his poems in many anthologies. He has lived in Florence for the past fifteen years and is currently Associate Professor of Renaissance History, Fine Arts and Literature in the Florence branches of both Syracuse and Stanford Universities.

GEORGE D. ASTLEY was educated at Haileybury College and Reading University. He was an actor on the London stage and a major in World War II. In January of 1971 he was appointed a Chevalier of the French *Ordre National du Mérite.* He has been with the Society of Authors for sixteen years, until recently as Registrar and now as Joint Secretary. He is also co-founder and director of The Translators' Association in London.

HELMUT BRAEM, born in Hanover, has been involved in the theatre both as actor and director and has written monographs on Eugene O'Neill and Edward Albee. He is co-author of *German Literature in the Twentieth Century* and his translations include works by Faulkner, Henry James and William Carlos Williams. Mr. Braem is married to the novelist, critic, and translator, Elizabeth Kaiser, and is president of the Association of German-Speaking Translators of Literary and Scientific Works. He has also edited a number of anthologies, among which is *American Short Stories.*

PIERRE BRODIN, born in Paris, has spent his life in the service of literature as author, teacher and translator. He is the holder of many university titles and five decorations and has been the Director of Studies at the *Lycée Français* in New York ever since its founding in 1935. He is the author of many books on history and literature and was the translator, for the Office of War Information, of three books by American writers.

MOURA BUDBERG got her first job as a translator after the October Revolution in 1917, in the Russian publishing house, World Literature, that Gorky had founded, and she rejoiced in his battle to preserve the cultural life of Russia. An aristocrat, she lost all her possessions in the Revolution except her self-possession, and as a citizen of the world, she has remained a link between Russia and the West. Among her many translations are *The Three Sisters* for Laurence Olivier's National Theater and *The Sea Gull* for Sidney Lumet's film.

AMIYA CHAKRAVARTY was born in Bengal and received a doctorate in philosophy at Oxford. He was for a time the literary secretary of Rabindranath Tagore, and for two years he accompanied Mahatma Gandhi on his peace marches through Indian villages. In 1970, Dr. Chakravarty received the Padma Bhushan, the highest award bestowed on eminent citizens by the Government of India. He has written twelve volumes of poetry and prose in Bengali, and his books in English include *The Dynasts and Post-war Poetry* and *A Tagore Reader*.

SHIH-HSIANG CHEN is Professor of Chinese and Comparative Literature at the University of California at Berkeley, as well as chairman of the Department of Oriental Languages and editor-in-chief of the University's translation series of Middle Chinese Dynastic Histories. Dr. Chen is also the director of the current Chinese Language Project at Berkeley and was the recipient of a Guggenheim fellowship in Chinese literature. His publications include *Modern Chinese Poetry* and *Ku Kai-Chih,* a biography, as well as many other works of literary criticism and philology in English, Chinese, French and Japanese.

JOY CHUTE, who signs her novels and short stories as B. J. Chute, was born in Minnesota and now lives in New York. She was president of American P.E.N. from 1959 to 1961 and was a judge of its Translation Prize Award in 1964. She has twice been a judge in the National Book Awards and is an Adjunct Associate Professor at Barnard College. Miss Chute's many published works include two collections of short stories and four novels, one of which, *Greenwillow,* was made into a Broadway musical in 1960.

DALE S. CUNNINGHAM did his undergraduate work at Hamilton College and post-graduate study at Princeton and the Sorbonne. A teacher, writer and translator, he has been since 1965 the director of "Into English Translations," an organization which handles medical and technical writing, editing and translating, and he is the newly elected president of the American Translators Association.

LEON DAMAS was educated in Martinique and then in Paris. Along with Aimé Césaire and Léopold Sédar Senghor he published the famous journal, *L'Etudiant noir,* and his collection of poems, *Pigments,* in 1937, was the first substantial artistic success of the champions of *négritude*. Since then he has traveled extensively, including several cultural missions, and has written stories, poems and essays that show his profound concern for the principle upon which he has based his literary career.

GUY DANIELS attended the University of Iowa, from which he graduated *summa cum laude*. His graduate work was interrupted by World War II, when he entered the Navy, and he wrote his first poems (published in *New Directions - 8*) in a Navy hospital. A full-time writer and translator since 1952, he is the author of a book of poems and a recent novel, *Progress U.S.A.* His many translations include Stendhal's *Racine and Shakespeare*, *The Complete Plays of Vladimir Mayakovsky*, *15 Fables of Krylov*, Leskov's *The Wild Beast* and *Russian Comic Fiction*.

IVAN ELAGIN, poet and translator, is Associate Professor of Russian Literature at the University of Pittsburgh. He has written four books of lyrics in Russian, some of them included in the London publication, *Anthology of Modern Russian Poetry*. He translated the works of various American poets into Russian for broadcasting over the Voice of America, and he did the Russian translation of *John Brown's Body* by Stephen Vincent Benét.

CHARLES BRACELEN FLOOD is the author of several novels and of a recently published study of the Vietnam War, *The War of the Innocents*. His articles and short stories have appeared in many periodicals. He is a member of the governing boards of the Authors League and the Authors Guild. From May 1969 to May 1971 he served as president of the American Center of P.E.N., and he gave his enthusiastic support to the P.E.N. Translators Conference held in May of 1970.

FRANCES FRENAYE was educated at Bryn Mawr College and then studied at the American Academy in Rome. She lived six years in Rome and Paris, and since 1961 she has worked for the *Istituto Italiano di Cultura* in New York. Her translations from the French include the work of Lenormand, Balzac, Zola, Troyat and Elie Wiesel, and those from the Italian include Silone, Alvaro, Marotta, Bachelli, Croce and Carlo Levi.

LEWIS GALANTIERE, for nearly half a century, has had one foot in international affairs and the other in literary. He began translating from French and German in the 1920's with versions of Cocteau, Wassermann and Mauriac, among many others. He went on to do Saint-Exupéry's *Wind, Sand and Stars* and, for the stage, Anouilh's *Antigone*. His *Goncourt Journals* remains a standard text. He was a director of the American Translators Association from 1962 to 1965, and, as president of the American P.E.N., organized the XXXIV International P.E.N. Congress, held in New York in June, 1966.

MIRRA GINSBURG was born in Russia, later moving to Canada and then to New York. Russian has remained her beloved language, while she originally learned English by reading poetry with the aid of a dictionary. Her many translations from the Russian include four works by Bulgakov, stories and essays by Zamyatin, two collections of Soviet science fiction, one of satires, folk tales from Siberia, fables and a picture book for children.

ELSA GRESS (WRIGHT) is an author, playwright and critic. She is also a translator and has not only translated Danish into English but has translated English, French and German into Danish. Miss Gress is a member of the board of the Danish Writers Union and president of Danish P.E.N.

GERALD GROSS has been interested in translation for the many years he has been in book publishing. He is Senior Vice President at the Macmillan Company, where he is in charge of the General Books Division, and before that he was Vice President at Pantheon Books. He has lectured at Columbia University and New

York University and was a founding member of the advisory board of The National Translation Center.

RICHARD HOWARD, born in Ohio, was educated at Columbia University and at the Sorbonne. One of his four books of poetry, *Untitled Subjects,* won the Pulitzer Prize for 1970, and his critical study of modern American poetry, *Alone with America,* was nominated for a National Book Award in 1969. He has translated over 150 works from the French, including the war memoirs of de Gaulle, books by Gide, Cocteau, Giradoux, Mauriac, Leiris, Camus, Sartre and the "New Novelists," and speculative works by Barthes, Foucault and Deleuze.

IRVING HOWE is Distinguished Professor of English at the City University of New York. He is the author of numerous critical works, including *Politics and the Novel, Thomas Hardy: A Critical Study* and *The Decline of the New.* He is co-editor with Eliezer Greenberg of *A Treasury of Yiddish Stories* and *A Treasury of Yiddish Poetry.*

YOUNGHILL KANG was born in Korea and educated in Asia, Europe and the United States. He has taught in various American universities and has been a member of the staff of the Metropolitan Museum of Art (with Alan Priest in the Oriental Department) and the Yale University Library. Dr. Kang has written two novels and a play; *The Grass Roof,* his study of his Korean childhood, was recently reprinted with an introduction by Rebecca West. He has been translating the works of a Zen priest, *Meditations of the Lover* (Yonsei Press, Seoul).

FRANCES KEENE is Chairman of the English Department of the Mannes College of Music in New York and Vice Chairman of the Translation Committee of the American Center of P.E.N. Her anthology, *Neither Liberty Nor Bread,* dealing with events under Fascism, has just been reissued, and her translations from the Italian include the works of Vittorini, Pavese, Borgese and Salvemini.

BRENDAN KENNELLY was born in Dublin, where he is now Fellow and Associate Professor of English at Trinity College and Dean of Gaelic Studies. He is the author of several books of poetry (his latest, *Selected Poems,* appeared in 1969) and in 1970 he completed the Penguin anthology of Irish Verse. He has twice recorded his own poems for Harvard University and has given readings in England, Ireland and the United States in both English and Gaelic. In 1967 he received the AE Memorial Prize, and he ranks as one of Ireland's leading translators from the Gaelic.

THOMAS LASK was born in London and chiefly educated in the United States. As a teacher, a staff member of The New York Times Book Review, and now as a daily reviewer for that newspaper, Mr. Lask has long been involved, in a practical functioning way, in the problems of translation of literary works in all languages. He is also the editor of *The New York Times Book of Verse.*

JOHN MACRAE III, a native New Yorker, has spent most of his working life editing books. He was first with Harper & Row and is now with E. P. Dutton, where he has been president since 1969. Both as a member of the P.E.N. Translation Committee and in his own firm, Mr. Macrae works to secure the widest possible readership for important foreign authors. Aside from books and authors, his major interest is ecology and he is an active member of the Mid-Atlantic Conservation Council and the Sierra Club.

FRANK MACSHANE is a writer and critic, his latest book being a study of Ford Madox Ford. He is also a translator and has done a number of books by the Chilean writer, Miguel Serrano. He started a translation seminar in the writing program of the School of the Arts at Columbia University. This seminar, now in its third year, has involved the cooperation of some of the leading translators of this country and abroad, including D. S. Carne-Ross, Richmond Lattimore, W. S. Merwin, Gregory Rabassa, William Jay Smith and Willard R. Trask.

CLARA MALRAUX, journalist, author and translator, was born in Paris. She married André Malraux in 1921 and shared many of his early adventures, particularly his voyage of discovery of Cambodian art. They were later divorced. During World War II, Mme. Malraux was active in the Maquis, working with the French Resistance. She continues to live in Paris, where she has done her many translations. Her own books include, *Par le plus long chemin, Contes de Perse, Java, Bali* and *Le bruit de nos pas.*

JOHN MISH is Chief of the Slavonic Division and Chief of the Oriental Division in The New York Public Library. Educated in the Universities of Breslau and Berlin, he taught Japanese and Chinese in many universities including Warsaw and Tokyo. He is an authority on Manchu, a translator of Japanese scientific journals, and fluent in some twenty other languages, including Malay, Arabic, Hindi, Sanskrit, Armenian and Basque.

IVAN MORRIS was educated both in England and the United States; at London's School of Oriental and African Studies he was a student of Arthur Waley. After working in the B.B.C. and the British Foreign Office, he studied in Japan and now teaches in the Department of East Asian Languages and Cultures at Columbia University. He has translated many works from Japanese, including the two-volume edition of *The Pillow Book of Sei Shonagon* and *The Temple of the Golden Pavilion* by Yukio Mishima. His own books include a study of *The Tale of Genji* and a memoir of Arthur Waley.

HELEN MUCHNIC, translator, scholar and critic, is Professor Emeritus of Smith College, where she taught first in the English Department and then as professor of Russian language and literature. She has also taught at Harvard, Yale and the University of Toronto. She has contributed articles and reviews to many journals and is the author of *Dostoevsky's English Reputation, 1881-1936, An Introduction to Russian Literature* and *From Gorky to Pasternak.* Her latest book is *Russian Writers: Notes & Essays.*

ROBERT PAYNE was born in Cornwall, England. He has been war correspondent, shipwright, armaments officer, and a professor in Chinese universities and in Alabama. The most recent of his many published works are his biographies of Gandhi and André Malraux, and among his many translations is an anthology of Chinese poetry, *The White Pony.* As chairman of the Translation Committee of the American P.E.N., Mr. Payne was the organizer of the Translation Conference of 1970.

FERNANDA SOTTSASS PIVANO, who was born in Genoa, found that an interest in American literature could be used as a kind of shield against Fascism, a discovery she shared with Cesare Pavese. Soon after the war she became established as a translator and translated Melville, Dos Passos and Hemingway. She wrote a book about American literature called *La balena bianca* (the white whale) and a biography of William Faulkner. More recently she has put out an anthology of translated "beat" poetry and befriended Kerouac and Ginsberg on their travels.

THEODORE M. PURDY has served as an editor at Macmillan and Appleton-Century, as Vice President at Putnam and President at Coward-McCann, and is now a consultant and Contributing Editor for Hawthorn and Meredith. He has translated works of Gobineau, Paul Morand and other European writers. He was a delegate to the Warsaw Translation Conference of 1958. Two years later he became the first chairman of the Translation Committee of the American Center of P.E.N., a post he held for four years.

GEORGE QUASHA, poet, editor and translator, teaches contemporary poetry at the State University of New York at Stony Brook. His books of poetry include *Five Blind Men* and *Delphine Transpositions,* and his transposition from Rilke's *Duino Elegies* received the American Literary Anthology Award. He edited an anthology of experimental poetry called *Open Poetry* and is also the editor of *STONY BROOK/Metapoetry,* which received a P.E.N. Citation for Translation in 1969.

GREGORY RABASSA graduated from Dartmouth College and served during World War II as a staff sergeant in North Africa and Italy. At present he is Professor of Romance Languages at Queens College, City University of New York. His translation of *Hopscotch* by Julio Cortázar received the National Book Award in 1967, and that of *One Hundred Years of Solitude* by Gabriel Garcia Márquez was nominated for an Award in 1971. Among the other authors he has translated are Asturias, Vargas Llosa, Mujica-Lainez and Piñon. He is the author of *The Negro in Brazilian Fiction* and was Associate Editor of *Odyssey Review.*

RAJA RAO, born in Mysore of an ancient Brahmin family, took his degree in English and history at Madras University and later studied at the Sorbonne under Professor Cazamian. He has traveled extensively, first in India and then over the greater part of the world, and his first stories were written in French and English. He is the author of *Kanthapura, The Cow of the Barricades, The Serpent and the Rope* and *The Cat and Shakespeare.* Like Dr. Chakravarty he received the Padma Bhushan Award, and he currently teaches at the University of Texas.

GEORGE REAVEY was educated in Belfast, in London, and at Cambridge University. He was in Russia in the first year of the Revolution and later returned as a Press Attaché. As a Rockefeller Fellow, he did research in Russian literature at Columbia and Stanford. His poetry has been published in many countries, and as editor and translator he has produced over twenty books from the French and Russian. He has been closely associated with Dylan Thomas, Boris Pasternak and Samuel Beckett and has translated works by major Russian writers from Gogol to Yevtushenko.

MURIEL RUKEYSER, poet, teacher and biographer, has just published her latest book, *The Traces of Thomas Hariot.* She began translating when she was fifteen, with an effort to turn Swinburne into French, and in college she did an English version of *Season in Hell.* Philip Rahv asked her to translate Aragon; Brecht himself asked her to translate Brecht. She has tried many things, ranging from Lucretius to a group of poems by Moa Tetua from the Marquesan. She has done the *Selected Poems* of Gunnar Ekelöf and translated three works by Octavio Paz, *Selected Poems, Sun Stone* and *Configurations*.

ISAAC BASHEVIS SINGER was born in Poland and came to the United States in 1935. He worked with Hebrew and Yiddish publications in Poland and with the *Jewish Daily Forward* in New York, and all his short stories and novels are written in Yiddish. They have been translated into English by a variety of writers with the help of the author himself, and so powerful is his control of the material that all the translations speak with a single voice.

KRYSTYNA TARNOWSKA was a very young woman at the outbreak of World War II but already engaged on her first translations from the English. Since then she has become one of Poland's foremost translators and thus able to translate books largely of her own choosing. These include Sterne's *Tristram Shandy*, Mark Twain's *Huckleberry Finn* and Thomas Wolfe's *Look Homeward, Angel*. She has translated works by Defoe, Dickens, Hemingway, Steinbeck, James Baldwin, Malcolm Lowry, Iris Murdoch and many others. She was given the first Marian Kister Memorial Award in 1964 and the translation prize of the Polish P.E.N. in 1967.

JULIUSZ ZULAWSKI, born in Poland, spent five years in a German prison camp. During his long career, he has written novels, biographies, poems, essays and short stories. He has translated more than fifty English and American poets, beginning with Spenser, Shakespeare and Milton, continuing through Pope, Keats, Browning and Whitman to Hart Crane and Robert Frost, and is currently working on a translation of Yeats. He received the translation prize of the Polish P.E.N. in 1969 and the Marian Kister Memorial Award in 1970.

RESOLUTION

The Translation Committee of the American P.E.N. has been holding a series of meetings on questions arising from translation. We feel that a new attitude towards translators is long overdue, and we have drawn up a list of nine urgent recommendations for the attention of translators and publishers.

Since the translator is the re-creator of a work, which is only as good as his final rendering, we believe he should be given *continuing* rights in the income arising from his work. We believe it is to the advantage of the publisher to extend to him these benefits. In this way publishers will attract more qualified translators and writers of proved literary ability, and at the same time improve the level of contemporary translations.

The P.E.N. Translation Committee believes that it is in the interests of publishers and translators alike that the following nine principles should be generally heeded in all agreements drawn up between them:

1. Translators shall receive contracts similar to those which are entered upon with authors.

2. The translator shall enjoy a *continuing* share in all the earnings of his work.

3. All payments made to translators shall be considered as installments against future earnings.

4. The translator's share in the royalties and subsidiary rights shall not be less than the equivalent of one third of the author's.

5. The copyright of the translation shall be in the name of the translator, and it shall be the publisher's responsibility to renew the copyright in his name.

6. The publisher shall make no changes in the copy without the approval of the translator.

7. The name of the translator shall be prominently displayed on the jacket, the title page and on all publicity concerning the work.

8. The translator shall receive ten or more free copies of his published translation.

9. The translator and the publisher shall agree that any dispute arising from the contract shall be referred to the American Arbitration Board, and their decision shall be binding.

MANIFESTO ON TRANSLATION

A Call for Action. The time has come for translators to come out into the open and to agree on a common course of action. For too long they have been the lost children in the enchanted forest of literature. Their names are usually forgotten, they are grotesquely underpaid, and their services, however skilfully rendered, are regarded with the slightly patronizing and pitying respect formerly reserved for junior housemaids.

Our culture, and indeed all cultures, are thoroughly rooted in translation, and the translator is the unacknowledged vehicle by which civilizations are brought about. We could have no Bible without Tyndale, no Proust without Scott-Moncrieff, no *Tale of Genji* without Arthur Waley. Most of what we know of the past has come to us through translation, and much of our future will inevitably depend on translation. We are the heirs of all the cultures of the past only because the translators have made these cultures available, and without the translator, the lost child, we are all lost.

Too often the translator is brushed aside as though he were some mechanical contrivance adept at converting one language into another. Since he is often poor, it is assumed that he came to his poverty honorably; and his name, if it appears at all, is usually printed in small type, in accordance with his reputation for humility. Reviewers rarely notice his existence. Publishers in their advertisements rarely pay any attention to him. Since the reviewer is the public's sole guide to the quality of the translation, and since only the publisher can give prominence to the translator's name, he remains largely anonymous and the quality of his work is unknown. As a consequence, the translator finds himself far too often in a shadowy no man's land, where he is scarcely distinguishable from the shadows.

Who knows the names of translators? Who cares? Yet the names deserve to be known, and it is necessary that we should care about them. It is absurd that they should be relegated to their own private no man's land, with no court of appeal and without recourse to the usual benefices reserved for authors. They are the proletarians of literature with nothing to lose but their chains.

The duties of translators are well known. Since the time of the first translators, they have always agreed that their task was to make a faithful rendering of the works they are translating. They know that it is not enough to convey the substance of these originals accurately; they must employ all their gifts of imagination and resourcefulness to make versions which mirror the original rhythms, assonances, structure and style. A sentence in Japanese, for example, has to be examined patiently, broken up into its separate parts and then refashioned before it can be expressed in English; and what is true of Japanese is equally true of all oriental languages, and to a lesser extent of all modern European languages. Translation is therefore reconstruction and re-creation, a creative act of immense difficulty and complexity. A translator may spend hours unraveling and recreating a single paragraph. He must somehow suggest the rhythm and structure of the original, and write in a style that conveys the style of the original. He must have a deep and far-reaching knowledge of two languages. The original author is luckier: he needs to know only one language.

Ideally, the best writers should be asked to make translations, and every good writer should at one time or another assume the burden of translation. Rilke translated Paul Valéry, Baudelaire translated Edgar Allen Poe, Dostoyevsky translated Balzac: but such happy conjunctions are very rare. In our own time great works of literature have been translated too often by writers with an insufficient command of the resources of the English language, but on the whole the level of translation has been higher than we had any right to expect under prevailing conditions. Obviously there are reasons why good writers often refuse to embark on translation. The rewards are small, the work arduous, the time can be spent more profitably. Nevertheless, the standard of translations improves every year, and every year there are more and more dedicated translators.

The duties of a translator are well known, but his rights have never been satisfactorily formulated. The P.E.N. Translation Committee believes that the time has come to re-examine the situation. A Bill of Rights for translators is long overdue, and it is proposed to call a Conference on Translation to discuss these rights in the spring of 1970.

The Rights of Translators. Among the subjects to be discussed are the following:

(a) The translator has the right to continuing royalties as long as his translation is in print. He is inseparable from the translation. Under no conditions whatsoever should he accept an outright fee for his work. Even if the royalty is very small, amounting to as little as 2%, such an arrangement is eminently necessary in order to guarantee his *continuing rights*. (This royalty should not be deducted from the author's royalties.) Without these, he becomes merely a pawn in the game, sacrificed as soon as he has fulfilled his elementary duty in the eyes of the publisher. A translator does not deserve to be treated as a pawn.

(b) A model contract suitable to publishers, authors and translators in preparation.

(c) The name of the translator should *always* appear on the title page and in the promotional matter issued by the publisher. It is not possible to insist on any relative size for the name of the translator on the title page, but in general it should be two-thirds the size of the name of the original author. The translator's name should also appear on the jacket.

(d) In general, the translator should retain the same proportional scale of royalties for his own work as does the author of the original work.

(e) Advances to translators based on fixed fees per thousand words, i. e. $20 per thousand words in current American practice, are clearly unworkable in cases of highly wrought imaginative fiction, and some new basis for computation is needed. It would be absurd to pay a translator of Thomas Mann or Paul Valéry at the same rate as a translator of any "sexpot" novel, but translators are in fact being paid according to the number of words and not according to the inherent difficulties of the task.

(f) Translators are continually faced with the need for special dictionaries, and it is suggested that in addition to an advance and royalties a translator should receive an honorarium to cover the cost of dictionaries.

(g) Translations made in England have been published in the United States only after large-scale revisions have been made, without any mention of the names of the translators responsible for the revisions. This is inherently dishonest, for the reader has no way of knowing who is ultimately responsible for the translation.

Translators' Conference. While the prime purpose of the Translators' Conference to be held in New York in the spring of 1970 will be to draw up a model contract and a Bill of Rights for Translators, there are other urgent matters to be discussed. Among them are the following:

Professorships of Translation. Although translations have been made since the beginning of recorded history and many of the best minds have been engaged in this appallingly difficult task, no chair of translation has ever been established. There have been "colleges" of translation instituted for the purpose of translating the Bible, but the art and craft of translation have never been taught as a major subject in a university.

This is a shocking state of affairs, which should be remedied as soon as possible. Such professorships should properly be established in all the major universities. Only in this way shall we have the possibility of constant professional study of the theory and practice of translation as distinguished from philology and linguistics. Exchange professorships with foreign countries are also urgently needed. The establishment of professorships will have the effect of producing an improvement in the quality of translations. Ultimately, it is a question of giving dignity to an art which has hitherto received only a grudging respect.

Exchange Fellowships. In addition to professorships there is need of exchange fellowships, because the art of translation is best pursued with constant meetings with translators from abroad. It is not so much a question of asking the foreign translators to take up positions in universities, but it is very necessary that they come to America and meet translators. This could be done under the auspices of P.E.N. It is especially desirable that translators from the African and Asian nations should be invited for a minimum period of two or three months. Ideally, of course, they would be attached to the universities, but this may not always be possible.

Prizes. The P.E.N. Translation Committee hopes to establish a number of regional prizes for translation. At the very least there should be prizes for the best translations from the literatures of Asia, Latin America, France, Germany, Italy, Spain and Scandinavia. We would also like to see an annual prize for the best translation from Russian, making no distinction whether the work comes from the Soviet

Union or from emigré writers. We would like to see prizes for the best translation from the Japanese and the languages of India-Pakistan. These prizes, if well publicized, would encourage publishers to produce more translations.

Publishers. There are already a number of publishers and editors on the P.E.N. Translation Committee, and it is hoped to add more. The Committee should keep in very close touch with them.

Translations from Russian. As long as the Soviet Union and other totalitarian regimes insist on censoring their writers and sending them to prison camps, their literature will be subject to intolerable strains. In these countries, the best writers write "for the drawer" against the day when, by a miracle, they will be allowed to write freely. Censorship was light under the Czars; under the Soviets it is all-pervasive, and not a word can be printed without the imprimatur of a government functionary. And this is true of all totalitarian regimes, and may become increasingly true throughout the world.

Like writers everywhere, Russian writers want to be read, they want to be known, they want their emotions to be shared and their ideas to be understood. They will go to almost any lengths to see that their books are read abroad if they cannot be read in Russia. Translators who receive their manuscripts then find themselves attempting to resolve intensely difficult moral problems, for they know that the publication of their translations will inevitably place the author in jeopardy and they will bear a moral responsibility for his fate. There are no simple solutions. We cannot say: "Let us publish, and be damned. We know that the author wanted his works to appear in translation and his intention outweighs all other considerations." Many imponderables have to be weighed, for no one has the right to sentence a man to a prison camp, which may also be a sentence of death.

The P.E.N. Translation Committee believes that there is need to re-examine the situation and to establish certain guide-lines in consultation with as many experts as possible. This is also a question to be discussed at the forthcoming Conference, at which time it is hoped to invite a representative of the Soviet and other government and any writers who have been heavily censored.

Untranslated Works. Translation has always been a rather haphazard affair depending on considerations which do not necessarily have anything to do with the real value of the works translated. The Arabs translated Greek works on philosophy, astronomy and medicine, because they needed them and thus saved them for posterity; they did not translate the plays of Aeschylus and Sophocles or the lyric poets, and we are therefore all the poorer. Some works translated by the Arabs are known to be lost. Chance has played its part, and even today translations often come about by chance.

Index of Translations. We need an Index of Translations, similar to the annual *Books in Print,* and we also need an Index of Works to Be Translated. This should properly be in the care of a university with a department of translation. A comparatively long list of works that need to be translated can be easily compiled, together with another list of works which have been translated inadequately. We have no adequate translations of Ariosto or Tasso. *The Dream of the Red Chamber,* acknowledged to be the greatest of the Chinese novels, has never been translated in full. There are no comprehensive anthologies of Indian or Japanese poetry. Strangely, there is no body of translations from the Vietnamese. As far as we know, neither the American Government nor any American university has made any conspicuous attempt to make Vietnamese culture known, and it is only with the greatest difficulty that one can find an occasional translation of a Vietnamese poem.

We have nothing from the Nepalese language, and precious little from the Arabic languages. If there is an outstanding novelist in Indonesia, we have not heard of him. Tibetan poetry is still unknown territory, and we are almost totally ignorant of the African languages. There is clearly a need for a comprehensive program to fill up the gaps, and we might very well begin with a serious study of the literature of the emerging African nations.

The question of inadequate translations is quite easily resolved when the books are out of copyright. What happens when the books are still in copyright? Edmund Wilson's strictures on the translation of *Doctor Zhivago* have not been satisfactorily answered, and there would seem to be a prima facie case for a new translation which would convey the poetry and rhythm of the original more adequately. Similarly, André Malraux's *Antimémoires* deserved a translator with a keener sense of the music of the original. In both cases, we are presented with modern classics in an English dress which fails to convey their extraordinary beauty. Under present circumstances nothing can be done and we shall have to wait until the works go out of copyright before a new translator can improve on them. This is not a very serious matter where minor works are concerned; it is a very serious matter indeed when it is a question of masterpieces.

Wherever we look, we find work for translators to do. There are urgent needs reflecting the contemporary situation, and we need a crash program for translations from modern Chinese and Vietnamese and from the African languages. But we are also living at a time when it has become necessary to re-examine our past and bring to light the important forgotten works of the past. We might begin by examining the 500 volumes of Migne's *Patrologia* to discover what the Christian Fathers were saying. It is not suggested that those immense volumes should be translated in full, but at least we should be permitted to have some idea of the treasures contained in them. What about Bruno's *De Immenso?* The more one contemplates our lack of translations, the more urgent appears the necessity of bringing into existence a publishing house supported by Foundations, which will be devoted solely to translations.

A Journal for Translators. We believe that each country should have a translator's journal which will present translations, reviews of translations, and a continuing commentary on the problems of translation. It should not be in the hands of a small academic élite, but represent the broad interests of translators all over the country. Many of the problems confronting translators would be solved by the existence of such a journal, which would provide them with a voice after an eternity of silence.

Although the journal would consist chiefly of translations and critical commentaries, it would also serve to promote the interests of translators and offer them a forum and a debating ground. They would learn what works are being translated and what works need to be translated. Through the journal serious efforts can be made to raise the standard of translation. Above all, the journal would serve as the translators' vehicle of communication with the outside world, which has rarely listened to them, because they have rarely been heard,

Translators are faced with a choice. Either they can continue to do nothing to improve their lot or they can join together to ensure that at long last they will receive their due. The choice is between apathy and active engagement in a struggle for recognition, between silence and the living voice. The world of translation is still largely undiscovered and unexplored, and the time has come to set the projects in order and to learn what can and what cannot be done.

P.E.N. Translation Committee
New York City
September, 1969